SIXTH EDITION

A Commonsense Guide to Grammar and Usage

Larry Beason

University of South Alabama

Mark Lester

Eastern Washington University

Bedford / St. Martin's

Boston ◆ New York

FOR BEDFORD/ST. MARTIN'S

Associate Editor: Alicia M. Young
Production Editor: Kerri A. Cardone
Senior Production Supervisor: Jennifer Peterson
Senior Marketing Manager: Christina Shea
Editorial Assistant: Kylie Paul
Copy Editor: Mary Lou Wilshaw-Watts
Indexer: Steve Csipke
Permissions Manager: Kalina K. Ingham
Senior Art Director: Anna Palchik
Text Design: Jean Hammond
Cover Art and Design: Donna Lee Dennison
Composition: NK Graphics
Printing and Binding: RR Donnelley and Sons

President: Joan E. Feinberg
Editorial Director: Denise B. Wydra
Editor in Chief: Karen S. Henry
Director of Marketing: Karen R. Soeltz
Director of Production: Susan W. Brown
Associate Director, Editorial Production: Elise S. Kaiser
Managing Editor: Elizabeth M. Schaaf

Library of Congress Control Number: 2011927766

Manufactured in the United States of America.

6 5 4 3 2
f e d c b

For information, write: Bedford/St. Martin's, 75 Arlington Street, Boston, MA 02116
  (617-399-4000)

ISBN: 978-0-312-69779-2

Preface for Instructors

A Commonsense Guide to Grammar and Usage, Sixth Edition, helps students write clear, error-free sentences by combining the easy access of a reference handbook with the practicality of a skills workbook. This book is intended for a range of students who need a firmer foundation in the grammar and usage of formal writing. These students might be enrolled in a beginning writing course, an ESL course, a first-year composition course, or a course in a discipline such as business, history, or science.

At the core of our approach is the firm belief that errors can be signs of risk taking, experimentation, and growth. Once students understand that errors are a part of the learning process, they can develop the confidence they need to recognize and correct sentence-level problems in their own writing—something they can do without an overwhelming amount of grammar terminology. We wrote this text because students, as well as teachers, need a book devoted to commonsense ways to avoid errors.

What Does This Book Offer — and Why?

The following combination of features makes this textbook a uniquely practical resource for instructors and students.

Emphasis on the most significant errors keeps students focused on essential skills. Using a straightforward, practice-oriented approach, *A Commonsense Guide* helps students learn how to identify and correct major problems in written English. On the basis of research, experience, and feedback from students and teachers, we concentrate on the grammar and usage problems that occur most frequently or are most distracting in the writing of first-year college students.

Easy-to-remember tips simplify grammar and usage. Each lesson includes at least one handy tip—a commonsense way of identifying or correcting an error. These tips, located in easy-to-find boxes, rely not on complex rules but on intuitive, practical strategies that writers actually use. Presented as friendly pieces of advice, these tips are easier for students to remember and apply than hard-and-fast rules or intimidating technical explanations.

Accessible, everyday language builds students' confidence.   The book's explanations and tips are written in clear, everyday language, so students will be confident about (rather than intimidated by) grammar. Unlike traditional handbooks, this book places special emphasis on learning how to identify and correct problems—*not* on learning terminology. We even include hand-edited example errors in the table of contents so students do not have to rely on grammar terms to find help for a specific problem.

Lessons *show* students—rather than tell them—how to avoid the most serious errors.   Each lesson involves hands-on practice so that students do not merely read about errors. Even before this practice, each lesson guides students through several examples so they can "see" how to identify and correct problems. Along these lines, the lessons are designed to engage visual learners, with ample charts and diagrams.

Modular approach to grammar breaks complex topics into manageable lessons.   To avoid overwhelming students, each lesson focuses on a single problem and follows a consistent organization.

- Brief diagnostic exercises in each lesson show whether students need help with a particular topic.

- Each lesson opens with at least two sample errors and corrections. We then offer a straightforward explanation of the errors. In so doing, we explain why even the most intelligent writer might be confused about formal English.

- Next, we offer correction strategies centered on each lesson's commonsense tips. We not only help students identify errors, we also equip them with practical strategies for revising.

How to Use This Book, on pages xv-xix, guides students through a sample lesson.

Abundant, carefully sequenced exercises build skills.   Each lesson concludes with many opportunities for students to practice what they learn, as they find and fix errors in sentences, paragraphs, and finally in their own writing.

Format allows students to use the book on their own.   Although lessons can be assigned as classwork or homework, several features allow the book to be used as a self-paced reference that students use on their own.

- The inside back cover offers a quick way to find major topics or grammatical issues (see Finding What You Need in This Book).

- The table of contents includes sample errors for each lesson, so students do not have to rely on grammar terms to locate specific topics.

- A chart of common correction symbols directs students to the right lessons.

- In the back of the book, answers to some exercises allow for self-study.

- The spiral binding, two-color format, tabbed unit dividers, and boxed tips and checklists make the book quick and easy to navigate.

Practical advice on reading, writing, and research makes *A Commonsense Guide* a complete reference. Unit Twelve: A Commonsense Writing Guide is a mini-rhetoric that balances two important issues. Students often want "bottom line" advice about what to do—and what not to do—as they write. However, many aspects of writing are too complex to reduce to fixed rules. Students need to understand that writers must react to their own writing situations—not to a formula. The following features help balance these important concepts:

- A lesson on critical reading provides an overview of the connections between reading and writing, along with helping students understand how to respond to what they read. Student examples illustrate the reading process, while tips and checklists highlight practical strategies.

- Commonsense tips offer practical advice for completing each stage of the writing process.

- Goal-oriented checklists and critical thinking questions guide students as they write expressive, informative, and persuasive paragraphs and essays.

- Sample student-written thesis statements, outlines, and drafts offer accessible models.

Two sections offer support for non-native speakers of English. Unit Nine: Choosing the Right Article and Unit Ten: Using Verbs Correctly are devoted to ESL issues. Throughout the rest of the book, ESL icons in margins point out topics that can be especially challenging to non-native speakers.

New to This Edition

As we planned the sixth edition of *A Commonsense Guide*, students and teachers asked us to make the book even easier to use while expanding our current coverage in key areas.

Expanded coverage of Grammar without Tears. With seven new grammar tests and lengthened discussions of subjects and predicates, independent and dependent clauses, and prepositional phrases, this section better helps students understand sentence structure and commonsense notions of language before they move on to identifying and fixing errors.

A new lesson on unnecessary commas and updated apostrophe lessons. Lesson 19 rounds out Unit Five: Using Commas Correctly by showing students not only when to use commas, but when *not* to use them. Unit 6: Using Apostrophes Correctly has been updated to reflect the latest trends on apostrophe usage, especially in regard to plural forms of special terms.

A new unit on documenting sources and avoiding plagiarism. Although not a true "grammar error," plagiarism is often the result of students' not understanding how quotation marks and other mechanical devices let readers know when a writer uses someone else's words or ideas. Two new lessons focus on how to quote from a source properly and how to attribute sources in citations and on a Works Cited page.

Updated MLA guidelines. The brief guide to MLA documentation has been updated to reflect the latest guidelines set forth by the Modern Language Association.

New APA Brief Documentation Guide. In addition to the updated MLA guidelines, we have added a Brief Documentation Guide for APA, which provides students with a quick reference for a second major documentation style used in college writing.

Up-to-date exercises with engaging content. A third of the Sentence Practice and Editing Practice exercises have been updated, with topics ranging from popular culture trivia to literary references to getting to class on time.

Practical Resources for Instructors and Students

Exercise Central 3.0, at **bedfordstmartins.com/exercisecentral,** is the largest online collection of grammar exercises available, providing over 9,000 exercise items. Conveniently arranged by topic and level, *Exercise Central* is a comprehensive resource for skill development and skill assessment. In addition to immediate feedback and reporting, *Exercise Central* can help identify students' strengths and weaknesses, recommend personalized study plans, and provide tutorials for common problems.

WritingClass, at **yourwritingclass.com**, is a customizable course space that helps keep students on track. At one easy-to-use site, your students can check for new assignments, complete activities, and check back to find out how they did. In addition to providing hundreds of diagnostics, tutorials, quizzes, and more, *WritingClass* features step-by-step lessons on grammar, punctuation, and writing skills that are adapted from the lessons in this very text, so your students get the same jargon-free, straightforward instruction that makes *A Commonsense Guide to Grammar and Usage* so practical. New **LearningCurve** activities also give students a flexible, supportive means of practicing and reviewing grammar skills: They help students build skills, rather than simply testing what they know, and they adapt the pace to each student—leading every student to success.

Re:Writing Basics, at **bedfordstmartins.com/rewritingbasics**, is an extensive collection of our most widely used online resources for the developmental writing course on a free, easy-to-access Web site. For students, there are helpful tutorials, exercises, research guides, bibliography tools, and more. For instructors, *Re:Writing Basics* offers such resources as *The Bedford Bibliography for Teachers of Basic Writing* and other free bibliographies, workshops, and online journals for professional development.

Re:Writing Basics **content for course management systems** is ready for use with Blackboard, WebCT, and other popular course management software. For more information about Bedford/St. Martin's course management offerings, visit **bedfordstmartins.com/cms**.

Make-a-Paragraph Kit with Exercise Central To Go gives students all the tools they need to write successful paragraphs. The visuals, sound, and interactivity appeal to all types of learning styles (ISBN-13: 978-0-312-45332-9, ISBN-10: 0-312-45332-9).

The Bedford/St. Martin's ESL Workbook, **Second Edition,** has been peer reviewed and crafted to focus on contemporary topics and dialogues. This outstanding resource covers grammatical issues for multilingual students with varying English-language skills and cultural backgrounds (ISBN-13: 978-0-312-54034-0, ISBN-10: 0-312-54034-5).

Testing Tool Kit: A Writing and Grammar Test Bank allows instructors to test students' writing and grammar skills by creating secure, customized tests and quizzes from a pool of nearly 2,000 questions covering 47 topics (ISBN-13: 978-0-312-43032-0, ISBN-10: 0-312-43032-9).

The Instructor's Resource Manual for **A Commonsense Guide to Grammar and Usage** offers the following support and resources for instructors:

- Advice on teaching grammar and usage

- Four sample syllabi that pair *A Commonsense Guide* with Bedford/St. Martin's readers

- A full chapter on teaching ESL students

- Lesson-by-lesson teaching tips for using *A Commonsense Guide* in the classroom or as a reference that students use on their own

- Answers to the Unit Review tests and the final practices in each lesson

- Supplemental exercises for additional practice, along with answers

- Tips on how to use *Exercise Central*

You can download a copy of this manual for free at **bedfordstmartins.com**.

Acknowledgments

We would like to thank the following instructors who completed questionnaires and reviews that allowed us to develop the sixth edition of this book: Merry Dennehy, Monterey Peninsula College; David D. Duncan, Palm Beach State College; Lexy Durand, Alamance Community College; Paul Friesen, Reedley College; Barbara Griest-Devora, Northwest Vista College; Jennifer Gurley, Le Moyne College; Michael Hall, Georgia Perimeter College; Gloria Heller, Santa Monica College; Barbara Henry, West Virginia State University; Joanna Howard, Montgomery College; Teresa Joy Kramer, Central Washington University; Jonathan Myerov, Middlesex Community College; Matt Oakes, Rock Valley College; Carl Olds, University of Central Arkansas; Ashley Oliphant, Pfeiffer University; Beverly Reilly, Rio Hondo College; Teresa Roberts, University of Maine at Farmington; Connie Ruzich, Robert Morris University; Victoria Sarkisian, Marist College; Dixie Shaw-Tillmon, University of Texas at San Antonio; Marguerite Stark, Monterey Peninsula College; Mary Stewart, Reedley College; Lori Stoltz, Saint Paul College; Bradley Waltman, Community College of Southern Nevada; Mel Waterhouse, Mira Costa Community College; Rebecca Wolfe, Cornerstone University; Theodore Worozbyt, Georgia Perimeter College – Newton Campus; and our anonymous reviewers from North Idaho College and Utah State University.

We extend special thanks to the people at Bedford/St. Martin's for their significant contributions to this revision: Alicia Young, developmental editor; Anne Leung, Karin Halbert, Shannon Leuma, Michelle Clark, and Amanda Bristow, for their work on previous editions of *A Commonsense Guide*; Kylie Paul, editorial assistant; Kerri Cardone, production editor; Mary Lou Wilshaw-Watts, copyeditor; Chuck Christensen, former president; Joan Feinberg, president; Denise Wydra, editorial director; Karen Henry, editor in chief; Elizabeth Schaaf, managing editor; Christina Shea, senior marketing manager; and Jean Hammond, text designer.

Finally, we wish to thank our wives, Colleen Beason and Mary Ann Lester, for their unwavering support and patience.

Larry Beason
Mark Lester

Why Use This Book? — For Students

Why use this book? We believe you have a right to an answer. Not only are you paying for this book, but you will also be asked to commit time and energy to its material.

Some people enjoy the study of grammar and formal rules that tell writers how to put words and sentences together. Most people, however, do not put such study at the top of their list of favorite things to do. We are not going to "sell" this book by claiming grammar is fun (though it can be). Rather, we want readers to understand why studying grammar and usage is worthwhile. In addition, we want you to know why this book takes a different approach than most grammar textbooks.

The most pressing reason why you should use this book is that it will help you in many college courses. Students are often surprised to learn how much writing is required outside the English department. Research has proven that history, business, computer science, education, and even math teachers—to name a few—frequently ask students to write. A physics teacher, for example, might ask you to write a detailed lab report so you will learn more about electricity. However, this teacher will not be able to tell if you have learned anything about physics unless your writing is clear. Errors such as fused sentences can make a report hard to follow.

Unless you understand certain rules and conventions, numerous teachers—not just English teachers—will be confused, distracted, and even annoyed. If you assume that only English teachers care about "good grammar," now is the time to realize that this assumption is dangerous—dangerous because it can harm your chances for succeeding in college.

People in the workplace can be even more strict about grammar and usage than college teachers. A study conducted by one of the authors of this textbook indicates that businesspeople are greatly affected by writers' errors in formal English. Professionals in the study frequently noted the importance of clear writing in jobs as diverse as health care, software development, and even laboratory work for gold mining companies. These people pointed out many instances when errors, such as comma splices and misspellings, confused readers. These businesspeople also made judgments, based on those errors, about the writers' workplace skills and attitudes. That is, businesspeople sometimes assume that errors reflect on the writers' ability to think logically or work effectively with other people. Such generalizations are not always valid, but it seems to be part of human nature to make large-scale judgments about people based on their language choices. We are not saying such judgmental behavior is right, but it's what people often do.

In short, this book can help you focus your readers' attention on the most important parts of your writing: its content, not the details of your language choices. Briefly, we want to point out why this book can help you in ways that other grammar books might not.

First, this textbook avoids, as much as possible, technical terms. By giving commonsense explanations and advice, we indicate how to avoid errors. For instance, each lesson focuses on a "tip" that is not really a rule but a piece of advice; this tip is easier to remember and understand than a drawn-out technical explanation. In addition, exercises focus on applying these tips so you will remember them. Too many textbooks rely on asking you to find and fix errors, as if you were just a proofreader. In this book, Sentence Practice exercises help you learn commonsense tips that draw on what you already know about language.

Second, we think you need more than just the quickest explanation possible. Thus, each lesson gives various types of guidance. We think it helps clear up confusion if you understand *why* many people make a certain type of error, so each lesson covers major misconceptions about whatever the lesson focuses on. But most information in each lesson is devoted to how to correct an error — not to rules.

Why use this book? We wrote it because we found that these strategies help you, as students, improve one important aspect of formal writing — grammar and usage. We believe the tools you take from this book will help you succeed in more than one classroom and in more than one stage of life.

Larry Beason
Mark Lester

How to Use This Book

A Commonsense Guide to Grammar and Usage is designed to offer you nuts-and-bolts strategies for improving your writing—especially for improving your sentences. Units One through Ten, which focus on grammar and usage, help you to identify, understand, and correct errors in your sentences with commonsense advice and plenty of opportunities for practice. Unit Eleven provides an overview of documenting outside sources and avoiding plagiarism in your writing. Unit Twelve, the writing guide, helps you to read, plan, draft, and revise a paragraph or an essay.

The grammar and usage lessons follow a consistent organization:

Example Errors and Corrections
Look at these examples to see whether you are making a similar error in your writing. (*Note:* Throughout the text, ungrammatical phrases and sentences are indicated by an ✗.) These examples are discussed in greater detail in the Fixing This Problem in Your Writing section of each lesson.

EXAMPLE 1	*Renamer Fragment*
Error:	Blocking my driveway was a car. ✗ A huge SUV.
Correction:	Blocking my driveway was a car. , a A huge SUV.
EXAMPLE 2	*Adverb Fragment*
Error:	I was really upset. ✗ Because I knew I would be late for work.
Correction:	I was really upset. because Because I knew I would be late for work.
EXAMPLE 3	*-ing Fragment*
Error:	I beeped my horn a couple of times. ✗ Letting the driver know I had to get out.
Correction:	I beeped my horn a couple of times. , letting Letting the driver know I had to get out.

What's the Problem?
This section explains a rule or convention of English that causes difficulty for many writers. If English is not your first language, you may want to pay special attention to material marked by this symbol: 🌐
ESL

Boldfaced words are defined in Appendix C: Guide to Grammar Terminology.

What's the Problem?

A **run-on sentence** contains two **independent clauses** that have been incorrectly joined together. (An independent clause is a group of words that can stand alone as a complete sentence.) Run-on sentences fail to show the reader where one idea ends and the next one begins.

The examples above illustrate two types of run-on sentence errors. When two independent clauses are joined with no punctuation at all, the error is called a **fused sentence**. When two independent clauses are joined with just a comma (without a coordinating conjunction like *and, but, or*), the error is called a **comma splice**. In both cases, the writer confuses the reader by failing to correctly signal the separation between two complete ideas.

In the following examples, notice how the clauses are separated by nothing at all or by just a comma.

Diagnostic Exercise
To find out if you need
help with the topic of the
lesson, do this exercise.
Then check your answers
in the back of the book.

Diagnostic Exercise

CORRECTED SENTENCES APPEAR ON PAGE 464.

Correct all errors in the following paragraphs using the first correction as a
model. The number in parentheses at the end of each paragraph indicates
how many errors you should find in that paragraph.

, earning
I need more money. There are only two ways to get more money/~~Earn-~~
~~ing~~ more or spending less. I am going to have to do a better job saving what
money I do earn. Because there is no realistic way that I can earn more
money. The first thing I did was to make a list of everything I bought. Starting last Monday. (2)

When I read over my list, the first thing I noticed was how much I
spent on junk food. Especially snacks and energy bars. It is really stupid
to spend so much money on stuff. That isn't even good for me. I can't just
do away with snacks, though. I work long, irregular hours, and so I can't
always have regular meals. Like everyone else. (3)

*Fixing This Problem
in Your Writing*
This section offers
practical strategies for
identifying and correcting
the error.

Fixing This Problem in Your Writing

Identifying Run-ons

Run-ons are easy to correct once you have identified them. The problem
is finding them to begin with. Here is a tip for spotting potential run-on
sentences in your writing.

Commonsense Tip
Use this concrete strategy
to identify or correct the
error.

IMAGINARY PERIOD TIP   If a sentence contains two separate ideas, put an
imaginary period between them. Now ask: Can BOTH parts stand alone as
complete sentences? If so, then the sentence might be a run-on.

Correction Sequence
This sequence shows
you how to apply the
commonsense tip to
correct the example errors.
Use this same step-by-step
strategy to help you
identify, understand,
and correct errors in your
writing.

A third way to punctuate two independent clauses is to combine them
with a comma and a **coordinating conjunction** (*for, and, nor, but, or, yet,
so*). We'll illustrate this method with Example 1 from the beginning of the
lesson.

Example 1:   ✗ I have a test on Thursday it should not be difficult.

Tip applied: I have a test on Thursday. It should not be difficult.
                                          ↑
              An imaginary period works, so the clauses are independent.

                                 , and
Correction: I have a test on Thursday it should not be difficult.
                                     ^
              Add a comma and conjunction where the imaginary period could go.

More Examples
Study the examples in
this section as a further
reminder of the concepts
in the lesson. *Note:* Only
some chapters include
this box.

MORE EXAMPLES

Error: ✗ Jamal is a physics major he plans to work for NASA.

Correction: Jamal is a physics major ~~he~~ . He plans to work for NASA.

Error: ✗ Traffic today was horrible I am thirty minutes late.

Correction: Traffic today was horrible , so I am thirty minutes late.

Putting It All Together
This checklist will help you
identify and correct the
error in your writing.

✳ **Putting It All Together**

Identify Fragments

____ Understand and look for the most common types of fragments: *renamers, adverbs,* and *-ing fragments.*

____ Proofread your paper starting at the last sentence and moving to the first, reading one sentence at a time.

____ Put *I realize* in front of each group of words that you think might be a fragment. The *I realize* sentence will not make sense if the word group is a fragment.

Correct Fragments

____ Attach each fragment to the previous sentence, or rewrite the fragment to make it a complete sentence if you want to emphasize it.

Sentence Practice
Do these exercises to practice applying the lesson's
tips. You can check your
answers to the first two
sets against the answer key
in the back of the book. A
box after the first exercise
set directs you to the Web
for further practice.

Sentence Practice 1

CORRECTED SENTENCES APPEAR ON PAGE 465.

Find the independent clauses in the following run-on sentences by using the Imaginary Period Tip. Correct each run-on by inserting a semicolon between the two independent clauses, by adding a comma and a coordinating conjunction, or by turning the imaginary period into a real one. If a sentence does not contain a run-on, write *OK* above it.

Example: My car is getting pretty old, it still gets me where I want to go.

Tip applied: My car is getting pretty old. It still gets me where I want to go.

Correction: My car is getting pretty old, but it still gets me where I want to go.

 For more practice correcting run-ons, go to **Exercise Central** at
bedfordstmartins.com/commonsense

Editing Practice
Do these exercises to practice identifying and correcting the error in a paragraph or mini-essay similar to one you might write. You can check your answers to the first one or two editing practices against the answer key in the back of the book.

Editing Practice 1

CORRECTED SENTENCES APPEAR ON PAGE 465.

Correct all run-ons in the following paragraph using the first correction as a model. The number in parentheses at the end of the paragraph indicates how many errors you should find.

I was late to my first class; my car broke down on the side of the
^
highway. This is the third time this fall that I have had to pull over because of an engine problem, I am not going to suffer through a fourth time. According to a mechanic, the problem has something to do with the fuel injector. I have replaced the fuse, and the mechanic has tried various other methods. Nothing has worked it does not make sense spending even more money on something that cannot be fixed. I might need a whole new fuel injector, I am considering buying a new car. The one I have is only six years old, so I hate buying a new one already. It all depends on what I can afford. (3)

Applying What You Know
Do this activity to demonstrate your ability to avoid the error in your own writing.

Applying What You Know

Select fifteen sentences from one of your textbooks, and use the Imaginary Period Tip to determine how many are composed of two or more independent clauses—complete ideas that can stand alone as separate sentences. How many of the fifteen sentences use a comma and a coordinating conjunction to separate independent clauses? How many use a semicolon?

The Bottom Line
Here is a final reminder of the main point of the lesson. The sentence is written so that it both demonstrates and describes the concept of the lesson.

| **The Bottom Line** | See if your sentence has two independent clauses, **and** make sure they are separated with a period, a semicolon, or a comma and coordinating conjunction. |

Using the Tabs

You may have noticed that there are tabs in the outside margins of this book. These tabs are designed to help you find your way around. If you open to a unit overview or unit review, the tab will indicate the unit number and whether you are in the overview or the review. If you flip through the book from front to back, you will notice twelve sets of tabs. These correspond to the twelve units in *A Commonsense Guide*.

Unit One

overview

If you open to an individual lesson, the tab will indicate the lesson number and a symbol for the topic of the lesson. For example, *frag* is the symbol used for Lesson 1: Fragments. You may notice that your instructor uses a similar system of symbols to indicate errors in your writing.

Lesson 1

frag

The last page of *A Commonsense Guide to Grammar and Usage* lists other common correction symbols.

Contents

Unit Three   **Using Correct Verb Tenses**   **68**

Unit Four   **Understanding Pronouns**   **87**

OVERVIEW   265

to
Mickey likes to bike, swim, and to go on long walks.
^

Our family took a plane to Chicago.
~~A plane was taken to Chicago by our family.~~
^

Nina's watch had to be thrown away.
Damaged beyond repair, ~~Nina threw her watch away~~.
^

REVIEW   291

OVERVIEW   293

There have been many studies about the effect of television
violence
~~violences~~ on children.
^

a
Masanori had ~~the~~ good idea.
^

The barn is always full of ~~some~~ mice.

REVIEW   318

OVERVIEW   322

am studying
I can't talk to you right now. I ~~study~~ for my exams.
^

Grammar without Tears

This brief overview of grammar basics will help you understand what sentences are and how they are built. This overview is divided into four parts and covers the following topics: (1) subjects and predicates, the two fundamental elements in all sentences; (2) the key grammatical components that make up subjects and predicates; (3) the difference between independent clauses (sentences) and dependent clauses; and (4) how to use prepositional phrases to expand a basic sentence with optional modifiers.

Subjects and Predicates

All grammatical sentences consist of two parts: a **subject** and a **predicate**. No matter how long or complicated a sentence is, it is easy to break it into the subject and predicate parts by identifying the subject. The subject of a sentence is always a noun or another structure that acts as a noun. Everything else in the sentence is part of the predicate. For example:

SUBJECT   PREDICATE

The defendant's lawyers delayed the trial for two weeks.

In this example, *the defendant's lawyers* is the subject, which means that the predicate consists of the verb *delayed* and its object (*the trial*) as well as the adverb phrase *for two weeks*.

Since the subject of a sentence is always a noun or another structure that plays the noun's role, the subject can always be identified by replacing it with a pronoun.

> **PRONOUN REPLACEMENT TIP** The subject of a sentence — whether it is a single-word noun or a long, complicated complete subject — can always be identified by replacing it with a subject pronoun: *he, she, it,* or *they.*

Let's apply the Pronoun Replacement Tip to the sample sentence above. The subject *the defendant's lawyers* can be replaced by the pronoun *they*:

1

They
The defendant's lawyers delayed the trial for two weeks.

Here are some more examples using the Pronoun Replacement Tip to identify subjects:

Example: *He*
The young man at the bank told us that our money was perfectly safe.

Example: *It*
What you don't know won't hurt you, most of the time, anyway.

Example: *It*
Finding out how much the payments would be made us reconsider buying a new car.

Grammar Test 1

Underline the subjects in the sentences below. Confirm your answers by applying the Pronoun Replacement Tip.

Example: The educated elite in most countries completely controls the government.

Answer: *It*
The educated elite in most countries completely controls the government.

1. The man behind the curtain was frantically pulling various levers.

2. Many of the fees that college students pay actually go to support athletics.

3. The high winds at the peak of the storm lifted the barn right off its foundation.

4. People who live in glass houses shouldn't throw stones.

5. Sally's getting a good grade on her first test really encouraged her to stay enrolled in the course.

Identifying Verbs

There are two fundamentally different types of verbs that can be used in a predicate: **action verbs** and **linking verbs**. Both the meaning and the grammatical structure of a sentence are totally dependent on which type of verb is used.

If an action verb is used, then the subject typically performs the action of the verb in the predicate. For example:

The children laughed.

In the sentence above, the subject *the children* performs the action described in the predicate—laughing. In action-verb sentences, this pattern of *actor (subject) + action (predicate)* is the norm.

If a linking verb is used, however, everything is different. The subject no longer performs an action because there is no action to perform. Instead, the subject is the topic of the sentence and the predicate gives information about that topic. For example:

Their modern house looks like a damaged UFO.

In the sentence above, the subject *their modern house* is not doing anything. It is just sitting there while the predicate describes it. The term *linking verb* refers to the fact that the verb links the information in the predicate back to the subject. In this example, the linking verb *looks like* links the appearance of a damaged UFO back to the subject *their modern house*.

The following chart summarizes the differences between action verbs and linking verbs:

	SUBJECT	PREDICATE
Action verb:	performer of action	action that is performed
Linking verb:	topic of sentence	describes the subject

Here are some additional examples of action verbs and linking verbs:

Action verb: I **ate** a banana.

Linking verb: Bananas **are** high in potassium.

Action verb: Everyone **smelled** the sandwiches in my coat pocket.

Linking verb: Dinner **smells** really good.

The last two examples show that some verbs, like *smell*, can be either action verbs or linking verbs depending on how they are used. Many jokes take advantage of this fact. Here's an amusing example:

First Man: My dog has no nose.

Second Man: How does he smell?

First Man: He smells awful!

Grammar Test 2

Label the boldfaced verbs in the following sentences as either action verbs or linking verbs.

> *linking verb*
> Example: The coffee **tastes** terrible.

> *action verb*
> Example: Eric **made** the coffee this morning.

1. Sam **answered** the phone on the first ring.

2. A blue truck **cut** right in front of us.

3. The flight **was** long and uncomfortable.

4. Jim and Louise **invited** us over for dinner on Friday.

5. The storm **seemed** to be getting worse by the minute.

While action verbs and linking verbs have equal grammatical status, they are far from equal in number. Though it is difficult to determine the exact numbers, there are probably around 200 linking verbs and more than 10,000 action verbs in the English language. In other words, more than 98 percent of English verbs are action verbs.

If linking verbs account for such a small percentage of all verbs, then why spend so much time talking about them? The answer is *frequency*. Though there are relatively few linking verbs, they are used all the time. For example, the linking verb *be* is by far the most commonly used verb in English. (This fact is still true even if we discount the use of *be* as a helping verb. For example: *They* **are** *waiting for your answer.*)

How can we tell if a verb is an action verb or a linking verb? Linking verbs are easy to recognize because they have two unique, related properties that define the entire class: (1) The subjects of linking verbs are topics, not actors, and (2) linking verbs always refer back to the subject of the sentence and give us information about it.

Unfortunately, there are no similar defining properties for the thousands of action verbs. It is true that many action verbs express action, but some do not. Here are three examples of such actionless "action" verbs:

We **lacked** the money to make such a large down payment.

Lacked does not express action at all; in fact, it almost emphasizes the inability to act.

Roberta **missed** the train this morning.

It is hard to see what action the subject *Roberta* is engaged in or how the object *the train* is a recipient of any action.

Our friends **own** a cabin in Colorado.

The verb *own* expresses an ongoing state or condition, but it does not express action.

The problem is that action verbs include all the verbs in the English language minus a couple hundred linking verbs. There is no simple way to define such a large and diverse group, except by exclusion: Action verbs are all the verbs in English that are not linking verbs.

Objects and Predicate Nouns

Action verbs and linking verbs affect the grammar of the rest of the predicate in very different ways. Both action verbs and linking verbs can be followed by nouns, but the relationship between the verb and the noun it follows is completely different depending on which category the verb belongs to.

In an action verb sentence, the noun that follows the verb is an **object**. An object is the thing or person acted on by the verb.

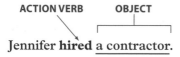

Jennifer **hired** a contractor.

In the sentence above, the object *a contractor* is the recipient of the action of Jennifer's hiring: In other words, the contractor is the person hired by Jennifer.

Here are some more examples of sentences in the *actor subject + action verb + object recipient* pattern, probably the most common pattern in English. The action verb is in boldface, and the object recipient is underlined:

Ralph **guessed** the answer.

The company **expanded** its plant in Malaysia.

I **took** my algebra final.

In a linking verb sentence, the noun that follows the verb is not an object; it is a **predicate noun**. A predicate noun is not the recipient of any action for the simple reason that there is no action to receive. Instead, the predicate noun describes, further identifies, or characterizes some aspect of the subject.

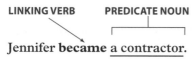

Jennifer **became** a contractor.

In the above example of a linking verb sentence, *a contractor* acts as a predicate noun that tells us something about the subject *Jennifer*.

Here are some more examples of sentences in the *topic subject + linking verb + predicate noun* pattern. The linking verb is in boldface, and the predicate noun is underlined:

> John **remained** <u>the head coach for years</u>.

> The tree **was** <u>a Norwegian pine</u>.

> Sally and I **have stayed** <u>best friends since childhood</u>.

Grammar Test 3

In the following sentences, label the underlined nouns that follow the boldfaced verbs as either objects or predicate nouns. Remember that objects are the recipients of action and predicate nouns describe the subject.

Example: Half the class **failed** <u>the exam</u> on their first attempt.   *[object]*

Example: The exam **came as** <u>a big surprise</u>.   *[predicate noun]*

1. The police finally **found** <u>our llama</u>.

2. Our biggest expense **is** <u>our car</u>.

3. Everyone **tasted** <u>the children's cookies</u>.

4. The dessert at the party **tasted like** <u>dryer lint</u>.

5. The garage **charged** <u>the battery</u>.

Predicate Adjectives

There is one additional characteristic of linking verbs that sets them apart from action verbs. Linking verbs can be followed by **predicate adjectives**, but action verbs cannot. Predicate adjectives describe the topic subject. For example:

> Be careful, those knives **are** <u>sharp</u>.

The predicate adjective *sharp* describes the subject *knives*. Here are some more examples with the linking verb in boldface and the predicate adjective underlined:

Example: Finally, after all his dieting, Ralph **got** <u>thin</u>. [*Thin* describes the subject *Ralph*.]

Example: The fruit in the market **looked** very <u>fresh</u>. [*Fresh* describes the subject *fruit*.]

Example: We **were** all <u>disappointed</u> when the game was rained out. [*Disappointed* describes the subject *we*.]

The biggest problem in recognizing predicate adjectives is that many of them (like *disappointed* in the example above) are derived from verbs and keep their *-ing* or *-ed* verb endings. If these predicate adjectives with such verb endings are used after any form of the helping verb *be* (*am, are, is, was, were, be, been, being*), they look just like the main verbs in the *helping verb + main verb* construction. For example, in the sentences below, which of the underlined *-ing* and *-ed* words are verbs and which are predicate adjectives?

We **are** moving next week.

We **are** upset by what happened.

They **were** encouraged.

They **were** helped by their friends.

At first glance, it seems impossible to tell predicate adjectives and verbs apart. Fortunately, there is simple tip that can help you do just that.

VERY TIP The word *very*, when used with verbs, never makes grammatical sense, but it can be used freely with nearly all predicate adjectives.

Here is the *Very* Tip applied to the example sentences above:

✗ We **are** very moving next week. [*Moving* is a verb.]

We **are** very upset by what happened. [*Upset* is a predicate adjective.]

They **were** very encouraged. [*Encouraged* is a predicate adjective.]

✗ They **were** very helped by their friends. [*Helped* is a verb.]

Grammar Test 4

Apply the *Very* Tip to determine whether the underlined words are predicate adjectives or verbs, and label them accordingly.

Example: 　　　　　*verb*
The job **was** attempted before we were really ready.

Confirmation: ✗ *The job was very attempted before we were really ready.*

Example: 　　　*predicate adjective*
The new iPad **is** striking.

Confirmation: *The new iPad is very striking.*

1. The presentation **was** interesting.
2. Their hockey game **was** recorded.

3.   The whole building **was** shaking.

4.   I **was** certainly tempted.

5.   The entire army **was** retreating.

Grammatical Components That Make Up Subjects and Predicates

As you have probably realized by now, the roles of subject, object, and predicate noun are played by nouns, pronouns, and other grammatical structures that function as nouns. As such, we need to be very clear about what nouns are and how we can recognize them.

The word **noun** comes from the Latin word *nomen*, meaning "name." Nouns are people, places, things, and abstractions. Nouns fall into two groups: **proper nouns** (capitalized) and **common nouns** (lowercase). Proper nouns are the names of specific things or individuals. Common nouns are the names of broader categories of people, places, and things. For example:

PROPER NOUN	COMMON NOUN
Alice	woman
Cincinnati	city
Burger King	restaurant

It is easy to recognize all proper nouns and those common nouns that refer to physical things. However, it can be tricky to identify nouns that refer to abstract things or ideas. For example, which of the following is a noun?

defend   defense

It is not easy to tell which of these words is a noun just by looking at it. Fortunately, there is a simple tip that can help you identify nouns.

> **THE TIP** If you can put *the* directly in front of a word and it makes sense, then that word is a noun.

Let's apply the *The* Tip to the two words given above:

✗ the defend   the defense

As you can see, *the* with the word *defend* makes no sense, but *the* with *defense* works. Using the *The* Tip reveals that *defense* is a noun and that *defend* is not (it is actually a verb). The *The* Tip is also especially reliable with abstract nouns, the type of noun that is the hardest to recognize.

Grammar Test 5

Apply the *The* Tip to the following word pairs, and underline each abstract noun.

	Example:	authority	authorize
	Answer:	*the* <u>authority</u>	✗ *the* authorize

1.	lengthen	length
2.	concede	concession
3.	discover	discovery
4.	performance	perform
5.	dedication	dedicate

Most of the time, we do not use common nouns by themselves. We use them in a package with articles like *a* and *the* and with modifying adjectives in front of the noun and with adjectival prepositional phrases or adjective clauses after the noun. For example:

the first three motions that were presented

In this example, the noun *motions* has an article (*the*) and two modifying adjectives in front of the noun (*first three*) as well as a modifying adjective clause following the noun (*that were presented*). This entire package of noun plus modifiers is called a **noun phrase**. No matter how long or how complicated a noun phrase is, it is still a single unit that functions just like the noun at its center functions.

Given that there are so many modifiers that we can use with nouns and such a variety of other structures that function as nouns, it is fortunate that there is a foolproof tip to identify noun phrases.

> **PRONOUN REPLACEMENT TIP** If a group of words can be replaced by a pronoun and the sentence retains grammatical sense, then that group is a noun phrase.

This tip means exactly what it says: Whatever can be replaced by a pronoun is a noun phrase—no more, no less. This test requires you to abandon the idea that pronouns *always* replace nouns. Pronouns often do replace nouns but only if the nouns have no modifiers. In the following examples, the pronouns *he* and *him* replace the noun *Bobby*:

He

Example: **Bobby** returned your call. [*He* replaces the singular masculine subject noun *Bobby*.]

him

Example: You need to call **Bobby** back. [*Him* replaces the singular masculine object noun *Bobby*.]

Now let's look at an example in which the noun does have modifiers. In the following sentence the noun is in boldface and its entire noun phrase is underlined:

We need to move <u>the **chairs** in the back of the room</u>.

If we took the traditional rule literally and replaced just the noun *chairs* with the appropriate pronoun, we would get this nonsensical result:

✗ We need to move the them in the back of the room.

As you can see, the pronoun must replace the noun along with all its modifiers, not just the noun at the heart of the noun phrase:

We need to move them. [*Them* = the chairs in the back of the room.]

Here again is the sample noun phrase given above:

the first three **motions** that were presented

We must replace the entire noun phase with one of the pronouns that would be appropriate for the noun *motions*. There are two pronouns that could be used, *they* or *them*, depending on whether the noun phrase is being used as a subject or as an object. Here are both possibilities:

They

Subject: <u>The first three **motions** that were presented</u> were rejected.

them

Object: The committee rejected <u>the first three **motions** that were presented</u>.

Grammar Test 6

Underline all the noun phrases in the following sentences. Confirm your answers by replacing the noun phrases with the appropriate pronouns. Label the functions of all the noun phrases (*subject, object, predicate noun*).

Example: The county clerk counted all the ballots.

                    He or she (subject)   *them (object)*
Answer: <u>The county clerk</u> counted <u>all the ballots.</u>

1. The candidates listed their qualifications.

2. My first omelet resembled a deflated yellow balloon.

3. The insurance agent viewed the fire damage.

4. Terry's suggestion was a great idea.

5. In 1814, ambassadors from the United States and Britain signed the Treaty of Ghent, ending the War of 1812.

So far we have established that nouns, pronouns, and noun phrases play the key roles of subjects, objects, and predicate nouns in sentences. The only major component that we have yet to discuss is the role of verbs in the predicate.

Verbs are the absolute heart of the **complement**—whatever the verb requires for the sentence to make sense. The verb agrees with the subject. The verb controls everything in the complement: It is either an action verb or a linking verb, and that in turn controls whether the noun following the verb is an object or a predicate noun.

Fortunately, verbs have a distinctive feature that makes them quite easy to recognize—**tense**. Verbs, and only verbs, can have present tense, past tense, and future tense forms. A good test for distinguishing verbs is to see if you can change the word to future tense by putting *will* in front of it.

> **WILL TIP**   Put *will* in front of the word you want to test. If the result makes grammatical sense, then the word is a verb. If the result doesn't make sense, then the word is not a verb.

Let's apply the *Will* Tip to these related words:

Example: postpone   postponement

Without using the *Will* Tip, it is not obvious which one is the verb. However, when we apply the *Will* Tip, it is perfectly clear:

Tip applied: *will* postpone   **✗** *will* postponement

The *Will* Tip shows us that *postpone* is a verb and that *postponement* is not.

Grammar Test 7

Apply the *Will* Tip to each of the following word pairs, and underline the verb.

Example:	realize	realization
Tip applied:	*will* realize	✗ *will* realization

1.	large	enlarge
2.	sale	sell
3.	authority	authorize
4.	choose	choice
5.	investment	invest

Distinguishing between Independent and Dependent Clauses

Sentences are **independent clauses**. To be independent, clauses must be able to stand alone (make sense by themselves) without being dependent on some other sentence. Clauses that fail to stand alone are called **dependent clauses**.

There are three types of dependent clauses: **noun clauses, adjective clauses**, and **adverb clauses**. Noun clauses function as nouns; adjective clauses, as adjectives; and adverb clauses, as adverbs. Here are examples of sentences that use each type of clause (which is underlined):

Noun clause:	Whatever dumb thing a politician says is sure to be posted on YouTube.
	I remember when I was your age.
Adjective clause:	The belt that I just bought is the wrong size.
	I bumped into some people whom I knew in high school.
Adverb clause:	After Cinderella finished the dishes, she went to the ball.
	The Prince eventually found her because she left her glass slipper.

If we take away the rest of the sentences and leave behind just the dependent clauses, none of them work as freestanding sentences:

Noun clause:	✗ Whatever dumb thing a politician says.
	✗ When I was your age.
Adjective clause:	✗ That I just bought.
	✗ Whom I knew in high school.

Adverb Clause: ✗ After Cinderella finished the dishes.

✗ Because she left her glass slipper.

An easy way to distinguish between independent clauses (sentences) and dependent clauses is to test the clause by putting *I realize* in front of it.

> **I REALIZE TIP** You can put *I realize* in front of independent clauses (sentences) and they make grammatical sense.

However, if you put *I realize* front of dependent clauses, the result will not make sense.

Here is the *I Realize* Tip applied to the six dependent clauses above:

✗ *I realize* whatever dumb thing a politician says.

✗ *I realize* when I was your age.

✗ *I realize* that I just bought.

✗ *I realize* whom I knew in high school.

✗ *I realize* after Cinderella finished the dishes.

✗ *I realize* because she left her glass slipper.

Grammar Test 8

Use the *I Realize* Tip to help you decide which of the following are independent clauses (sentences) and which are dependent clauses and then label them accordingly.

Example:
dependent clause
After it began to rain.

Confirmation: ✗ *I realize* after it began to rain.

Example:
independent clause (sentence)
We have to catch the 6:15 train.

Confirmation: *I realize* we have to catch the 6:15 train.

1. As soon as we get finished here.

2. What they wanted to do.

3. It's getting pretty late.

4. Whom we were just talking about.

5. The frost has killed all our petunias.

Compound Sentences

A **compound sentence** consists of two independent clauses joined by a **coordinating conjunction**. Here is an example:

I work in the city, but I commute in from the suburbs.

The two independent clauses are joined together by the coordinating conjunction *but* to form a single sentence. (Note the use of the comma before the coordinating conjunction *but*. This comma is obligatory—for details, see Lesson 13, "Commas with *And, But, Or,* and Other Coordinating Conjunctions.")

The three most common coordinating conjunctions used to join independent clauses are *and, but,* and *or*. Here are some examples of compound sentences:

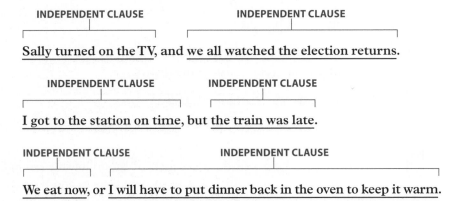

Sally turned on the TV, and we all watched the election returns.

I got to the station on time, but the train was late.

We eat now, or I will have to put dinner back in the oven to keep it warm.

To form a compound sentence, both parts must be complete and freestanding independent clauses. However, we often delete the subject in the second clause because it is redundant. When this happens, the structure of the sentence changes. For example, compare the following two versions of the same message:

1. Henry picked up the phone, and he called for a taxi.
2. Henry picked up the phone and called for a taxi.

Obviously, both sentences mean the same thing. However, the first version is a compound sentence. The second version is not a compound sentence because *called for a taxi* is not an independent clause—it has no subject. Notice also the difference in punctuation. Version 1 has a comma before the coordinating conjunction *and*; version 2 has no comma. The comma in version 1 is required because the coordinating conjunction joins two independent clauses. The *and* in version 2 does not join two independent clauses, so putting a comma after it would be grammatically incorrect.

Grammar Test 9

Underline the independent clauses in the sentences below. If a sentence contains two independent clauses, label it *compound sentence*. If a sentence contains only one independent clause, label it *not a compound*.

Example:
not a compound
The lifeguard yelled at the children and told them to stop running.

Example:
compound sentence
The first tremor didn't cause any damage, but the second one destroyed many houses.

1. The government should agree to the demands, or there will be a major strike.

2. I turned off the lights at 10 P.M. and went to sleep.

3. There were several pencils on the desk but no pens.

4. The shoes were the right color, but they didn't fit all that well.

5. The waiter brought the menus, and we ordered some wine.

Using Prepositional Phrases to Expand the Basic Sentence

Prepositional phrases consist of two components: prepositions and the objects that follow those prepositions. In the following examples, the prepositions are in boldface and the objects are underlined:

after dinner

during the intermission

beside the front door

with a screwdriver

near me

The objects of prepositions are exactly the same group of words as are the objects of action verbs: nouns, noun phrases, object pronouns (like *me*), and other nounlike structures.

Many prepositions refer to space (*above, across, around, behind, beneath, beside, inside, near, on, over, under*) or time (*after, before, during, past, since, throughout, till, until*). However, many prepositions (for instance, *as, but, by, concerning, except, for, like, of, with*) defy simple classification.

The word *preposition* means "to place before." In a prepositional phrase, the preposition always comes before its object. They are locked together as a unit and can never be separated. (*Note:* There is another, totally different use of prepositions in *verb + preposition* compounds. For example, in the sentence *I **took down** the notice*, the compound *took down* means "removed." These *verb + preposition* compounds are discussed at length in Lesson 34, "Two-Word Verbs.")

The function of prepositional phrases is to expand the basic framework of *subject + predicate* sentences by adding optional modifiers to the nouns and verbs that make up the sentence. For example, we can use prepositional phrases (underlined) to expand this basic sentence:

Basic sentence: All my friends heard the news.

Expanded sentence: All my friends at work heard the news about the merger over the weekend.

Prepositional phrases that modify nouns are called **adjective prepositional phrases**, and prepositional phrases that modify verbs are called **adverb prepositional phrases**. (These modifying prepositional phrases are so common that they are often referred to merely as **adjective phrases** and **adverb phrases**.) Below are some examples of prepositional phrases modifying nouns and verbs. The prepositional phrases are underlined, and the words they modify are in boldface.

Adjective prepositional phrases:

The **clerk** at the hardware store recommended the **roller** with the longer handle.

My **roommate** in college wrote a **movie** about his family.

Her favorite book was a **novel** by Barbara Kingsolver.

Adverb prepositional phrases:

There **was** a big snow storm during the weekend.

After dinner we **watched** some TV.

Speakers often **warm up** their audiences by telling some jokes.

Adjective prepositional phrases always immediately follow the nouns they modify and give more information about those nouns. Adverb prepositional phrases usually give information about *where, when,* or *how* the action of the verb takes place.

Grammar Test 10

Underline the prepositional phrases in the following sentences. If the prepositional phrase modifies a noun, label it *adjective*. If it modifies a verb, label it *adverb*.

adverb
Example: We had dinner <u>at a nearby restaurant</u>.

adjective
Example: I couldn't remember the title <u>of the book</u>.

1. They built their new house with their own hands.

2. We lost the game in the last second.

3. I am taking some classes at a community college.

4. The soil on the farm is amazingly rich.

5. The report of the accident was finally released on Monday.

Understanding the Basic Sentence

OVERVIEW

The Nuts and Bolts of Understanding the Basic Sentence

This unit will help you understand the most basic concept in writing: the correct punctuation of complete sentences. A **complete sentence** has the following characteristics:

- It contains both a **subject** and a **verb**.

- It expresses a complete thought—a freestanding, self-contained idea.

The two lessons in this unit present the two ways that a sentence can be mispunctuated: as a **fragment** or as a **run-on**.

Lesson 1 shows you how to identify and correct fragments. In a fragment, something less than a complete sentence has been punctuated as though it were one. Here is an example of a fragment:

Fragment: Celeste found a cat. ✗ Which she promptly took home.

Correction: Celeste found a cat╱ ~~Which~~ ,which she promptly took home.

The fragment *which she promptly took home* contains both a subject and a verb, but it cannot stand alone as a self-contained idea. Most fragments are continuations of the preceding sentence, so the easiest way to correct fragments is to attach them to the preceding sentence.

Lesson 2 shows you how to identify and correct run-ons. In a run-on, two complete sentences have been joined together incorrectly and punctuated as though they were a single sentence. Here is an example of a run-on:

Run-on: ✗ The boss liked my idea, she said she would take it to the board of directors.

Correction: The boss liked my idea╱ ; she said she would take it to the board of directors.

This kind of run-on is called a **comma splice** because it incorrectly uses a comma to join two complete sentences. If the two sentences had been put together without any punctuation at all, it would be another kind of run-on called a **fused sentence**. Writers sometimes create run-ons when they try to keep closely related ideas together within the same sentence. Two good ways to achieve the same goal are to join the related sentences with a comma and a **coordinating conjunction** (*for, and, nor, but, or, yet, so*) or with a semicolon (;).

Fragments

EXAMPLE 1   *Renamer Fragment*

Error: Blocking my driveway was a car. ✗ A huge SUV.

                                                , a

Correction: Blocking my driveway was a car/ A huge SUV.

EXAMPLE 2   *Adverb Fragment*

Error: I was really upset. ✗ Because I knew I would be late for work.

                                      because

Correction: I was really upset/ ~~Because~~ I knew I would be late for work.

EXAMPLE 3   *-ing Fragment*

Error: I beeped my horn a couple of times. ✗ Letting the driver know I had to get out.

                                             , letting

Correction: I beeped my horn a couple of times/ ~~Letting~~ the driver know I had to get out.

What's the Problem?

ESL

A **fragment** is a group of words that cannot stand alone as a **complete sentence** but is mistakenly punctuated as though it were. In English, a subject, a verb, and a complete thought are needed for a complete sentence. Many fragments lack a verb, as in Example 1, or lack a subject, as in Example 3. Example 2 has a subject and a verb, but it does not express a complete thought.

Fragments are hard for writers to spot because they sound normal. In the quick give-and-take of conversation, fragments are used as a way of clarifying, elaborating on, or emphasizing what was just said without stopping and reformulating the previous sentence. In formal, written language, however, fragments are inappropriate. Readers expect formal writing to be carefully planned.

Diagnostic Exercise

CORRECTED SENTENCES APPEAR ON PAGE 464.

Correct all errors in the following paragraphs using the first correction as a model. The number in parentheses at the end of each paragraph indicates how many errors you should find in that paragraph.

, earning

I need more money. There are only two ways to get more money. ~~Earning~~ more or spending less. I am going to have to do a better job saving what money I do earn. Because there is no realistic way that I can earn more money. The first thing I did was to make a list of everything I bought. Starting last Monday. (2)

When I read over my list, the first thing I noticed was how much I spent on junk food. Especially snacks and energy bars. It is really stupid to spend so much money on stuff. That isn't even good for me. I can't just do away with snacks, though. I work long, irregular hours, and so I can't always have regular meals. Like everyone else. (3)

The second thing I noticed was how much I was spending on drinks. Such as coffee and bottled water. I was dropping four or five dollars every time I went to Starbuck's. Which is way more than I can afford. What really got my attention, though, was the cost of bottled water. I resolved to save some bottles and fill them from a drinking fountain. After all, you can get water for free. (2)

Fixing This Problem in Your Writing

Identifying Fragments

A fragment is almost always a continuation of the preceding sentence. To find and then fix a fragment, we need to separate it from the previous sentence. When a fragment is by itself, isolated from preceding sentences, we are much

frag

more likely to notice it doesn't make sense on its own. Here is one tip that will help you isolate fragments.

> **LIKELY FRAGMENTS TIP**   Most fragments fall into one of three categories: *renamers*, *adverbs*, and *-ing fragments*. If you are aware of what the most common types of fragments are, you are more likely to spot them.

Renamers. These fragments rename or give further information about the last noun in the preceding sentence. Example 1 illustrates this type of fragment.

FRAGMENT

Example 1:   Blocking my driveway was a <u>car</u>. ✗ <u>A huge SUV</u>.

The fragment renames the noun *car*.

Another common type of renamer begins with *which*:

FRAGMENT

Along the curb, there was a <u>car</u>. ✗ <u>Which was completely blocking my driveway</u>.

The fragment gives further information about the car.

Adverbs.   In this category are adverb clauses that tell when, where, and especially why something happened. Example 2 illustrates this type of fragment.

FRAGMENT

Example 2:   <u>I was really upset</u>. ✗ <u>Because I knew I would be late for work</u>.

The fragment expands on the entire previous sentence, explaining why the writer was upset.

-ing *Fragments*. These fragments begin with the *-ing* form of a verb. Example 3 illustrates this type of fragment.

FRAGMENT

Example 3:   <u>I beeped my horn a couple of times</u>. ✗ <u>Letting the driver know I had to get out</u>.

frag

Typically, *-ing* fragments explain something about the meaning of the preceding sentence. In this example, the *-ing* fragment explains why the writer beeped the horn.

Here is a tip to help you spot all three types of fragments.

> **BACKWARD PROOFREADING TIP** Proofread your paper backward, one sentence at a time. Use one hand or a piece of paper to cover up all but the last sentence in each paragraph. See if that sentence can stand alone. If it can, then uncover the next-to-last sentence to see if it can stand alone, and so on.

Backward proofreading is a standard and quite effective way of identifying fragments because fragments generally don't make sense when they are separated from preceding sentences. Try this tip on the Diagnostic Exercise at the beginning of this lesson.

Here is a third tip to help you catch fragments.

> **I REALIZE TIP** You can put *I realize* in front of most complete sentences and make a new grammatical sentence. However, when you put *I realize* in front of a fragment, the result will not make sense.

The *I Realize* Tip is a particularly handy way to test whether something is actually a fragment. Here is how it would be applied to each of the three sample fragments:

Tip applied: ✗ <u>I realize</u> a huge SUV.

Tip applied: ✗ <u>I realize</u> because I knew I would be late for work.

Tip applied: ✗ <u>I realize</u> letting the driver know I had to get out.

The *I Realize* Tip confirms that these examples are fragments: They do not make sense when you put *I realize* in front of them.

Correcting Fragments

Once you identify a fragment, the easiest way to correct it is to attach it to the preceding sentence. Use the following guidelines in deciding how to punctuate the new sentence.

- If the fragment is a renamer or an *-ing* fragment, you will probably need to add a comma.

- If it is an adverb fragment, you will usually need no punctuation to attach it to the previous sentence. A comma is required only if the

frag

fragment begins with a word or phrase such as *although* or *even though*, to show a strong contrast.

Alternatively, you could expand the fragment to make a complete sentence in its own right. Decide if the material in the fragment is worth emphasizing. If it is, expand the fragment to a full sentence. If it is not that important (most of the time, this is the case), attach it to the preceding sentence.

Let's use the *I Realize* Tip to identify fragments in three new examples. We'll then correct each fragment using both methods: connecting the fragment to the preceding sentence and expanding the fragment to make a complete sentence.

RENAMER FRAGMENT

Example: I have to commute on the beltway. ✗ The Highway from Hell.

Tip applied: ✗ <u>I realize</u> the Highway from Hell.

Connected: I have to commute on the beltway. *, the* ~~The~~ Highway from Hell.

Use a comma to connect a renamer fragment.

Expanded: I have to commute on the beltway. *It is called the* ~~The~~ Highway from Hell.

ADVERB FRAGMENT

Example: Yesterday's traffic was worse than usual. ✗ Because there was an accident.

Tip applied: ✗ <u>I realize</u> because there was an accident.

Connected: Yesterday's traffic was worse than usual. *because* ~~Because~~ there was an accident.

Don't use a comma to connect most adverb fragments.

Expanded: Yesterday's traffic was worse than usual. Because there was an accident. *, it took me over an hour to get to work.*

-ING FRAGMENT

Example: Today, I actually left home on schedule. ✗ Showing that I can be on time if I try.

Tip applied: ✗ I realize showing that I can be on time if I try.

Connected: Today, I actually left home on schedule/ S̶h̶o̶w̶i̶n̶g̶ , showing that I can be on time if I try.

Use a comma to connect an *-ing* fragment.

Expanded: Today, I actually left home on schedule. S̶h̶o̶w̶i̶n̶g̶ ̶t̶h̶a̶t̶ See, I can be on time if I try.

✳ *Putting It All Together*

Identify Fragments

____ Understand and look for the most common types of fragments: *renamers*, *adverbs*, and *-ing fragments*.

____ Proofread your paper starting at the last sentence and moving to the first, reading one sentence at a time.

____ Put *I realize* in front of each group of words that you think might be a fragment. The *I realize* sentence will not make sense if the word group is a fragment.

Correct Fragments

____ Attach each fragment to the previous sentence, or rewrite the fragment to make it a complete sentence if you want to emphasize it.

Sentence Practice 1

CORRECTED SENTENCES APPEAR ON PAGE 464.

Find the fragments by using the *I Realize* Tip. Write *OK* above each complete sentence. Write *frag* above each fragment and identify which of the three types it is: *renamer*, *adverb*, or *-ing fragment*. Correct the fragment by combining it with the complete sentence next to it. (Use a comma if the fragment

frag

is a renamer or an *-ing* fragment. Do not use a comma if the fragment is an adverb.)

Example: A few years ago, there was only one kind of eating apple that you could buy. The Red Delicious.

OK
Tip applied: <u>I realize</u> a few years ago, there was only one kind of eating apple that you could buy.

frag, renamer
✗ <u>I realize</u> the Red Delicious.

Correction: A few years ago, there was only one kind of eating apple
, the
that you could buy̶.̶ ̶T̶h̶e̶ Red Delicious.
^

1. Growers loved the Red Delicious apple variety. Because it stayed ripe for a long time.

2. Growers kept changing the Red Delicious variety over the years. Making the apples redder and even more long lasting.

3. Unfortunately, there was a negative side effect to their changes. Taste.

4. I didn't really like the old Red Delicious apples. I thought their skins were bitter.

5. A lot of people must have agreed. Because the sales of Red Delicious slowed down.

 For more practice correcting fragments, go to **Exercise Central** at **bedfordstmartins.com/commonsense**

Sentence Practice 2

CORRECTED SENTENCES APPEAR ON PAGE 464.

Find the fragments by using the *I Realize* Tip. Write *OK* above each complete sentence. Write *frag* above each fragment and identify which of the three types it is — *renamer*, *adverb*, or *-ing fragment*. Correct the fragment by combining it with the complete sentence next to it. (Use a comma if the fragment is a renamer or an *-ing* fragment. Do not use a comma if the fragment is an adverb.)

Example: One of the most popular apples in the world comes from Japan. The Fuji apple.

Tip applied: *OK*
               I <u>realize</u> one of the most popular apples in the world comes from Japan.

               frag, renamer
               X I <u>realize</u> the Fuji apple.

Correction: One of the most popular apples in the world comes from
                               , the
               Japan/ ~~The~~ Fuji apple.
                   ^

1. The public loves Fuji apples. Because they are sweet and crisp.

2. Apple growers love them. Since they keep for up to six months.

3. Apple researchers in Japan developed the Fuji apple. Using our old friend the Red Delicious.

4. The Fuji apple is a cross between two American apples. The Red Delicious and the Virginia Ralls Genet.

5. The researchers who developed the apple named it. Calling it "Fuji" after the name of their research station.

Sentence Practice 3

Combine the following pairs of sentences by turning the second sentence into a renamer, an adverb clause, or an *-ing* expression as directed and then attaching the revision to the first sentence.

Example: a. The Florida Keys are actually hundreds of little islands.

              b. The islands run from the mainland to Key West. (*-ing* expression)

Answer: The Florida Keys are actually hundreds of little islands running from the mainland to Key West.

1. a. The bigger keys end at Key West.

    b. Key West is the westernmost of the bigger keys. (renamer)

2. a. The road to Key West is a series of bridges.

    b. The bridges span from key to key. (*-ing* expression)

3. a. The bridges were built on a previously existing causeway.

    b. The causeway is the remains of an abandoned railway line. (renamer)

4. a. Building the railway line was a huge task.

b. There are many hurricanes that strike the keys. (adverb clause)

5. a. However, what doomed the railway was a different problem.

b. The problem was the lack of docking facilities on Key West. (renamer)

6. a. In 1935, a large hurricane came through the keys.

b. The hurricane tore out big parts of the railway. (*-ing* expression)

7. a. The railway was abandoned after the storm.

b. Rebuilding the railways would be prohibitively expensive. (adverb clause)

8. a. Today, Key West is connected to the mainland by a highway.

b. The highway is a causeway built on land filled in for the old railway. (renamer)

9. a. The highway is an amazing construction.

b. The construction runs for 127 miles. (*-ing* expression)

10. a. We know that the highway is well built.

b. The highway survived a major hurricane in 2005. (adverb clause)

Editing Practice 1

CORRECTED SENTENCES APPEAR ON PAGE 464.

Correct all fragment errors in the following paragraph using the first correction as a model. The number in parentheses at the end of the paragraph indicates how many errors you should find.

for

Key West is a great place to visit/ ~~For~~ a lot of reasons. First of all,
                                    ^
the physical setting is magnificent. Blue sky and beautiful ocean views.

Being on an island makes you much more aware of the water and the sky.

Unlike the often cloudless skies on the Pacific coast, the skies in the keys

often have small puffy clouds. Giving a sense of space and depth to the sky.

The color of the water is always changing. Because the coral reefs reflect

the continually changing play of sun and cloud. The fact that the ocean

around Key West is so shallow and so varied gives the water vibrant colors.

frag

With dozens of shades of green and blue everywhere you look. The beaches in California are quite drab by comparison. Because they are mostly made up of uniform, gray sandy bottoms. (5)

Editing Practice 2

CORRECTED SENTENCES APPEAR ON PAGE 464.

Correct all fragment errors in the following paragraph using the first correction as a model. The number in parentheses at the end of the paragraph indicates how many errors you should find.

It is interesting to compare Key West with a similar ocean-side destination in California/, Santa Barbara, for instance. Besides being beach destinations, they share another important feature. A lengthy Spanish heritage. Key West today doesn't feel Spanish at all. Even though it (and the rest of Florida) was part of the Spanish empire for nearly three hundred years. There was never any permanent Spanish settlement there. Because there was no source of fresh water on the island. Key West was a temporary home for fishermen and pirates. A source of much humor today. Santa Barbara, on the other hand, is overflowing with its Spanish heritage. Especially in its architecture. Santa Barbara today looks classically Spanish. With its white buildings and red tile roofs. (6)

Editing Practice 3

Correct all fragment errors in the following paragraph using the first correction as a model. The number in parentheses at the end of the paragraph indicates how many errors you should find.

There is one huge difference between Key West and Santa Barbara/ The
, the
climate. Key West is in the Caribbean. A shallow, warm tropical sea. As a result, Key West is uniformly warm. And excessively humid. The sun and humidity generate a lot of clouds. Resulting in almost daily rain showers.

Lots of sun and rain support luxurious tropical vegetation. And plenty of bugs. Santa Barbara is almost the exact opposite. Southern California is essentially a desert. Resulting in distinctly un-lush, drought-tolerant vegetation. Even though the beaches in Santa Barbara are beautiful, very few people actually go in the water. Because it is bone-numbingly cold. On the other hand, there are very few bugs. (6)

Applying What You Know

On your own paper, write a paragraph or two comparing the advantages and disadvantages of two places you have been on vacation. Use the Putting It All Together checklist on page 25 to make sure that there are no fragments.

The Bottom Line	**I realize** you can use *I realize* to spot fragments.

Run-ons: Fused Sentences and Comma Splices

EXAMPLE 1	***Fused Sentence***
Error:	✗ I have a test on Thursday it should not be difficult.
Correction:	I have a test on Thursday ⌃*, and* it should not be difficult.
EXAMPLE 2	***Comma Splice***
Error:	✗ The student-government election is this week, I have no idea who is running.
Correction:	The student-government election is this week, ⌃*but* I have no idea who is running.

What's the Problem?

A **run-on sentence** contains two **independent clauses** that have been incorrectly joined together. (An independent clause is a group of words that can stand alone as a complete sentence.) Run-on sentences fail to show the reader where one idea ends and the next one begins.

The examples above illustrate two types of run-on sentence errors. When two independent clauses are joined with no punctuation at all, the error is called a **fused sentence**. When two independent clauses are joined with just a comma (without a coordinating conjunction like *and, but, or*), the error is called a **comma splice**. In both cases, the writer confuses the reader by failing to correctly signal the separation between two complete ideas.

In the following examples, notice how the clauses are separated by nothing at all or by just a comma.

INDEPENDENT CLAUSE   INDEPENDENT CLAUSE

Fused Sentence: ✗ I went to the store it was closed.

Problem: Nothing separates the two clauses.

run-on

INDEPENDENT CLAUSE   INDEPENDENT CLAUSE

Comma Splice: ✗ I went to the store, it was closed.

Problem: Only a comma separates the two clauses.

Diagnostic Exercise

CORRECTED SENTENCES APPEAR ON PAGE 465.

Correct all run-on errors in the following paragraph using the first correction as a model. The number in parentheses at the end of the paragraph indicates how many errors you should find.

, but

I go to school on the West Coast my family lives on the East Coast. My family is very close-knit, they all live within a hundred miles of each other. When I applied to college, I submitted applications to schools nearby I also submitted an application to one West Coast school. To my great surprise, I got in to the West Coast school. They had exactly the program I wanted to study and they gave me a really good financial aid package. At first, the idea of going seemed impossible the school just seemed so far away. My family was not at all happy, most of them said I should go to school in state. The one person who thought I should go to the West Coast was my aunt she said I should go to the best school I could get in to no matter where it was. I am really glad that I followed her advice, I have really come to love my West Coast school. (7)

Fixing This Problem in Your Writing

Identifying Run-ons

Run-ons are easy to correct once you have identified them. The problem is finding them to begin with. Here is a tip for spotting potential run-on sentences in your writing.

IMAGINARY PERIOD TIP   If a sentence contains two separate ideas, put an imaginary period between them. Now ask: Can BOTH parts stand alone as complete sentences? If so, then the sentence might be a run-on.

Here is the Imaginary Period Tip applied to the fused sentence and the comma splice from the beginning of the lesson:

Example 1:   ✗ I have a test on Thursday it should not be difficult.

Tip applied: I have a test on Thursday. It should not be difficult.

A period added between the separate ideas creates two sentences.

Example 2:   ✗ The student-government election is this week, I have no idea who is running.

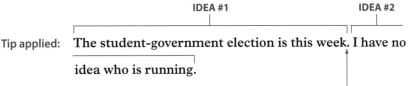

Tip applied: The student-government election is this week. I have no idea who is running.

A period added between the separate ideas creates two sentences.

In both cases, the two new sentences created by the Imaginary Period Tip can stand alone. In other words, each part of the Tip Applied sentence is a complete sentence, not a fragment. (See Lesson 1 if you need help recognizing a complete sentence.)

Correcting Run-ons

The Imaginary Period Tip does not prove that a sentence is a run-on. It only helps you determine whether a sentence contains two independent clauses and *might* be a run-on. Now you must determine if the two independent clauses are correctly separated. The easiest way to correctly separate two independent clauses is with a period. The Tip Applied step in the examples above illustrates this method.

Another way to separate two independent clauses is with a semicolon (;). A semicolon allows you to keep two closely related ideas together within the same sentence. (See Lesson 24 for more on semicolons.) Here is an example of how to correct a run-on with a semicolon.

Example: ✗ I did pretty well on the last test I got an 82.

Tip applied:	I did pretty well on the last test. I got an 82.
	An imaginary period works, so the clauses are independent.
Correction:	I did pretty well on the last test; I got an 82.
	Add a semicolon where the imaginary period could go.

A third way to punctuate two independent clauses is to combine them with a comma and a **coordinating conjunction** (*for, and, nor, but, or, yet, so*). We'll illustrate this with Example 1 from the start of the lesson.

Example 1:	✗ I have a test on Thursday it should not be difficult.
Tip applied:	I have a test on Thursday. It should not be difficult.
	An imaginary period works, so the clauses are independent.
	, *and*
Correction:	I have a test on Thursday it should not be difficult.
	Add a comma and conjunction where the imaginary period could go.

Example 2 (the comma splice) has only half of what we need: a comma but no coordinating conjunction. A comma alone should not separate two independent clauses.

Example 2:	✗ The student-government election is this week, I have no idea who is running.
Tip applied:	The student-government election is this week. I have no idea who is running.
	An imaginary period works, so the clauses are independent.
	but
Correction:	The student-government election is this week, I have no idea who is running.
	Use a comma and conjunction where the imaginary period could go.

MORE EXAMPLES

Error:	✗ Jamal is a physics major he plans to work for NASA.
	. *He*
Correction:	Jamal is a physics major. he plans to work for NASA.
Error:	✗ Traffic today was horrible I am thirty minutes late.
	, *so*
Correction:	Traffic today was horrible I am thirty minutes late.

Error: ✗ On a cold day in December, my car broke down on the highway, it is parked there.

Correction: On a cold day in December, my car broke down on the highway ̷ **;** it is parked there.
                                         ^

Error: ✗ George has two sons, they are both in elementary school.

                                        and
Correction: George has two sons, they are both in elementary school.   ^

✳ *Putting It All Together*

Identify Run-ons

____ Insert an imaginary period between two ideas in a sentence. If both ideas can stand alone as complete sentences, the original sentence might be a run-on.

____ Check to see whether the two ideas are correctly separated. A semi-colon or a comma plus a coordinating conjunction (such as *and* or *but*) should come between the two ideas.

Correct Run-ons

____ Join two independent clauses with a semicolon or with a comma and a coordinating conjunction in the spot where you placed the imaginary period.

____ Alternately, turn the imaginary period into a real one, making each idea into a separate sentence.

Sentence Practice 1

CORRECTED SENTENCES APPEAR ON PAGE 465.

Find the independent clauses in the following run-on sentences by using the Imaginary Period Tip. Correct each run-on by inserting a semicolon between the two independent clauses, by adding a comma and a coordinating conjunction, or by turning the imaginary period into a real one. If a sentence does not contain a run-on, write *OK* above it.

run-on

Example: My car is getting pretty old, it still gets me where I want to go.

Tip applied: My car is getting pretty old. It still gets me where I want to go.

but
Correction: My car is getting pretty old, it still gets me where I want to go.
                                                                    ^

1. I slipped on the ice going to work I wrenched my left knee.

2. The math homework is getting pretty hard I am thinking of getting a tutor.

3. Trying to sell a house in this economic climate is tough nobody can get a loan.

4. Daylight saving time doesn't end until after Halloween the trick-or-treaters don't have go out in the dark.

5. Please call your mother she's been trying to reach you all day.

 For more practice correcting run-ons, go to **Exercise Central** at **bedfordstmartins.com/commonsense**

Sentence Practice 2

CORRECTED SENTENCES APPEAR ON PAGE 465.

Find the independent clauses in the following run-on sentences by using the Imaginary Period Tip. Correct each run-on by inserting a semicolon between the two independent clauses, by adding a comma and a coordinating conjunction, or by turning the imaginary period into a real one. If a sentence does not contain a run-on, write *OK* above it.

Example: I usually work from home, once a week I go into the office.

Tip applied: I usually work from home. Once a week I go into the office.

but
Correction: I usually work from home, once I week I go into the office.
                                                            ^

1. Please come here, I need some help.

2. There is a grinding noise every time I put the car in reverse.

3. I don't watch much TV anymore, I still read *TV Guide*.

4. We are taking out the kitchen counter we are putting in a granite one.

5. He is going back to school as soon as he saves enough money.

Sentence Practice 3

Combine each pair of sentences by attaching the second sentence to the first with a comma and an appropriate coordinating conjunction (*for, and, nor, but, or, yet, so*).

> Example: My sister plans to go to college next year. She is sending out dozens of applications now.

> Answer: My sister plans to go to college next year/ ~~She~~ is sending
> *, so she*
> out dozens of applications now. ^

1. We are going to San Diego in September. Then we are going to Los Angeles in October.

2. My iPod isn't working. Maybe it just needs to be recharged.

3. She had to stay up late last night. This morning she is sleeping in.

4. I am coming down with a cold. My allergies are really acting up.

5. I am coming down with a cold. Unfortunately, I still have to go to work.

6. It looked like rain. I decided to take my umbrella.

7. It looked like rain. I decided not to take my umbrella because I had no place to keep it if it got wet.

8. It looked like it would rain at any minute. Not surprisingly, it began to pour a few minutes later.

9. I hate having lunch alone. I always look for a friend to eat with.

10. I hate having lunch alone. Sometimes I have to.

Editing Practice 1

CORRECTED SENTENCES APPEAR ON PAGE 465.

Correct all run-ons in the following paragraph using the first correction as a model. The number in parentheses at the end of the paragraph indicates how many errors you should find.

I was late to my first class; my car broke down on the side of the
                                   ^
highway. This is the third time this fall that I have had to pull over because

of an engine problem, I am not going to suffer through a fourth time.

According to a mechanic, the problem has something to do with the fuel

injector. I have replaced the fuse, and the mechanic has tried various

other methods. Nothing has worked it does not make sense spending even

more money on something that cannot be fixed. I might need a whole new

fuel injector, I am considering buying a new car. The one I have is only six

years old, so I hate buying a new one already. It all depends on what I can

afford. (3)

Editing Practice 2

CORRECTED SENTENCES APPEAR ON PAGE 465.

Correct all run-ons in the following paragraph using the first correction as a
model. The number in parentheses at the end of the paragraph indicates how
many errors you should find.

                                                                 , and
At my college, on-campus parking can be extremely difficult the
                                                                 ^
situation will soon be worse. Currently, the college has eight parking lots

for students, two of them hold only about a dozen cars. During the

summer, construction will begin on a new library, which we certainly need.

The construction will last a year, two parking lots will be closed

during the construction phase. When the library opens up next year,

only one of the two lots will be reopened the other will have vanished

because the library will cover it. Almost everyone believes we need a new

library, it is too bad that the administration has not made plans regarding

the parking problem, which is only going to get more dire. (4)

run-on

Editing Practice 3

Correct all run-ons in the following paragraphs using the first correction as a model. The number in parentheses at the end of each paragraph indicates how many errors you should find.

Most people do not really know what an infinitive is, it is *to* + the `is. It or is; it` dictionary form of a verb, for example: *to work, to sleep, to laugh.* However, there is one thing that everybody can tell you about infinitives, it is bad grammar to split them. Here is an example of a sentence with a split infinitive: "He promised to *always* use good grammar." This is a split infinitive because the adverb *always* comes in between (i.e., splits) the words of the infinitive *to use.* So, why is it considered bad grammar to split an infinitive? (1)

To answer this question we must go back in time. People have been happily splitting infinitives since at least the fourteenth century nobody noticed or cared. Splitting infinitives was never an issue until the early grammar books for English were written in the eighteenth century. These grammar books based their analysis of English on Latin grammars they were the only model of grammar that eighteenth-century grammarians had. In Latin grammar, the infinitive is a single-word construction, unlike English there is no *to*. Since it is literally impossible to split the one-word infinitive in Latin, these grammarians decreed that it was, therefore, improper to split an infinitive in English. (3)

Modern grammarians know that there is no valid reason to condemn split infinitives after all, English and Latin are totally different languages. However, since so many people are absolutely convinced that it is wrong to split infinitives, grammarians advise writers to avoid them, not because there is anything actually wrong with split infinitives, but because they bother some people why upset people needlessly? (2)

run-on

Applying What You Know

Select fifteen sentences from one of your textbooks, and use the Imaginary Period Tip to determine how many are composed of two or more independent clauses—complete ideas that can stand alone as separate sentences. How many of the fifteen sentences use a comma and a coordinating conjunction to separate independent clauses? How many use a semicolon?

The Bottom Line	See if your sentence has two independent clauses, **and** make sure they are separated with a period, a semicolon, or a comma and coordinating conjunction.

Understanding the Basic Sentence

REVIEW

To write effectively, you must be able to recognize and correctly punctuate basic sentences. Every basic sentence has these components:

- a subject and a verb
- a self-contained, complete idea

Another term for a basic sentence is an independent clause. The following chart points you to the tips that will help you avoid errors when punctuating basic sentences.

TIPS	QUICK FIXES AND EXAMPLES
Lesson 1. Fragments	
The Likely Fragments Tip (p. 22) helps you remember the most common types of fragments. The Backward Proofreading Tip (p. 23) and the *I Realize* Tip (p. 23) help you spot fragments in your writing.	Attach a fragment to the previous sentence, or re-write the fragment to make it a complete sentence if you want to emphasize it. **Error:** Laura has been exhausted. ✗ Since she has been working on the weekends. **Correction:** Laura has been exhausted/ *since* ~~Since~~ she has been working on the weekends. ^
Lesson 2. Run-ons	
The Imaginary Period Tip (p. 33) helps you determine whether a sentence contains two independent clauses so you can make sure they are punctuated correctly.	Separate the two independent clauses of a run-on with a period, a semicolon, or a comma and a coordinating conjunction (such as *and, but, or*). **Error:** ✗ Laura is exhausted she has been working weekends. . *She* **Correction:** Laura is exhausted ~~she~~ has been ^ working weekends.

Review Test

Correct fragment and run-on errors in the following paragraphs using the first correction as a model. The number in parentheses at the end of each paragraph indicates how many errors you should find.

        after
I read an article on washing clothes~~.~~ ~~After~~ I shrank an expensive
                                        ^
sweater. I thought I could just toss everything in the washer. Without

checking the color or type of fabric. I learned a valuable lesson I just wish it

hadn't been such an expensive lesson. (2)

Most items made of heavy cotton can be washed in very hot water,

they won't shrink. It is best if white cotton items are washed by themselves.

Because they can pick up colors from other things being washed. Light-

weight cottons do best in warm water. Unless they are dark colors. Which

always require cold water. (4)

Badly soiled laundry needs to be washed in very hot water. Unless the

garment label says otherwise. That is how I ruined my sweater, I simply

didn't know to look at its label. (2)

Making Subjects and Verbs Agree

OVERVIEW

The Nuts and Bolts of Subject-Verb Agreement

This unit will help you make your subjects and verbs agree in your writing. By "agree," we mean that the **subject** of any sentence must match the **verb** in number. For example, a singular subject (one person, place, or object) should be paired with the singular form of a verb. A plural subject (more than one person, place, or object) should be paired with the plural form of a verb.

Singular: The <u>student</u> <u>uses</u> the Internet for research.

Plural: The <u>students</u> <u>use</u> the Internet for research.

One basic rule to follow in making subjects and verbs agree is to add an *-s* to the **present tense** form of the verb if the subject is *he*, *she*, or *it* or if the subject can be replaced by one of these **personal pronouns**. The lessons in this unit deal with three common errors writers make in **subject-verb agreement**.

Lesson 3 shows you how to make the subject and verb agree when the subject phrase is so long or complicated that the actual subject gets lost. Here is an example of an error involving a lost subject.

Example: ✗ The cost of all the repairs we needed to make were more than we could afford.

Correction: The cost of all the repairs we needed to make ~~were~~ *was* more than we could afford.

The verb in this sentence must agree with the subject *cost*, not the nearby noun *repairs*.

Lesson 4 shows you how to make the subject and verb agree when the subject follows the verb, as in sentences that begin with *there is* or *there was*. Here is an example of this type of error.

Example: ✗ There is usually some leftovers in the refrigerator.

Correction: There ~~is~~ usually some leftovers in the refrigerator.
                                are
                        ^

The verb in this sentence must agree with the subject *leftovers*.

Lesson 5 shows you how to make the subject and verb agree when the sentence includes a **compound subject** (two or more subjects joined by *and*). Here is an example of an error involving a compound subject.

Example: ✗ Good planning and careful follow-through is necessary for success in any field.

Correction: Good planning and careful follow-through ~~is~~ necessary for success in any field.
                                                          are
                                                          ^

The verb in this sentence must agree with the compound subject *planning and follow-through*.

LESSON 3

Nearest-Noun Agreement Errors

EXAMPLE 1   *Plural Subject with a Singular Verb*

Error: ✗ The <u>advantages</u> of this entertainment system <u>is</u> that
it is more compact and less expensive than others on
the market.

Correction: The <u>advantages</u> of this entertainment system ~~is~~ *are* that it
is more compact and less expensive than others on
the market.

EXAMPLE 2   *Singular Subject with a Plural Verb*

Error: ✗ Last night, <u>one</u> of the new cottages <u>were</u> damaged in
the storm.

Correction: Last night, <u>one</u> of the new cottages ~~were~~ *was* damaged in
the storm.

What's the Problem?

When a sentence contains a **subject–verb agreement** error, most often the
problem is that the **verb** in the sentence is agreeing with a word that is not
the actual **subject**—usually it is agreeing with a noun that is closer to the
verb than the actual subject. We call this error the "nearest-noun" agreement
error.

Let's look once again at the two examples of nearest-noun agreement
errors that started the lesson. In Example 1, the verb *is* mistakenly agrees
with the nearest noun, *entertainment system*, rather than with the actual subject of the sentence, *advantages*.

ACTUAL SUBJECT   NEAREST NOUN

Example 1:   ✗ The <u>advantages</u> of this <u>entertainment system</u> <u>is</u> that . . .

In Example 2, the problem is that the verb *were* mistakenly agrees with the nearest noun, *cottages*, rather than with the actual subject of the sentence, *one*.

ACTUAL SUBJECT   NEAREST NOUN

↓   ↓

Example 2:   ✗ Last night, <u>one</u> of the new <u>cottages</u> <u>were</u> damaged in the storm.

It is easy to make nearest-noun agreement errors when many words separate the subject of the sentence from the verb or when another noun comes between the subject of the sentence and the verb.

Diagnostic Exercise

CORRECTED SENTENCES APPEAR ON PAGE 466.

Correct all subject-verb agreement errors in the following paragraph using the first correction as a model. The number in parentheses at the end of the paragraph indicates how many errors you should find.

dates

The beginning of the first public schools in the United States ~~date~~
        ^

from the early 1800s. The pressure to create public schools open to children

of working-class parents were a direct result of the union movements in large

cities. In response, state legislatures gave communities the legal right to levy

local property taxes to pay for free schools open to the public. By the middle

of the nineteenth century, control of the school policies and curriculum were

in the hands of the state government. As school populations outgrew one-

room schoolhouses, the design of school buildings on the East Coast were

completely changed to accommodate separate rooms for children of different

ages. Before this time, all children in a schoolhouse, regardless of age, was

taught together in the same room by the same teacher. (4)

Fixing This Problem in Your Writing

To avoid making nearest-noun agreement errors, your first job is to find the correct subject of the sentence. The subject is *usually* the first noun (or pronoun) in the sentence. When you look for the subject, remember not to be fooled by nouns that are nearer to the verb than the actual subject is.

Lesson 3

s-v
agr

One exception to the rule that the subject is the first noun in a sentence is when a sentence begins with an introductory element that contains a noun, as in the following example:

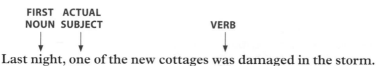

FIRST   ACTUAL
NOUN SUBJECT   VERB
  ↓   ↓   ↓
Last night, <u>one</u> of the new cottages <u style="text-decoration: double underline">was</u> damaged in the storm.

Here the first noun in the sentence is *night*. However, *night* is not the subject of the sentence because it is part of an introductory element and does not make sense as the subject (the *night* was not damaged in the storm). To find the subject, you therefore need to find the first plausible noun *after* any introductory phrase. In this case, the word *one* is the subject.

Use the following tip to find the correct subject in a sentence.

FINDING THE SUBJECT TIP   To find the correct subject of a sentence, jump back to the beginning of the sentence and find the *first* noun (or pronoun) that makes sense as the subject and is not part of an introductory element. Once you find the correct subject, make sure that the verb agrees with that subject.

In the following examples, see how jumping back to the beginning of the sentence and finding the first plausible noun correctly identifies the subject:

Example 1:   ✗ The advantages of this entertainment system is that it is more compact and less expensive than others on the market.

SUBJECT   ✗

Tip applied: The (advantages) of this entertainment system <u style="text-decoration: double underline">is</u> that it is . . .

Correction: The advantages of this entertainment system ~~is~~ *are* that it is . . .

In this example, the first noun in the sentence (*advantages*) is the subject, not the noun closest to the verb (*entertainment system*). The subject is plural, so the verb should also be plural.

Example 2:   ✗ Last night, one of the new cottages were damaged in the storm.

SUBJECT   X

Tip applied: Last night, (one) of the new cottages <u>were</u> damaged in the storm.

was

Correction: Last night, one of the new cottages ~~were~~ damaged in the storm.
                                                        ^

In this example, the subject (*one*) is the first noun after the introductory phrase, not the first noun in the sentence (*night*) or the noun closest to the verb (*cottages*). The subject is singular, so the verb should also be singular.

✳ *Putting It All Together*

Identify the Subject

____ Jump back to the beginning of the sentence to find the first noun or pronoun that makes sense as the subject and that is not part of an introductory element.

Correct Nearest-Noun Agreement Errors

____ Use a singular verb form for a singular subject and a plural verb form for a plural subject.

Sentence Practice 1

CORRECTED SENTENCES APPEAR ON PAGE 466.

In the following sentences, the verb is in **boldface** type. Jump to the beginning of the sentence and find the first word that makes sense as the subject. Underline this subject and then make the verb agree with it. If the form of the verb is correct, write *OK* above it.

seem

Example: The <u>suggestions</u> about cutting the budget always ~~seems~~ terribly simplistic.
                                                                   ^

1. The integration of so many different ideas **take** a lot of time and effort.

2. The ranking of all the qualifying teams **are** always controversial.

3. Examination of the entirety of documents clearly **show** that the defendant is innocent.

4. The losses at the start of the season **makes** it hard to win the conference.

5. One of the trees in our neighborhood **have crashed** down onto the power line.

 For more practice correcting nearest-noun agreement errors, go to **Exercise Central** at **bedfordstmartins.com/commonsense**

Sentence Practice 2

CORRECTED SENTENCES APPEAR ON PAGE 466.

In the following sentences, the verb is in **boldface** type. Jump to the beginning of the sentence and find the first word that makes sense as the subject. Underline this subject and then make the verb agree with it. If the form of the verb is correct, write *OK* above it.

Example: The <u>construction</u> of new buildings promised by the
                                was
            developers ~~were~~ never completed.
                        ^

1. Any communication between the defendants and the witnesses **are** strictly prohibited.

2. During the afternoon, the temperatures inside the warehouse complex **is** unbearable.

3. The ads created by their Madison Avenue advertising firm **was** the talk of the industry.

4. The legal status of many Greek artifacts taken out of Greece **is** unclear.

5. As a result of the accident, all flights into and out of the city **have** been canceled.

Sentence Practice 3

Check each of the following sentences for nearest-noun agreement errors and then correct the errors. Write *OK* in front of the sentences that do not contain a subject-verb agreement error. Then confirm your answer by rewriting each sentence to eliminate all words between the subject and the verb so that the subject and verb are next to each other. In the new sentence, underline the subject once and the verb twice.

Example: Most programs on the History Channel ~~is~~ quite
                     informative.
                                                                    ^
                                                    are

Rewrite: *Most <u>programs</u> <u>are</u> quite informative.*

1. The reporters covering the story for the local station has already left.

2. A movie based on a collection of the author's short stories are being filmed.

3. The hearings chaired by Senator Blather was a complete waste of time.

4. The files kept in the locked cabinet in the main office is never to leave the office.

5. The family involved in the fire at the warehouse deserves some privacy.

Editing Practice 1

CORRECTED SENTENCES APPEAR ON PAGE 466.

Correct all nearest-noun agreement errors in the following paragraph using the first correction as a model. The number in parentheses at the end of the paragraph indicates how many errors you should find.

    Owning a pet, even the least demanding of creatures, ~~are~~ never
                                                                                    is
                                                                                  ^

easy. Over the years, we have had a number of cats, each of which

have had a unique personality. Sometimes people seek out cats,

and sometimes cats, instinctively knowing the house with the most

defenseless owner, chooses where to live. One of the cats that fall into

the latter category is a big yellow tomcat we call Ferdinand. If cats

could belong to political parties, Ferdinand would be a pacifist. Absolutely

nothing that happens around him seem to upset him. For example, every

one of the cats that we had before as pets were terrified of the vacuum

cleaner. Ferdinand, however, completely ignores it. When he is sleeping

on the rug, I have to vacuum around him. (5)

Editing Practice 2

CORRECTED SENTENCES APPEAR ON PAGE 466.

Correct all nearest-noun agreement errors in the following paragraph using the first correction as a model. The number in parentheses at the end of the paragraph indicates how many errors you should find.

       A researcher who has studied the history of cats ~~believe~~ *believes* that

the ancestor of today's domestic cats were a species of small wildcats

native to northern Africa and southern Europe. The first evidence of cats

being domesticated animals kept by humans were found in Egypt. An

Egyptian official who oversaw large government grain storehouses were

apparently the first to use cats to control rats and mice. In fact, in Egypt,

the pet cats of an important official was considered sacred. When a

favored cat died, it was not uncommon to mummify the cat and to

give it tiny mummified mice to play with throughout eternity. (4)

Editing Practice 3

Correct all nearest-noun agreement errors in the following paragraph using the first correction as a model. The number in parentheses at the end of the paragraph indicates how many errors you should find.

       The universe of pet owners ~~are~~ *is* divided into two groups: cat

owners and dog owners. Of course, there are a few who actually keeps

both cats and dogs, but they do not count because they are the kind of

universal animal lovers who also end up with pet rabbits, gerbils, goldfish,

and nasty things that creep and crawl. The choice of animals, to a

certain degree, reflect the personality of the owner. Typically, the cat

lover, like cats, have a tendency to be an introvert who needs a lot of quiet

time alone. Many dog lovers, on the other hand, are like their pets. They

are both extroverts, social beings who dislike being alone. (3)

Applying What You Know

On your own paper, write a paragraph or two about your experience with pets. Draw an arrow from each subject to its verb. How many of the subjects are the first noun or pronoun in the sentence?

The Bottom Line	If the verb is far away from the beginning of the sentence, **jump back** to the beginning and find the first subject that makes sense with the verb.

Agreement with *There is* and *There was*

EXAMPLE 1 **Plural Subject Follows a Singular Verb**

Error: ✗ There is a million stories in every big city.

  are
Correction: There is a million stories in every big city.
  ^

EXAMPLE 2 **Plural Subject Follows a Singular Verb**

Error: ✗ There was dozens of books piled on the couch.

  were
Correction: There was dozens of books piled on the couch.
  ^

What's the Problem?

English, like most languages, has a special construction used to point out the existence of something. This type of sentence is constructed using *there* plus some form of the verb *be* (or a similar verb like *seem* or *appear*). For example, you might call your server's attention to a fly floating in your soup by saying, "Waiter! *There is* a fly in my soup!"

In sentences that begin with *There is* or *There was*, the subject is not in its normal position. Instead, it *follows* the verb. In our sentence about the soup, for example, the verb (*is*) agrees with the subject that follows it (*fly*):

There is a fly in my soup.

Subject-verb agreement errors occur in this type of sentence when the **subject** is **plural** but the preceding **verb** is **singular**, as in the two example sentences that started the lesson. Why do such errors occur? The problem is a conflict between casual spoken English and the more formal requirements of the written language. When speaking English, we tend to use a singular verb, *is* (present tense) or *was* (past tense), even when the subject following it may be plural. Look at the two example sentences at the beginning of the

ESL

53

Lesson 4

*s-v
agr*

lesson. If you heard those two sentences in a casual conversation, odds are you might not have noticed that they were actually ungrammatical.

Diagnostic Exercise

CORRECTED SENTENCES APPEAR ON PAGE 466.

Correct all errors in the following paragraph using the first correction as a model. The number in parentheses at the end of the paragraph indicates how many errors you should find.

                                          are

    Despite the fact that there ~~is~~ lots of movies coming out every month, there is surprisingly few choices open to us. Most movies are designed to fall into a few easily marketed categories. There is action movies for teens, romantic comedies for first dates, and slasher movies for people I don't want to even think about. Since most new movies are only in the theaters for a short period of time, there is only a few weeks for studios to advertise the movies. If there was unusual aspects or features to a new movie, the studio wouldn't have time to find and reach an audience that falls outside the predictable categories. As a result, we get to see the same few types of movies over and over. (4)

Fixing This Problem in Your Writing

Because subject-verb agreement errors with *there is* and *there was* are common in everyday speech, you may not be able to trust your ear to tell you when a sentence beginning with these words is ungrammatical. When you begin a sentence with *There is* or *There was*, check that it is grammatically correct with the following tip.

> **THERE IS/THERE WAS TIP**   When a sentence begins with *There is* or *There was*, the subject, which comes AFTER the verb, is the first noun (or pronoun) that makes sense as the subject. Make sure the verb agrees with this subject.

    Let's apply the tip to our two example sentences to find the correct subject and make sure the verb agrees with it:

Example 1:   ✗ There is a million stories in every big city.

SUBJECT

✗

Tip applied: ✗ There is a million (stories) in every big city.

The plural subject *stories* does not agree with the singular verb *is*.

are

Correction: There ~~is~~ a million stories in every big city.
^

Example 2:   ✗ There was dozens of books piled on the couch.

SUBJECT

✗

Tip applied: ✗ There was (dozens) of books piled on the couch.

The plural subject *dozens* does not agree with the singular verb *was*.

were

Correction: There ~~was~~ dozens of books piled on the couch.
^

✳ *Putting It All Together*

Identify There is/There was *Errors*

_____ When you use a sentence that begins with *There is* or *There was*, check to make sure that the verb agrees with the actual subject— the first noun (or pronoun) that follows the verb and makes sense as the subject.

Correct There is/There was *Errors*

_____ If the subject and verb do not agree, change the form of the verb to match the subject. Use a singular verb form for a singular subject and a plural verb form for a plural subject.

Sentence Practice 1

CORRECTED SENTENCES APPEAR ON PAGE 467.

Using the *There is/There was* Tip, underline the first word or words following the verb that make sense as the subject. If there is an error in subject-verb agreement, write the correct form of the verb above the incorrect verb. If there is no error, write *OK* above the verb.

Example: There ~~is~~ a lot of problems with their proposal.
_____*are*_____
                         ^

1.   There is never enough napkins to go around.

2.   After the storm ended, there was dozens of trees down all over the city.

3.   There is a couple of movies that I would like to see.

4.   You could never tell that there was any difficulties with the stage lighting.

5.   Before the children's game started, there was a dispute about who was the home team.

   For more practice with subject-verb agreement, go to **Exercise Central** at **bedfordstmartins.com/commonsense**

Sentence Practice 2

CORRECTED SENTENCES APPEAR ON PAGE 467.

Using the *There is/There was* Tip, underline the first word or words following the verb that make sense as a subject. If there is an error in subject-verb agreement, write the correct form of the verb above the incorrect verb. If there is no error, write *OK* above the verb.

                         are
Example: There ~~is~~ a bookstore and a coffee shop in the building.
                         ^

1.   There was an old woman who lived in a shoe.

2.   Since it had snowed all night, there was only some trucks on the road.

3.   There is some cookies and pastries to go with the coffee.

4.   Fortunately, there was a flashlight and some candles in the closet.

5.   There is lots of things for the children to do there.

Sentence Practice 3

Rewrite the following sentences as *There is/There was* sentences.

Example: An opener is in the drawer.

Answer: *There is an opener in the drawer.*

1.   A tavern is in the town.

2.   A really nasty flu is going around.

3. A light golden haze is on the meadow.

4. Some good movies are playing this weekend.

5. Lots of fish are in the ocean.

6. Several fountains were spraying water in the courtyard.

7. People were waiting to be served.

8. A suite is available if you want to stay there.

9. Paint and masking tape were all over the floor where he had been working.

10. Is an airport in Coeur d'Alene?

Lesson 4

S-V
agr

Editing Practice 1

CORRECTED SENTENCES APPEAR ON PAGE 467.

Correct all the *there is/there was* errors in the following paragraph using the first correction as a model. The number in parentheses at the end of the paragraph indicates how many errors you should find.

       are
     There is̶ lots of reasons to visit Spain. First of all, there is all those
         ^
wonderful, long, sunny afternoons. Even though Spain is west of England,
Spain uses the same time zone as France and Italy, essentially giving Spain
year-round daylight savings time. Moreover, when Spain goes on daylight
savings time in the summer with the rest of Europe, there is actually two
extra hours of daylight in Spain. The extra daylight in the afternoon means
that when the stores reopen after the siesta at 6 P.M., there is still plenty of
daylight when people are out and about. Most businesses and offices open
at 8 or 9 in the morning to take advantage of the fact that there is many
hours of relative coolness in the morning before the sun gets high enough
to make it unbearable. (3)

Editing Practice 2

CORRECTED SENTENCES APPEAR ON PAGE 467.

Correct all the *there is/there was* errors in the following paragraph using the first correction as a model. The number in parentheses at the end of the paragraph indicates how many errors you should find.

Another reason to visit Spain is to explore the art and architecture.

are

Lesson 4

There ~~is~~ some of the world's greatest museums, art galleries, and

s-v
agr

churches in Spain. In Madrid, there is half a dozen great art collections,

the most famous being the Prado. The Prado has the world's greatest

collection of Spanish paintings: There is innumerable paintings by Goya,

Velazquez, and El Greco. The enormous wealth Spain acquired from its

conquests in the New World allowed Spanish kings to purchase numerous

collections of great art masterpieces from the rest of Europe. In the Prado

there is fantastic collections of Dutch and Flemish paintings. For example,

there is nearly one hundred paintings by Rubens alone. (4)

Editing Practice 3

Correct all the *there is/there was* errors in the following paragraph using the
first correction as a model. The number in parentheses at the end of the paragraph indicates how many errors you should find.

are

Another reason to visit Spain is that it is a lot of fun. There ~~is~~

wonderful local dishes and wines. A great way to sample local food is to

order *tapas*—small snacks or appetizers. There is a huge variety of

tapas. Every bar and restaurant has its tapas menu. Tapas are usually

eaten standing up at a counter with a glass of wine or beer. There is

usually two or three seafood dishes, several kinds of dried hams, and, of

course, a Spanish omelet. The dried hams, more or less like Italian pro-

sciutto, are really quite special. There is literally dozens of types of dried

hams with a wide range of prices. The upscale ones are quite expensive.

With your tapas, you might want a glass of local wine. Spain has become

one of the world's major wine producers. There is deep, earthy reds and

surprisingly good sparkling white wines—all at quite reasonable prices.

Enjoy. (3)

Applying What You Know

Skim through a magazine or newspaper article and find five examples of sentences beginning with *There* plus some form of the verb *be*. Draw an arrow from the subject back to the verb it follows. Do you find any mistakes?

Lesson 4

s-v
agr

The Bottom Line	There **is** always a **subject** after the verb in a *there is* or *there was* construction.

Agreement with Compound Subjects

EXAMPLE 1   *Compound Subject with a Singular Verb*

Error: ✗ The <u>pencils</u> and some <u>paper</u> is on the desk.

Correction: The <u>pencils</u> and some <u>paper</u> ~~is~~ *are* on the desk.

EXAMPLE 2   *Compound Subject with a Singular Verb*

Error: ✗ Our genetic <u>makeup</u> and our personal <u>experience</u> <u>defines</u> us.

Correction: Our genetic <u>makeup</u> and our personal <u>experience</u> ~~defines~~ *define* us.

What's the Problem?

When two (or more) subjects are joined by *and*, they are called a **compound subject**. Compound subjects can cause **subject-verb agreement** errors when writers incorrectly think of the compound subject as a single unit and therefore use a singular verb. Compound subjects, however, are almost always plural and therefore must use plural verbs.

Diagnostic Exercise

CORRECTED SENTENCES APPEAR ON PAGE 467.

Correct all errors in the following paragraph using the first correction as a model. The number in parentheses at the end of the paragraph indicates how many errors you should find.

    I work in a busy law office. Even though we now have voice mail, answering the phone and writing down messages ~~takes~~ *take* up a lot of my time. I am also responsible for maintaining the law library, although most of the time I do nothing more glamorous than shelving. The law books and reference material is always left scattered around the library, and some of the lawyers even leave their dirty coffee cups on the tables. I used to have a relatively comfortable working area, but the new computer terminal and modem has now taken up most of my personal space; that's progress, I guess. Despite all the stress, meeting the needs of clients and keeping track of all the information required in a modern law office makes it a fascinating job. (3)

Fixing This Problem in Your Writing

Whenever your sentence contains *and*, check to see whether the *and* has joined two subjects to create a compound subject. If so, then the subject is plural, and you must use a plural verb. Use the following tip to help you identify compound subjects and get the right form of the verb.

> **THEY TIP** Whenever *and* is used in the subject part of a sentence, see whether you can replace the entire subject portion of the sentence with the pronoun *they*. If you can, then the subject is a compound, and the verb must be made plural to agree with *they*.

Here is how the *They* Tip identifies the compound subject and the right form of the verb in the two example sentences:

Example 1:   ✗ The pencils and some paper is on the desk.

Tip applied: ✗ They is on the desk.

> *They* does not agree with *is*. It requires a plural verb.

Correction: The pencils and some paper ~~is~~ *are* on the desk.

Example 2:   ✗ Our genetic makeup and our personal experience defines us.

Lesson 5

S-v
agr

Tip applied: ✗ They <u>defines</u> us.

They does not agree with *defines*. It requires a plural verb.

Correction: Our genetic makeup and our personal experience
               define
               ~~defines~~ us.
               ^

✳ *Putting It All Together*

Identify Compound-Subject Errors in Your Writing

_____ When you see *and* in the subject part of your sentence, use the *They* Tip to determine whether you have a compound subject.

_____ If *they* makes sense when it replaces the subject, the subject is compound and requires a plural verb.

Correct Compound-Subject Errors in Your Writing

_____ If the verb in a sentence with a compound subject does not agree with *they*, change the verb to the plural form.

Sentence Practice 1

CORRECTED SENTENCES APPEAR ON PAGE 467.

Underline the entire subject portion of the sentence. If the subject portion contains *and*, replace the underlined portion of the sentence with *they*. Circle the verb form that agrees with the subject *they*.

                        They
Example: <u>Vegetables and fruit</u> (is/(are)) important for a good diet.

1. Weekends and holidays always (feel/feels) too short.

2. A runny nose and a sore throat (is/are) good indicators of a cold.

3. Oops! The groceries and the milk (is/are) still in the car.

4. Peanuts, pretzels, and a cookie (is/are) about all you get to eat when you fly coach today.

5. During the summer, the thunder and the lightning in our area (is/are) just amazing.

For more practice with subject-verb agreement, go to **Exercise Central** at
bedfordstmartins.com/commonsense

Lesson 5

S-V
agr

Sentence Practice 2

CORRECTED SENTENCES APPEAR ON PAGE 467.

Underline the compound subjects in the following sentences. If there is an
error in subject-verb agreement, correct the error and confirm your answer
by replacing the compound subject with *they*. If there is no error, write *OK*.

Example: A <u>hamburger, fries, and a Coke</u> ~~has~~ *have* been my normal
lunch for years.
              They

1. Loud drums and thunderclaps frighten my little sister.

2. What "football" means in America and what it means in the rest of the
world is totally different things.

3. The light in the garage and the light over the sink needs replacing.

4. Fortunately, the captain and the crew of the sunken boat was safe.

5. The characters and the plot of his latest book is just like those in all his
other books.

Sentence Practice 3

Combine the following sentences by making a compound subject. Make the
verb agree with the new subject. Underline the subject once and the verb
twice in your new sentence.

Example: The dishpan is under the sink. The soap is under the sink.

Answer: The <u>dishpan and the soap</u> <u>are</u> under the sink.

1. Time waits for no man. Tide waits for no man.

2. Communism was a powerful force in the middle of the century.
Fascism was a powerful force in the middle of the century.

3. The captain was reviewing the troops. The major was reviewing the
troops.

4. What we say is important. What we do is important.

5. The advancing storm was enough to make us turn back. The gathering
darkness was enough to make us turn back.

6. A hammer is in the garage. A chisel is in the garage.

7. The kitchen is in pretty bad shape. The bathroom is in pretty bad shape.

8. Her imagination makes her one of the best new novelists. Her strong sense of place makes her one of the best new novelists.

9. An officer was manning the checkpoint. A group of enlisted men was manning the checkpoint.

10. The ship's constant rocking was making us feel queasy. The smell of diesel fuel was making us feel queasy.

Editing Practice 1

CORRECTED SENTENCES APPEAR ON PAGE 468.

Correct all the compound-subject errors in the following paragraph using the first correction as a model. The number in parentheses at the end of the paragraph indicates how many errors you should find.

                                            are
     Many stories, plays, and even a famous opera ~~is~~ based on the
                                          ^

legend of Don Juan. Don Juan's charm and wit supposedly makes him

utterly irresistible to women. The most famous treatment of the Don

Juan legend is in Mozart's opera *Don Giovanni* (*Giovanni* is the Italian

form of the Spanish name *Juan*, or *John* in English). Mozart's opera is

highly unusual in that comedy and villainy is mixed together in almost

equal parts. For example, the actions and behavior of the Don constantly

keeps the audience off balance. His charm and bravery makes him almost

a hero at times. However, at other times, his aristocratic arrogance and

deliberate cruelty to women reveals he is far from a true hero. The delicate

seduction of a willing woman and a violent rape is all the same to him. (6)

Editing Practice 2

Correct all the compound-subject errors in the following paragraph using the first correction as a model. The number in parentheses at the end of the paragraph indicates how many errors you should find.

The role and character of Don Giovanni's servant Leporello is *[are]*
also quite unusual. Leporello and Don Giovanni often works together to
carry out a seduction. At first, his constant complaining and caustic asides
to the audience makes Leporello seem to be just a conventional comic
sidekick. Yet in some ways, Leporello's comments on and reactions to his
master's behavior becomes the focus of the opera. Leporello's grudging
admiration for the Don's charm and his repulsion at the Don's behavior
reflects the audience's equally mixed feelings. (4)

Lesson 5

s-v
agr

Applying What You Know

Using the Editing Practice essays in this lesson as models, write a paragraph
or two about a fictional character from a movie, play, or book. What are the
personality features that make this person interesting? Try to use as many
examples of compound subjects as you can. Then, use the *They* Tip to show
that the verbs you have used with compound subjects are correct.

The Bottom Line	A noun/pronoun and another noun/pronoun joined by *and* **make** a compound subject and **require** a plural verb.

Making Subjects and Verbs Agree

REVIEW

Writers make errors in subject-verb agreement when they make the verb agree with a word that is not the actual subject of the sentence. The following chart points you to the tips that will help you avoid these kinds of errors.

TIPS	QUICK FIXES AND EXAMPLES
Lesson 3. Nearest-Noun Agreement Errors	
The Finding the Subject Tip (p. 47) helps you find the real subject of a sentence so you can check for subject-verb agreement.	Find the real subject of long sentences by jumping back to the beginning of the sentence. Error: ✗ The <u>plan</u> that we have developed for city roads <u>are</u> ready for approval. Correction: The plan that we have developed *is* for city roads ~~are~~ ready for approval. ^
Lesson 4. Agreement with *There is* and *There was*	
The *There is/There was* Tip (p. 54) helps you find the subject of a sentence that begins with *There is* or *There was* so you can check for subject-verb agreement.	Make sure the verb agrees with the first noun (or pronoun) *after* the verb that makes sense as the subject. Error: ✗ There <u>is</u> a dozen <u>things</u> that could go wrong with your plan. *are* Correction: There ~~is~~ a dozen <u>things</u> that could ^ go wrong with your plan.
Lesson 5. Agreement with Compound Subjects	
The *They* Tip (p. 61) helps you identify compound subjects (*diet and exercise*) so you know to use a plural verb.	If you can replace the subject portion of the sentence with *they*, use a plural verb. Error: ✗ The <u>sun and the wind</u> <u>was</u> chapping my lips. *were* Correction: The <u>sun and the wind</u> ~~was~~ chapping ^ my lips.

Review Test

Underline the subjects in every sentence. Then, correct all errors using the first correction as a model. The number in parentheses at the end of each paragraph indicates how many errors you should find.

Although European explorers came to the New World in search of
were
gold, the <u>fruits</u> and <u>vegetables</u> of the New World ~~was~~ much more important
                                                              ^
to the Old World than all the gold they ever found. Before contact with

the New World, there was no tomatoes, corn, or potatoes in the Old World.

However, for many of us, the greatest gift of all the New World's many

agricultural products were the food and beverage that we call *chocolate*.

All products containing chocolate in any form comes from the seeds of the

cacao tree. The Mayas in Central America was the first to discover how to

produce chocolate from cacao seeds. (4)

A number of large, melon-shaped pods grow directly on the trunk

and larger branches of the cacao tree. Each of these pods contain up to

forty almond-shaped seeds. The seeds, after being removed from the pod,

fermented, and dried, is transformed into the commercial cocoa bean. (2)

The first step in producing chocolate from the cacao beans are to

remove the outer shells. What remains after the shells have been removed

are called *nibs*. Nibs contain a high percentage of a natural fat called *cocoa*

butter. When nibs are heated and ground, the cocoa butter is released. The

mixture of cocoa butter and finely ground nibs form a liquid called *chocolate*

liquor. The chocolate liquor, after being cooled and molded into little cakes,

are what we know as baking chocolate. Baking chocolate and sugar is at the

heart of all those wonderful chocolate goodies that we would all die for. (5)

UNIT THREE

Using Correct Verb Tenses

OVERVIEW

The Nuts and Bolts of Verb Tenses

Verb *tense* indicates when the action in a sentence occurred. The lessons in Unit Three show you how to use the past tense, the present tense, and the perfect tense correctly.

Lesson 6 shows you how to avoid improper *tense shifting* between the present and past tenses. Knowing when to shift from one to the other requires an understanding of the fundamentally different roles of the two tenses. The **present tense** is used to state facts or make generalizations. The **past tense** is used to narrate events completed in the past.

Example: ✗ Michelle took the bus whenever she has to work.

Correction: Michelle ~~took~~ the bus whenever she has to work.
                        takes

Lesson 7 shows you how to use the **perfect tenses**, which are made with the **helping verb** *have* (in some form) followed by a verb in the **past participle** form. If you use a present tense form of *have*, you create a *present perfect* verb (*Jesse has seen that movie dozens of times*). If you use the past tense *had*, you create a *past perfect* verb (*Aisha had seen the movie before she read the book*). Sometimes writers mistakenly use the past tense when they should use either the present perfect or the past perfect.

Example: ✗ I felt much more secure ever since we installed a home alarm system.

Correction: I felt much more secure ever since we installed a home
                  have
              alarm system.

Present, Past, and Tense Shifting

EXAMPLE 1 *Verbs Shift Tenses*

Error: ✗ Whenever we <u>went</u> to a restaurant, Robert always <u>makes</u> a fuss about ordering the best wine.

Correction 1: Whenever we went to a restaurant, Robert always
made
~~makes~~ a fuss about ordering the best wine.
     ^
[*Both verbs are in past tense.*]

Correction 2: Whenever we ~~went~~ to a restaurant, Robert always
         go
       ^
makes a fuss about ordering the best wine.

[*Both verbs are in present tense.*]

EXAMPLE 2 *Verbs Don't Shift Tense*

Error: ✗ She <u>went</u> to Trident Technical College, which <u>was</u> in South Carolina.

Correction: She went to Trident Technical College, which ~~was~~ in
         is
South Carolina.
                    ^

What's the Problem?

Readers usually expect a piece of writing to maintain a consistent use of verb **tense** from beginning to end. For instance, in Example 1, the writer starts in the **past tense** and then inappropriately shifts to the **present tense**:

PAST TENSE

Example 1: ✗ Whenever we <u>went</u> to a restaurant, Robert always

PRESENT TENSE

<u>makes</u> a fuss about ordering the best wine.

However, sometimes the opposite is true: The sentence is wrong if we don't shift verb tenses. For instance, in Example 2, the writer needs to shift the past tense *was* to the present tense *is* because, as the sentence is written, it implies something that the writer does not mean: that Trident Technical College is no longer in South Carolina.

Diagnostic Exercise

CORRECTED SENTENCES APPEAR ON PAGE 468.

Correct all verb tense errors in the following paragraph using the first correction as a model. The number in parentheses at the end of the paragraph indicates how many errors you should find.

Last summer we took a trip to Provence, a region in the southeast corner of France, which ~~bordered~~ *borders* Italy. The name *Provence* referred to the fact that it was the first province created by the ancient Romans outside the Italian peninsula. Today, Provence still contained an amazing number of well-preserved Roman ruins. While there were a few big towns on the coast, Provence was famous for its wild country and beautiful scenery. Provence was especially known for its abundance of wildflowers in the spring. These flowers were used to make some of the world's most expensive perfumes. (6)

Fixing This Problem in Your Writing

To shift or not to shift? Past tense and present tense have different uses, and we shift between the two tenses as we have need for those uses.

The past tense is used to describe events that happened in the past. Most stories and novels use the past tense as the basic vehicle of narration, for example:

My mother <u>called</u> us during dinner last night.

She <u>wanted</u> my sister's new phone number.

Fortunately, I <u>had</u> it in my Palm Pilot.

The present tense is used to make "timeless" statements or generalizations that are not only true for the time of the story but will continue to be true indefinitely. For example:

My mother always <u>seems</u> to call at the most inconvenient moment.

She <u>lives</u> in a different time zone.

She never <u>remembers</u> to take the time change into account.

Here are two tips that will help you decide which tense to use.

PAST TENSE TIP Use the past tense when telling a story about something that was completed in the past.

PRESENT TENSE TIP Use the present tense to make "timeless" statements of fact or generalizations that are true now and will continue to be true indefinitely unless something happens to change the situation.

Let's return to the two examples that started the lesson:

PAST TENSE NARRATION

Example 1: ✗ Whenever we <u>went</u> to a restaurant, Robert always

PRESENT TENSE GENERALIZATION

<u>makes</u> a fuss . . .

In this example, the writer couldn't decide whether he or she was telling a story (past tense) or making a generalization about Robert's wine ordering practices (present tense). The writer's jumping from past tense to present tense is an example of improper tense shifting. The solution is to be consistent: Either tell a story in the past tense (following the Past Tense Tip) or make a generalization in the present tense (following the Present Tense Tip):

- **Tell a story.** Use the past tense to describe a specific event or events that happened in the past.

PAST TENSE

Tip applied: Whenever we <u>went</u> to a restaurant, Robert always

PAST TENSE

<u>made</u> a fuss about ordering the best wine.

- **Make a generalization.** Use the present tense to generalize about something that will continue to be true indefinitely unless something happens to change the situation.

PRESENT TENSE

Tip applied: Whenever we <u>go</u> to a restaurant, Robert always

PRESENT TENSE

<u>makes</u> a fuss about ordering the best wine.

Lesson 6

shift

Let's look at the other example.

| PAST TENSE | PAST TENSE |
| NARRATION | NARRATION |

Example 2:   ✗ She <u>went</u> to Trident Technical College, which <u>was</u> in South Carolina.

In this sentence, a shift in tense is necessary. *She* has finished attending Trident Technical College, so the use of the past tense in this part of the sentence is correct. However, the college is still, and probably always will be, in South Carolina. So, in the second part of the sentence, the verb must shift to the present tense:

| PAST TENSE | PRESENT TENSE |
| NARRATION | STATEMENT OF FACT |

Tip applied: She <u>went</u> to Trident Technical College, which <u>is</u> in South Carolina.

✳ *Putting It All Together*

Identify Problems with Verb Tense and Tense Shifting

_____ Identify every present and past tense verb in your sentence.

_____ Ask yourself whether the verb is used in a narrative that deals with past events or whether the verb is used to make a statement of fact or a generalization.

Correct Problems with Verb Tense and Tense Shifting

_____ Use the past tense when describing or discussing events that happened or were completed in the past.

_____ Use the present tense to make statements of fact or generalizations.

_____ If your sentence combines narratives of past events with statements of fact or generalizations, shift tenses accordingly.

Sentence Practice 1

CORRECTED SENTENCES APPEAR ON PAGE 468.

For each of the following sentences, decide whether the sentence is (1) telling a story or (2) making a "timeless" statement or generalization. If 1, write *Tell a story*, and make the verb (in boldface) past tense. If 2, write *Make a statement*, and make the verb (in boldface) present tense.

Lesson 6

shift

> Example: Reno, Nevada, **be** actually farther west than Los Angeles, California.
>
> Answer: Reno, Nevada, ~~be~~ *is* actually farther west than Los Angeles, California. *Make a statement*
>
> Example: Our car **break** down just outside Reno, Nevada.
>
> Answer: Our car ~~break~~ *broke* down just outside Reno, Nevada. *Tell a story*

1. Headlights that stay on all the time **has** significantly reduced automobile accidents.

2. Young people **be** using their landlines less and less often.

3. I **get** a very surprising phone call.

4. The team's bus **have** a minor accident and they **miss** their first game.

5. Halloween often **frighten** young children.

 For more practice with past and present tense shifting, go to **Exercise Central** at **bedfordstmartins.com/commonsense**

Sentence Practice 2

CORRECTED SENTENCES APPEAR ON PAGE 468.

Each of the sentences below contains two verbs in boldface. Correct the present and past tense errors by drawing a line through each error and writing the correct verb tense above it. If the sentence is correct, write *OK* above it.

> Example: It always **seems** *OK* to rain whenever we **go** on a picnic.
>
> Example: This past Christmas, we ~~go~~ *went* to Chicago, where my parents **live**.

1. I **leave** my towel in the locker that **be** nearest the door.

2. The fact that Hawaii **do** not go on daylight savings time always **confuse** people.

3. I usually **check** my e-mail as soon as I **get** back from lunch.

Lesson 6

4. He **deposit** the money in an account that he **keep** at the local credit union.

shift

5. The accident **occur** on a stretch of road that **have** a reputation for being dangerous.

Sentence Practice 3

Circle the correct form of the verb in the following sentences.

> Example: We all know that Boxing Day (is / was) the day after Christmas.

1. I think that a matinee performance typically (started / starts) at two.

2. I got a shock when I (plug / plugged) that old lamp in.

3. She always calls her children when she (is / was) going to be late.

4. Artists today are still influenced by the art styles that (originate / originated) in prewar Germany.

5. After all our work, we discovered that the answer (is / was) in the back of the book.

6. He makes it sound like every little problem (is / was) a major crisis.

7. My parents always traveled first class, which (seems / seemed) ostentatious today.

8. The guide informed us that the trains for Rome (leave / left) from Platform 3.

9. It is amusing that the governor (pretends / pretended) that he was a simple man of the people.

10. It is really true; the French (do / did) go on vacation all of August.

Editing Practice 1

CORRECTED SENTENCES APPEAR ON PAGE 468.

Correct all the verb tense errors in the following paragraphs using the first correction as a model. The number in parentheses at the end of each paragraph indicates how many errors you should find.

Even though Shakespeare died in 1616, performances of his plays
have
~~had~~ continued without interruption right up to today. I recently attend
‸
the Oregon Shakespeare Festival in Ashland, Oregon. In planning the

performances, the director has to make some big decisions about how to

stage plays that were more than 350 years old. The biggest problem for

all directors today was whether to present Shakespearian plays in period

costume or in more modern dress. (4)

Staging the plays in modern dress made the plays more interesting

and often a lot more fun. For example, in a performance of *Henry IV,*

Part I at Ashland a few years ago, Falstaff comes on stage for the first time

on a motor scooter with a case of beer strapped on behind. Sometimes,

staging plays in different time periods allowed the director to make

political or social comments. An outstanding example of this was the 1995

movie version of *Richard III* with Ian McKellen in an imaginary Fascist

England in the 1930s. McKellen's performance as an all-powerful, sadistic

ruler in an authoritarian state chilled the viewers' blood. Nobody could see

this film and not be terrified of unrestrained government power. (5)

Editing Practice 2

CORRECTED SENTENCES APPEAR ON PAGE 469.

Correct all the verb tense errors in the following paragraph using the first
correction as a model. The number in parentheses at the end of the paragraph indicates how many errors you should find.

began
Ashland's Shakespeare Festival ~~begins~~ almost by accident as
‸
an outgrowth of the old Chautauqua circuit. Chautauqua provides

entertainment to rural America before the days of radio and movies.

Chautauqua is a mix of popular lecturers, music, and vaudeville acts—

something that seems strange today. After the collapse of Chautauqua,

Ashland finds itself with a good-sized summer theater facility. After unsuccessfully trying a variety of entertainments, including boxing matches, the faculty from the local college decides to stage a few Shakespearian plays. The plays proved to be so successful that the Oregon Shakespeare Festival is born and has grown to become a highly successful theatrical company today. (5)

Lesson 6

shift

Editing Practice 3

Correct all the verb tense errors in the following paragraph using the first correction as a model. The number in parentheses at the end of the paragraph indicates how many errors you should find.

                is

Shakespeare ~~was~~ certainly the most influential playwright in the

               ^

history of drama. Given the fact that his plays are written about four hundred years ago in a language that is now quite hard to follow, it was a testament to his importance that so many of his plays were still staged today. Another measure of Shakespeare's importance was the number of his plays that appeared as operas, ballets, and movies. Three movies based on Shakespeare's plays had won Oscars for best picture. They are *Hamlet* in 1948; *West Side Story* (based on *Romeo and Juliet*) in 1961; and *Shakespeare in Love* (about the writing of *Romeo and Juliet*) in 1998. (6)

Applying What You Know

On a separate sheet of paper, write about a play or movie you have seen recently. Try to mix past tense descriptions of the action and present tense generalizations about the meaning or effectiveness of the play or movie.

The Bottom Line	**Keep** the verbs in a sentence in the same tense unless you **have** a reason for mixing past tense narration with present tense generalizations or statements of fact.

The Past and the Perfect Tenses

EXAMPLE 1   *Past Tense Used Instead of Present Perfect Tense*

Error: ✗ We <u>regretted</u> our choice ever since we bought that car.

Correction: We regretted *have* our choice ever since we bought that car.

EXAMPLE 2   *Past Tense Used Instead of Past Perfect Tense*

Error: ✗ When we bought the house last year, it <u>was</u> empty for ten years.

Correction: When we bought the house last year, it ~~was~~ *had been* empty for ten years.

What's the Problem?

The **perfect tenses** are formed with the helping verb *have* in some form followed by the **past participle** form of a second verb. When the present tense forms of *have* (*has* or *have*) are used, the **present perfect tense** is formed. When the past tense *had* is used, the **past perfect tense** is formed. Here are some examples:

PRESENT PERFECT TENSE	PAST PERFECT TENSE
has walked, have walked	had walked
has sung, have sung	had sung
has been, have been	had been

The present perfect and past perfect tenses allow us to express subtle differences in the time relationship of past events. The *present perfect tense* is used to indicate an action that began in the past and continues to the present. The *past perfect tense* is used to indicate an action that took place in the past before another past action. Many writers mistakenly use the past tense when they should use either the present perfect tense (Example 1) or the past perfect tense (Example 2). We'll discuss these examples in detail below.

Diagnostic Exercise

CORRECTED SENTENCES APPEAR ON PAGE 469.

Lesson 7

vt

Correct all verb tense errors in the following paragraph using the first correction as a model. The number in parentheses at the end of the paragraph indicates how many errors you should find.

have been

Unfortunately, most people ~~were~~ involved in an automobile
^

accident at some time. I was involved in several, but my luckiest

accident was one that never happened. Just after I got my driver's

license, I borrowed the family car to go to a party. Although it was

a very tame party, I left feeling a little hyper and silly. It was night, and

there were no streetlights nearby. I parked a little distance from the

house, so my car was by itself. I got into the car and decided to show

off a little bit by throwing the car into reverse and flooring it. I went

about twenty yards backward before I thought to myself that I was

doing something pretty dangerous. I slammed on the brakes in a panic.

I got out of the car and found that my back bumper was about four inches

from a parked car that I never saw. Whenever I feel an urge to push my

luck driving, I remind myself of the accident that almost happened. (6)

Fixing This Problem in Your Writing

Understanding the Perfect Tenses

The key to using the perfect tenses correctly is understanding the difference in meaning between the past tense and the two perfect tenses. The following are brief descriptions of these three tenses.

- The **past tense** is used to refer to an event that is over and done with. The event could have happened at a single moment in time or lasted for years. In either case, the event is now history.

Past tense: Elliot <u>lived</u> in Chicago for ten years. [He no longer lives there.]

TIME

ELLIOT'S STAY IN CHICAGO

When Elliot	When Elliot	Present
moved to	left Chicago	time
Chicago		

- The **present perfect tense** is used to refer to an event that began at some point in the past and continues into the present time.

Present perfect   Elliot <u>has lived</u> in Chicago for ten years. [He still lives tense: there.]

TIME

ELLIOT'S STAY IN CHICAGO

When Elliot	Present
moved to	time
Chicago	

- The **past perfect tense** is used to indicate that a particular event in the past was completed *before* some more recent past event took place. Here is an example:

Past perfect   Elliot <u>had lived</u> in Chicago ten years before we met. tense: [Elliot had lived in Chicago ten years before he met the writer, and he may or may not still live there today.]

TIME

ELLIOT'S STAY IN CHICAGO

When Elliot	When	Present
moved to	we met	time
Chicago		

Choosing between Past Tense and Present Perfect Tense

The basic distinction between the past tense and the present perfect tense is whether the past event is over and done with (past tense) or whether it continues up to the present (present perfect). Here is a tip to help you know when to use the present perfect tense.

PRESENT PERFECT TIP   Use the present perfect tense to emphasize that a past action has continued over a span of time up to the present moment.

Let's apply this tip to the first example sentence:

PAST TENSE

Example 1: ✗ We <u>regretted</u> our choice ever since we bought that car.

Tip applied: ✗ Past tense = *regretted* = We no longer regret the choice.

✓ Present perfect tense = *have regretted* = We still regret the choice.

Correction: We regretted our choice ever since we bought that car.
have

In this example, the use of the past tense *regretted* is incorrect because the writer still regrets the choice of car, even today. Therefore, the present perfect tense should be used instead.

Choosing between Past Tense and Past Perfect Tense

As noted above, the past tense is used to describe an event that happened in the past. The past perfect tense emphasizes the before-and-after sequence of *two* past events. Here is a tip to help you know when to use the past perfect tense.

> **PAST PERFECT TIP** Use the past perfect tense to show that one event in the past was completed *before* a more recent past event took place.

Let's apply the tip to the second example sentence:

PAST TENSE

Example 2: ✗ When we bought the house last year, it <u>was</u> empty for ten years.

Tip applied: ✗ Past tense = *was* = The house was empty (but when?).

✓ Past perfect tip = *had been* = The house was empty before we bought it.

Correction: When we bought the house last year, it ~~was~~ empty for ten years.
had been

There are two past events here: (1) a ten-year period before last year during which time the house had stood empty and (2) the moment last year when the writer bought the house. The sentence is much clearer if we use the past perfect tense to emphasize the time sequence between the two different past events.

Writers often use the past perfect tense to imply that one past event *caused* a later past event. For example, the sentence *They had gotten into a big fight just before they broke up* implies that they broke up *because* of their big fight.

✳ *Putting It All Together*

Identify Errors in Using the Past and the Perfect Tenses

___ Identify past tense verbs in your sentence.

___ Ask yourself whether you are describing an event that began and ended entirely in the past or one that began in the past and continues into the present.

___ Check to see whether you are describing two past events in a definite sequence or with a cause-and-effect relationship.

Correct Errors in Using the Past and the Perfect Tenses

___ If you are describing an event that began and ended entirely in the past, use the past tense (usually the *-ed* form of the verb).

___ If you are describing an event that began in the past and continues into the present, use the present perfect tense (*has* or *have* + past participle).

___ If you are connecting two past events in a single sentence, use the past perfect tense (*had* + past participle).

Sentence Practice 1

CORRECTED SENTENCES APPEAR ON PAGE 469.

The errors in the sentences below all involve choosing between the past tense and the present perfect. If the past action covers a span of time, write *Continuous* and check to see if the verb is in the present perfect. If the verb is in the present perfect, write *OK*. If it is not, make the necessary correction.

Example: I ~~was~~ interested in history for years. *Continuous*

(*have been*)

If the past action deals with an event that is over and done with, write *Single event* and check to see if the verb is in the past tense. If the verb is in the past tense, write *OK*. If it is not, make the necessary correction.

Example: He ~~has~~ wrecked his knee on the first play of the game.
                Single event

1. I worked overtime for the past six months.

2. The company bought up empty houses since the beginning of the year.

3. The game began about an hour ago.

4. It snowed every day this winter since Christmas.

Lesson 7

5. She climbed every peak over 14,000 feet in North America.

vt

> For more practice using the past and perfect tenses, go to **Exercise Central** at **bedfordstmartins.com/commonsense**

Sentence Practice 2

CORRECTED SENTENCES APPEAR ON PAGE 469.

Each sentence below contains two clauses; both are written using the past tense. If the events in the sentence's clauses occurred in roughly the same time period and the past tense is correct, write *OK* above it. If one event was completed before the more recent event started, use the past perfect tense for the earlier event.

Example: We **had** dinner and **watched** the game.   *OK*

Example: The storm ~~closed~~ the runway before we **got** clearance to take off.   *had closed*

1. After the book became a big hit in Europe, American publishers were willing to take a chance on it.

2. We decided to cancel our trip because it snowed so much during the night.

3. I didn't need to go through the line because I already paid for my ticket online.

4. We painted the walls and ripped out the old carpet.

5. After I finished assembling the bike, I found a leftover part.

Sentence Practice 3

Combine the following sentences by adding the underlined information in the second sentence to the first sentence. Change the past tense of the first sentence to the present perfect or past perfect tense as appropriate.

Example: The board met. They met <u>every Monday this past year.</u>

                                                  has met
Answer: The board <s>met</s> every Monday this past year.
                                        ^

1. The whistle already sounded. This was <u>before the ball went into the net.</u>
2. We worked on our car. We worked <u>since early this morning.</u>
3. I just stepped into the shower. I did that <u>when the phone rang.</u>
4. Our team played together. They did that <u>for three seasons now.</u>
5. Fortunately, Elvis already left the building. He left <u>before the reporters arrived.</u>

Lesson 7

vt

Editing Practice 1

CORRECTED SENTENCES APPEAR ON PAGE 469.

Correct all tense errors in the following paragraph using the first correction as a model. The number in parentheses at the end of the paragraph indicates how many errors you should find.

                                                                                    has
        The number of deaths resulting from traffic accidents declined
                                                                                   ^
steadily over the past decade. In recent years, researchers cited a number

of different reasons: improved safety of vehicles, increased use of seat

belts and airbags, and fewer drunk drivers. Automobile manufacturers

were reluctant to even talk about safety until the federal government

began mandating standards in the 1980s. Over the years, manufacturers

continued to resist installing even inexpensive safety features. For example,

manufacturers were very slow to produce cars with daytime headlights,

even though in recent years many Canadian researchers demonstrated

that this no-cost item results in significantly fewer accidents. (5)

Editing Practice 2

Correct all tense errors in the following paragraph using the first correction as a model. The number in parentheses at the end of the paragraph indicates how many errors you should find.

Lesson 7

vt

Actually, two large factors in reducing automobile accident

have been

deaths over the last decade ~~were~~ changes in driver behavior. First,

we became much more consistent in routinely using seat belts for

ourselves and car seats for our children. Now, most of us would never start

the car until we first fastened the seat belts and buckled the children in.

It is appalling to think how common it was even a few years ago to see

children standing up on the seats of cars. How quickly that sight became

a rarity. Second, in recent years there was a general decline in the use of

alcohol. As a result, alcohol-related accidents, although still too common,

became a lot less frequent than they used to be. In the last few years, there

was a real change in society's tolerance of drinking and driving. (6)

Applying What You Know

On your own paper, write a short essay about some aspect of automobile safety. Try to use a mixture of the past tense and the two perfect tenses. Use the Putting It All Together checklist on page 81 to make sure that the tenses in your essay are correct.

The Bottom Line	Use the present perfect tense for an action that **has continued** up to the present. Use the past perfect tense to emphasize that an earlier event **had ended** before a more recent event started.

Using Correct Verb Tenses

REVIEW

Unit Three discusses how to use verb tenses correctly. The following chart points you to the tips that will help you avoid verb-tense errors.

TIPS	QUICK FIXES AND EXAMPLES
Lesson 6. Present, Past, and Tense Shifting	
The Past Tense Tip (p. 71) and Present Tense Tip (p. 71) help you remember the difference between the two tenses so you know when it is appropriate to shift tenses and when it is not.	Use the past tense when telling a story and the present tense to make "timeless" statements of fact or generalizations. Error: ✗ Denver was on the eastern slopes of the Rockies. Correction: Denver ~~was~~ *is* on the eastern slopes of the Rockies.
Lesson 7. The Past and the Perfect Tenses	
The Present Perfect Tip (p. 79) and Past Perfect Tip (p. 80) help you understand the difference between the two perfect tenses.	Use the present perfect (*has* or *have* + *walked*) when a past action continues up to the present moment. Use the past perfect (*had* + *walked*) to show that one event in the past (in this case, the walking) was completed before another event. Error: ✗ I saw the memo before the announcement was made public. Correction: I ~~saw~~ *had seen* the memo before the announcement was made public.

Review Test

Correct the verb errors in the following paragraphs using the first correction as a model. The number in parentheses at the end of each paragraph indicates how many errors you should find.

Thanks to federal regulations, industrial pollution ~~was~~ *has been* significantly reduced over the past several decades. However, we begin to realize that there is another form of water pollution that was completely outside state and federal regulation: "nonpoint-source" pollution. Existing regulations dealt with pollution that has a distinct point of origin—a particular factory or plant, for example, whose unregulated discharge can be directly measured. "Point-of-origin" pollution consists of relatively high levels of pollutants in a small area. The effects that a particular point-of-origin had on the immediate area are easy to identify, and we can cost them out. (4)

Nonpoint-source pollution is a different matter altogether. Every time we get into our car and start it up, we release a relatively small amount of various pollutants into the atmosphere. These pollutants are dispersed over such a wide area that nobody can tell where they came from or even when they are put into the air. The problem that defeated environmental agencies for years is how to deal with such overwhelming numbers of little polluters. A similar problem existed for years with runoff. Every time it rains, water dissolves the grease and oil on our driveways and washes it off into nearby streams. The amount of pollution per square foot of paved surface is not very great, but the cumulative effect from millions of square feet of pavement can be devastating. (3)

Understanding Pronouns

OVERVIEW

The Nuts and Bolts of Understanding Pronouns

Pronouns are an important part of many languages. As noun replacers, they help us avoid having to use the same words over and over (as in *Ms. Ramone stopped by yesterday, and Ms. Ramone took us for a ride in Ms. Ramone's new car*). Pronouns are useful because they can fit into almost any sentence.

But the adaptability of pronouns also creates problems. Because they can refer to so many things, writers must take care to make the reference of each pronoun clear. The lessons in this unit address some common difficulties involving pronouns.

Lesson 8 shows you how to make a pronoun and the word it refers to either both singular *or* both plural.

Example: ✗ The person who called didn't leave their phone number.

Correction: The person who called didn't leave ~~their~~ *her* phone number.

Lesson 9 shows you how to make clear what a pronoun refers to.

Example: ✗ Our dog gets so mad at the cat that it chases its tail.

Correction: Our cat gets the dog so mad it chases its own tail.

Lessons 10 and 11 help you choose between similar pronouns: *I* or *me*? *she* or *her*? *he* or *him*? (see Lesson 10); *who, whom,* or *that*? (see Lesson 11).

Example: ✗ Dolly and me went skiing.

Correction: Dolly and ~~me~~ *I* went skiing.

Example: ✗ Our group decided whom would type our paper.

                                                who
Correction: Our group decided ~~whom~~ would type our paper.
                                              ^

Lesson 12 helps you to use nonsexist language to ensure that nouns and pronouns refer, as appropriate, to both males and females.

Example: ✗ Everyone should have completed his assignment.

                                                        the
Correction: Everyone should have completed ~~his~~ assignment.
                                                       ^

Unit Four

overview

Pronoun Agreement

EXAMPLE 1

Error: ✗ A <u>teacher</u> should explain <u>their</u> assignments carefully.

Correction: *Teachers*
              ~~A teacher~~ should explain their assignments carefully.
              ^

EXAMPLE 2

Error: ✗ Did <u>everybody</u> cast <u>their</u> vote in the last election?

Correction: Did everybody ~~cast their~~ vote in the last election?

What's the Problem?

Personal pronouns include *I, he, she, it, they, we,* and all their varied forms, such as *me, him, his, her, its, their,* and *them.* A personal pronoun often refers back to a person, place, or thing (called a **pronoun antecedent**). This pronoun and antecedent should be in **agreement**; that is, they should match in number, person, and gender. In the following example, the pronoun *they* refers back to its antecedent, *voters.* Both *they* and *voters* are plural, so they agree.

Example: The <u>voters</u> turned out even in pouring rain, and <u>they</u> reelected the mayor.

This lesson focuses on the most common problem with pronoun agreement: making sure a personal pronoun agrees in number with its antecedent. Let's look at the two example sentences from the beginning of the lesson, which illustrate this problem.

Example 1:   ✗ A <u>teacher</u> should explain <u>their</u> assignments carefully.

The pronoun *their* is plural, but *teacher* is singular.

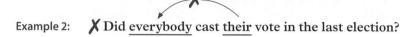

Example 2:   ✗ Did <u>everybody</u> cast <u>their</u> vote in the last election?

The pronoun *their* is plural, but *everybody* is singular.

Lesson 8

*pron
agr*

It is easy to see why these errors occur. Words such as *everybody*, *every-one*, *anybody*, and *someone* seem plural; *everybody* in particular appears to refer to many people. In Example 1, *teacher* similarly refers to an entire category of people, not just one particular teacher. Nonetheless, these words are always grammatically singular. Another reason this error occurs is that writers do not want to be sexist. If Examples 1 and 2 used *his* instead of *their*, the writer would avoid an agreement error but might be considered sexist for excluding females. Writers should learn ways to avoid both kinds of problems—agreement errors and sexist language. (See Lesson 12 for more on sexist language.)

Diagnostic Exercise

CORRECTED SENTENCES APPEAR ON PAGE 470.

Correct all the pronoun agreement errors in the following paragraph using the first correction as a model. The number in parentheses at the end of the paragraph indicates how many errors you should find.

    Politicians have

~~A politician has~~ to play a hundred different roles in meeting the

expectations of their constituents. One key role for every politician is to

pay special attention to the concerns and problems of their constituents.

The other key role is to actually participate in the process of governing.

Not that long ago, there was a broad middle-of-the road consensus on most

public issues. Not so today. Now, if a politician from one party proposes

anything, they are automatically attacked by politicians from the other

party. In the past, a politician would campaign on their own ideas and

agendas. Now, it is almost irrelevant for a politician to develop proposals to

attract voters to their campaign. What a politician does today is air vicious

negative ads attacking their opponents, often with malicious half-truths

and even outright lies. As a result, the average voter is less and less inter-

ested in following politics, and they are even giving up casting their votes. (6)

Fixing This Problem in Your Writing

Identifying Pronoun Agreement Errors

Most pronoun agreement errors involve one particular pronoun (*they*) and its various forms (*their*, *them*). *They*, *their*, and *them* are always plural. This first tip helps you determine if an antecedent is singular or plural.

> **ARE TIP** When using *they*, *their*, or *them*, make sure the antecedent is also plural. If you can use the plural verb *are* after the antecedent, it is indeed plural and in agreement with *they*, *their*, or *them*. If *are* does not seem to fit, there is an agreement error.

Lesson 8

*pron
agr*

In Example 1, the *Are* Tip shows us that there is a problem with pronoun agreement.

ANTECEDENT   PRONOUN

Example 1:   ✗ A <u>teacher</u> should explain <u>their</u> assignments carefully.

Tip applied: ✗ A teacher *are*?

The test sentence sounds strange because *are* is not a verb you would use with *teacher*: *teacher* is singular while *are* is plural. Thus, the *Are* Tip shows us that the singular noun *teacher* cannot agree with the plural pronoun *their*.

Correcting Pronoun Agreement Errors

In the following tip, we explain one of the easiest ways to correct pronoun agreement errors involving *they*, *their*, and *them*.

> **PLURAL TIP** To correct most agreement errors involving forms of the pronoun *their*, replace the singular antecedent with a plural one.

In Example 1, we corrected the agreement error by making the antecedent plural.

Teachers
Correction: ~~A teacher~~ should explain their assignments carefully.

The plural pronoun *their* now agrees with the plural antecedent *teachers*.

Example 2 is trickier because *everybody* has a plural "feel" to it. But would you ever say *Everybody are?*

ANTECEDENT   PRONOUN

Example 2:   ✗ Did everybody cast their vote in the last election?

Tip applied: ✗ Everybody *are?*

Because *everybody* fails the *Are* Tip test, we know that it is singular and does not agree with the plural *their*. Using the Plural Tip, we could change *everybody* to a plural term:

Lesson 8

pron
agr

all members   votes
Correction: Did everybody cast their vote in the last election?

> The plural pronoun *their* now agrees with the plural antecedent *all members*. Because *all members* is plural, *vote* must change to *votes*.

A second strategy is to revise so you don't need the pronoun *their*. Eliminating the pronoun eliminates the problem with pronoun agreement. (Notice also that the revised sentence is more concise.)

Correction: Did everybody cast their vote in the last election?

A third way to correct pronoun agreement errors is to use *his or her* instead of *their* with a singular subject.

his or her
Correction: Did everybody cast their vote in the last election?

> The singular pronoun combination *his or her* now agrees with the singular antecedent *everybody*.

MORE EXAMPLES

Error: ✗ Everyone in my dorm parks their car in Lot B.

All residents   park   cars
Correction: Everyone in my dorm parks their car in Lot B.

Error: ✗ Somebody at the airport forgot to bring their ID card.

an
Correction: Somebody at the airport forgot to bring their ID card.

Error: ✗ Almost every <u>woman</u> who has dated Ralph did not let him meet <u>their</u> parents.

Correction: Almost every woman who has dated Ralph did
not let him meet ~~their~~ parents.
                                      her
                                       ^

✳ *Putting It All Together*

Identify Pronoun Agreement Errors

____ Most pronoun agreement errors involve *they*, *their*, or *them*, so look for these pronouns, which are always plural.

____ Does each of these pronouns have an antecedent — a word that the pronoun refers back to? If so, the antecedent should also be plural.

____ To make sure the antecedent is plural, use the *Are* Tip. If *are* sounds odd after the antecedent, the antecedent is singular, meaning it does not agree with *they*, *their*, or *them*.

Correct Pronoun Agreement Errors

____ The Plural Tip is one easy way to correct most agreement errors. Revise the antecedent so that it is plural.

____ Other correction strategies are to reword the sentence so that you do not need a pronoun at all, or to use *his*, *her*, or *his or her* instead of *their* with a singular subject.

Lesson 8

*pron
agr*

Sentence Practice 1

CORRECTED SENTENCES APPEAR ON PAGE 470.

In each sentence, underline the pronoun once and the antecedent twice. Write *plural* or *singular* above the pronoun and its antecedent. Correct any agreement problems. If a sentence has no such error(s), write *OK* above it.

                singular   *plural*
Example: <u>Everyone</u> got instructions on how to fill out <u>their</u> forms.

                                                      his or her
Correction: Everyone got instructions on how to fill out ~~their~~ forms.
                                                             ^

1. A college freshman has no idea what they are going to major in.

2. A customer is always right, but that doesn't mean they know what they are talking about.

3. Anyone who is late with their term papers will lose a full grade.

4. Every parent has a responsibility to ensure that their children get immunized.

5. Any car will skid if you drive them too fast around curves.

 For more practice with pronoun agreement, go to **Exercise Central** at
bedfordstmartins.com/commonsense

Lesson 8

pron
agr

Sentence Practice 2

CORRECTED SENTENCES APPEAR ON PAGE 470.

In each sentence, underline the pronoun once and the antecedent twice.
Write *plural* or *singular* above the pronoun and its antecedent. Correct any
agreement problems. If a sentence has no such error(s), write *OK* above it.

>   *singular*   *plural*
> Example: Every teacher is giving their final exam on the same day!

>   *All teachers are*   *exams*
> Correction: ~~Every teacher is~~ giving their final ~~exam~~ on the same day!
>   ^   ^

1. Someone parked their car in a place where it will be towed.

2. Almost everyone brought his or her book to class today.

3. Most people who can recall the assassination of John F. Kennedy seem
   able to remember exactly what they were doing when they heard the
   news.

4. Did somebody take my pen instead of theirs?

5. Out of thirty people in their class, nobody knew that Becca and Alyssa
   are sisters.

Sentence Practice 3

Combine the following sentences with *and*, *but*, or *or*. Make whatever changes
are necessary to eliminate errors in pronoun agreement.

> Example: Sometimes, a teacher has to act like a drill sergeant.
>   They also need the patience of a saint.

> Answer: *Sometimes, teachers have to act like drill sergeants, but they*
>   *also need the patience of a saint.*

1. A driver needs to be careful. They might have a wreck.

2. Everyone here needs to be quiet for a moment. They can continue talking after I finish adding these numbers.

3. A mall is a convenient place to shop. They all seem the same.

4. Someone ate at this table before us. They were sloppy.

5. Each book in this room is old. These are part of a valuable collection.

6. A lab assistant is available. They will come to you if you raise your hand.

7. Replace worn-out fan belts. It might break when you are on the road.

8. Final course examinations are normally given in the morning. Not if it is for a lab course.

9. Get their names. Help get him seated as soon as possible.

10. The restaurant is nearby. They aren't very good.

Lesson 8

pron agr

Editing Practice 1

CORRECTED SENTENCES APPEAR ON PAGE 470.

Correct all the pronoun agreement errors in the following paragraphs using the first correction as a model. The number in parentheses at the end of each paragraph indicates how many errors you should find.

My brother has been collecting certain cards that have been
                      People
popular in the last few years. ~~Someone~~ might merely collect these
                ^
cards, or they might actually play games with them. Many years ago,

a card collector would have likely collected sports cards, but nowadays they

collect cards based on strange creatures or superhuman characters from

comics and TV shows. Many of these cards are based on Japanese popu-

lar culture, and they are especially likely to deal with magical beings that

engage in duels. (1)

At one time, Pokémon was the most popular card game. The person

who created these cards must have made a great deal of money from their

creations. Another Japanese-inspired game is called Yu Gi Oh, and it is still popular. In Yu Gi Oh, a player selects a card from their hand to play. The opponent likewise picks a card they will duel with. I thought this was a mindless game until I saw how much math and strategy are involved in the dueling stage. The game is so complex that somebody learning the game needs all the help they can get from an experienced player. I doubt I will collect or play this game, but I won't make fun of it anymore either. (4)

Lesson 8

pron
agr

Editing Practice 2

Correct all the pronoun agreement errors in the following paragraph using the first correction as a model. The number in parentheses at the end of the paragraph indicates how many errors you should find.

When I was young, sports were only available through the schools. That meant that during the summer, a̶ ̶c̶h̶i̶l̶d̶ *children* had absolutely no access to organized sports when they actually had free time to engage in them. The situation is completely different for children today. The big problem for them is having so many options that he doesn't know what to pick. Should children play Little League baseball, should he do tennis at Parks and Recreation, or should they take swimming lessons at the "Y"? Should they take karate or should he take tae kwon do? It sometimes seems to me that children today are absolutely lost in a sea of options, making it easy for him to flit from one sport to another without ever getting very good at any one of them. Maybe it is not so critical with individual sports or martial arts because it can be started up again without too much loss of skills. A team sport is a totally different matter because they take a long time to build team spirit or a sense of group cohesiveness. (6)

Applying What You Know

Using *they*, *their*, or *them* at least five times, write a paragraph or two on how you would help a child decide on what activities he or she should engage in during the summer. Help him or her weigh the pros and cons of different kinds of activities.

The Bottom Line	**Pronouns** should agree with **their** antecedents.

Lesson 8

pron agr

Vague Pronouns: *This, That,* and *It*

EXAMPLE 1 **Two Possible Antecedents**

Error: Two of Ryland's hobbies are fishing and skiing.

   ✗ It requires a lot of money for good equipment.

Correction: Two of Ryland's hobbies are fishing and skiing.
       Skiing
   ~~It~~ requires a lot of money for good equipment.
      ^

EXAMPLE 2 **Missing Antecedent**

Error: Contrary to her campaign promises, the governor announced cutbacks in welfare and an increase in education spending. ✗ That is sure to anger voters.

Correction: Contrary to her campaign promises, the governor announced cutbacks in welfare and an increase in
                 announcement
education spending. That is sure to anger voters.
          ^

What's the Problem?

Many pronouns refer back to a previous noun or pronoun: the **pronoun antecedent**. A problem occurs when the antecedent is unclear or missing. In Example 1, it is not clear *which* of Ryland's hobbies is expensive. In Example 2, the writer is vague about *what* "is sure to anger voters." The following guidelines will help you avoid vague pronouns.

- The antecedent should be a specific person, place, or thing that the pronoun refers to.

- The antecedent should be in the same sentence as the pronoun or in the previous sentence.

- Avoid using other nouns between the pronoun and its antecedent.

- If you must include an "interrupting" noun between the pronoun and antecedent, make sure readers could not logically mistake this noun for the antecedent.

The following example satisfies all four guidelines.

My car has not been running well, so Paul took it to a mechanic.

ANTECEDENT   **PRONOUN**

The pronoun (*it*) refers clearly to a specific antecedent (*car*). Although an "interrupting" noun (*Paul*) comes between the pronoun and the antecedent, *it* cannot logically refer to *Paul*.

A speaker can use pronouns such as *this, that,* or *it* without clear antecedents because physical gestures (such as pointing) can clarify what *this* or *that* refers to. Unfortunately, people often carry over their uses of vague pronouns into their writing.

This lesson focuses on *this, that,* and *it,* which account for most problems involving vague pronouns. However, the concepts in this lesson apply to all pronouns that require an antecedent (*many, few,* and *they,* for example).

Diagnostic Exercise

CORRECTED SENTENCES APPEAR ON PAGE 470.

Correct all vague uses of *this, that,* and *it* in the following paragraph using the first correction as a model. The number in parentheses at the end of the paragraph indicates how many changes you should make.

"Star Wars" was the name of a military program as well as a movie.
The program
~~It~~ was a large research program calling for military defense in outer
^
space. This was initiated by President Reagan in the 1980s, and it had the

official title of "Strategic Defense Initiative." The public never embraced

that as much as the catchier title "Star Wars." This project was heavily

funded for years, but it underwent major cutbacks once the cold war

ended. (2)

Fixing This Problem in Your Writing

To avoid vague pronouns, see if you can easily locate the antecedent by using the following tip.

> **ANTECEDENT TIP**   Locate what you think the pronoun refers to, and make sure this antecedent is a *noun*—a person, place, or thing. Next, make sure there is no "want-to-be antecedent"—another noun that the pronoun could possibly refer to.

Lesson 9

pron
ref

In Example 1, *It* seems to refer to either *fishing* or *skiing*. Both are nouns, so the sentence passes the first part of the Antecedent Tip.

NOUN   NOUN

Tip applied: Two of Ryland's hobbies are fishing and skiing. It requires a lot of money for good equipment.

The sentence does not, however, pass the second part of the tip. If the writer assumes that only one of these hobbies (fishing or skiing) is expensive, then the other hobby is a "want-to-be antecedent." In other words, one noun is the real antecedent; the other is in a position that could make readers think it is the real antecedent.

The simplest way to correct this sentence is to replace *It* with the word being renamed. We'll assume the author had *skiing* in mind.

Skiing

Correction: Two of Ryland's hobbies are fishing and skiing. ~~It~~
requires a lot of money for good equipment.   ^

Now look at Example 2, which does not pass the first part of the Antecedent Tip. The pronoun *That* seems to refer to the entire idea of the first sentence, not to a specific noun.

Tip applied: Contrary to her campaign promises, the governor

announced cutbacks in welfare and an increase in

?

education spending. ✗ That is sure to anger voters.

That does not refer to any specific noun in the first sentence.

Keep in mind the word *pronoun* comes from *for a noun* (as in *pronoun*). The origin of the word will help you remember that a pronoun should stand only for a noun (or another pronoun). In Example 2, we're guessing that the writer was trying to refer to the entire group of words in the first sentence.

One way to correct this error is to revise the sentence before the pronoun to provide a specific antecedent, the noun *reversal*.

Correction: ~~Contrary to her campaign promises, the~~ *The* governor

announced cutbacks in welfare and an^ increase in

, a reversal of her campaign promises.

education spending**/** That is sure to anger voters.

Another way to correct the error in Example 2 is to apply this next tip.

Lesson 9

THIS/THAT TIP   Add a noun after *this* or *that* to clarify your meaning.

pron ref

Adding a noun after *this* or *that* turns these pronouns into **adjectives**, eliminating the need to worry about antecedents.

Correction: Contrary to her campaign promises, the governor

announced cutbacks in welfare and an increase in

ADJECTIVE   NOUN

announcement

education spending. That is sure to anger voters.
^

Because *That* is now an adjective describing *announcement*, it does not require an antecedent. Although *this* and *that* can correctly be used as pronouns, your writing will often be clearer if you use these words as adjectives instead.

MORE EXAMPLES

This, That, and It *Used as Pronouns with Clear Antecedents*

Do you know how to make <u>tortilla soup</u>? I'm craving <u>that</u> for dinner.

My weekend <u>plan</u> was ruined because <u>it</u> depended on our having good weather.

This *and* That *Used as Adjectives to Avoid Vague Pronouns*

The college president decided tuition would be increased to give teachers a raise. <u>This decision</u> was appreciated by teachers but not by students.

You need a haircut, a shave, and a bath because you have been camping for a week. I cannot help you with <u>that problem</u>.

✳ *Putting It All Together*

Identify Vague Pronouns

_____ The most common vague pronouns are *this*, *that*, and *it*, so look for these pronouns in your writing.

_____ Each of these pronouns should have a clear antecedent — a previous, nearby noun (or pronoun) that means the same thing.

_____ If readers see more than one logical choice for the antecedent, the pronoun is vague.

Correct Vague Pronouns

_____ Make sure the antecedent is close to its pronoun, either in the same sentence or in the previous sentence. Often, you can correct a vague pronoun by either moving it closer to the antecedent or vice versa.

_____ Replace the vague pronoun with the noun that it refers to, or revise the sentence to provide a specific antecedent (a noun or a pronoun).

_____ Alternatively, add a noun after *this* or *that* to turn the pronoun into an adjective.

Lesson 9

pron
ref

Sentence Practice 1

CORRECTED SENTENCES APPEAR ON PAGE 470.

If the underlined pronoun is vague, correct the sentence using one of the methods described in this lesson. If the pronoun is not vague, write *OK* above it and underline the antecedent.

This kind of politicization

Example: Global warming has gotten caught up in politics. ~~This~~ is
                   what I was afraid of.
                                                                          ^

1. In 1930, Pluto was declared a planet. <u>It</u> was reclassified as a dwarf planet in 2006.

2. We did not hear about our proposal. We need to talk about <u>that</u>.

3. John slammed the door while we were talking to him. <u>This</u> really upset us.

4. The budget cutback has hurt higher education. Students are protesting <u>it</u>.

5. The weather forecast did not predict the storm. There was a lot of damage because of <u>this</u>.

For more practice correcting vague pronouns, go to **Exercise Central** at
bedfordstmartins.com/commonsense

Sentence Practice 2

CORRECTED SENTENCES APPEAR ON PAGE 471.

Find the vague pronoun in the following sentences and correct it by using
one of the methods described in this lesson.

Lesson 9

*pron
ref*

Example: There is a new lecture series on the Civil War. *The series* will last
all quarter.

1. There was an accident on the freeway. This causes everyone to stop and
    stare.

2. San Francisco is one of the most photographed cities in the world. This
    makes it a natural tourist destination.

3. The governor and the legislature are virtually at war with each other.
    That has brought the state to its knees.

4. We need to get a new car, but that's not too likely in the near future.

5. Amy Brown won her election in a landslide. That came as a surprise to
    everyone.

Sentence Practice 3

The second sentence in each pair contains a vague pronoun that is underlined. Rewrite the second sentence so that it makes a clear reference.

Example: My roommate met an old friend recently. <u>She</u> is going to
graduate school now.

Answer: *Her friend is going to graduate school now.*

1. A squirrel appeared outside the window of my bedroom. <u>It</u> is not
    pretty.

2. My algebra teacher kept us ten minutes after we were supposed to
    leave. <u>This</u> made me mad.

3. The crack in my windshield is getting bigger. I knew <u>that</u> might
    happen.

4. Besides bringing a shovel, Dalit brought food for us to eat on our camping trip. We might not need <u>it</u>, but the food will come in handy.

5. In his speech, Louis argued that the best way to increase involvement in student government is to give a tuition break to members of the student senate. <u>That</u> happened last week.

Editing Practice 1

Lesson 9

pron
ref

CORRECTED SENTENCES APPEAR ON PAGE 471.

Correct all errors in the following paragraphs using the first correction as a model. The number in parentheses at the end of each paragraph indicates how many errors you should find.

> *This practice*

Some credit card companies are taking advantage of students. ~~It~~ is
                                                              ^
becoming increasingly common. I see salespeople from the card

companies almost every week on my campus, and it seems even more

common in the spring semester when students are graduating. Most

students have little experience with credit companies, and the

representatives know that. (2)

The companies give away T-shirts or candy bars to get students'

attention. This gimmick sparks students' interest, and then the salespeople

tell students that they are "preapproved" and can get a card immediately.

It seems to work because I always see students signing up for these cards.

The salespeople often forget a small detail: That little card is going to cost

an annual fee plus 21 percent interest on all charges. Most students seem

to think it is still great, but they will change their minds when they see the

bills adding up. Believe me, it happened to me. (3)

Editing Practice 2

CORRECTED SENTENCES APPEAR ON PAGE 471.

Correct all errors in the following paragraphs using the first correction as a model. The number in parentheses at the end of each paragraph indicates how many errors you should find.

My college finally decided to invest in a new system for allowing

students to register online without having to come to campus during

registration. *The new system* ~~It~~ is a good idea. In fact, I am surprised this has taken

so long to implement here. This has been used at other colleges in the

region. That is not unusual, however. I like my school, but it often seems

behind the times in terms of technology. (3)

Lesson 9

*pron
ref*

Under the new system, students will be given passwords allowing

them to access their student accounts. Initially, it will be automatically

assigned to each student, but the password can be changed later. By

following the onscreen directions, students can pick and choose which

classes they want to take, and this can be changed anytime up to the first

day of the semester. Students can now pay tuition online as well by using

their credit cards. That is good, even though I live across the street from

our campus. This new procedure is especially convenient for people who

commute a long distance to school. (3)

Editing Practice 3

Correct all errors in the following paragraph using the first correction as a model. The number in parentheses at the end of the paragraph indicates how many errors you should find.

This past summer, the National Spelling Bee was televised on two

telecast major networks. This is not exactly new. ESPN began showing the final

rounds of the contest during the early 1990s. It is not really an athletic

contest, but the network decided to broadcast the event because of the

competitive nature of spelling bees. This has apparently paid off for ESPN,

considering the high ratings the broadcast usually receives. The popularity

of the bees has greatly increased in the last few years. That can be seen by

the release of two major films and a Broadway musical that focus on

spelling bees. (3)

Applying What You Know

Write a paragraph or two describing your first efforts to learn a new sport, game, or hobby. Use *this*, *that*, and *it* (any combination and any use) at least five times. Use the two tips discussed in this lesson to make sure you use these three terms correctly.

<table>
<tr><td>Lesson 9</td><td>**The Bottom Line**</td><td>When using a **pronoun**, be sure **it** has a clear antecedent.</td></tr>
<tr><td>*pron ref*</td><td></td><td></td></tr>
</table>

Choosing the Correct Pronoun Form

EXAMPLE 1 *Pronoun as Subject*

Error: ✗ Jennifer Wong and <u>me</u> both took the same art class.

Correction: Jennifer Wong and ~~me~~ *I* both took the same art class.

EXAMPLE 2 *Pronoun as Object*

Error: ✗ They sang a song just for <u>she</u>.

Correction: They sang a song just for ~~she~~ *her*.

What's the Problem?

Most personal pronouns have one form when they are used as subjects and a second form when they are used as objects. Here is a complete list of the subject and object forms of all personal pronouns:

SINGULAR

Subject:	**I**	you	**he**	**she**	it
Object:	**me**	you	**him**	**her**	it

PLURAL

Subject:	**we**	you	**they**	**they**	**they**
Object:	**us**	you	**them**	**them**	**them**

The pronoun forms in boldface show a difference between subject and object forms.

As the names indicate, subject pronouns play the role of subjects of verbs; object pronouns play the role of objects of verbs or objects of prepositions. In Example 1, the object form *me* is incorrectly used where a subject pronoun is needed. In Example 2, the subject form *she* is incorrectly used as the object of a preposition.

The examples illustrate the two places where the large majority of subject/object pronoun errors occur: in compounds and in the use of subject pronouns where we should use object pronouns. Let's look at these two situations in more detail.

Lesson 10

*pron
case*

Pronouns in compounds. Compounds are two grammatical elements of the same kind joined by coordinating conjunctions. Here are some examples of pronouns (in boldface) in compounds: *Sally and **I**; **you** and Fred; the Smiths and **us**; **you** and **me**.* Whether the pronoun is in the subject form or the object form depends entirely on how the compound is used. If the compound is used as a subject, then the pronoun is in the subject form; if the compound is used as an object, then the pronoun is in the object form. For example:

Subject: Lois and **I** are going out tonight.

Object: They left a note for Lois and **me**.

For some reason, people find the pronouns in compounds (especially if the pronoun is in the second position within the compound) extremely difficult to monitor for correctness. Errors involving pronouns in compounds are one of the few grammatical errors that commonly occur in the speech of sophisticated people such as news broadcasters and educators.

Subject pronouns in object positions. The most common place for this error is following prepositions, for example:

✗ They went shopping with <u>we</u>.

✗ The paint store matched the sample for <u>he</u>.

✗ The girls sat down next to <u>I</u>.

It is not very easy to understand why this mistake is so common. There is some evidence that people assume that subject forms of pronouns are somehow more formal or proper than object forms. In other words, we have a kind of unconscious bias against object pronoun forms. This would explain why the reverse error of incorrectly using object pronouns in subject positions is quite rare. For example, nobody would make the following mistake unless he or she was trying (not very successfully) to be funny:

✗ <u>**Him**</u> went to the beach.

Diagnostic Exercise

CORRECTED SENTENCES APPEAR ON PAGE 471.

Correct all pronoun errors in the following paragraph using the first correction as a model. The number in parentheses at the end of the paragraph indicates how many errors you should find.

A friend and ~~me~~ *I* visited her cousin Jim, who lives in a cabin he built from scratch. My friend asked Jim if he would mind if her and me could stay in the cabin with he for a few days this summer. He said that was fine if we would work with he building a new storeroom he wanted to add onto his cabin. My friend told him that neither her nor me had any real experience building things. Jim said that it was OK. He would work with we. Both my friend and me learned how to measure and cut lumber, pound nails, and paint without getting it all over ourselves. Jim was very good-natured about the whole thing, even though my friend and me were probably more trouble than we were worth. (9)

Fixing This Problem in Your Writing

Here is a very useful tip for checking to see if the pronouns in a compound are correct.

> **PLURAL PRONOUN TIP** Replace compounds with a plural pronoun and test for grammatical correctness. If a plural subject pronoun such as *they* is correct, use a subject pronoun in the compound. If a plural object pronoun such as *them* is correct, use an object pronoun in the compound.

This tip works because by replacing the compound with a plural pronoun, we get around the problem of monitoring compounds. In other words, we are much less likely to make a mistake with a pronoun that appears by itself than we are to make a mistake with a pronoun that appears in a compound. Here is the tip applied to Example 1:

Example 1: **✗** Jennifer Wong and <u>me</u> both took the same art class.

Tip applied: <u>We</u> both took the same art class.

Tip applied: ✗ <u>Us</u> both took the same art class.

> The Plural Pronoun Tip shows us that we must use a subject pronoun in the compound.

Correction: Jennifer Wong and ~~me~~ both took the same art class.
             I

Lesson 10

Here is a tip to help you tell if you are using subject form pronouns incorrectly in positions where you should be using object form pronouns.

pron case

> **NO VERB, NO SUBJECT TIP**   Use the object form for every pronoun *unless* there is a verb right after it that enters into a subject-verb relationship with that pronoun.

The implication of this tip is that you should use object forms for pronouns unless you know for a fact that the pronoun is playing the role of a subject. Here is the No Verb, No Subject Tip applied to Example 2:

Error: ✗ They sang a song just for <u>she</u>.

Since the subject pronoun *she* is not followed by a verb, we must change *she* to the corresponding object form *her*:

Correction: They sang a song just for ~~she~~.
                                        her

Note that the No Verb, No Subject Tip requires that the subject form pronoun be followed by a verb that enters into a subject-verb relationship with the pronoun. The reason for the subject-verb relationship provision is that often object pronouns are followed by present and past participle verb forms. These participle forms cannot enter into subject-verb relations with pronouns; only present and past tense verbs can do that. Here are some examples of object pronouns followed by participles:

Present participle: We heard <u>her</u> singing in the next room.

Past participle: The <u>children</u> found them hidden in the attic.

We cannot use subject pronouns in these positions because there is no true subject-verb relationship:

Present participle: ✗ We heard <u>she</u> singing in the next room.

Past participle: ✗ The children found <u>they</u> hidden in the attic.

MORE EXAMPLES

Subject Pronoun Followed by a Verb

Nicole and <u>he</u> traveled by plane to El Paso.

Next spring, Rahim and <u>they</u> are driving all the way to Denver.

Object Pronoun Not Followed by a Verb

The decision is not up to Sue and <u>him</u>.

Our only hope is <u>them</u> coming up with the necessary funding.

Note that *them* is followed by a verb (*coming up*) but not a verb form that can enter into a subject-verb relationship.

✳ *Putting It All Together*

Identify Errors in Pronoun Forms

_____ Identify the five personal pronouns in your own writing that have different subject and object forms: *I/me; he/him; she/her; we/us; they/them*.

_____ When using a pronoun in a compound phrase, replace the compound phrase with a single plural pronoun.

_____ Check to see whether the pronoun is followed by a verb.

Correct Errors in Pronoun Forms

_____ If a pronoun is followed by a verb that can enter into a subject-verb relationship, use the subject form: *I, he, she, we, they*.

_____ Otherwise, use the object form: *me, him, her, us, them*.

Sentence Practice 1

CORRECTED SENTENCES APPEAR ON PAGE 471.

The pronouns in the following sentences are used in compounds. Underline both elements of the compound. Replace the compound with the appropriate plural pronoun. If the original pronoun is grammatical, write *OK* above it. If the original pronoun is wrong, replace it with the correct one.

> *They*
> Example: ✗ Her and her little dog eventually returned to Kansas.
>
> *She*
> Correction: ~~Her~~ and her little dog eventually returned to Kansas.
>   ^

1. They ordered it specially for my mother and I.

2. The manager asked Harriet and she to trade assignments.

3. Several of their friends and they are planning a vacation in Hawaii next winter.

4. I hesitated to ask Alicia and she such a big favor.

5. Roberta and him will graduate next spring.

 For more practice using pronouns, go to **Exercise Central** at **bedfordstmartins.com/commonsense**

Sentence Practice 2

CORRECTED SENTENCES APPEAR ON PAGE 472.

Underline all the object pronouns in the following sentences. If the object form is correct, write *OK* above it. If the object form is incorrect, replace it with the appropriate subject form. Confirm subject pronoun answers by underlining twice the verb that immediately follows the subject pronoun.

> *OK*   *I*   *OK*
> Example: John told him that ~~me~~ was going to meet them at the
>   restaurant.   ^

1. Him advised us that them had already gotten approval from her.

2. Them were worried about how them had not had a chance to talk to them.

3. Did him ever figure out what them should have said to her?

4. Them explained what them expected us to say about him.

5. Me expected that them would not have time to see them.

Sentence Practice 3

Replace the underlined noun with the appropriate pronoun.

Example: I assumed that Shirley and ~~Ray~~ were engaged.
                              he ^

1.   The landlord and <u>Ms. Gray</u> are meeting with us today about the security problem.

2.   That pie is for <u>Mark</u>.

3.   Carl and <u>Stacy</u> will be leaving soon.

4.   The request was made by <u>Kim</u>, not <u>Hank</u>.

5.   Dr. Wang asked her students to write a letter to <u>the dean</u> describing their concerns over the tuition increase.

6.   <u>Wilbur</u> asked <u>Orville</u> to gas up the plane.

7.   <u>A team of scientists</u> were reviewing the report.

8.   Jayne was thinking of moving to Austin so that she could be near <u>her children</u>.

9.   <u>Lord Banbury and Lady Agatha</u> were expecting <u>guests</u> for tea that afternoon.

10.   We noticed <u>the horse</u> grazing in the pasture behind the barn.

Lesson 10

pron case

Editing Practice 1

CORRECTED SENTENCES APPEAR ON PAGE 472.

Correct all errors in the following paragraphs using the first correction as a model. The number in parentheses at the end of each paragraph indicates how many errors you should find.

When I was in high school, my father and ~~me~~ would build a new
                                            I ^
house every other summer. My father and mother were both teachers, so them always had summers off. During the first summer, my father and me would pour the foundation and do the framing and roofing. During the school year, a contractor would supervise the plumbing, wiring, and other specialties. The following summer, my father and me would finish the interior work. During the next school year, my mother would take charge of all the interior decoration, and then her would put the house on the market. (4)

The key to making this scheme work was having the contractor; without he, we could never have done it. When we first started building houses, we needed he for his expertise. Later on, that was not the case. We needed he because he could control the subcontractors. (3)

Editing Practice 2

Correct all errors in the following paragraph using the first correction as a model. The number in parentheses at the end of the paragraph indicates how many errors you should find.

When you build a house, most of the work is actually done by specialized subcontractors: plumbing, wiring, drywall, cabinetry, tile work, and so on. If my father built a house by himself, without a

contractor, ~~him~~ *he* would be unable to get the subcontractors to do the work. The problem is not hiring they—they are delighted to sign contracts. The problem is getting they to actually show up and do the work. Typically, contractors are working three or four jobs at once. The subcontractors would know that them would never work for my father again. Thus, my father would be the lowest priority; the contractors would work on our house only when them had time available, which could be once a week or once a month. Since these specialized jobs are sequenced (electrical and plumbing, for example, have to be done before the drywall contractor can close up the walls), delays in one subcontractor's work snowball and cause huge delays for the other subcontractors. Our contractor, on the other hand, could call up a subcontractor and say to he, "Listen, if you ever want to work for I again, you will finish the job by next Wednesday." Guess what? Them would show up and finish the job by next Wednesday. (7)

Applying What You Know

Write a paragraph or two describing how you and another person worked together on some project. Use as many of the following pronouns as you can: *I/me, he/him, she/her, we/us, they/them.*

The Bottom Line	Subject forms of personal pronouns are fairly predictable. Usually, **they are followed** by verbs.

Lesson 10

pron
case

Who, Whom, and That

EXAMPLE 1   **That** *Used Instead of* **Who/Whom**

Error: ✗ The student <u>that</u> read my draft said it was clear.

Correction: The student ~~that~~ *who* read my draft said it was clear.

EXAMPLE 2   **Who** *Used Instead of* **Whom**

Error: ✗ Bobbie met a person <u>who</u> you might know.

Correction: Bobbie met a person ~~who~~ *whom* you might know.

What's the Problem?

Who, *whom*, and *that* usually function as pronouns, and writers are often confused about which one of them to use in a given sentence. Many times, writers use *that* when they should use either *who* or *whom* (as with Example 1). But even if writers know that *that* is the wrong choice, they might not know whether *who* or *whom* is correct (as with Example 2).

You can avoid these two errors by first understanding how *who*, *whom*, and *that* often refer back to a previous noun (or another pronoun), as seen in the following correct examples.

I once had a <u>crack</u> in my windshield <u>that</u> prevented me from driving.

I had it fixed by <u>someone</u> <u>whom</u> I could trust.

The previous word that the pronoun refers back to is called a **pronoun antecedent**—a noun or pronoun that essentially means the same thing as *who*, *whom*, or *that* in the sentence. *Crack* and *someone* are the antecedents in the example sentences above.

In general, do not use *that* when the antecedent is a person. Example 1 is incorrect because *that* refers back to a person (a *student*). Writers often incorrectly use *that* because they hope to avoid having to choose between *who* or *whom*, which indeed is a more difficult decision.

To decide whether to use *who* or *whom*, you need to determine how the pronoun functions in the sentence.

- If the pronoun functions as a subject, use *who* (the subject form):

  I have a friend <u>who</u> wears a red hat every Valentine's Day.

  Who functions as a subject: It performs the action (*wears*).

- If the pronoun is a direct object or an object of a preposition, use *whom* (the object form):

  She got the hat from someone <u>whom</u> she once loved.

  Whom functions as an object. Here, it is receiving the action of the verb (*loved*).

Lesson 11

pron case

Diagnostic Exercise

CORRECTED SENTENCES APPEAR ON PAGE 472.

In the following paragraph, every *that* is underlined. Using the first correction as a model, change each inappropriate *that* to *who* or *whom*. The number in parentheses at the end of the paragraph indicates how many errors you should find.

An experience <u>that</u> we all have had is working for a bad boss. One

   whom
boss ~~that~~ we have all had is the petty tyrant, a person <u>that</u> loves to find
   ^

fault with every employee <u>that</u> works in the building. It seems like the petty

tyrant is more interested in finding employees <u>that</u> he or she can belittle

than in getting the job done. Even worse than the petty tyrant is a super-

visor <u>that</u> is inconsistent. An inconsistent boss is a person <u>that</u> the employees

can never trust. A game <u>that</u> this kind of boss loves is playing favorites. One

day, this boss is everyone's best buddy; the next day, the boss acts as if he or

she doesn't know the name of a person <u>that</u> has worked with the company

for ten years. (6)

Fixing This Problem in Your Writing

Knowing When to Use *That*

The following tip simplifies the guidelines on when to use *that*.

> **THAT THING TIP**   Use *that* only if it refers back to a nonhuman thing (such as an object, an idea, a place, or an animal).

The *That Thing* Tip reveals the problem with Example 1. The antecedent is a human, not a thing. Thus, we should not use *that*.

Example 1:   ✗ The student that read my draft said it was clear.

NOT A THING
✗
Tip applied: ✗ The student that read my draft said it was clear.

Student is not a thing, so *that* is wrong.

At this point, we have determined only that it is incorrect to use *that* in the sentence. We still need to decide whether to use *who* or *whom*, which takes us to the next step.

Exception: Some people believe it is fine to use *that* if it refers to a type of person — not to a real person (as in *I need a lawyer that I can trust*). Not everyone agrees with this exception, and you are never wrong to use *who/whom* to refer to a person or type of person. Thus, we suggest always avoiding *that* to refer to people.

Choosing between *Who* and *Whom*

As noted earlier, use *who* when the pronoun is the subject of a verb. Use *whom* when the pronoun serves as an object (a direct object or an object of a preposition). The following tip will help you make the right choice between *who* and *whom*.

> **WHO + VERB TIP**   Look at the word following (usually immediately following) *who* or *whom*. If this word is a verb, use *who*.

The *Who* + Verb Tip works because the subject form (*who*) is used when the pronoun is a subject of a verb, and verbs normally appear very soon after a subject. Now we know how to correct Example 1. There is a verb right after the pronoun, so *who* is the right choice:

Example 1:   ✗ The student that read my draft said it was clear.

WHO   +   VERB

Tip applied: The student [who/whom] read my draft said it was clear.

A verb comes after the pronoun, so *who* is the correct choice.

who
Correction: The student ~~whom~~ read my draft said it was clear.
               ^

Lesson 11

*pron
case*

Compare this example with Example 2, however. In this second example, the pronoun is followed by a pronoun, not a verb. Thus, our correction changes *who* to *whom*.

Example 2:   ✗ Bobbie met a person who you might know.

WHOM + PRONOUN

Tip applied: Bobbie met a person [who/whom] you might know.

The pronoun is *not* followed by a verb, so we use *whom*.

whom
Correction: Bobbie met a person ~~who~~ you might know.
               ^

It is possible for adverbs to come between *who* and its verb (as in *I know a man who always wears hats*). Still, the *Who* + Verb Tip provides an easy way to remember the basic rules: Use *who* as the subject of a verb.

MORE EXAMPLES

Sentences Using **That** *Correctly*

My cousin bought a computer that has a built-in webcam.

Dr. Zeikowitz has a parrot that he has taught over two dozen words.

Sentences Using **Who** *Correctly*

I need a spouse who will be supportive of my emotional needs.

Who brought the cheesecake?

Sentences Using **Whom** *Correctly*

Mayor Beach is a leader whom the people trust and admire.

Adair is a person in whom you should place little trust.

✳ *Putting It All Together*

Identify Errors in Using Who, Whom, *and* That

_____ Look for the words *who*, *whom*, and *that* in your writing. These words are normally pronouns that require an antecedent. An antecedent is a previous noun (or pronoun) that the pronoun is referring to.

Correct Errors in Using Who, Whom, *and* That

_____ Use *that* only when referring to nonhuman things (such as an object, an idea, a place, or an animal). Do not use *that* to refer to people.

_____ Use *who* when the pronoun is the subject of a verb. Normally, a verb should follow *who* almost immediately.

_____ Use *whom* when the pronoun is the object of the sentence. There should *not* be a verb immediately following *whom*.

Sentence Practice 1

CORRECTED SENTENCES APPEAR ON PAGE 472.

Underline all occurrences of the pronoun *that*. Next, underline twice the noun or pronoun to which *that* refers (its antecedent). If the antecedent is nonhuman, write *OK*. If the antecedent refers to people, then replace *that* with *who* or *whom* as appropriate.

Example: Did you notice the <u><u>couple</u></u> ~~that~~ was next to me in the
who
elevator?

1. I shined the shoes that I would wear to the meeting the next morning.
2. I asked if he knew any residents that were interested in leasing their apartments.
3. The candidate thanked all the volunteers that had worked so hard on the campaign.
4. I couldn't find the clerk that had sold me the shirt.
5. We really liked the plans that we had looked at first.

 For more practice using pronouns, go to **Exercise Central** at
bedfordstmartins.com/commonsense

Sentence Practice 2

CORRECTED SENTENCES APPEAR ON PAGE 472.

Underline all occurrences of the pronoun *who*. Underline twice the word or phrase that immediately follows *who*. If that following word or phrase is a verb, write *OK*. If that following word or phrase is not a verb, then replace *who* with *whom*.

CORRECTED SENTENCES APPEAR ON PAGE 472.

> *whom*
>
> Example: Everybody talked about the man ~~who~~ the police had
> arrested in the garage.

1. Everyone liked the actors who had played the parts on Broadway.

2. Nobody knew the stage manager who the new director had hired.

3. The people who we were scheduled to meet with never showed up.

4. Unfortunately, the architect who had designed the building was no longer in the area.

5. You have to trust the people who you have hired to do the job.

Sentence Practice 3

Change the capitalized word(s) in the second sentence into *who* or *whom* and combine the sentences so that the second part modifies the underlined word in the first part.

> Example: I found someone. SOMEONE will help me study.
>
> Answer: *I found someone who will help me study.*

1. Yogi Berra is the baseball player. THE PLAYER holds the World Series record for most times on a winning team.

2. He is also a cultural icon. AN ICON is known for his humorous sayings.

3. We need to call the person. You spoke to THE PERSON.

4. Over there is the man. You want to avoid THE MAN.

5. A student angered the teacher. THE TEACHER asked the class to stop talking.

Editing Practice 1

CORRECTED SENTENCES APPEAR ON PAGE 472.

Correct all errors in the following paragraph using the first correction as a model. The number in parentheses at the end of the paragraph indicates how many errors you should find.

Lesson 11

pron case

                        whom
    My boss is someone ~~who~~ you might consider strange. I work

part time at a convenience store that is located outside the city. My boss,

Ms. McDonald, is someone who wants everything exactly her way. If you

ever disagree with her, she tells you to hush and then covers her ears.

She is married to a man that sells exotic goats for a living, and he occa-

sionally brings them to the store. Last weekend, one goat bit a customer

who was buying tomatoes that the goat wanted. Ms. McDonald, who the

goat also tried to bite, called the police. By the time they arrived, both

the goat and my boss's husband had escaped. The customer whom was

bitten said he would sue the store; Ms. McDonald simply told him to hush

and covered her ears. The officers, whom were all too familiar with her

strange behavior, said she could no longer have goats in the store. It's not

exactly a funny situation, but she certainly makes my job interesting. (4)

Editing Practice 2

CORRECTED SENTENCES APPEAR ON PAGE 473.

Correct all errors in the following paragraphs using the first correction as a model. The number in parentheses at the end of each paragraph indicates how many errors you should find.

                         who
    Many Americans, even those ~~that~~ are knowledgeable about differ-

ent cultures, know little about many religions. One example is Buddhism.

This religion was founded in India by Siddhartha Gautama, whom

is known as Buddha, and it has over 300 million followers worldwide.

Another example is Confucianism. This religion is based on the teachings of Confucius, a Chinese philosopher that stressed the importance of relationships among people, families, and members of society. (2)

Some lesser-known religions were actually founded by people that migrated to America. The Amish Mennonites can be traced back to the birth of the Mennonite religion in Switzerland during the 1500s. In 1693, however, the followers of Jacob Ammann broke from other Mennonites, but a great many rejoined the main group in the eighteenth century. The remainder, whom stayed loyal to Jacob Ammann's views, migrated to Pennsylvania. These are the followers that became known as Amish Mennonites. Today, there are some forty thousand Amish Mennonites in the world. (3)

Lesson 11

*pron
case*

Editing Practice 3

Correct all errors in the following paragraph using the first correction as a model. The number in parentheses at the end of the paragraph indicates how many errors you should find.

who
Several students ~~that~~ are in my calculus class have taken the course
^
more than once. Paul, whom has taken the course three times, said many students fail because they do not complete all the homework. He said that not attending class also poses a problem for students that struggle with math. I also spoke with my friend Inez, who passed the course with an A. She formed a study group with three students that were in her class, and they all passed. Inez also received help from her teacher, who she frequently consulted during his office hours. Math does not come easily to me, so I'll need to plan ahead on finding additional help with the course. (4)

Applying What You Know

In groups of three, investigate the varied uses of *who, whom,* and *that.* These three words are not always pronouns having antecedents. See if you can identify the different uses of *who, whom,* and *that* covered in this lesson. Each member of your group should be assigned one of these words.

All group members should find their own magazine article; it must have at least three uses of the word the member was assigned. Each member does one of the following tasks:

1. Circle every *that* and put a check by each one that is a pronoun. Put a check also by the antecedent, if there is one.
2. Circle every *who*. If *who* is the subject of a verb, put a check by the verb.
3. Circle every *whom*. One function of *whom* is to serve as the object of a verb (see **direct object** in the Guide to Grammar Terminology on page 441). Place a check by the verb that is affecting each *whom* you circled.

This task is more difficult than it might seem, so go through your findings with your group.

Lesson 11

pron
case

| The Bottom Line | The word *that* is a pronoun **that** should refer to ideas and things—not to people. |

Eliminating Sexist Pronouns

EXAMPLE 1

Error: ✗ Everybody should bring <u>his</u> book to class tomorrow.

Correction: Everybody should bring ~~his~~ book to class tomorrow.
his or her

EXAMPLE 2

Error: ✗ A kindergarten teacher helps <u>her</u> students gain social as well as academic skills.

Correction: ~~A kindergarten teacher helps her~~ students gain social as well as academic skills.
Kindergarten teachers help their

What's the Problem?

Sexist language, even when unintentional, is unacceptable in college and professional communication. Such language excludes one gender or the other, and it is demeaning. A writer who uses sexist language is likely to offend readers, who in turn will be less likely to respect the point that the writer is trying to make.

Sexist language takes many forms, but this lesson focuses on one of the most common forms: pronouns used in ways that exclude or ignore one gender. That is, sexist language occurs when certain **personal pronouns**—*he, his, him, she,* and *her*—are used in ways that indicate *only* males or *only* females are being discussed.

For instance, Example 1 suggests that only males should bring their books, while Example 2 indicates that all kindergarten teachers are female. Of course, you can use pronouns such as *he* or *her* when the pronouns logically refer only to males (a father or a member of an all-male class) or only to females (a bride or a pitcher on a women's softball team), but make such generalizations *only* if there is no chance of excluding people who are in the category.

At one time, it seemed acceptable to use the so-called generic *he* to refer to all people, meaning that sentences such as Example 1 would have been satisfactory to some readers. It also seemed appropriate at one time to associate one gender with particular roles or professions (such as nurses = female; doctors = male). Thus, Example 2 might have once seemed acceptable. Today, however, people are aware of the subtle discrimination involved in using such language, and therefore it is no longer sufficient, even if the writer or speaker is not intentionally being sexist.

Lesson 12

sexist pron

Diagnostic Exercise

CORRECTED SENTENCES APPEAR ON PAGE 473.

Correct all instances of sexist language in the following paragraph using the first correction as a model. The number in parentheses at the end of the paragraph indicates how many problems you should find.

My psychology teacher, Ms. Crystal, had each member of the class
complete a questionnaire that would help him *or her* choose an appropriate
career. I had already decided on a profession, ^but she said the questionnaire would offer me other options. I've always wanted to be an electrical
engineer because I like to design things; an engineer spends much of his
time drawing designs and writing specifications. Ms. Crystal said my
survey results indicated I should consider being an accountant. She also
told me, however, that the survey was just one resource for choosing a
career. I agree. Each person has to consider what he knows better than
anyone else: his own interests. (3)

Fixing This Problem in Your Writing

Identifying Sexist Pronouns

Many writers do not check their sentences for gender-biased language because few people consider themselves sexist. However, the following tip provides a way for you to check your writing for even unintentional problems.

> **ABSTRACT-REFERENCE TIP**   First, look for *abstract* references to people (words that deal with a type of person or to people in general, not specific individuals). Second, check to see whether you use personal pronouns to refer back to these abstract references later in your writing. If these pronouns exclude one gender, the language is probably sexist.

Let's apply the Abstract-Reference Tip to Example 1. In this example, *everybody* is an abstract reference because *everybody* could refer to anyone, not to a specific individual. However, the writer uses the personal pronoun *his*, which excludes females. Unless no females are in the class, the sentence contains sexist language.

Lesson 12

sexist pron

Example 1:   ✗ Everybody should bring his book to class tomorrow.

ABSTRACT
REFERENCE

"ONE GENDER"
PRONOUN

Tip applied: ✗ <u>Everybody</u> should bring <u>his</u> book to class tomorrow.

As the above example illustrates, sexist pronouns tend to follow a predictable pattern:

Abstract Reference + "One Gender" Pronoun = Sexist Language

Example 2 has the same pattern. *A kindergarten teacher* is a general reference to a type of person; it could again be almost anyone. This time, the pronoun after this reference excludes males:

Example 2:   ✗ A kindergarten teacher helps her students gain social as well as academic skills.

ABSTRACT
REFERENCE   +

"ONE GENDER"
PRONOUN   =

SEXIST
LANGUAGE

Tip applied: ✗ <u>A kindergarten teacher</u> helps <u>her</u> students gain social as well as academic skills.

Correcting Sexist Pronouns

Here are two ways to revise these sentences to avoid sexist language:

1. Reword the sentence so that any abstract reference to people is in the plural form. Do the same with personal pronouns (such as *they* or *their*; see Lesson 8 on pronoun agreement).

   PLURAL   PLURAL
   Abstract Reference + Pronoun = Nonsexist Language

Our correction of Example 2 follows this correction pattern:

> *Kindergarten teachers help their*
> Correction: ~~A kindergarten teacher helps her~~ students gain social as
> well as academic skills.
>
> PLURAL Abstract Reference (*teachers*) + PLURAL Pronoun
> (*their*) = Nonsexist Language

Lesson 12

*sexist
pron*

2. If you want to keep the singular form, you can include both genders by using some form of all three words *he or she* instead of using just *he* or just *she*:

> **SINGULAR**
> Abstract Reference   +   *He or She*   =   Nonsexist Language

We corrected Example 1 by keeping the singular *everybody* but changing *his* to *his or her*:

> *or her*
> Correction: Everybody should bring his book to class tomorrow.
>
> SINGULAR Abstract Reference (*Everybody*) + *his or her* = Nonsexist Language

---

MORE EXAMPLES

Error: ✗ A supervisor who values his employees' rights is greatly needed here.

> *Supervisors who value their*   *are*
> Correction: ~~A supervisor who values his~~ employees' rights ~~is~~
> greatly needed here.

Error: ✗ If you see a professor, tell her to go to Room 264.

> *him or*
> Correction: If you see a professor, tell her to go to Room 264.

✳ Putting It All Together

Identifying Sexist Pronouns

____ Look for abstract references to people — very general nouns or pronouns that do not deal with particular people or individuals.

_____ Are there singular personal pronouns such as *he*, *his*, *she*, or *her* soon after these references? If so, these pronouns are sexist if they inappropriately exclude or ignore one gender.

Correcting Sexist Pronouns

_____ Use plural references and plural pronouns so that you can use inclusive pronouns such as *they*, *them*, and *their*.

_____ Another option is to use phrases such as *he or she* to include both genders.

Sentence Practice 1

CORRECTED SENTENCES APPEAR ON PAGE 473.

The sentences below contain sexist singular pronouns that refer back to abstract references to people. Underline both the sexist pronoun and the abstract reference. Eliminate the sexist language by making both the pronoun and the abstract reference plural. If needed, change the verb to agree with the new plural subject.

Example: I like <u>a teacher</u> who really <u>knows his</u> material.
(with corrections above: *teachers* ... *know their*)

1. Every parent should strive to make his child independent.
2. No employer wants his employees to be without health insurance.
3. A politician must choose his words carefully.
4. We want every eligible voter to cast his ballot in favor of the school bond.
5. Every CEO has to take full legal responsibility for his actions.

 For more practice eliminating sexist pronouns, go to **Exercise Central** at **bedfordstmartins.com/commonsense**

Sentence Practice 2

CORRECTED SENTENCES APPEAR ON PAGE 473.

Underline all sexist pronouns in the following sentences. Correct the sexist pronoun and make the necessary changes to the rest of the sentence. If the sentence does not contain a sexist pronoun, write *OK* above it.

Example: *he or she*
When we hire the new secretary, we must be sure that ~~she~~ can use the accounting software.
                                                          ^

1. I never met an accountant who didn't keep his office compulsively neat.

2. Could everybody give me his attention, please!

3. Whoever mixed the paint didn't keep good records on what proportions he used.

Lesson 12

*sexist
pron*

4. Every car salesperson makes it his business to call you by your first name at least five times in the first three minutes after he meets you.

5. My next-door neighbor wants us to help him get his car started.

Sentence Practice 3

In the spaces provided, add an appropriate personal pronoun. You might also need to change the subject of some sentences and make other revisions.

Example: Nobody in class did _____ homework correctly.

Answer: Nobody in class did *his or her* homework correctly.

1. Everybody watching the movie got _____ money's worth.

2. Each employee who uses the restroom must wash _____ hands before returning to work.

3. A good spouse knows when to keep _____ mouth shut.

4. If you see someone breaking curfew, report _____ immediately.

5. When you meet a superior officer, _____ must be saluted.

Editing Practice 1

CORRECTED SENTENCES APPEAR ON PAGE 473.

Correct all instances of sexist language in the following paragraph using the first correction as a model. The number in parentheses at the end of the paragraph indicates how many problems you should find.

          students   *themselves*
In American high schools and colleges, ~~a student~~ can avail ~~himself~~ of
                    them   ^   ^
a number of free activities open to ~~him~~. This is completely different from
                                      ^
European schools where a student has virtually no extracurricular

activities available to him. In Europe, a school-aged athlete must find (and pay for) a private, after-school sports club that he can join. When a European student comes to the United States, he is astonished at the extracurricular activities routinely available to him. Often an exchange student will single out the extracurricular activities that he participated in as the most enjoyable part of his experience in the United States. Europeans point out that one reason why test scores for the average American are so low (by international standards) is that the American student spends too much of his school day in nonacademic activities. Whether or not the American student is well served by his extracurricular experience is obviously a matter of debate. (8)

Lesson 12

sexist
pron

Editing Practice 2

Correct all sexist language in the following paragraphs using the first correction as a model. The number in parentheses at the end of each paragraph indicates how many problems you should find.

It seems to me that ~~a young person~~ *young people* today ~~has~~ *have* fewer opportunities for part-time and summer work than ~~he~~ *they* did a generation ago. For example, it used to be that a high school student could find as much work as he wanted. He could even find work in his neighborhood doing yard work or child care. If the teenager had a car, there were lots of jobs within his driving range. Virtually every labor-intensive business in town could find a use for him doing low-skilled jobs. (5)

A teenager today lives in a world where he has very different needs than he did a generation ago. Today, a teenager needs to work on getting into the college of his choice. He needs to build up his résumé. Rather than working for money to help out his family or to pay for his own expenses, a teen today is more likely working to pull up his grades in school or to try to prepare for his SATs. If he does work, it may well be in a nonprofit humanitarian organization, either because he believes in its mission or because it will look good on his college application (or both). (12)

Applying What You Know

People sometimes use sexist pronouns because they incorrectly assume only women do a certain type of work, only men are a certain way, all men do certain things, and so on. On a piece of paper, write three common generalizations about men or women that you believe are or are not valid. Share these in groups of three or four. Decide whether the generalizations other group members develop are valid, and explain your reasoning.

Lesson 12

sexist pron

The Bottom Line	**Writers** can avoid sexist pronouns if **they** use plural nouns for references to people.

Understanding Pronouns

REVIEW

Pronouns replace nouns (and sometimes other pronouns) in a sentence. The following chart points you to the tips that will help you avoid common pronoun problems.

TIPS	QUICK FIXES AND EXAMPLES
Lesson 8. Pronoun Agreement	

The *Are* Tip (p. 91) helps you check whether an antecedent agrees with the plural pronouns *they*, *their*, or *them*. The Plural Tip (p. 91) helps you correct errors involving these pronouns.	To correct an agreement error with *they*, *their*, or *them*, revise the antecedent so that it is plural. For other strategies, see page 91.
	
	 Error: ✗ Everyone should turn off their cell phone.
	
	 All students
	 Correction: ~~Everyone~~ should turn off their cell
	            s
	 phone.
	    ^

Lesson 9. Vague Pronouns: *This*, *That*, and *It*	

The Antecedent Tip (p. 100) helps you make sure that a pronoun has a clear antecedent. The *This/That* Tip (p. 101) also helps you clarify the meaning of a pronoun.	Move the pronoun closer to its antecedent, or revise the sentence to provide a specific antecedent. You could also add a noun after *this* or *that*.
	
	 Error: I slipped and fell on the ice while walking to class. ✗ That made me late.
	
	 Correction: I slipped and fell on the ice while
	                   accident
	 walking to class. That made me late.
	              ^

Lesson 10. Choosing the Correct Pronoun Form	

The Plural Pronoun Tip (p. 109) helps you use the correct pronoun in a compound structure. The No Verb, No Subject Tip (p. 110) helps you choose between the subject and object form of pronouns.	If a pronoun is followed by a verb, use the subject form: *I, he, she, we, they*. Otherwise, use *me, him, her, us, them*.
	
	 Error: ✗ Jay and me went for a walk.
	
	                 I
	 Correction: Jay and ~~me~~ went for a walk.
	             ^

TIPS	QUICK FIXES AND EXAMPLES
Lesson 11. *Who, Whom,* and *That*	

The *That Thing* Tip (p. 118) tells you when to use *that*. The *Who* + Verb Tip (p. 118) helps you choose between *who* and *whom*.	Use *that* only when referring to nonhuman things. Use *who* when a verb immediately follows the pronoun; otherwise, use *whom*.
	
	Error: ✗ We called a friend that is good at math.
	
	     who
	Correction: We called a friend ~~that~~ is good at math.
	                    ^

Lesson 12. Eliminating Sexist Pronouns	

The Abstract-Reference Tip (p. 127) will help you check your writing for sexist language.	Make the pronoun reference plural and change the gender-exclusive pronoun to *they, them,* or *their.* Other strategies are replacing the pronoun with *his or her* or revising the sentence to avoid personal pronouns altogether.
	
	Error: ✗ I asked everyone to bring his own lunch to the meeting.
	
	                           or her
	Correction: I asked everyone to bring his own
	                                              ^
	lunch to the meeting.

Review Test

Correct all errors in the following paragraph using the first correction as a model. The number in parentheses at the end of the paragraph indicates how many errors you should find.

                                                                    who
     Yesterday, I received a call from my neighbor Elena, ~~whom~~
                                                                    ^
wanted me to meet her friend Janie. She has just arrived in town and

is staying with Elena for a short time. Elena and me have been friends

a long time, so I was glad to meet a friend of hers. Janie, who is an

electrician, is looking for a job, and I know a number of contractors

that work in the area. An electrician can get a job if he is really

experienced and willing to work his way up the pay scale. Typically,

an electrician is experienced because their skills are so technical that

they do a lot of hands-on learning to acquire these skills. (6)

Using Commas Correctly

OVERVIEW

The Nuts and Bolts of Using Commas Correctly

This unit will help you with one of the most challenging aspects of written English: when to use (or not to use) commas. These seven lessons cover the most common or most bothersome types of errors involving commas (see Lessons 2 and 23 as well). Some of these "comma lessons" are clearly inter-related (especially Lessons 15 and 16). Others, however, have their own distinct rules and guidelines on commas.

Lesson 13 shows you how to combine two independent clauses with a comma and a coordinating conjunction. This lesson also explains when you do not use a comma before a coordinating conjunction that separates two parts of a sentence.

Example:	✗ Thelma ran away from the charging lion but she was unable to run fast enough.
Correction:	Thelma ran away from the charging lion, but she was unable to run fast enough.

Lesson 14 shows you how to punctuate transitional terms. A transitional term (often called a conjunctive adverb) clarifies the relationship between two ideas. Below is a correction involving two ideas that are separated by a semicolon. The transitional term (*however*) helps readers understand just how closely connected these two ideas are. A comma is usually placed after the transitional term in this sort of sentence.

Example:	✗ My toast was badly burnt, however, I decided to eat it.
Correction:	My toast was badly burnt; however, I decided to eat it.

Lesson 15 shows you how to combine two clauses when one clause begins with a subordinating conjunction. Here is an example:

    Example: ✗ Because I was in a hurry I had no time to call you.

    Correction: Because I was in a hurry, I had no time to call you.
                                  ^

Lesson 16 shows you how to punctuate introductory elements. Some introductory elements require a comma, while for others a comma is optional. Failure to use a comma with introductory elements is one of the most common errors in the writing of college students.

    Example: ✗ While I was revising my paper my hard drive crashed.

    Correction: While I was revising my paper, my hard drive crashed.
                                   ^

Unit Five

overview

Lesson 17 shows you how to punctuate adjective clauses. If the clause does not significantly alter the meaning of the noun it modifies, it is said to be nonessential to the meaning of the sentence. A nonessential adjective clause should be set off from the rest of the sentence with commas. If the adjective clause does significantly alter meaning, it is said to be essential. Essential adjective clauses do not require commas.

    Example: ✗ I wanted to go to a place, where I could relax.

    Correction: I wanted to go to a place,/where I could relax.

Lesson 18 shows you how to punctuate appositives. Appositives are nouns or pronouns that rename or modify the nouns they follow. If the appositive does not significantly alter the meaning of the noun it renames, it is said to be nonessential to the meaning of the sentence. A nonessential appositive should be set off with commas. If the appositive does significantly alter the meaning of the noun, it is said to be essential to the meaning of the sentence and does not require commas.

    Example: ✗ I recently visited Julia my aunt.

    Correction: I recently visited Julia, my aunt.
                                   ^

Lesson 19 discusses three types of unnecessary commas not covered elsewhere in this unit. The three categories involve commas needlessly used (1) after coordinating conjunctions, (2) between a subject and verb, and (3) before lists. Below are examples of these errors.

    Example 1:   ✗ Pepper wants cake, but, I want ice cream.

    Correction: Pepper wants cake, but,/I want ice cream.

Example 2:   ✗ The fly that landed on my nose earlier today, is now on yours.

Correction: The fly that landed on my nose earlier today,/ is now on yours.

Example 3:   ✗ This book has information on, China, Japan, and Thailand.

Correction: This book has information on,/ China, Japan, and Thailand.

Unit Five

overview

LESSON 13

Commas with *And, But, Or,* and Other Coordinating Conjunctions

---

EXAMPLE 1   *Missing Comma*

Error: ✗ Derek finally finished writing his book of poems <u>but</u> his publisher was not satisfied.

Correction: Derek finally finished writing his book of poems_∧ but his publisher was not satisfied.

EXAMPLE 2   *Unnecessary Comma*

Error: ✗ A moose wandered into town, <u>and</u> scared several boys.

Correction: A moose wandered into town⁄ and scared several boys.

What's the Problem?

Using **coordinating conjunctions** is the most common way to join **independent clauses** (see Lesson 1 for tips on identifying an independent clause, a group of words that can stand alone as a complete sentence). This lesson focuses on the most common coordinating conjunctions: *and, but,* and *or.* The easiest way to remember all seven coordinating conjunctions is by the term FANBOYS, formed from the first letter of each conjunction:

FANBOYS = <u>F</u>or, <u>A</u>nd, <u>N</u>or, <u>B</u>ut, <u>O</u>r, <u>Y</u>et, <u>S</u>o

Coordinating conjunctions, or FANBOYS, are punctuated in two different ways depending on what the conjunctions join. As you can see in Example 1, a comma must go in front of the FANBOYS when the FANBOYS joins two independent clauses.

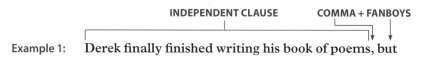

INDEPENDENT CLAUSE   COMMA + FANBOYS

Example 1:   Derek finally finished writing his book of poems, but

INDEPENDENT CLAUSE

his publisher was not satisfied.

When one of the FANBOYS joins just parts of sentences, you should not use a comma. In Example 2, no comma is needed because *and* does not join two independent clauses.

INDEPENDENT CLAUSE   FANBOYS

Example 2:   A moose wandered into town and scared several boys.

> *Scared several boys* cannot stand alone as a sentence, so no comma is needed with the FANBOYS.

It is easy to understand why punctuation errors occur with coordinating conjunctions. Both examples above *seem* similar because each conjunction joins a group of words. The key to knowing when to use a comma with a coordinating conjunction is to determine what the FANBOYS joins together—word groups that could be complete sentences or just parts of sentences. You can avoid punctuation problems by looking at what comes before and after the coordinating conjunction.

Lesson 13

coord

Diagnostic Exercise

CORRECTED SENTENCES APPEAR ON PAGE 474.

Correct all comma errors in the following paragraph using the first correction as a model. The number in parentheses at the end of the paragraph indicates how many errors you should find.

Africa was the home of humans long before recorded history, and

scientists believe humanlike creatures roamed eastern Africa at least three

million years ago. Today, most archaeologists believe it was in Africa that

humans became differentiated from other primates but relatively little

is known of the beginnings of African religion. Several sites include rock

paintings, and burial remains that suggest ancient religious activity in

Africa. Many objects associated with religious activity do not survive long

in Africa's tropical climates so archaeological finds are limited in terms of

what they reveal about early African religion. Available finds have pro-

vided information on the development of some African religions in some areas but little is known of the beginnings of religions south of the Sahara Desert. (4)

Fixing This Problem in Your Writing

The following tip helps determine whether you should use a comma with FANBOYS.

> **IMAGINARY PERIOD TIP**   Pretend there is a period right before the FANBOYS. If *both* parts divided by the imaginary period can stand alone as complete sentences, use a comma before the FANBOYS in the original sentence. Otherwise, omit the comma.

Lesson 13

coord   In other words, if an imaginary period works in the sentence, you should use a comma before the FANBOYS. Like a period, a comma before a coordinating conjunction lets readers know that you are moving on to a new idea—to a new subject and a new verb.

Here is how the Imaginary Period Tip can be applied to the two example sentences.

Example 1:   ✗ Derek finally finished his book of poems but his publisher was not satisfied.

Tip applied: Derek finally finished his book of poems. But his publisher was not satisfied.

Imaginary period works, confirming that *but* is used with two independent clauses. A comma must be added.

Correction: Derek finally finished his book of poems, but his publisher was not satisfied.

Usually, it is what comes *after* the imaginary period that tells you if you should use a comma. In Example 2, a comma is unnecessary because the phrase after the imaginary period—*scared several boys*—cannot stand alone.

Example 2:   ✗ A moose wandered into town, and scared several boys.

Tip applied: A moose wandered into town. ✗ And scared several boys.

Imaginary period does not work, so no comma is needed.

Correction: A moose wandered into town / and scared several boys.

This example contains a **compound verb**, two lengthy verbs combined with a conjunction (*wandered into town and scared several boys*). Because the two verbs are being combined, a comma should not separate them. The following diagram will help you remember this rule.

No Comma before a FANBOYS

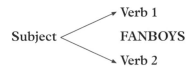

```
                          ↗ Verb 1
   Subject  ⟨              FANBOYS
                          ↘ Verb 2
```

Let's look at an example that correctly follows this formula:

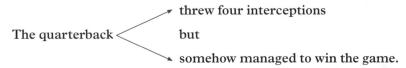

```
                              ↗ threw four interceptions
   The quarterback ⟨           but
                              ↘ somehow managed to win the game.
```

Also, avoid using a comma immediately *after* any FANBOYS. Some people mistakenly insert a comma because they pause at that point when reading the sentence aloud, but only rarely is a comma needed after a coordinating conjunction.

Lesson 13

coord

MORE EXAMPLES

Error: ✗ You must return my car by Thursday or I will not allow you to borrow it again.

Correction: You must return my car by Thursday, or I will not allow
you to borrow it again.
　　　　　　　　　　　　　　　　　^

Error: ✗ We ate at a nearby restaurant, but could not get back to campus on time.

Correction: We ate at a nearby restaurant/ but could not get back to campus on time.

✳ *Putting It All Together*

Identify Errors in Using Coordinating Conjunctions

___ Put an imaginary period before each coordinating conjunction
(the FANBOYS).

_____ Check to see if what comes before and after the imaginary period can stand alone as two complete sentences.

Correct Errors in Using Coordinating Conjunctions

_____ If both parts can stand alone, use a comma in front of the coordinating conjunction.

_____ If one or both parts cannot stand alone, do not use a comma.

Sentence Practice 1

CORRECTED SENTENCES APPEAR ON PAGE 474.

Lesson 13

coord

Correct any comma errors in the following sentences. If there is no error, write *OK* above the sentence. Confirm your corrections by applying the Imaginary Period Tip.

> Example: **This paper is torn,/but can still be used for scratch paper.**
>
> Confirmation: *This paper is torn. But can still be used for scratch paper.* [*Imaginary period does not work, so no comma is needed.*]

1. Soviet-made airplanes once accounted for 25 percent of the world's aircraft but this proportion has drastically changed.

2. Someone called for you this morning, and left a strange message.

3. The town of Longyearbyen forbids people from dying there, for it is so cold in this Arctic town that bodies do not decompose.

4. My first class officially ends at noon but the teacher keeps us late every day.

5. Most Americans are terrified of being bitten by a shark, yet far more people are killed each year by dogs.

 For more practice using commas, go to **Exercise Central** at **bedfordstmartins.com/commonsense**

Sentence Practice 2

CORRECTED SENTENCES APPEAR ON PAGE 474.

Correct the comma errors in the following sentences. If there is no error, write *OK* above the sentence. Confirm your corrections by applying the Imaginary Period Tip.

Example: **My friend Al didn't need a car, nor could he afford one.**
                                   ^

Confirmation: *My friend Al didn't need a car. Nor could he afford one.*
                     [Imaginary period works, so a comma is needed.]

Non-native speakers of English will notice the odd fact that after the coordinating conjunction *nor* the subject and verb are reversed—*could he* rather than *he could.* This is grammatically correct. Be sure, however, to use a comma before *nor* when it joins two independent clauses.

ESL

1. Jeremy did not arrive on time today, nor was he on time yesterday.

2. My roommate was ill this morning, so she missed class.

3. My father bought an old sword in England but the old relic is not worth much.

4. After class, Jan asked me if I would loan her my notes, and I was more than happy to do so.

5. Bahir is dropping by my place later so I suppose I should try to clean up a bit.

Lesson 13

coord

Sentence Practice 3

Combine each pair of sentences using a coordinating conjunction of your choice. If you want to keep both as independent clauses, you must use a comma with the coordinating conjunction. If you reduce one of the sentences to less than an independent clause, do not use a comma with the coordinating conjunction. When possible, combine sentences both ways.

Example: **My hat doesn't fit very well. It keeps falling off when I ride my bike.**

                                          , so it
Answer: **My hat doesn't fit very well./ I̶t̶ keeps falling off when I ride my bike.**
                                       ^

                                          and
            My hat doesn't fit very well./ I̶t̶ keeps falling off when I ride my bike.
                                       ^

1. The water at the beach is cold today. It will be even colder tomorrow.

2. This desk is too big. That one is too small.

3. My coach told us not to be late. He comes in late often.

4. I downloaded software from the Internet. I am supposed to send money to the author of the software.

5. Ellen wrote you a check. She will put it in the mail tomorrow.

6. The giant armadillo has almost one hundred teeth. They are very small.

7. The giant anteater has no teeth. It uses a long tongue to catch its food.

8. A cell phone rang during the middle of my math class. The teacher was really annoyed.

9. My roommate said it would rain today. It rained 2 inches in less than an hour.

10. The Anglo-Zanzibar War occurred in 1896. The conflict ended after some forty-five minutes.

Lesson 13

Editing Practice 1

CORRECTED SENTENCES APPEAR ON PAGE 474.

coord   Correct all errors involving commas and coordinating conjunctions in the following paragraph using the first correction as a model. The number in parentheses at the end of the paragraph indicates how many errors you should find.

Writing is a form of visible language, but there is a form of writing
                                        ^
that is not meant to be seen. Braille is written as a series of dots or bumps

and visually impaired people can "read" it with their fingers. It is written

as a series of cells and each cell contains dots that can be variously

arranged. Each particular arrangement of dots has its own meaning

but what the dots represent depends on the style of Braille. There are

two forms of Braille: Grade 1, and Grade 2. Grade 1 Braille is a system

in which the dots represent letters, and some very short words. Grade 2

Braille is not a completely different system but it is a shorthand version of

Grade 1 that is much harder to read. (6)

Editing Practice 2

CORRECTED SENTENCES APPEAR ON PAGE 474.

Correct all errors involving commas and coordinating conjunctions in the following paragraph using the first correction as a model. The number in parentheses at the end of the paragraph indicates how many errors you should find.

The wedding ring has been around for many centuries, and its
                                                        ^
history is more complex than people might think. Ancient Greeks are

often credited with inventing this tradition but many historians believe

it started with the Egyptians or Hebrews. We do know the first rings were

not made of precious metals. Many of the earliest rings were made of iron,

and did not have a gemstone. The ring was usually placed on the woman's

fourth finger for it was believed a nerve behind this finger led directly

to the heart. In the United States, the ring is placed on the left hand but

it is traditionally placed on the right hand in many other countries, such

as Russia and Germany. In many areas of the world, the ring is an

important part of the wedding ceremony, yet this is often not the case

in some countries. In Eastern Orthodox religions, the ring is part of the

formal engagement ceremony, but its role in the actual wedding is small.

Around the world, the wedding ring has become part of a multimillion-

dollar industry. (4)

Lesson 13

coord

Editing Practice 3

Correct all errors involving commas and coordinating conjunctions in the following paragraph using the first correction as a model. The number in parentheses at the end of the paragraph indicates how many errors you should find.

Liechtenstein is one of the smallest countries in the world, but was

once one of the 343 states that made up the enormous Holy Roman

Empire. In 1806, Napoleon invaded this empire, and it soon began to fall

apart. Liechtenstein was forced to become a "protectorate" of France

but this arrangement ended a few years later. The country then became

part of the German Confederation yet this alliance also failed to last.

In 1868, Liechtenstein declared itself independent and neutral. However, it remained closely allied with varying countries, such as Switzerland and the Austrian Empire. Liechtenstein might be small, and its history might be turbulent. Nonetheless, it is now a prosperous country and its royal head of state is one of the richest in the world. (3)

Applying What You Know

Write seven sentences about your past week, but do not put periods at the end of these sentences. Next, use each of the seven FANBOYS to connect each of your sentences to a new thought (for example, *My girlfriend cut her hair this week, yet I could not see any difference*). Use a different coordinating conjunction for each sentence.

Trade your sentences with a classmate and use the Imaginary Period Tip to see if your partner's sentences are correctly punctuated.

Lesson 13

coord

| The Bottom Line | See whether what comes before and after *and*, *but*, or *or* can stand alone, **and** use a comma if they both can. |

Commas with Transitional Terms

EXAMPLE 1   *Comma Splice*

Error: ✗ The Hope diamond is the best-known diamond, <u>however</u>, the Cullinan diamond was larger before it was cut.

Correction: The Hope diamond is the best-known diamond/; however, the Cullinan diamond was larger before it was cut.

EXAMPLE 2   *Missing Comma*

Error: Ancient Egyptians used various substances to brush their teeth. ✗ For instance they used a powder made from the ashes of burnt ox hooves.

Correction: Ancient Egyptians used various substances to brush their teeth. For instance, they used a powder made from the ashes of burnt ox hooves.

What's the Problem?

Transitional terms (sometimes called **conjunctive adverbs**) are words such as *furthermore* and *however*. Usually, transitional terms are just one word, although they can consist of two or more words (as with *in fact* and *for example*).

These terms have little meaning by themselves, but they are important "signpost" words that allow readers to see a connection between two ideas. A transitional term might connect two ideas within the same sentence or show how an entire sentence relates to a previous sentence.

Transitional terms can lead to two types of punctuation errors. Example 1 illustrates the most significant error: a **comma splice**, the use of just a comma to separate what could be two separate sentences, or **independent clauses** (see Lesson 2). As Example 1 shows, a transitional term *cannot* be used with just commas to join two independent clauses. A semicolon (or even a period) must be used before the transitional term.

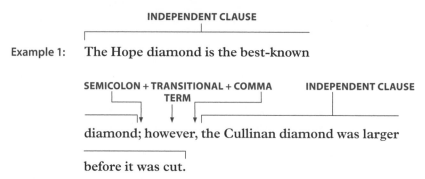

INDEPENDENT CLAUSE

Example 1:   The Hope diamond is the best-known

SEMICOLON + TRANSITIONAL + COMMA   INDEPENDENT CLAUSE
TERM

diamond; however, the Cullinan diamond was larger

before it was cut.

Lesson 14

trans

The second type of error is less severe: the omission of commas around transitional terms that do not separate independent clauses. When a transitional term begins a sentence, as in Example 2, you should usually follow the term with a comma. The following examples show other cases in which a transitional term does not separate two independent clauses and, therefore, is set off with just commas.

> I saw several classmates at the movie last night. Kate and Trisha, <u>for example</u>, were sitting right behind me.
>
> *Kate and Trisha* and *were sitting right behind me* cannot stand alone as complete sentences, so <u>for example</u> is set off with commas.
>
> Jay looked very tired when he arrived at baseball practice. He played better than usual, <u>however</u>.

Handbooks and teachers do not always agree on whether it is necessary to set off transitional terms with commas. In fact, some readers might not consider Example 2 from the beginning of the lesson to be an error at all. It is this sort of inconsistency that makes the "rule" confusing. We suggest using commas because they draw attention to the transitional terms, helping readers make clearer connections between ideas. Most teachers seem to prefer the more formal guideline of using commas to set off transitional terms, so this is the safest approach in college-level writing.

Diagnostic Exercise

CORRECTED SENTENCES APPEAR ON PAGE 474.

Correct all errors involving transitional terms in the following paragraph using the first correction as a model. The number in parentheses at the end of the paragraph indicates how many errors you should find. (Only one error is counted per transitional term—semicolon and comma errors are not counted separately.)

Many places around the globe have universal appeal. They are, however, not necessarily accessible to the general public. An international committee has designated some sites as World Heritage Sites, which are sites having international value and responsibility. In the United States for example the committee has chosen Yosemite Park and the Statue of Liberty, both of which are part of our national parks system. We tend to take our parks system for granted, however, it is really quite unusual. Very few developed countries have extensive public land, consequently their important public sites are little more than individual buildings. The vast size of some national parks in the American West makes them unique, therefore they attract visitors from every country. (4)

Lesson 14

trans

Fixing This Problem in Your Writing

Identifying Transitional Terms

The first step in punctuating transitional terms is recognizing them. This chart lists common transitional terms grouped into categories according to their meaning.

TRANSITIONAL TERMS

In Addition	For Example	On the Other Hand	As a Result
again	for instance	however	accordingly
also	in fact	instead	consequently
besides	in particular	nevertheless	subsequently
further(more)	namely	nonetheless	therefore
likewise	specifically	on the contrary	thus
moreover		otherwise	
similarly		still	

Look for such words that establish a relationship between two ideas. Then, use the following tip to determine if indeed there is a transitional term.

> **TRANSITIONAL TERM MOVEMENT TIP**   A transitional term can be moved around in a sentence (or even deleted). Move *only* the term you are testing — not anything else.

ESL

If a word (or very brief group of words) establishing a relationship between ideas can be moved, it is probably a transitional term. Coordinating conjunctions such as *and* or *but* cannot be moved. Words such as *because* and *while* also cannot be moved, despite seeming similar to transitional terms.

Lesson 14

trans

How do you know *where* a transitional term can be moved in a sentence? The Movement Tip relies on a person's intuition about whether a word sounds right when it is moved around. A non-native speaker of English might need to consult a native speaker on this matter.

Example 1 still makes sense when we use the Movement Tip to shift *however* to the end of the sentence:

Example 1:   ✗ The Hope diamond is the best-known diamond, however, the Cullinan diamond was larger before it was cut.

Tip applied: . . . the Cullinan diamond was larger before it was cut, however.

Because *however* provides transition and can be moved around, it is a transitional term.

In Example 2, we can move *for instance.* This time, the transitional term works in the middle of a sentence:

Example 2:   ✗ For instance they used a powder made from the ashes of burnt ox hooves.

Tip applied: They used, for instance, a powder made from the ashes of burnt ox hooves.

Punctuating Transitional Terms

Once you find a transitional term in your writing, first make sure you do not create a comma splice in using it. That is, use a semicolon before the term *if* it joins what could be two separate sentences. Do not leave out commas completely, though. Normally, a comma goes after a transitional term used with a semicolon.

Because the transitional term in Example 1 separates what could be two separate sentences, we know that it cannot be used with just commas.

Correction: The Hope diamond is the best-known
diamond**/;** <u>however</u>, the Cullinan diamond was larger
before it was cut.

A semicolon corrects the comma splice, and a comma is still needed
after the transitional term.

In Example 2, the transitional term does *not* separate two independent
clauses, so the original sentence needs only a comma after the transitional term.

Correction: <u>For instance</u>**,** they used a powder made from the
ashes of burnt ox hooves.

The transitional term is set off with a comma.

If the transitional term is in the middle of a sentence and does *not* separate
two independent clauses, a comma should come before and after the term.

Lesson 14

They used, <u>for instance</u>, a powder made from the ashes of
burnt ox hooves.

trans

✳ *Putting It All Together*

Identify Transitional Terms

____ Look for words that establish a clear connection between two ideas.

____ See if you can move the word (or words) around in the sentence. If so,
it is probably a transitional term.

Correct Errors in Punctuating Transitional Terms

____ To avoid a comma splice, use a semicolon before the transitional
term if what comes before and what comes after the term could each
be separate sentences. Then, be sure to use a comma right after the
transitional term.

____ Otherwise, set off a transitional term with at least one comma.

Sentence Practice 1

CORRECTED SENTENCES APPEAR ON PAGE 475.

Underline the transitional terms in the following sentences, and punctuate
each sentence correctly. Confirm your answer by moving the transitional
term to another position in the sentence. If the sentence contains no transitional terms, write *none* above the sentence.

Example:
none
In the early 1800s, Tecumseh roused most tribes east of the Mississippi in an attempt to drive out the whites. His forces, however, were defeated by General Harrison.

Confirmation: *However, his forces were defeated by General Harrison.*

1. Bill said he might be late. Indeed he was four hours late.

2. Little is known about the Pilgrim ship *Mayflower*; we do know however that it weighed about 180 tons.

3. English is the predominant language in the United States, nevertheless, over three hundred languages are spoken within U.S. borders.

4. The oldest known weapon is a broken spear found in Great Britain; it is estimated to have been made around 200,000 B.C.

5. A serious accident has caused major delays. In fact some commuters have decided to stay home.

For more practice using transitional terms, go to **Exercise Central** at **bedfordstmartins.com/commonsense**

Sentence Practice 2

CORRECTED SENTENCES APPEAR ON PAGE 475.

Underline the transitional terms in the following sentences, and punctuate each sentence correctly. Confirm your answer by moving the transitional term to another position in the sentence. If the sentence contains no transitional terms, write *none* above the sentence.

Example: Most fans believe a football team must have a coach; nonetheless, the Chicago Bears won the 1943 championship without a head coach.

Confirmation: *The Chicago Bears, nonetheless, won the 1943 championship without a head coach.*

1. Sean Connery is remembered most for his James Bond movies. However he won an Oscar for a different role in *The Untouchables*.

2. Scott Joplin wrote over sixty musical compositions. He wrote for instance an opera entitled *Treemonisha*.

3. Some people consider Scotland part of England, but both are part of the United Kingdom.

Lesson 14

trans

4.   The top position in the British army is field marshal. The top position in Britain's navy in contrast is admiral of the fleet.

5.   The singer Prince has gone by more than one name, for example, his birth name is Prince Rogers Nelson.

Sentence Practice 3

Combine the two short sentences with a semicolon and an appropriate transitional term (see the list on page 149). Underline the transitional term.

Example: My parents want me to major in accounting/ I want to major in drama.

; however,

Lesson 14

trans

1.   The doctors diagnosed the problem. They were able to recommend a treatment.

2.   There has been a 20 percent increase in fertilizer use. Food production has increased substantially.

3.   The legislature has set new limits on enrollments. Each school must reassess its admission policies.

4.   The experiment had failed. It had damaged the equipment badly.

5.   The witch had frightened Dorothy and her friends. They decided to continue their trip.

6.   Many people believe that nothing rhymes with *orange*. The term *sporange* is one word that does.

7.   The water in our city tastes awful. The citizens are planning to complain to the mayor.

8.   Most cucumbers are 95 percent water. They have few calories.

9.   Alfred Butts invented Scrabble, an enormously successful game. He invented a game called "Alfred's Other Game," which did not do so well.

10.   I like card games. Solitaire is one of my favorites.

Editing Practice 1

CORRECTED SENTENCES APPEAR ON PAGE 475.

Correctly punctuate all transitional terms in the following paragraphs using the first correction as a model. The number in parentheses at the end of each paragraph indicates how many errors you should find.

I am facing a difficult decision/; however, it is one I have to make
          ^
soon. My family would like me to help with our family business after I

graduate from college. My parents own a construction company, and my

major is accounting. Consequently I believe that I would have a lot to

offer my parents' company once I finish my degree. I could for example

help them develop more precise estimates for construction projects.

My plans seemed so clear and logical at one time. (2)

Lesson 14

trans

      I enjoy talking with my parents about different accounting methods,

nevertheless, I have lately been considering moving to a different part

of the country and working in a different type of business. New England

would be a great place to live for example. Additionally I am considering

working as an accountant for a company that manufactures computer

parts. Even though I want the family business to do well, I want to try

something very different. My parents have always supported my choices,

still, I know they will be disappointed if I do not work for them. (4)

Editing Practice 2

Correctly punctuate all transitional terms in the following paragraphs using the first correction as a model. The number in parentheses at the end of each paragraph indicates how many errors you should find.

      Ancient Egyptian religion embraced a remarkable variety of gods and
             In fact,
goddesses/. in fact, many regions had their own deity. The most striking
    ^ ^
feature however was not the sheer quantity of Egyptian gods. Rather Egyp-

tian religion was distinguished by the remarkable qualities of its deities. (2)

      These gods were thought of either as complete animals or as semi-

human forms. Horus was represented, for instance, by a human body and

a falcon's head. Hathor had a woman's head and cow's body, while Anubis

featured a man's body and the head of a jackal. In contrast other deities appeared as complete animals, such as a crocodile, a cat, and an eel. Ancient Egyptians might have fully understood why their deities took these varied forms. Nonetheless modern scholars have several competing theories on these origins. (2)

Applying What You Know

Write down five transitional terms and switch lists with someone in the class. Using each of the transitional terms on your partner's list, write five sentences. Punctuate these sentences correctly, using a semicolon at least twice. The ideas you connect within each sentence should be logically related, but the sentences can be on different topics. When you have finished, switch papers and check your partner's sentences for correct punctuation.

Lesson 14

trans

The Bottom Line	Transitional terms clarify how ideas connect; **however,** you must punctuate these terms correctly.

Commas with Adverb Clauses

EXAMPLE 1 **Missing Comma**

Error: ✗ <u>When Paula and I go to a movie</u> I always have to buy the popcorn.

Correction: When Paula and I go to a movie, I always have to buy the popcorn.

EXAMPLE 2 **Unnecessary Comma**

Error: ✗ Steven was late for class, <u>because the bus was unusually slow.</u>

Correction: Steven was late for class/ because the bus was unusually slow.

What's the Problem?

An **adverb clause** is a group of words that answers the question *when, where, why, how,* or *to what degree* about the verb in the sentence. Adverb clauses are **dependent clauses:** They have a subject and a verb, but they cannot stand alone.

Some writers become confused about when to use a comma with an adverb clause. What's important is the *position* of the adverb clause in the sentence. A comma is needed in Example 1 because the adverb clause is lengthy and appears at the beginning of the sentence; the comma signals to readers where the introductory adverb clause ends and the main clause begins. When an adverb clause appears at the end of a sentence, as in Example 2, a comma is rarely needed.

Here are more examples:

```
        ADVERB CLAUSE              MAIN CLAUSE
```
As soon as the rain stopped, we continued our hike.

```
        MAIN CLAUSE              ADVERB CLAUSE
```
We continued our hike as soon as the rain stopped.

Diagnostic Exercise

CORRECTED SENTENCES APPEAR ON PAGE 475.

Correct all errors involving adverb clauses in the following paragraph using the first correction as a model. The number in parentheses at the end of the paragraph indicates how many errors you should find.

> After everybody was asleep Monday night, there was a fire in the
> ^
> dorm next door. Fortunately, a smoke detector went off, when smoke got
> into the staircase. While the fire department was fighting the fire six rooms
> were totally destroyed. A friend of mine in another part of the building lost
> her computer, because of the smoke and water damage. If school officials
> close down the dorm for repairs she will have to find a new place to stay.
> I heard they will make a decision today, as soon as they receive a report
> from the fire inspectors. (5)

Lesson 15

adv
cl

Fixing This Problem in Your Writing

Identifying Adverb Clauses

The first step in correcting problems with adverb clauses is to locate them in your writing. Adverb clauses begin with **subordinating conjunctions**, flag words that tell readers an adverb clause will follow. Here is a list of the most common ones grouped according to meaning.

SUBORDINATING CONJUNCTIONS

Cause	Condition	Contrast	Place	Time
as	as if	although	where	after
because	assuming that	even though	wherever	as soon as
since	if	though		before
so that	in case			since
	unless			until
	when			when
	whether			whenever

In an adverb clause, a subject and verb follow the flag word. Note that an adverb clause must always be part of a complete sentence; it can never stand alone.

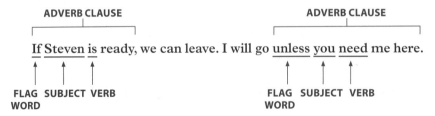

ADVERB CLAUSE

ADVERB CLAUSE

If Steven is ready, we can leave. I will go unless you need me here.

FLAG   SUBJECT   VERB
WORD

FLAG   SUBJECT   VERB
WORD

Here is an easy way to identify an adverb clause.

Lesson 15

adv
cl

ADVERB CLAUSE MOVEMENT TIP   An adverb clause is the only type of dependent clause that can be moved around in a sentence.

We know that the sentences above contain adverb clauses because we can move them to another part of the sentence.

Tip applied: (If Steven is ready,) we can leave.   [*We can leave if Steven is ready.*]

Tip applied: I will go (unless you need me here.)   [*Unless you need me here, I will go.*]

Punctuating Adverb Clauses

Once you have identified an adverb clause in your writing, make sure it is punctuated correctly. In Example 1, the adverb clause is at the beginning of the sentence, so a comma should come after the clause to let readers know where it stops:

Example 1:   ✗ When Paula wants to go to a movie I always have to buy the popcorn.

Tip applied: (When Paula wants to go to a movie) I always have to buy the popcorn.   [*I always have to buy the popcorn when Paula wants to go to a movie.*]

The clause can be moved around, so it is an adverb clause.

Correction: When Paula wants to go to a movie**,** I always have to buy the popcorn.
                                        ^

Use a comma after an introductory adverb clause.

In some cases, particularly in business writing, it is acceptable to omit a comma after a very short introductory clause. In college writing, however, it is best to use the comma. Most instructors prefer that you use one to show where the introductory clause ends and the main part of the sentence begins.

In Example 2, no comma is needed because the adverb clause comes at the end of the sentence.

Example 2:   ✗ Steven was late for class, because the bus was unusually slow.

Tip applied: Steven was late for class, (because the bus was unusually slow). [*Because the bus was unusually slow, Steven was late for class.*]

The clause can be moved around, so it is an adverb clause.

Correction: Steven was late for class/because the bus was unusually slow.

Omit a comma before a sentence-ending adverb clause.

Sometimes rules have exceptions. If an adverb clause conveys a strong sense of contrast by using a flag word such as *although*, *even though*, or *though*, the clause must always be set off with a comma even if it is at the end of the sentence.

I didn't like the movie, <u>even though it received excellent reviews</u>.

Lesson 15

adv
cl

MORE EXAMPLES

Introductory Adverb Clauses

<u>Whenever I go to the mall</u>, I seem to forget my credit card.

<u>Unless it rains</u>, class will be held under the oak tree.

Sentence-Ending Adverb Clauses

Someone shut the door on my foot <u>as I was leaving the building</u>.

You need to study hard <u>because the next test will cover the entire textbook</u>.

Lesson 15

adv
cl

✳ *Putting It All Together*

Identify Adverb Clauses

____ Look for groups of words in your writing that answer the question *when, where, why, how,* or *to what degree* about the verb in a sentence.

____ Determine if the clause follows this formula: *Flag Word + Subject + Verb.*

____ Try moving the clause around in the sentence. If it can be moved, it is an adverb clause.

Correct Errors in Punctuating Adverb Clauses

____ Use a comma after an adverb clause that begins a sentence.

____ Do not use a comma before an adverb clause that ends a sentence, unless the clause strongly contrasts with the first part of the sentence. Contrasting adverb clauses usually begin with *although, even though,* or *though.*

Sentence Practice 1

CORRECTED SENTENCES APPEAR ON PAGE 475.

In each of the following sentences, underline the adverb clause and correct the comma error. Confirm your answer by moving the adverb clause to another position in the sentence.

Example: When we got the tests back, we all went out for coffee.

Confirmation: *We all went out for coffee when we got the tests back.*

1. When I visit my parents in New Mexico I always bring them something from my part of the country.

2. I will go with you, after I finish eating.

3. After Omar competed in the third basketball tournament of the season he was not eager to travel again.

4. Because the test included over a hundred questions I could not finish it in just fifteen minutes.

5. Stephanie wants to leave, because she smells a strange odor in the room.

For more practice using adverb clauses, go to **Exercise Central** at **bedfordstmartins.com/commonsense**

Sentence Practice 2

CORRECTED SENTENCES APPEAR ON PAGE 475.

In each of the following sentences, underline the adverb clause and correct the comma error. Confirm your answer by moving the adverb clause to another position in the sentence.

Example: I was upset,/ because I should have known better.

Confirmation: *Because I should have known better, I was upset.*

1. My roommate must not realize the word *dormitory* comes from an ancient term meaning "sleep," because he stays up very late every night.

2. Because it always appears sleepy the dormouse gets its name from the same ancient term (*dorm*).

3. While I was walking to my first class of the day a mouse ran across the sidewalk.

4. Even though I am not fond of mice, I did not let this incident delay me.

5. When I am awake late because of a noisy roommate who does not let me sleep I do not have time to worry about a mouse.

Sentence Practice 3

Combine each pair of sentences by turning the second sentence into an adverb clause. Choose an appropriate subordinating conjunction, or flag word, from the list on page 157. Underline the adverb clause, and show that it can be used both at the beginning and at the end of the sentence. Punctuate each version correctly.

Example: I need to hang up. I have to go to class now.

Answer: *I need to hang up because I have to go to class now.*
            Because I have to go to class now, I need to hang up.

1. We cannot leave. You are not ready to go.

2. I am not going to play this game. You want to play also.

3. Peter told us a strange story about your history teacher. You were not here.

4. Someone called for you. You left.

5. Keisha came to class. She has a bad cold.

6. Your dog ran away. A cat wandered into the backyard.

7. Napoleon Bonaparte was a famous military leader. He was afraid of cats.

8. You will need to repay the money I loaned you. You have the money.

9. I used ketchup to clean the candleholder. Ketchup is good for cleaning brass.

10. People receive a lot of spam e-mails. Spammers need to send thousands of e-mails to receive the response they want.

Lesson 15

adv
cl

Editing Practice 1

CORRECTED SENTENCES APPEAR ON PAGE 476.

In the following paragraphs, correctly punctuate each sentence that contains an adverb clause. The number in parentheses at the end of each paragraph indicates how many errors you should find.

Because I am a full-time student, my income is limited. I don't want to borrow money from my family, unless no other option is available. Twice, I have used a government loan to pay for my tuition, fees, and books. Without those loans, I would not have been able to attend college. Although I would prefer not to take out any more student loans I will likely have to do so again. (2)

My part-time job does not pay well, since it is a minimum-wage position. Although I can't afford any luxuries living on this meager income is manageable. In a few years, I will likely be able to improve my standard of living greatly, so my situation is not depressing. When I graduate from college I should be able to find a job, because my field is very much in demand. Until then, I will be able to get by on an occasional student loan. (4)

Editing Practice 2

In the following paragraphs, correctly punctuate each sentence that contains an adverb clause. The number in parentheses at the end of each paragraph indicates how many errors you should find.

Although many people may not be aware of it, Pearl Buck was
the first American woman to win a Nobel Prize in Literature. After her
parents had spent years as missionaries in China they returned to the
United States for a short time in the early 1890s, during which time Pearl
was born. When she was just three months old Pearl returned to China
with her parents. She grew up speaking Chinese, because her family lived
among the Chinese rather than in a Western compound. (3)

While they were living in China there were many protests against
the Western governments that had controlled China's economy for years.
Since she had lived among ordinary people Pearl was aware of their daily
struggles for bare survival. Because she had such a depth of personal
experience in China her most famous novel, *The Good Earth*, reflected
her compassion for the Chinese and their culture. When Pearl Buck died
President Nixon said that she had served as a "human bridge between the
civilizations of the East and West." (4)

Lesson 15

*adv
cl*

Applying What You Know

Write a paragraph describing the field you are concentrating in and why it interests you. In a second paragraph, imagine what you might be doing in that field ten years from now. Try to use as many adverb clauses as possible, punctuating them as discussed in this lesson.

The Bottom Line	**If you use an introductory adverb clause,** set it off with a comma.

Commas with Introductory Elements

EXAMPLE 1 *Long Introductory Element*

Error: ✗ While I was taking my morning walk a car almost hit me.

Correction: While I was taking my morning walk, a car almost hit me.

EXAMPLE 2 *Short but Confusing Introductory Element*

Error: ✗ When you called Sam was in the backyard.

Correction: When you called, Sam was in the backyard.

What's the Problem?

In college writing, an **introductory element** is usually set off with a comma. This comma tells the reader where the introductory element ends and the "real" sentence begins. Inserting a comma after an introductory element is especially important when the introductory element is long. Example 1 above is easier to read when a comma is used, telling the reader where to "take a breath" before proceeding.

However, even short introductory elements might require commas. In Example 2, *When you called* is short, but if the comma is left out, the reader might mistakenly think the introductory element is *When you called Sam.*

Punctuation errors involving introductory elements often occur because writers are confused about when they should use commas. Some introductory elements *must* be followed by a comma, while other types do not require one. In addition, some people have strong feelings about when commas should be used with introductory elements, no matter what the "rules" are. Many teachers prefer that commas be used even when optional, whereas many people in the business world prefer that commas not be used after most introductory elements.

Diagnostic Exercise

CORRECTED SENTENCES APPEAR ON PAGE 476.

Correct all the comma errors in the following paragraph using the first correction as a model. The number in parentheses at the end of the paragraph indicates how many problems you should find.

Until the relatively recent development of technology, most people throughout history were largely ignorant of the world. Travelers might bring stories of distant places, but only the literate few could read about those places. For most people around the globe information traveled slowly. For instance the Battle of New Orleans was fought two weeks after a treaty ended the War of 1812. The combatants were unaware of the treaty's signing. Later on in the nineteenth century the railroad and telegraph brought the world closer. Even so coverage was still slow and spotty. (4)

Lesson 16

intro

Fixing This Problem in Your Writing

Identifying Introductory Elements

Here are several examples of types of introductory elements that *always* require a comma:

- **Transitional terms always require commas** (see Lesson 14).

  However, there is no reason to vote against him.

- **Long adverb clauses always require commas** (see Lesson 15).

  When you leave to go to the library, lock the front door.

- **Infinitive phrases always require commas.**

  To finish on time, we had to write quickly.

- **Participial phrases always require commas.**

  Seeing that the game was almost over, the crowd started to leave.

Commas with other types of introductory elements are optional. We show some examples of these cases in the More Examples section on page 167. With all these types of introductory elements, knowing when a comma is optional can be confusing. We recommend a simple approach for college writing: Identify introductory elements in your writing, and—in most cases—punctuate them with a comma.

Here is a tip that will help you identify introductory elements.

> **DELETION TIP**   To make sure you have found an introductory element, see if you can delete it. If what remains is a complete sentence, what you deleted is an introductory element.

Unlike most parts of a sentence, an introductory element can always be deleted without creating an ungrammatical sentence. The Deletion Tip confirms that Example 1 has an introductory element:

Error: ✗ While I was taking my morning walk a car almost hit me.

Tip applied: ~~While I was taking my morning walk~~ A car almost hit me.

Using the tip, we can delete the introductory element (*While I was taking my morning walk*) and still have a grammatical sentence (*A car almost hit me*).

Punctuating Introductory Elements

Once you have determined that a sentence contains an introductory element, use this next tip to help you decide whether you should insert a comma after the introductory element.

> **COMMA TIP**   Unless you know that readers prefer otherwise, use a comma after *all* introductory elements.

Although some readers might *prefer* that you not use a comma in cases when the comma is optional, using a comma after an introductory element is never a grammatical error. In contrast, leaving out the comma after certain introductory elements is always a grammatical mistake. Thus, we suggest using the comma *unless you know your reader believes in the "don't use it unless you have to" philosophy of commas.*

Using the Comma Tip, we can correct the errors in Examples 1 and 2:

Correction: While I was taking my morning walk, a car almost hit me.

Correction: When you called, Sam was in the backyard.

MORE EXAMPLES

Long Prepositional Phrases   *Commas are required:*

<u>In a state of rage over the drastic increase in taxes</u>, the voters elected a new governor.

<u>At a bookstore in the Bronx</u>, Chuck found a karate manual.

Short Prepositional Phrases   *Commas are optional if the omission of a comma does not cause confusion:*

<u>In my day</u>, we used typewriters for our college papers.

<u>After lunch</u> Bijan went to the library.

Long Adverb Clauses   *Commas are required:*

<u>Even though the teacher gave everyone two more days to study</u>, the test was still difficult.

<u>Because the employee parking lot is being painted</u>, you must park elsewhere.

Short Adverb Clauses   *Commas are optional:*

<u>When the storm ended</u> we jogged for an hour.

<u>If it's sunny</u> we'll go to the lake.

Lesson 16

intro

✳ *Putting It All Together*

Identify Introductory Elements

_____ Use the Deletion Tip to identify introductory elements. Introductory elements come in many types, but all can be deleted without creating a fragment.

Correctly Punctuate Introductory Elements

_____ Whether a comma is required or optional after an introductory element depends on the type of element and your readers' preferences. If you know that your readers do not like optional commas, leave out commas after short introductory elements unless the omission causes confusion.

_____ If you do not know what your readers prefer, use a comma after all introductory elements.

Sentence Practice 1

CORRECTED SENTENCES APPEAR ON PAGE 476.

Correct the following sentences. Confirm your answer by applying the Deletion Tip.

> Example: When we got the test back, nobody even thought about
> sleeping.
>   ^
>
> Confirmation: *Nobody even thought about sleeping.*

1. Although Wally Amos is best known for his brand of cookies he was also the first African American talent agent for the William Morris Agency.

2. In France shepherds once carried small sundials as pocket watches.

3. Even though he was best known as an actor Jimmy Stewart was a brigadier general in the U.S. Air Force Reserve.

4. After eating our cat likes to nap.

5. Whenever I walk our dog likes to go with me.

 For more practice using introductory elements, go to **Exercise Central** at **bedfordstmartins.com/commonsense**

Sentence Practice 2

CORRECTED SENTENCES APPEAR ON PAGE 476.

Correct the following sentences. Confirm your answer by applying the Deletion Tip.

> Example: According to a recent study, more women than men
>   ^
> take Oreo cookies apart to eat the middle.
>
> Confirmation: *More women than men take Oreo cookies apart to eat the middle.*

1. To keep people from sneaking up on him Wild Bill Hickok placed crumpled newspapers around his bed.

2. Before his career was suddenly ended Jesse James robbed twelve banks and seven trains.

3. Therefore he was a successful criminal for a time.

Lesson 16

intro

4. Believe it or not the state "gem" of Washington is petrified wood.

5. When she was in a high school band singer Dolly Parton played the snare drum.

Sentence Practice 3

Rewrite each of the following sentences by inserting an introductory element of your own. Use various types of introductory elements, and use a comma after each.

Example: I was getting cold.

Answer: *Because I was getting cold, I put on a sweater.*

1. My favorite fish died this weekend.

2. Claire prefers vanilla ice cream.

3. The predator moved slowly and cautiously.

4. The paper reported that a blizzard is headed our way.

5. The vultures circled overhead.

6. Many people are absent.

7. Someone sent me an odd text message.

8. Joshua wants his coffee with a lot of cream.

9. Three mice scurried into the kitchen.

10. A police car is waiting for you outside.

Editing Practice 1

CORRECTED SENTENCES APPEAR ON PAGE 476.

Correct the errors in the following paragraph using the first correction as a model. The number in parentheses at the end of the paragraph indicates how many errors you should find.

When I tried to start a student organization on campus last semester**,** I was surprised by the difficulties and hurdles. I wanted to establish a club for students who enjoy science fiction. After being encouraged by several friends I contacted the school official who oversees campus organizations. She informed me I would need a faculty sponsor and had to go through an

Lesson 16

intro

approval process that could take several weeks. Upon reading some twelve pages of forms and directions I almost gave up. Fortunately a couple of friends agreed to help me fill out the forms and gather signatures from students interested in the club. However the work was still not finished. We had to arrange a schedule of events and apply for funding. It took three months before the science fiction club was approved by various committees and school administrators. Now that the club has had three successful meetings I feel that all the work was worthwhile. (5)

Editing Practice 2

CORRECTED SENTENCES APPEAR ON PAGE 477.

intro

Correct the errors in the following paragraph using the first correction as a model. The number in parentheses at the end of the paragraph indicates how many errors you should find.

Though most professional orchestras today include a pianist, the
                                                                ^
piano is a relatively new addition to the symphony. In older times when pianos were not as common as they are today the orchestra regularly included a different keyboard instrument, the harpsichord. This older keyboard instrument is much simpler than today's piano. Nonetheless the advantage of virtually any keyboard instrument is that it can play chords and full harmony as well as melodies. To put this more simply a person can play a whole piece of music on a keyboard instrument without requiring other musicians at all. As a result of this fact solo music for piano, harpsichord, and organ is much more extensive than solo music for other instruments. (4)

Editing Practice 3

Correct the errors in the following paragraph using the first correction as a model. The number in parentheses at the end of the paragraph indicates how many errors you should find.

When I have time for recreation, sometimes I like to play video
games. I have other interests, but playing video games is fun as well.
Contrary to what many people believe there is a social aspect to playing
many games. Obviously some games are meant to be played solo.
However a game such as Halo 3 can be played alone or with multiple
players. When you play a multiplayer game you can be in the same room
as other people or you can play them online. Either way you do more than
just simply fight these other people on the screen. With many multiplayer
games that are played online you can converse with teammates by using
a headset to discuss strategy. By playing such games over the last couple
of years I have been able to meet new people and make friends. To me
playing games is one aspect of socializing, so I disagree with those people
who say that playing video games means a person lacks a social life. (8)

Lesson 16

intro

Applying What You Know

Knowing how to punctuate introductory elements might seem confusing, but
introductory elements are useful because they help clarify your ideas and add
variety to your writing style. Write five sentences without introductory elements. The sentences need not be related to one another. Trade sentences
with someone else and add an introductory element to each sentence. Notice
how these elements add new ideas or clarify the writing in some way. Work
with your partner to make sure each introductory element uses a comma
correctly.

The Bottom Line	**When you use an introductory element,** set it off with a comma.

Commas with Adjective Clauses

EXAMPLE 1	*Unnecessary Comma*
Error:	✗ Sally met a teacher, <u>who will be teaching composition this fall.</u>
Correction:	Sally met a teacher/ who will be teaching composition this fall.

EXAMPLE 2	*Missing Comma*
Error:	✗ I called Ms. Watson <u>who lives in Atlanta.</u>
Correction:	I called Ms. Watson, who lives in Atlanta.

What's the Problem?

An **adjective clause** is a group of words that describes a person, a place, a thing, or an idea. Adjective clauses usually begin with a **relative pronoun** (*who, whom, whose, which,* or *that*) or with a relative adverb (*when* and *where*). Unlike a one-word adjective such as *big* or *red*, an adjective clause appears *after* the noun it modifies, not before. In Example 1, the adjective clause *who will be teaching composition this fall* describes the noun *teacher*. In Example 2, *who lives in Atlanta* describes the noun *Ms. Watson*.

Writers often make punctuation errors with adjective clauses because some clauses *must* be set off from the rest of the sentence with a comma(s), whereas others *must not*. To punctuate adjective clauses correctly, you must first understand that there are two types of adjective clauses: *essential* (or **restrictive**) **clauses** and *nonessential* (or **nonrestrictive**) **clauses**. The following chart explains their functions and correct punctuation.

Adjective clause	Function	Punctuation
Essential	Provides important identifying information about the noun it describes	Do *not* set off with a comma (see Example 1).

Adjective clause	Function	Punctuation
Nonessential	Provides extra information about the noun, but the meaning of the noun would not significantly change if the clause were deleted	Set off with a comma (see Example 2).

The following is a summary of what to remember about adjective clauses:

Essential Clause = Essential Information = No Comma

Nonessential Clause = "Extra" Information = Comma

Unfortunately, there is no simple grammatical rule you can use to determine whether an adjective clause is essential or nonessential. Instead, you must consider how the meaning of the adjective clause affects the noun it modifies. The following examples illustrate how meaning determines the distinction between essential and nonessential clauses.

Lesson 17

adj
cl

Essential: All my friends who went to the party were late for class.

Nonessential: All my friends, who went to the party, were late for class.

In the first sentence, some friends went to the party and some did not. The ones who were late for class were the ones who went to the party (not the ones who stayed home). In the second sentence, *all* the friends went to the party, and thus *all* the friends were late for class.

Diagnostic Exercise

CORRECTED SENTENCES APPEAR ON PAGE 477.

Correct all the comma errors in the following paragraph using the first correction as a model. The number in parentheses at the end of the paragraph indicates how many commas you should either add or delete.

The first true clocks were built in the thirteenth century, which was
an era when accurate timekeeping became increasingly important. Other
timekeeping devices had been used in situations, that were not ideal.
Sundials were useless at night when there was insufficient sunlight for casting a shadow. The wind could blow out candles which also could be used

to estimate the time. Other timekeeping devices used streams, but these could freeze in winter. By the thirteenth century, the European monastery was a major type of social organization, that depended on precise and reliable timing. Their cooperative work efforts required people to coordinate their duties in terms of timing. This was an important need that called for a machine that could keep reliable time. Thus, the modern clock was devised. (4)

Fixing This Problem in Your Writing

adj
cl

Essential adjective clauses change the meaning of the nouns they modify by providing specific, identifying information. Because they contain information necessary to understanding the intended meaning of the sentence, essential clauses should *not* be set off from the rest of the sentence with a comma(s). Here is a tip that will help you determine whether an adjective clause is essential.

> **DELETION TIP**   Delete the adjective clause and look again at the noun it modified. If the noun is still clear, the clause is not essential. If deleting the clause creates confusion, the clause is essential.

When we apply the Deletion Tip to Example 1, a vague sentence results.

Example 1:   ✗ Sally met a teacher, <u>who will be teaching composition this fall</u>.

?

Tip applied: Sally met a teacher, ~~who will be teaching composition this fall~~.

By deleting the underlined clause, we have removed crucial information about *which* teacher Sally met. The clause identifies the teacher as someone who will teach composition this fall. That information is important to understanding the sentence, so the clause is essential. To punctuate the sentence correctly, we apply the guideline described earlier.

Correction: Sally met a teacher/ who will be teaching composition this fall.

Essential Clause = Essential Information = No Comma

If we apply the tip to Example 2, however, we find that the sentence still makes sense even after the adjective clause is deleted.

Example 2:   ✗ I called Ms. Watson <u>who lives in Atlanta.</u>

✓

Tip applied: I called Ms. Watson ~~who lives in Atlanta~~.

This adjective clause is considered nonessential because it just adds extra information—"gravy" that provides detail that might be useful but is not crucial in terms of identifying *Ms. Watson*. This does not mean we should permanently delete the adjective clause. In fact, effective writers frequently use nonessential clauses to provide further clarification and detail. To punctuate the sentence correctly, we apply the guideline described earlier.

Correction: I called Ms. Watson, who lives in Atlanta.
                                   ^
Nonessential Clause = "Extra" Information = Comma

Lesson 17

adj
cl

It is not unusual for one sentence to have both types of adjective clauses, but you should follow the same guidelines discussed so far. In this final example, the first clause is a nonessential clause, so it is set off with commas, but the second clause is not set off with commas because it is essential:

NONESSENTIAL CLAUSE (COMMAS)

Mr. Gordon, who is my math teacher, owns the house

ESSENTIAL CLAUSE (NO COMMA)

that is across from mine.

MORE EXAMPLES

Essential Clauses   *Do not set off with a comma(s):*

Jonathan lives next to a woman <u>who is from Denmark.</u>

Somebody <u>who was in a hurry</u> asked me to give you this note.

Nonessential Clauses   *Set off with a comma(s):*

I am leaving for San Diego, <u>where I was born and raised.</u>

My car, <u>which is fifteen years old</u>, has never needed a repair.

✳ *Putting It All Together*

Identify Adjective Clauses

_____ Find the adjective clauses in your writing. An adjective clause is a group of words that functions as an adjective. Adjective clauses usually begin with relative pronouns (*who, whom, that, which*) or relative adverbs (*when, where*).

_____ Determine whether the adjective clause is essential or nonessential. If you can delete the clause without confusing readers or changing the meaning of the sentence, the clause is nonessential. If the clause is necessary for readers to understand the sentence, then the clause is essential.

Correctly Punctuate Adjective Clauses

_____ If the adjective clause is essential, do *not* set it off with a comma(s).

_____ If the adjective clause is nonessential, set it off with a comma(s).

Lesson 17

*adj
cl*

Sentence Practice 1

CORRECTED SENTENCES APPEAR ON PAGE 477.

Label the underlined adjective clauses in the following sentences as *essential* or *nonessential*, and punctuate accordingly. If a sentence is already punctuated correctly, write *OK* next to it.

essential
Example: Houses⁄ that are made of wood⁄ often survive major earthquakes.

1. Bo is reading a novel <u>that was written by J. R. R. Tolkien</u>.

2. Bo is reading *The Silmarillion* <u>which was written by J. R. R. Tolkien</u>.

3. She wanted to go to a place <u>where she could be alone</u>.

4. This neighborhood café <u>which first opened in 1939</u> is one of my favorite places to drink coffee.

5. My parents were married in the Middle Eastern country of Yemen <u>where a wedding feast can last three weeks</u>.

For more practice using commas with adjective clauses, go to **Exercise Central** at **bedfordstmartins.com/commonsense**

Sentence Practice 2

CORRECTED SENTENCES APPEAR ON PAGE 477.

Label the underlined adjective clauses in the following sentences as *essential* or *nonessential*, and punctuate accordingly. If a sentence is already punctuated correctly, write *OK* next to it.

> Example: I bumped into my second-grade teacher, *whom I hadn't seen in years.*   [nonessential]

Lesson 17

*adj
cl*

1. During Thanksgiving break, I have to drive to Denver <u>which is 600 miles away</u>.

2. Three actors from the film *Predator*, <u>which stars Arnold Schwarzenegger</u>, have run for the office of governor.

3. One of these actors is Sonny Landham <u>who was unsuccessful in becoming the governor of Kentucky</u>.

4. I need someone <u>whom I can trust</u>.

5. Jack Kerouac, <u>who wrote several novels</u>, could type one hundred words a minute.

Sentence Practice 3

Add an adjective clause to each sentence below by using a relative pronoun or relative adverb. The clause should describe the underlined noun. Determine if you need to use a comma to set off each clause you add.

> Example: The <u>truck</u> is mine.
>
> Answer: *The truck that is parked in the driveway is mine.*

1. I once owned a <u>dog</u>.

2. My favorite place to eat is a <u>restaurant</u>.

3. <u>Jay</u> does not feel well.

4. Someone broke this <u>computer</u>.

5. On Saturday, my roommate traveled to <u>Chicago</u>.

6. We need a football <u>coach</u>.

7. *Star Wars* is still a popular movie.

8. My mother was born in <u>1976</u>.

9. I really dislike <u>chocolate</u>.

10. Do you ever visit <u>New Orleans</u>?

Editing Practice 1

CORRECTED SENTENCES APPEAR ON PAGE 477.

Correct all errors in the following paragraph using the first correction as a model. The number in parentheses at the end of the paragraph indicates how many commas you should add or delete.

Lesson 17

adj
cl

    I recently purchased a green-cheeked conure, which is a type of small parrot. It is an intelligent bird, that is becoming increasingly popular as an exotic pet. *Pyrrhura molinae* which is the bird's scientific name is mostly green. The green-cheeked conure obtains its name from the bright green feathers on its cheeks. It is a very playful and active bird. My father who generally dislikes all birds even likes my bird, which I named Pepper because she likes to eat raw peppers. Most of the time, Pepper eats a blend of colored pellets that I buy at the pet store. Like many conures, Pepper is capable of mimicking speech but is not a great talker. She mainly whistles and makes a variety of odd noises, that often wake me early in the morning. (6)

Editing Practice 2

CORRECTED SENTENCES APPEAR ON PAGE 477.

Correct all errors in the following paragraph using the first correction as a model. The number in parentheses at the end of the paragraph indicates how many commas you should add or delete.

    I am rooming with Harold Lee, who is very practical. We couldn't afford to spend much for Christmas gifts this year, so we decided to can some vegetables. First, we made a relish, that was primarily composed of tomatoes, onions, and cabbage. The tomatoes which we bought at the local market had to be completely green. The jars had to be carefully sterilized, and the directions confused us. Luckily, we received advice from my mom whom I called in a panic. Once we understood the process better, we went on to asparagus which has always been my favorite. I'm not sure we saved much time or money, but the experience was fun. (5)

Editing Practice 3

Correct all errors in the following paragraph using the first correction as a model. The number in parentheses at the end of the paragraph indicates how many commas you should add or delete.

Lesson 17

adj
cl

   I live in a small town,/ that is on the Gulf of Mexico. Gulf Shores, which is the name of this Alabama town, is a tourist attraction for people, who want to sunbathe or enjoy the ocean. Gulf Shores has more than one beach, but the beach, where most people go, is practically in the middle of town. Traffic can be really bad in summer which of course is the best time to go to the beach. Unfortunately, there is only one road that can take you to the main beach. Noon is the time, when you probably do not want to travel to the beach. Anyone who really wants to avoid the congestion can do so by arriving at the beach no later than 9:00 A.M., when relatively few people are coming or going. You might not think such a small town could have significant traffic problems, but I promise that you will change your mind if you visit this beach in summer. (5)

Applying What You Know

Even though nonessential adjective clauses are not truly essential to a sentence's meaning, they can add details and information that help readers better understand what the writer is trying to say. To illustrate this point, write five sentences that state a fact but that do not use any nonessential clauses. Trade your sentences with someone else and add a nonessential adjective clause to each of your partner's sentences so that each sentence is more detailed. Each nonessential clause should be set off with a comma (or two). Start each nonessential clause with one of the following relative pronouns: *who, whom, whose, which,* or *that.*

The Bottom Line	Nonessential clauses, **which can always be deleted,** should be set off with commas.

Lesson 17

adj cl

LESSON 18

Commas with Appositives

What's the Problem?

An **appositive** is a noun (or pronoun) that renames a previous noun (or pronoun). In Example 1 above, *Macbeth* is an appositive renaming the noun *play*.
An appositive and the word it renames mean the same thing. For instance,
you could think of Example 2 above as making the following claim:

   our governor = Seth Nodar

   Writers often make punctuation errors with appositives because some
appositives *must* be set off from the rest of the sentence with a comma(s),
whereas others *must not*. Whether a comma is necessary depends on whether
the appositive is *essential* or *nonessential*. In this way, appositives are similar to
adjective clauses (see Lesson 17). Let's look at the definition of each type of
appositive and how each type is punctuated.

Appositive	Function	Punctuation
Essential	Provides important identifying information about the noun it renames	Do *not* set off with a comma (see Example 1).

181

Appositive	Function	Punctuation
Nonessential	Provides extra information about the noun being renamed; removing the appositive doesn't make the noun any less clear	Set off with a comma (see Example 2).

Without essential appositives, readers might not be able to identify the person, place, or thing that the appositive renames. In the following example, the appositive (*Adam*) is essential because the writer likely has several friends. The appositive indicates which friend is being referred to:

WORD BEING
RENAMED   APPOSITIVE

My friend Adam is thirty years old.

Which friend? The appositive is essential because it provides necessary information about the noun.

In contrast, the appositive in this next example is nonessential because the word being renamed (*Fort Worth*) is already specific:

WORD BEING
RENAMED   APPOSITIVE

I am flying to Fort Worth, a large city near Dallas.

The word being renamed is specific, so the appositive is nonessential.

The rules for commas with appositives can be summarized this way:

Essential Appositive = Essential Information = No Comma

Nonessential Appositive = "Extra" Information = Comma

Diagnostic Exercise

CORRECTED SENTENCES APPEAR ON PAGE 478.

Correct all the comma errors in the following paragraph using the first correction as a model. The number in parentheses at the end of the paragraph indicates how many appositive errors you should find. (Each error involves a pair of commas unless the appositive is at the end of a sentence.)

Every summer, I visit my Aunt Carol, a vigorous woman of
                                          ^
sixty-five. Aunt Carol lives in a small town in Minnesota a state in the

northern part of the American Midwest. Even though I love her, we argue about one thing coffee. Like many midwesterners, she drinks coffee all day, and her coffee is very weak. The problem is that I am from Seattle the home of Starbucks. Starbucks one of the fastest growing companies in the United States has made espresso into a lifestyle choice. My favorite drink a double mocha has the caffeine equivalent of a dozen cups of Aunt Carol's coffee. The first time I made coffee at her house, she had a fit. She not only threw out all the coffee I made but also made me wash the pot. From then on, she made the coffee the kind you can see through. (6)

Lesson 18

appos

Fixing This Problem in Your Writing

Identifying Appositives

The first step in correcting appositive errors is identifying appositives in general. Knowing that appositives are nouns or pronouns that rename a previous noun or pronoun helps, but here is another tip.

> **FINDING THE APPOSITIVE TIP**   Try using *only* what you think is the appositive in the sentence, deleting the previous noun it renames. If the sentence still makes sense and is grammatically correct, you have identified the appositive.

Remember the "equation" noted earlier regarding Example 2. Because the appositive = the word being renamed, you should be able to use *just* the appositive in the sentence, letting it replace the word it renames. Let's apply this tip to our example sentences. Don't worry about commas yet; just note how it is possible to delete the word being renamed.

Example 1: ✗ Shakespeare's play, *Macbeth*, was recently made into a movie again.

Tip applied: ~~Shakespeare's play,~~ *Macbeth* was recently made into a movie again.

Example 2: ✗ Our governor Seth Nodar is making an important speech at my campus.

Tip applied: ~~Our governor~~ Seth Nodar is making an important speech at my campus.

As you can see, these sentences make sense even after we delete the words the appositives rename. The tip confirms that *Macbeth* and *Seth Nodar* are indeed appositives.

Punctuating Appositives

Once you identify appositives in your writing, determine whether they are *essential* appositives (which don't use commas) or *nonessential* appositives (which require commas). Use the following tip to determine whether an appositive is essential or nonessential.

> **GENERAL-NOUN TIP**   Identify the word(s) that the appositive renames. The more general this noun phrase is, the more likely that its appositive is essential.

Lesson 18

appos

In this tip, *noun phrase* refers not just to the noun being renamed but to its modifiers as well. It's the whole phrase that determines whether the idea is vague. Vague noun phrases tend to pair with essential appositives. Noun phrases that are already specific do not.

In Example 1, the appositive *Macbeth* renames *Shakespeare's play*. At first, *Shakespeare's play* seems specific, but Shakespeare wrote many plays, so the noun phrase is general. Thus, the appositive *Macbeth* is essential and should not be set off with commas.

GENERAL NOUN PHRASE

Tip applied: ✗ (Shakespeare's play) *Macbeth*, was recently made into a movie again.

The appositive is essential because it renames a general, vague noun phrase.

Correction: Shakespeare's play∕ *Macbeth*∕ was recently made into a movie again.

Essential Appositive = Essential Information = No Comma(s)

In contrast, the noun renamed in Example 2 is specific. *Our governor* could mean only one person, so the appositive is not necessary and should be set off with commas.

SPECIFIC NOUN PHRASE

Tip applied: ✗ (Our governor) Seth Nodar is making an important speech at my campus.

The noun phrase is specific, so the appositive is nonessential.

Correction: **Our governor, Seth Nodar, is making an important speech at my campus.**

Nonessential Appositive = "Extra" Information = Comma(s)

MORE EXAMPLES

Essential Appositives   *Do not set off with a comma(s):*

My neighbor <u>Cindy</u> works part-time in a lawyer's office.

I need to read the story "<u>Snow</u>" by Friday.

Nonessential Appositives   *Set off with a comma(s):*

I was taught to respect fire by my father, <u>a retired firefighter</u>.

My brother, <u>Gary</u>, lives in Boston.*

*This last example could be either essential or nonessential. If the writer has only one brother, the sentence is fine. But if the writer has *more* than one brother, the appositive is essential and we must remove the commas.

✳ *Putting It All Together*

Identify Appositives in Your Writing

_____ Look for appositives—nouns or pronouns that rename a previous noun or pronoun. To confirm that a word or group of words is an appositive, delete the previous noun it renames. If the sentence still makes sense and is grammatically correct, you have identified an appositive.

_____ Next, determine whether the appositive is essential or nonessential. Essential appositives tend to rename noun phrases that are general and vague. Nonessential appositives rename noun phrases that are already specific and clear to readers.

Correctly Punctuate Appositives in Your Writing

_____ If the appositive is essential, do NOT set it off with a comma(s).

_____ If the appositive is nonessential, set it off with a comma(s).

Sentence Practice 1

CORRECTED SENTENCES APPEAR ON PAGE 478.

All the appositives in the following sentences are nonessential. Underline each appositive, and add the necessary commas. Confirm your answer by applying the Finding the Appositive Tip.

> Example: The university is in the capital of Thailand, Bangkok.
>
> Confirmation: *The university is in Bangkok.*

1. Ian Fleming the creator of 007 named James Bond after the author of a book about birds.

2. Ian Fleming also wrote *Chitty Chitty Bang Bang* a children's book.

3. Tim's mother a registered nurse thinks I have a virus.

4. Richard a guy in my geology class fell asleep during the lecture.

5. Spanish Fort a town in south Alabama was the site of one of the last battles of the Civil War.

Lesson 18

appos

 For more practice using appositives, go to **Exercise Central** at
bedfordstmartins.com/commonsense

Sentence Practice 2

CORRECTED SENTENCES APPEAR ON PAGE 478.

Underline the appositives. Label them *essential* or *nonessential*, and punctuate them correctly. If a sentence is already punctuated correctly, write *OK* next to it. Using the General-Noun Tip, circle the noun phrases that the appositives rename and write *general* or *specific* above them.

>   *specific*   *nonessential*
> Example: (My English assignment), a ten-page essay, is due
>   next week.

1. Eleven of the twelve astronauts who walked on the moon were in the Boy Scouts an organization that began in 1910.

2. I rarely see my neighbor a woman who works the night shift at the hospital.

3. Cuba a country that struggled for years to produce sufficient electricity has lifted most of its bans on air conditioners, toasters, and other household appliances.

4. My psychology professor a noted scholar suggested I participate in a study she is conducting.

5. Although he was never seriously considered, Adolf Hitler was nominated in 1939 for the Nobel Peace Prize a prestigious international award.

Sentence Practice 3

Create an appositive for either set of underlined words in each sentence. Confirm the appositive by using the Finding the Appositive Tip. Then, use the General-Noun Tip to determine if your appositive needs commas.

> Example: My **grandparents** still recall **Black Thursday**.
>
> Answer: *My grandparents still recall Black Thursday, the day the stock market crashed in 1929.*

Lesson 18

appos

1. Jack's mother owns a revolver.
2. My friends are planning to move to Miami.
3. More than 90 percent of rubies come from Myanmar.
4. Sonya asked if I wanted to watch *The Wizard of Oz*.
5. On my birthday, I am going to watch my favorite singer.
6. Your advisor suggested you make an appointment with Dr. Olfason.
7. There are more people named Chang in China than there are people in Germany.
8. Jo Ann wants to meet with you on October 31.
9. Shakespeare's play can be seen this weekend at my old high school.
10. Cynthia left but returned just in time to visit with my friend.

Editing Practice 1

CORRECTED SENTENCES APPEAR ON PAGE 478.

Correct all errors in the following paragraphs using the first correction as a model. The number in parentheses at the end of each paragraph indicates how many commas you should add or delete.

World War II, one of the best-known wars of all time, was followed a few years later by a conflict that still is not well understood.

The Korean War, a conflict between the United Nations and North Korea, was never officially a war. Harry Truman the U.S. president at the time of the conflict never asked Congress to declare war. The U.S. troops fought as part of the UN forces. The conflict was therefore called a "police action." (2)

This war caused many problems for the United States, possibly because its status and purpose were not clear. General Douglas MacArthur the commander of the UN forces was removed from office for insubordination to President Truman the commander in chief. After the landings at Inchon a major turning point the North Koreans were pushed back. Neither side completely achieved its goals, and a truce was signed in 1953. (5)

Lesson 18

appos

Editing Practice 2

Correct all errors in the following paragraphs using the first correction as a model. The number in parentheses at the end of each paragraph indicates how many commas you should add or delete.

I received an unusual gift on July 1, my nineteenth birthday. My oldest brother, Gary, gave me a gift certificate for a free ride on a biplane at an airstrip outside Foley, our hometown. The pilot was a young man who had rebuilt the old plane so he could sell rides lasting thirty minutes. The plane was a Travelair an open-cockpit biplane built in the late 1920s. I was nervous about riding in an old plane, but when I arrived at the airstrip, I was impressed by how sturdy and well kept the plane appeared. (3)

Jerry Burns the pilot gave me a set of goggles to wear as he escorted me to the passenger's seat. It was located right behind his seat in the *Bird of Paradise* the name he gave his plane. The motor was incredibly loud, and the plane vibrated greatly when we finally took off. Before long,

the ride became much smoother, and I could see all of Gulf Shores the

nearest city. I have ridden many times in a commercial plane, yet this

was a totally different experience I will always remember. (4)

Applying What You Know

Write a paragraph or two describing places that you enjoy, but do not use appositives yet. Then, to show how nonessential appositives play a useful role in providing extra detail, revise by adding at least three nonessential appositives. Underline these appositives.

Trade your paper with a partner so that you can have someone see if (1) you used appositives, (2) these are nonessential appositives, and (3) you used commas correctly with these appositives. Use the Finding the Appositive Tip and General-Noun Tip to check your work.

Lesson 18

appos

The Bottom Line	A nonessential appositive, **the optional "gravy,"** is always set off with a comma or commas.

Unnecessary Commas

EXAMPLE 1	*Unnecessary Comma after Coordinating Conjunction*
Error:	Sakura left the classroom. ✗ <u>But</u>, we pretended not to notice.
Correction:	Sakura left the classroom. But╱we pretended not to notice.
EXAMPLE 2	*Unnecessary Comma between Subject and Verb*
Error:	✗ <u>Keeping up</u> with my classes while working at a lumber yard, <u>is</u> difficult.
Correction:	Keeping up with my classes while working at a lumber yard╱is difficult.
EXAMPLE 3	*Unnecessary Comma before a Series*
Error:	✗ My grocery list includes, <u>juice, oranges, and candy</u>.
Correction:	My grocery list includes╱juice, oranges, and candy.

What's the Problem?

Writers should know not only when to use commas but also when *not* to use them. Besides being distracting, unnecessary commas can confuse readers by suggesting that the sentence structure is different from what it really is. This problem is especially likely in sentences like Example 2. The comma could be misinterpreted as the first of two commas that set off an unimportant idea. In truth, what comes after this comma is highly important to the meaning of the sentence, and a second comma never appears.

Why are commas often used unnecessarily? First, they have so many functions that it is easy for a writer to assume they can be used for yet another reason. Second, many people accept the very misleading but common suggestion that if you would naturally pause at a certain point while saying a sentence aloud, then you should put a comma there. Commas can, indeed, suggest a pause, but no two people pause the same way when they speak.

You might pause after using a word such as *and*, but other people might not. Avoid inserting a comma unless you know the guideline for using it. For most of us, a better rule of thumb for commas is *if in doubt, leave it out.*

Although there are various types of unnecessary commas, there are some common tendencies. Previous lessons offer information on these common errors:

Lesson 13: Unnecessary comma between two verbs

Lesson 15: Unnecessary comma before an adverb clause

Lesson 17: Unnecessary comma with an important adjective clause

Lesson 18: Unnecessary comma with an essential appositive

This lesson focuses on three other types of comma errors: unnecessary commas used (1) after coordinating conjunctions, (2) between a subject and a verb, and (3) before lists.

Lesson 19

no ‸

Diagnostic Exercise

CORRECTED SENTENCES APPEAR ON PAGE 478.

Correct all comma errors in the following paragraph using the first correction as a model. The number in parentheses at the end of the paragraph indicates how many errors you should find.

Tens of millions of people around the globe / contributed to the outcome of World War II. Sacrifice, determination, mistakes, and luck, were combined with, brains, courage, leadership, and material resources to bring about the Allied victory. Undoubtedly, one indispensable factor was the alliance among the major powers, particularly, the United States, Great Britain, and the Soviet Union. Fighting alone, none of the Allies could have prevailed against Germany. But, working together enabled them to defeat what had been the strongest military power in the world. (4)

Fixing This Problem in Your Writing

If you use too many commas rather than too few, consider the aforementioned suggestion: *If in doubt, leave it out.* Also, consider the following three tips (along with those in Lessons 13, 15, 17, and 18).

> **NOT AFTER FANBOYS TIP**   Avoid using a comma right after a coordinating conjunction.

As discussed in Lesson 13, a coordinating conjunction combines words (or groups of words) that share the same grammatical function. One way to memorize the seven coordinating conjunctions is by using the acronym FANBOYS:

FANBOYS = For, And, Nor, But, Or, Yet, So

Avoid putting a comma immediately after any of the FANBOYS. This error often occurs when a writer begins a sentence with a conjunction (see Example 1). Once you recognize the problem, correcting it is easy—simply remove the comma.

Example 1:   Sakura left the classroom. ✗ But, we pretended not to notice.

Correction: Sakura left the classroom. But we pretended not to notice.

Even if you paused when saying *but* aloud, you should not use just a single comma immediately after a FANBOYS.

If, however, the conjunction is followed by a structure requiring *two* commas, you can put a comma after the conjunction—but *only* if there is a second corresponding comma (usually fairly close to the first one). In the following example, for instance, there is a clause that requires a comma before as well as after it.

Sakura left the classroom. But, <u>because we knew she did not feel well,</u> we pretended not to notice.

A comma is used after a FANBOYS, but it is one of two commas that set off the underlined clause. The comma after *but* is linked to the underlined clause—not to the FANBOYS. Some people believe a proper sentence should never begin with a FANBOYS anyway. While this is not a firm rule, sentences beginning with coordinating conjunctions should be used sparingly in formal writing. In light of this, another way to correct Example 1 would be to combine the sentences and to move the comma *before* the FANBOYS.

Sakura left the classroom, but we pretended not to notice.

As this correction indicates, you should also avoid a single comma after a FANBOYS that combines two sentences.

Here are more examples of sentences in which two independent clauses are joined with a comma and a coordinating conjunction. Note that a comma appropriately comes *before* (not after) the underlined FANBOYS.

Lesson 19

no ⌃,

I shot the sheriff, <u>but</u> I didn't shoot the deputy.

Yesterday, Todd called for you, <u>and</u> I told him you were at work.

In sentences that contain a FANBOYS, you only use a comma before the coordinating conjunction if what follows it could be a separate grammatical sentence (see Lesson 13).

Another type of unnecessary comma separates a subject from its verb. Chances are you would not use a comma in a sentence like this:

Error: ✗ The eagle, dropped its food.

Obviously, a comma is needlessly used between the subject (*eagle*) and verb (*dropped*). This error is easier to overlook when several words come between a subject and its verb. Nevertheless, just as you would not use a comma in the short sentence above, do not use a single comma in a longer sentence. A subject and its verb have such a strong relationship that you should not needlessly place just one comma between them.

In Example 2, the simple subject is underlined once, and its verb is underlined twice.

Example 2:   ✗ <u>Keeping up</u> with my classes while working at a lumber yard, <u><u>is</u></u> difficult.

Correction: <u>Keeping up</u> with my classes while working at a lumber yard⁄ <u><u>is</u></u> difficult.

Most commas incorrectly separating a subject and its verb appear right before the verb, not after the subject. Thus, remember the next tip to help you avoid this error.

> **NOT BEFORE A VERB TIP**   Avoid using just a single comma immediately before a verb.

Remember this tip when a subject and verb seem separated by several words, as also seen in the next example. The simple subject is underlined once and the verb twice.

Error: ✗ The most important <u>thing</u> you almost forgot to pack, <u><u>is</u></u> a clean pair of pants.

Correction: The most important <u>thing</u> you almost forgot to pack⁄ <u><u>is</u></u> a clean pair of pants.

Some people might be confused by what *appears* to be an exception to this tip: There are times when inserting *two* commas between a subject and

Lesson 19

no ^,

verb is correct. When used after a subject, several structures should be set off by a pair of commas, as shown in the following, correct sentence.

Albert, an old friend of mine, <u>e-mailed</u> me today.

The subject and verb are separated by a few words (*an old friend of mine*) that rename *Albert*. Such a nonessential appositive is, indeed, set off by commas (see Lesson 18). Thus, although at first it appears that a comma is used between a subject and verb in the above example, in reality the sentence correctly uses *two* commas — a familiar pattern that rarely confuses readers.

Our final type of unnecessary comma involves its use with a series of two or more grammatically similar words. Essentially, this is a list of things, people, or actions. Such lists can be worded in different ways, and the wording determines what punctuation, if any, is needed (see Lesson 25, for instance, on using colons with lists). Remember the following tip to help you punctuate lists.

Lesson 19

no $\hat{,}$

> **NOT BEFORE A SERIES TIP**   Avoid using a single comma immediately before the first item in a list.

This tip will help you avoid one type of error, but it does not help you determine if the comma should be replaced by some other punctuation, such as a colon. For now, consider this rule of thumb: Avoid any punctuation immediately before a list unless the result would be a truly odd sentence. This highly intuitive approach to list punctuation does not work for everyone, but usually writers err by putting too much, rather than too little, punctuation before lists. Again we suggest *if in doubt, leave it out*.

In Example 3, below, each item in the list is underlined. A comma incorrectly appears before the initial item. As the Not before a Series Tip suggests, avoid such a comma. The correction is easy enough: Remove the comma. Because there is nothing odd about the resulting sentence, do not place any punctuation before the list.

Example 3:   ✗ My grocery list includes, <u>juice</u>, <u>oranges</u>, and <u>candy</u>.

Correction: My grocery list includes/<u>juice</u>, <u>oranges</u>, and <u>candy</u>.

In the next two examples, no comma appears right before the first item in each list, so the sentences are correct.

William asked for a wine that goes with <u>chicken</u>, <u>lemons</u>, and <u>squash</u>.

The test will cover several subjects, including but not limited to the <u>Great Depression</u>, <u>World War II</u>, and the <u>Cold War</u>.

In the second sentence, a comma appears before *including*. Applying the Not before a Series Tip shows that the comma is correct because it is not immediately before the first item in the list. Possible exceptions to this third tip are rare. Remember the tip, and you will avoid most unnecessary commas before lists.

✳ Putting It All Together

Identify Unnecessary Commas

____ Look for single commas that appear *immediately* (1) after a coordinating conjunction, (2) before a verb, and (3) before the first item in a list.

Correct Unnecessary Commas

____ If it is just a single comma (not a pair), you usually should delete the comma.

Lesson 19

no ⌃,

Sentence Practice 1

CORRECTED SENTENCES APPEAR ON PAGE 478.

Delete the unnecessary comma in each sentence below. Use the three tips to help you detect errors.

Example: Wishing for something you can't have**/** is normal behavior.

1. Remember to bring, a pen, paper, and your grammar book.

2. Thomas Jefferson is credited with several inventions, such as, a revolving bookstand and the first swivel chair.

3. And, he sat in a swivel chair while drafting the Declaration of Independence, according to some sources.

4. Each week, Candice paid a tutor to help her pass sociology, but, nothing helped.

5. My biology teacher, Ms. Anderson, required a great deal of homework this week, beginning with, reading three chapters and completing several exercises.

 For more practice using commas, go to **Exercise Central** at
bedfordstmartins.com/commonsense

Sentence Practice 2

CORRECTED SENTENCES APPEAR ON PAGE 479.

Delete any unnecessary commas in the following sentences. Use the three tips to help you detect errors. Write *OK* above each correct comma.

                    OK   OK
Example: Alex, my former boss, asked me to have coffee with him.

1. Delete the comma in this sentence if you think you should, but it is actually necessary.

2. But, there is a comma in this sentence that should be deleted, unless you intentionally want the sentence to be incorrect.

Lesson 19

3. When a city's name is followed by the country's name, place a comma before and, after the country.

no ⌄,

4. Florence, Italy, was the first European city to pave virtually all its streets.

5. For many people, commas can be a confusing form of punctuation, along with, semicolons, colons, and quotation marks.

Sentence Practice 3

Turn each phrase below into a complete sentence that correctly uses any commas provided or any you add. Avoid adding unnecessary commas.

Example: This computer,

Answer: *This computer, which I bought four years ago, needs a memory upgrade.*

1. My roommate,

2. Don't buy needless items such as

3. A pet that requires a great deal of attention

4. It was not supposed to rain today, yet

5. Don't forget to buy

6. I need to take a shower. But

7. For this recipe, you need several ingredients, including

8. Dr. Turner,

9. One reason why you have to leave right now

10. And

Editing Practice 1

CORRECTED SENTENCES APPEAR ON PAGE 479.

Delete all unnecessary commas in the following paragraph using the first correction as a model. The number in parentheses at the end of the paragraph indicates how many commas you should delete.

A major development in the evolution of film/ was the arrival of nickelodeons. This was a type of movie theater whose name is a combination
of, the admission price and the Greek word for *theater*. According to media
historian Douglas Gomery, these small and uncomfortable makeshift
theaters were often converted storefronts redecorated to mimic vaudeville
theaters. Usually, a piano player added live music, and, sometimes theater
operators used sound effects to simulate gunshots or loud crashes. Because
they showed silent films that usually transcended language barriers, nickelodeons flourished during the great European immigration to America
at the turn of the twentieth century. These theaters filled a need for many
newly arrived people who faced challenges such as, struggling to learn
English and seeking an inexpensive escape from the hard life of the city.
These nickelodeons, which were often managed by immigrants, required a
minimal investment: just a secondhand projector and a large white sheet.
The craze reached its greatest popularity in 1910. But, entrepreneurs soon
began to seek more affluent spectators, attracting them with, larger facilities and more lavish buildings. (5)

Lesson 19

no ⌃,

Editing Practice 2

Delete all unnecessary commas in the following paragraph using the first correction as a model. The number in parentheses at the end of each paragraph indicates how many commas you should delete.

By the 1910s, movies were a major industry, and/ Thomas Edison
was among the first to try to dominate this business. He formed the

Motion Picture Patents Company, also known as the Trust, in 1908. This association of American and French film producers, used several tactics to achieve their goal, such as, sharing patents with one another to control film technology, acquiring major film distributorships, and signing exclusive manufacturing deals. George Eastman, one major manufacturer, agreed to supply movie film only to Trust-approved companies. (2)

Yet, some producers refused to bow to the Trust. Their reasons were based on, public demand for films, the money to be made, and the fact that there were ways to avoid the Trust's scrutiny. Some producers left the centers of film production in New England and moved to places such as, Cuba and Florida. But, it was Hollywood that became the film capital of the world. The area's advantages included, cheap labor, diverse scenery for outdoor shooting, and a mild climate for year-round production. Independent producers located in faraway Hollywood, could also easily slip over the border into Mexico to escape prosecution by the Trust for violation of its patents. (6)

Lesson 19

no ⌃ ,

Applying What You Know

Print out one or two pages of an informal Internet blog in which commas are used at least ten times. Be prepared to explain in class why each comma is either correct or in error. If you are not sure whether a comma is correct, explain why you think the writer used it, even if the blogger did so incorrectly.

The Bottom Line	Commas, a common form of punctuation, should be used as needed, but they are often used needlessly with sentence elements such as lists and coordinating conjunctions.

Using Commas Correctly

REVIEW

Commas are used in so many ways that knowing when to use (and not use) a comma can be particularly challenging. This chart helps you avoid the most common problems involving commas.

TIPS	QUICK FIXES AND EXAMPLES
Lesson 13. Commas with *And*, *But*, *Or*, and Other Coordinating Conjunctions	
The Imaginary Period Tip (p. 140) helps you determine whether a sentence contains two independent clauses so you can join them with correct punctuation.	If a FANBOYS is connecting two independent clauses, use a comma before the FANBOYS. Otherwise, do not use a comma.
	Error: ✗ My physics instructor was not in class today but another teacher took her place.
	Correction: My physics instructor was not in class today**,** but another teacher took her place. ^
Lesson 14. Commas with Transitional Terms	
The Transitional Term Movement Tip (p. 150) helps you identify transitional terms so you can punctuate them correctly.	If the transitional term separates two independent clauses, use a semicolon before it and a comma after it. If it comes at the beginning or end of a sentence, set it off with just a comma.
	Error: ✗ My bus was late, therefore, I could not make it to class on time.
	Correction: My bus was late**/;** therefore, I ^ could not make it to class on time.
Lesson 15. Commas with Adverb Clauses	
The Adverb Clause Movement Tip (p. 158) helps you identify adverb clauses so you can punctuate them correctly.	Set off most introductory adverb clauses with a comma. Use no comma with a sentence-ending clause unless it conveys a strong sense of contrast.
	Error: ✗ While we were taking a test in my astronomy class a fire alarm went off.
	Correction: While we were taking a test in my astronomy class**,** a fire alarm went off. ^

TIPS	QUICK FIXES AND EXAMPLES
Lesson 16. Commas with Introductory Elements	
The Deletion Tip (p. 166) helps you identify introductory elements, and the Comma Tip (p. 166) helps you remember when to use a comma with them.	Use a comma after all introductory elements unless your readers prefer otherwise. Error: ✗ In the middle of the movie someone began snoring. Correction: In the middle of the movie, someone began snoring. ^
Lesson 17. Commas with Adjective Clauses	
The Deletion Tip (p. 174) helps you determine whether an adjective clause is essential or nonessential so you can punctuate it correctly.	Do not use commas with essential clauses. Use commas with nonessential clauses. Error: ✗ I called Dr. Perez who referred me to another doctor. Correction: I called Dr. Perez, who referred me to another doctor. ^
Lesson 18. Commas with Appositives	
The Finding the Appositive Tip (p. 183) helps you identify appositives. The General-Noun Tip (p. 184) tells you whether an appositive is essential or nonessential.	Do not use commas with essential appositives. Use commas with nonessential appositives. Error: ✗ My old friend, Rusty, called me last night. Correction: My old friend / Rusty / called me last night. ^ ^
Lesson 19. Unnecessary Commas	
The Not after FANBOYS Tip (p. 192) helps you avoid comma errors occurring right after a coordinating conjunction. The Not before a Verb Tip (p. 193) helps you avoid comma errors between a subject and verb. The Not before a Series Tip (p. 194) helps you avoid commas that needlessly appear before the first item in a series.	Avoid placing a single comma right after a coordinating conjunction, right before a verb, and right before the first item in a list. Error: ✗ The child holding the broken toy, asked me to help her, but, I have too many things to do, such as, meeting my friend for a ride and getting to work on time. Correction: The child holding the broken toy / asked me to help her, but / I have too many things to do, such as / meeting my friend for a ride and getting to work on time.

Review Test

Correct the comma problems in the following paragraphs using the first correction as a model. The number in parentheses at the end of each paragraph indicates how many commas you should add or delete.

My English teacher, Ms. Gonzales, asked us to find three magazine articles for our next essay assignment. My paper which will deal with solar energy is a fairly easy one to research. I found fourteen articles in less than an hour and almost all of these appear to be credible and useful. (3)

Some of these articles were online, but most can be found only in a hard copy of the magazine. However it did not take long for me to go to the library, and find the ones I needed. Even though Ms. Gonzales asked for only three articles I decided to find several more and choose the best for my paper. I needed some advice picking the best sources, so I asked for help from my roommate, who is an English major. She did not read them thoroughly, but gave me advice on how to determine which magazines were most credible. I am confident, therefore, that I have chosen effective sources for my next paper. (4)

Unit Five

review

Using Apostrophes Correctly

OVERVIEW

The Nuts and Bolts of Using Apostrophes Correctly

An apostrophe (') is a mark of punctuation used to indicate (1) missing letters in a contraction and (2) possession or ownership. Your writing may be unclear to your readers if you misplace or misuse apostrophes.

Lesson 20 explains how to use contractions with apostrophes. Contractions are shortened forms of words. For example, *I'll* is short for *I will*; *didn't* is short for *did not*; and *what's* is short for *what is*. Writers use an apostrophe to take the place of the missing letters.

> Example: ✗ Wasnt that course canceled last semester?
>
> Correction: Wasn't that course canceled last semester?

Lesson 21 covers the use of possessive apostrophes. Writers use an apostrophe to show that someone possesses something. The placement of the apostrophe depends on whether the "owner" is singular (the *girl's books* = the books of one girl) or plural (the *girls' books* = the books of two or more girls). This lesson covers the use of apostrophes and spelling of contractions.

> Example: ✗ Five students cars were towed from the parking lot.
>
> Correction: Five students' cars were towed from the parking lot.

Lesson 22 shows you when *not* to use an apostrophe. Sometimes writers use an apostrophe when there is no need for one. This error tends to occur when people add an apostrophe to form the plural of words.

> Example: ✗ Your sentence has too many apostrophe's.
>
> Correction: Your sentence has too many apostrophe/s.

Apostrophes in Contractions

EXAMPLE 1

Error: ✗ Henry Pym wasnt in class today.

                                wasn't
Correction: Henry Pym ~~wasnt~~ in class today.
                              ^

EXAMPLE 2

Error: ✗ I heard its going to rain this weekend.

                        it's
Correction: I heard ~~its~~ going to rain this weekend.
                      ^

What's the Problem?

Contractions are shortened forms of words, and—for better or worse—they add an informal tone as well as some conciseness. Many readers prefer that writers not use contractions in formal writing, so one way to avoid contraction errors is to avoid using contractions altogether. However, many writers want the option of using contractions, so here we describe how they can be correctly "assembled."

An error occurs when a contraction lacks an apostrophe or when the apostrophe appears in the wrong place. We focus on the "missing apostrophe" error because it is more frequent. Example 1 has a contraction error because *wasnt* (*was not*) lacks an apostrophe between *n* and *t*. Example 2 requires an apostrophe to show that *its* stands for *it is*.

Contractions are common in speech. In fact, many writers use contractions to provide the relaxed, natural tone found in conversation. Thus, it is easy to overlook the apostrophe since we do not worry about it in speech. In addition, there is particular confusion about the contraction *it's* (meaning *it is*) and the possessive *its* (as in *The fish ate its neighbor*). Most spell-checkers and grammar-checkers are unable to catch the error that results when writers confuse these two words.

Diagnostic Exercise

CORRECTED SENTENCES APPEAR ON PAGE 479.

Correct all errors in the following sentences.

> *can't*
> **Example:**   We ~~cant~~ leave until I brush my teeth.
>   ^

1. On the television show *Seinfeld*, Kramer's first name wasnt used often.

2. I didnt realize until recently that his first name is Cosmo.

3. Its too late to eat supper, but let's have a snack.

4. In the original books featuring Tarzan, his pet chimp isn't named Cheetah; rather, it's name is Nkima.

5. If youre going sightseeing, remember to bring your camera.

Lesson 20

Fixing This Problem in Your Writing

This editing tip will help you avoid contraction errors.

> **EXPANSION TIP**   Reread any word that might possibly be a contraction to see if you can "expand" that word by filling in missing letters. If you can, make sure that there is an apostrophe in the spot where the missing letters would appear.

Here are some examples of contractions showing first the contracted form and then the expanded form that fills in the missing letters. The filled-in letters in the expanded form are underlined:

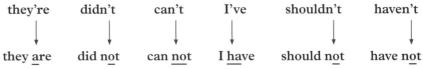

they're	didn't	can't	I've	shouldn't	haven't
they <u>a</u>re	did <u>n</u>ot	can <u>n</u>ot	I ha<u>ve</u>	should <u>n</u>ot	have <u>n</u>ot

Notice that the missing letters are vowels or sometimes both a vowel and a consonant (for example, *ha* in *I have*). For complicated historical reasons, there is one contraction that does not fit the normal pattern: The contracted form of *will not* is *won't*.

The Expansion Tip shows that Examples 1 and 2 each contain a word that can be expanded:

Example 1:　　✗ Henry Pym <u>wasnt</u> in class today.

Tip applied:　Henry Pym <u>was not</u> in class today.

Correction 1:　Henry Pym <u>wasn't</u> in class today.

Correction 2:　Henry Pym <u>was not</u> in class today.

The Expansion Tip shows that *wasnt* is really an incorrectly formed contraction of *was not*. We can correct the error in one of two ways: (1) use an apostrophe to show the place where the letters are missing—*wasn't*, or (2) use the uncontracted form *was not*. Both choices are perfectly grammatical. If you want your writing to have a conversational tone, then you will probably want to use the contracted form *wasn't*. On the other hand, if you want to be more formal, then you will probably want to use the uncontracted, expanded form *was not*.

Example 2:　　✗ I heard <u>its</u> going to rain this weekend.

Tip applied:　I heard <u>it is</u> going to rain this weekend.

Correction 1:　I heard <u>it's</u> going to rain this weekend.

Correction 2:　I heard <u>it is</u> going to rain this weekend.

The Expansion Tip shows that *its* is really an incorrectly formed contraction of *it is*. Again, we can correct the error either by using an apostrophe to show the missing letters in the contracted form or by using the full, uncontracted form.

It's is by far the most troublesome contraction because there are actually two *its* that are easily confused: the contraction of *it is* and the possessive pronoun *its* as in *The dog bit **its** tail*. The Expansion Tip is very useful for helping you tell the two *its* apart. We can always expand the contracted *it's* to *it is*. We can never expand the possessive pronoun *its* to *it is*. Here is the Expansion Tip applied to both uses of *its*:

Contraction:　✗ <u>Its</u> a nice day.

Tip applied:　<u>It is</u> a nice day.

Correction:　<u>It's</u> a nice day.

The fact that we can expand *its* to *it is* tells us that *its* is a contraction that must be spelled with an apostrophe.

Possessive:　The car had been parked with <u>its</u> headlights still on.

Tip applied:　✗ The car had been parked with <u>it is</u> headlights still on.

The fact that the Expansion Tip gives us an incorrect answer tells us that this *its* is not a contraction of *it is*. Therefore, *its* must be the possessive pronoun, which is never used with an apostrophe because there are no missing letters.

✳ *Putting It All Together*

Identify Contraction Errors

_____ Proofread to see if any word can be "expanded" into two words. If so, that word is a contraction.

_____ Look at every use of *its* and *it's*. If its can be expanded to *it is*, it is the contraction *it's*; if *its* cannot be expanded, it is the possessive pronoun *its*.

Correct Contraction Errors

_____ Make sure all contractions have apostrophes in the spots where letters were omitted.

_____ In formal writing, consider using the uncontracted forms.

Lesson 20

Sentence Practice 1

CORRECTED SENTENCES APPEAR ON PAGE 479.

If a sentence does not have a contraction error, write *OK* above it. If there is an error, cross it out. Then, write out the full form of the words. In addition, supply the correct form of the contraction.

Example: I think ~~its~~ time to leave.
            it is (it's)

1. My roommate wont be awake for at least another hour.

2. Its supposed to rain today, but I'm not sure that will happen.

3. The killer whale isnt a whale; it's actually the largest member of the dolphin family.

4. A rhinoceros has three toes on each foot, yet you cant see them because they're each encased in a hoof.

5. The British Empire isn't what it once was; the tiny Pitcairn Islands are the last of it's Pacific territories.

For more practice using contractions, go to **Exercise Central** at
bedfordstmartins.com/commonsense

Sentence Practice 2

CORRECTED SENTENCES APPEAR ON PAGE 479.

If a sentence does not have a contraction error, write *OK* above it. If there is
an error, cross it out. Then, write out the full form of the words. In addition,
supply the correct form of the contraction.

Example: *There is (There's)*
~~Theres~~ no business like show business.
            ^

1.   We're all going to the concert this weekend, unless it rains.

2.   Platinum wasnt highly valued at one time, so Russia used this rare
     metal in the early 1800s to make coins.

3.   The town of Hibbling, Minnesota, was entirely relocated because
     companies couldnt otherwise mine the iron ore underneath it.

4.   Martha Jane hasn't changed her e-mail address in twelve years.

5.   My snake shed its skin last night.

Sentence Practice 3

Rewrite the sentences below using at least one contraction in each sentence.

Example: I do not see the problem.

Answer: *I don't see the problem.*

1.   We will have to keep in touch.

2.   There is no reason to be upset.

3.   I have decided it is time to eat.

4.   We will not have to take your car, right?

5.   They are not sure if you will have to continue your medication.

Editing Practice 1

CORRECTED SENTENCES APPEAR ON PAGE 479.

Correct all errors in the following paragraphs using the first correction as a
model. The number in parentheses at the end of each paragraph indicates
how many errors you should find.

Lesson 20

Rice might seem to be a common (and perhaps dull) subject to

Americans. However, ~~its~~ *it's* such an important part of life in other parts of

the world that rice has an honored place in many cultures. Youve probably

long known about the tradition of throwing rice at newlyweds when

theyre leaving a church. But you probably did not know that in India rice

is traditionally the first food a bride offers her husband. In Indonesia,

tradition has it that a woman cant be considered for marriage until she can

skillfully prepare rice. (3)

Rice isnt associated with just marriage. Even the word itself is special.

Ive been to one region in China where the word for rice is also the word for

food. In Japan, the word for cooked rice is also the word for meal. Its also

common for rice fields in Japan to be given names as if they were people. (3)

Lesson 20

Editing Practice 2

Correct all errors in the following paragraphs using the first correction as a
model. The number in parentheses at the end of each paragraph indicates
how many errors you should find.

Like a lot of people, ~~Ive~~ *I've* been trying to lose some weight lately. I think

that part of the problem that were all facing is that our lifestyles are

working against us. Most of us work in an office or behind a desk, places

where its impossible to engage in any physical activity at all. When we go to

work, we have to commute such long distances that we cant possibly walk

or bicycle. I dont know about you, but my job is pretty stressful. For me,

one of the worst consequences of stress is that I tend to compulsively snack

on things that are quick and convenient (and loaded with calories). Lets

not kid ourselves; no one snacks on apple slices. (5)

A friend of mine just got back from a trip to Italy. She said that she

pretty much ate her way across northern Italy. She and her friends had three-course lunches and dinners with plenty of local wine. She thought

that when she got back that she wouldve gained ten pounds. In fact, she

didnt gain a pound—she actually lost five pounds. "Ive been thinking

about it," she said. "I think therere two things I did differently: I didnt

snack at all, and I walked all day long." (5)

Applying What You Know

Formal writing tends to use few contractions, but sometimes they can be effective. Find at least three examples of published writing that use contractions, and be ready to explain whether you think the contractions are useful or not. For at least one of your examples, find something that is not from the Internet and not taken from a short story or novel.

The Bottom Line	If you use a contraction, **you'll** need to use an apostrophe.

Lesson 20

Apostrophes Showing Possession

EXAMPLE 1 *Missing Apostrophe*

Error: ✗ The judges robe was torn and dirty.

              judge's
Correction: The ~~judges~~ robe was torn and dirty.
               ^

EXAMPLE 2 *Misplaced Apostrophe*

Error: ✗ Those student's cars are illegally parked.

              students'
Correction: Those ~~student's~~ cars are illegally parked.
               ^

What's the Problem?

Writers normally add an apostrophe and an *s* to indicate that somebody (or something) possesses something, as seen in this correct example:

This person owns this.

I paid for <u>Randy's ticket</u>.

The apostrophe lets readers know the *s* is added to show *possession*, not plurality. In Example 1, the apostrophe has been incorrectly left out, so at first it seems the sentence is referring to more than one judge. The apostrophe in the corrected version lets readers know that ownership is involved, not plurality.

A different problem occurs when the apostrophe is *misplaced*. This error is most likely to occur when the noun needing an apostrophe is plural (see Example 2). The solution is usually simple: If a noun ends in *s* because it is plural, you just add an apostrophe after this *s* to indicate possession.

Diagnostic Exercise

CORRECTED SENTENCES APPEAR ON PAGE 480.

Correct all errors in the following paragraph using the first correction as a model. The number in parentheses at the end of the paragraph indicates how many errors you should find.

      family's
    Paul Ortega has been one of my ~~familys~~ best friends over the years.
       ^
Although he was born in Mexico, he speaks English like a native because

his fathers employer relocated his family to Arizona when Paul was

six. In a few years, Pauls English was as good as anyones. Nearly every

summer, however, Paul and his sisters went back to Mexico City, where

they stayed at a relatives' house. As a result, he is completely at home in

either countrys culture. He and my father have been business partners for

many years. The companys success has been due largely to Paul's ability to

conduct business in both Mexico and the United States. (6)

Lesson 21

; ✓

Fixing This Problem in Your Writing

Identifying Possession

An apostrophe is used to show possession, but another way to indicate ownership is to reword the sentence. Here is a tip to help you identify possessive forms.

> **OF TIP** If a pair of words involves possession, you can usually reword the phrase using *of*.

    If a pair of words passes the *Of* Tip, possession is involved, so an apostrophe is normally required. Example 1 passes the *Of* Tip, proving the sentence indicates possession.

    Example 1:   ✗ The judges robe was torn and dirty.

    Tip applied: The robe <u>of</u> the judge . . .

Example 2 also passes the *Of* Tip, proving it is possessive.

Example 2:   ✗ Those student's cars are illegally parked.

Tip applied: Cars <u>of</u> those students . . .

Sometimes, the *Of* Tip produces a "double possessive." This occurs when possession is shown in two ways: with *of* AND an apostrophe. A double possessive is grammatical, as seen in this correct example:

Example: We were angered by Maria's statement.

Tip applied: . . . statement <u>of</u> Maria's.

                 Double possessive is OK.

At times, a phrase might involve only what could be loosely defined as "ownership." Often such phrases deal with particular amounts of something—such as time, weight, or distance.

today's news	last year's report	a moment's notice
arm's length	a dollar's worth	a pound's worth

Fortunately, the *Of* Tip usually works reasonably well with these expressions. As shown in the following example, using *of* might not sound as natural, but both versions essentially mean the same thing.

Example: Tomorrow's headline will shock you.

Tip applied: The headline of tomorrow will shock you.

Using the Apostrophe

The *Of* Tip can help you find possessive words, but next you must make sure the apostrophe is in the correct place. The good news is that there is a standard guideline. The bad news is that there are some exceptions and options that might confuse people. Let's start with the standard guideline, which works most of the time.

> **STANDARD TIP** For most singular possessive nouns, use an *'s* at the end of the word.

The *Of* Tip showed us that Example 1 involves possession. Because the sentence is referring to only one judge, we use the Standard Tip to show possession, adding the apostrophe before the *s* that is already there:

Example 1:   ✗ The <u>judges</u> robe was torn and dirty.

                 Singular possession: One judge owns the robe.

Lesson 21

Correction: The ~~judges~~ *judge's* robe was torn and dirty.

^

Singular possessive nouns need an *'s*, so put an apostrophe before the final *s*.

The tip works with these correct examples as well: Each is a singular noun ending in *'s*.

My <u>mother's</u> car is red.   I saw <u>Jin's</u> dog.

<u>Sue's</u> house is big.   My <u>boss's</u> tie is ugly.

The last example (*boss's*) involves a singular word already ending in *s*, but we followed the Standard Tip and made sure there was a final *'s* at the end of the word.

Exception: Most readers prefer you add *'s* to a singular word that already end in *s*, unless the result is a tongue twister that is difficult to say aloud. For example, *Sarah Connors' son* is easier to say than *Sarah Connors's son*.

The Standard Tip is for singular nouns. This next tip helps with most plural nouns.

PLURAL POSSESSION TIP If the possessive noun is plural, begin with the plural form. Then add *just* the apostrophe if the plural form ends in *s*.

Let's look at Example 2. The *Of* Tip proved that this sentence involves possession. Because the possession clearly deals with more than one student, we know that we should use the Plural Possession Tip to correctly place the apostrophe. Plural possessives show two separate things: plurality and possession. Thus, this tip involves two separate steps to construct the right form:

Example 2:   ✗ Those student's cars are illegally parked.

Tip applied, Step 1:   <u>students</u>

Start with the plural form.

Tip applied, Step 2:   students'

Add an apostrophe to show possession.

students'

Correction: Those ~~student's~~ cars are illegally parked.

^

Most plural nouns in English end in *s*, so usually you just add an apostrophe to show possession:

My <u>parents</u>' house is tiny.

These <u>cats</u>' bowls are empty.

The <u>students</u>' votes were counted.

Add just an apostrophe because plural forms already end in *s*.

Some plurals do not end in *s*, so add *'s* to make them possessive. The Plural Possession Tip still works, but you must now use *'s* at the end of the plural form:

Example: ✗ The <u>childrens</u> toys are broken.

Tip applied, Step 1:   children

                       Start with the plural form.

Tip applied, Step 2:   children<u>'s</u>

                       Plural form does not end in *s*, so use *'s* to show possession.

                                children's
Correction: The ~~childrens~~ toys are broken.
                               ^

MORE EXAMPLES

Possessive Singular Nouns   Add 's:

The <u>man's</u> arm was fractured in two places.

<u>Tess's</u> boyfriend lives in England.

Possessive Plural Nouns Ending in s   Add just an apostrophe:

All of my <u>teachers</u>' offices are in the Humanities Building.

The <u>Smiths</u>' house was vandalized this weekend.

Possessive Plural Nouns Not Ending in s   Add 's:
The <u>men's</u> score was considerably higher than usual.
My <u>teeth's</u> enamel is badly worn.

✱ Putting It All Together

Identify Possessives

_____ Look for possessive forms in your writing: nouns that "own" something right afterward.

_____ Look for possessive forms even when the possession is very general, usually involving measurements of distance, weight, and — in par-ticular — time (as in *a day's worth*).

_____ To confirm that possession is involved, reword the phrase using *of* to show possession (*the cat's tail* becomes *tail of the cat*)

Show Possession Using an Apostrophe

_____ Use an apostrophe to show possession.

_____ If a noun is singular, form the possessive by adding *'s* (as in *mouse's tail*). Most singular nouns that end in *s* still need *'s* added at the end (as in *Gus's store*).

_____ If a noun is plural and already ends in *s*, add *just* an apostrophe (as in *neighbors' cars*).

_____ If a noun is plural and does not already end in *s*, add *'s* (as in *mice's cage*).

Lesson 21

Sentence Practice 1

CORRECTED SENTENCES APPEAR ON PAGE 480.

Correct the possession error in each of the following sentences. Confirm your correction by applying the *Of* Tip.

>   *visitors'*
> **Example:**   They put all the ~~visitors~~ suitcases in the hall.
> **Confirmation:**   *They put the suitcases of all the visitors in the hall.*

1. My husbands watch is broken.

2. John Lennons middle name was Winston.

3. A starfishs eyes are located at the tip of each arm.

4. I need help with tomorrows homework.

5. The student council agreed that the schools name should be changed.

 For more practice using apostrophes, go to **Exercise Central** at **bedfordstmartins.com/commonsense**

Sentence Practice 2

CORRECTED SENTENCES APPEAR ON PAGE 480.

Correct the possession error in each of the following sentences. Confirm your correction by applying the *Of* Tip.

Example: The ~~couples~~ *couple's* car was parked in the driveway.

Confirmation: *The car of the couple was parked in the driveway.*

1. The guppys name comes from the name of the man who discovered this species.

2. The saxophones inventor was named Adolphe Sax.

3. Hold the acid at arms length.

4. Russells girlfriend is throwing him a birthday party this Friday.

5. My composition teachers pet peeve is the misuse of apostrophes.

Lesson 21

Sentence Practice 3

Turn the *of* structures in the following sentences into possessive structures.

Example: ~~The collapse of Enron~~ *Enron's collapse* sent shock waves throughout the energy sector.

1. Sharon ignored the suggestions of her tutor.

2. The business district of my hometown has fallen on bad times.

3. The last scene of that movie was disappointing.

4. I am worried that the decline of the dollar will hurt the economy further.

5. The husband of my best friend has a history class with me.

6. Are you going to watch the beginning of the game?

7. The future of this nation depends on a strong educational system.

8. I witnessed the dismissal of my coworker.

9. The deadline of tomorrow is approaching quicker than I expected.

10. You are not the boss of Helen.

Editing Practice 1

CORRECTED SENTENCES APPEAR ON PAGE 480.

Correct all possession errors in the following paragraph using the first correction as a model. The number in parentheses at the end of the paragraph indicates how many errors you should find.

    You have probably never heard Alfred ~~Wegeners~~ *Wegener's* name. Wegener was born in Berlin in 1880. He got a PhD in astronomy, but his lifes work was the new field of meteorology (the study of weather). As a young man, he became interested in ballooning and, for a time, held the worlds record for altitude. As a balloonist he was well aware of the fact the winds direction and speed on the earths surface did not correspond at all with the winds movement high above the surface. He was the first person to exploit the balloons ability to carry weather instruments high into the atmosphere and to track wind movement at various altitudes. He was one of a group of early researchers who studied a remarkable current of air that circulated around the North Pole. The researchers had discovered what we now call the jet stream. In 1930, he and a colleague disappeared on an expedition to Greenland. His and his colleagues frozen bodies were found a year later. (7)

Lesson 21

Editing Practice 2

Correct all possession errors in the following paragraphs using the first correction as a model. The number in parentheses at the end of each paragraph indicates how many errors you should find.

    Today, ~~Wegeners~~ *Wegener's* name is associated with his highly original theory of continental drift. If you have ever looked at a globe, you couldn't help noticing that the huge bulge on South Americas eastern coastline exactly matches the equally huge indentation on Africas western coastline. Wegener became fascinated with the idea that at some distant time in the past, South Americas and Africas coastlines were joined together in a single continent. If that were indeed the case, then the ancient land formations and fossils of eastern South America should be identical with the ancient land formations and fossils of western Africa. Once Wegener started looking, scientists work in many fields showed the connections. For example, fossils of highly unusual land lizards on South Americas eastern coast were also found on Africas western coast, and nowhere else. Since the lizards couldn't swim, Wegener argued, they must have originated in a single spot that was later split apart by the continents separation. (8)

Wegeners 1915 book, *The Origin of Continents and Oceans*, argued that all of the different continents today had once been part of a single giant supercontinent that he called Pangaea. Needless to say, the scientific communitys reaction was overwhelmingly negative. The books great weakness was its inability to show any mechanism that could split the continents apart and then drive them thousands of miles away from each other. Research in the mid-Atlantic Ocean in the 1950s and 1960s supplied Wegeners missing explanation: plate tectonics. We now know that all the continents are rafts floating on deep, liquid magma and that the continents are driven around by the magmas currents. (5)

Lesson 21

Applying What You Know

Write a paragraph or two describing someone's innovative idea. It could be the work of a scientist or the novel approach of a writer or musician. Try to use at least three possessive forms. Use the *Of* Tip and the Plural Possession Tip to show that your possessives are formed correctly.

The Bottom Line	A **writer's use** of the apostrophe can be checked by using the *Of* Tip.

Unnecessary Apostrophes

EXAMPLE 1 *Nouns with Unnecessary Apostrophes*

Error: ✗ Your sentence has four comma's in it.

                                    commas
Correction: Your sentence has four ~~comma's~~ in it.
                                      ^

EXAMPLE 2 *Last Names with Unnecessary Apostrophes*

Error: ✗ Two George Bush's have been elected president.

                        Bushes
Correction: Two George ~~Bush's~~ have been elected president.
                          ^

What's the Problem?

The apostrophe (') is commonly used to show that letters have been left out of a word to form a *contraction* (Lesson 20) or to show *possession* (Lesson 21). For practically all words, however, it is incorrect to use an apostrophe to show that there is more than one of something. Example 1 illustrates this serious error.

Example 2 shows a particular form this error often takes: Many people mistakenly add an apostrophe and an *s* to form the plural of a last name. An apostrophe should *not* be used to pluralize last names. Even if a last name already ends in *s* (or *sh*), the plural is formed by adding *es*, not an apostrophe. For example, when you are writing about more than one Clinton or Bush, the correct plural forms are *Clintons* and *Bushes*.

Diagnostic Exercise

CORRECTED SENTENCES APPEAR ON PAGE 480.

Correct all errors in the following paragraph using the first correction as a model. The number in parentheses at the end of the paragraph indicates how many errors you should find.

friends
Some old ~~friend's~~ of mine stopped by my apartment for coffee. My
^
roommate's coffeepot was broken, so I made them some instant coffee. I'm

not good at making coffee, but everybody had two cup's apiece. The coffee

was pretty old, yet nobody seemed to care. We talked about our schedule's

for next semester, and we decided we should try to leave some time open

for getting together every now and then. (2)

Fixing This Problem in Your Writing

Here are three tips you can use to determine whether you truly need an apostrophe in your writing. You should apply all three tips, but we introduce each
tip individually for clarity's sake.

Lesson 22

no ⁏

> **OF TIP**   Possessive words can usually be reworded using *of*. Possessive nouns
> need an apostrophe.

The following example passes the *Of* Tip, showing us that *driver's* is
possessive and does, indeed, require an apostrophe:

Example: Our driver's eyesight was poor.

                              ✓
Tip applied: The eyesight <u>of</u> our driver . . .

However, try applying this tip to Example 1:

Example 1:   ✗ Your sentence has four comma's in it.

Tip applied: ✗ ? <u>of</u> the comma

                What does the comma possess? Cannot reword using *of*.

In Example 1, *comma* possesses nothing, so it is impossible to use the *Of* Tip
to correctly rearrange the sentence. Thus, there is no need for a possessive
apostrophe. The word *comma* is merely plural. To correct the sentence, delete
the apostrophe:

                                            commas
Correction: Your sentence has four ~~comma's~~ in it.
                                              ^

> **EXPANSION TIP**   If you can expand a word containing an apostrophe to make up two different words without the apostrophe, then the apostrophe is used as a legitimate contraction of two words. However, if you cannot expand the word with an apostrophe to make two different words, then the apostrophe is not used as a legitimate contraction.

For example, the apostrophe in the following sentence is correctly signaling a legitimate contraction:

Example: We're about ready to leave.

Tip applied: We are (or we were) about ready to leave.

The Expansion Tip shows that the apostrophe in *we're* is a valid use of the apostrophe for making a contraction.

Compare the example above with the following:

Example: I knew that we we're about ready to leave.

Tip applied: ✗ I knew that we we are (or we were) about ready to leave.

                               were
Correction: I knew that we ~~we're~~ about ready to leave.
                                ^

Here the Expansion Tip shows that *we're* contains an unnecessary (and invalid) use of an apostrophe because the two words formed are nonsensical.

Here is the Expansion Tip applied to Example 2:

Example 2:   ✗ Two George Bush's have been elected president.

Bush's cannot be expanded to form two new, uncontracted words, so the apostrophe does not correctly indicate a contraction.

                          Bushes
Correction: Two George ~~Bush's~~ have been elected president.
                             ^

There is one final tip is worth noting, although it covers a rare structure in most students' writing: "special terms" and their plural forms. These terms include abbreviations, numerals for years, symbols, letters used as letters or as grades, numbers, and other unusual characters or figures that are often not even thought of as "words." In the past, some grammar guides permitted the use of an apostrophe to indicate, for example, the plural form of a year. Even now, the guides are not in complete agreement, so we offer the following advice—the safe approach.

Lesson 22

no '

> **"SPECIAL TERM" TIP**   Do not use an apostrophe to form the plural of "special terms" such as years and abbreviations unless the special term is an individual letter.

Letters of the alphabet are the only exceptions (as in *She made all A's* or *There are two* x's *in this word*). Even here, some grammar guides state that you should use an apostrophe *only* with lowercase letters, not with capitals. To be safe, avoid the "plural apostrophe" with all special terms unless you can confer with your teacher (or primary reader) about his or her preference.

Here are examples of special terms in correct plural form:

three DVDs	in the 1990s	no *if*s, *and*s, or *but*s
several 100s	two TVs	five &s

Lesson 22

no ❦

✳ *Putting It All Together*

Identify Unnecessary Apostrophes

____ Use apostrophes only to show ownership (*the captain's hat*) or to indicate there is a contraction (*I'll go*).

____ Do not use an apostrophe to indicate more than one of something. (The only exception involves forming the plural of individual letters, as in *two d's*).

Correct Apostrophe Errors

____ Remove apostrophes that do not fit one of the two situations described above. Most likely, your word should simply end in *s* or *es* rather than *'s*.

Sentence Practice 1

CORRECTED SENTENCES APPEAR ON PAGE 480.

Refer to the tips in this lesson and write *OK* above each correct apostrophe. Then label each correct apostrophe as *contraction* or *possession*. If there is an error, make the necessary change by deleting the apostrophe.

Example: The ~~students'~~ laughed at the teacher's shirt.
          students   *OK — possession*

1. I have three essay's to complete this month.

2. Maria's best friend went on a cruise last summer.

3. All four radio's in my apartment need batteries.

4. My parents went to college back in the 1980's.

5. One of the two Joe Smiths' in this class is an old friend of mine.

 For more practice using apostrophes, go to **Exercise Central** at **bedfordstmartins.com/commonsense**

Sentence Practice 2

CORRECTED SENTENCES APPEAR ON PAGE 481.

Refer to the tips and write *OK* above each correct apostrophe. Then label each correct apostrophe as *contraction* or *possession*. If there is an error, make the necessary change by deleting the apostrophe.

Lesson 22

no ⸮

wrappings

Example: The toys were still inside the plastic ~~wrapping's~~.
                                                              ^

1. You have several class's with me this semester.

2. I need to burn two CD's on your computer.

3. When someone's cell phone went off in class, my English teacher became upset.

4. We aren't ready to leave.

5. Did you see all the camera's in the hallway?

Sentence Practice 3

Rewrite the underlined *of* expression to produce a correct possessive apostrophe.

election's outcome

Example: The ~~outcome of the election~~ was in doubt.
                              ^

1. The success of the team was completely unexpected.

2. The coastline of Canada is absolutely immense.

3. An accident was averted thanks to the vigilance of the crew.

4. We got caught up in the <u>excitement of the children</u>.

5. The <u>worth of the stamps</u> was difficult to establish.

Editing Practice 1

CORRECTED SENTENCES APPEAR ON PAGE 481.

Correct all errors in the following paragraph using the first correction as a model. The number in parentheses at the end of the paragraph indicates how many errors you should find.

Lesson 22

no ˇ

The word *parasite* comes from a Greek word meaning a flunky who
does no honest work but depends entirely on ~~handout's~~ *handouts* from wealthy and
powerful patrons. In biology, the term was adopted to describe a huge
variety of creature's that steal their nourishment from hosts, often causing
their hosts' death. The behavior of parasites' strikes all of us as profoundly
vicious and ugly. One of the best fictional depiction's of parasites is in the
1979 science fiction movie *Alien*. In that movie, the crew of a spaceship investigates a clutch of egg's left on an otherwise lifeless planet. As one of the
crew examines an egg, a crablike thing bursts out of the shell and wraps a
tail around the crewman's neck. By the next day, the crablike thing has
disappeared and the crewman seems normal. Later, the crewman clutches
his stomach in terrible pain, and a little knobby-headed alien pierces
through his skin and leaps out. The alien has laid an egg in the crewman's
abdomen; the egg has hatched and has been devouring his intestines. This
horrible scenario is in fact based on the real behavior of parasitic wasps'
that lay their eggs' in living caterpillars. As the eggs' mature, they devour
the internal organs of the caterpillar, sparing only the organs' necessary
to keep the caterpillar alive. When the eggs are fully mature, they erupt
through the skin of the caterpillar, leaving behind their hollowed-out host
to die. (8)

Editing Practice 2

Correct all errors in the following paragraphs using the first correction as a model. The number in parentheses at the end of each paragraph indicates how many errors you should find.

    By far the worst parasite from the perspective of ~~human's~~ *humans* is malaria. Malaria experts' estimate that as many as half of all the human's who have ever lived on Earth died of malaria. One reason that malaria is such a terribly effective killer is that it has been evolving for a very long time. A substantial number of dinosaur's probably died of malaria. (3)

    As you may know, malaria is spread by only one particular type of mosquito, the female *anopheles*. When a female anopheles mosquito bites an animal that is infected with malaria, thousands of malaria parasites' are sucked up with the victim's blood. The parasites travel to the mosquito's gut, where the parasites' mate with parasites from other bites. The parasites' offspring migrate up to the mosquito's salivary gland, where they are ready to be injected into any and all other creatures' that the mosquito bites. And thus the cycle starts all over again. (3)

Lesson 22

no '

Applying What You Know

Write a paragraph describing what you like to do when you have spare time. Skip lines so that you can revise later. When you are done, see if you can use the apostrophe at least three times (you might have already done so). Trade your paragraph with a partner who will proofread it to determine if all your apostrophes are needed.

The Bottom Line	Writers sometimes add unnecessary apostrophes to plural words. However, only individual letters use apostrophes to form plurals.

Using Apostrophes Correctly

REVIEW

Apostrophes (') are used for several different purposes. This unit presented situations in which apostrophes are required and those in which apostrophes are unnecessary. The following chart points you to the tips that will help you avoid four problems writers encounter in using apostrophes.

TIPS	QUICK FIXES AND EXAMPLES
Lesson 20. Apostrophes in Contractions	
The Expansion Tip (p. 204) helps you place an apostrophe in the correct place in a contraction.	Use an apostrophe in the spot where letters were omitted in a contraction. Error: ✗ You cant believe everything you hear. _can't_ Correction: You ~~cant~~ believe everything ⌃ you hear.
Lesson 21. Apostrophes Showing Possession	
The _Of_ Tip (p. 211) helps you identify possessive forms so you know that an apostrophe is needed. The _Of_ Tip also shows you when an apostrophe should be used with expressions of time or measurement (_a moment's notice_). The Standard Tip (p. 212) tells you how to make most singular nouns possessive. The Plural Possession Tip (p. 213) helps you make plural nouns possessive.	Add _'s_ to make most singular nouns possessive. For plural nouns that already end in _s_, add just an apostrophe; for those that do not, add _'s_. Error: ✗ We looked for Jaynes pet turtle everywhere. _Jayne's_ Correction: We looked for ~~Jaynes~~ pet turtle ⌃ everywhere.

TIPS	QUICK FIXES AND EXAMPLES
Lesson 22. Unnecessary Apostrophes	
The tips in Lessons 20 and 21 help you remember the *only* instances in which apostrophes should be used.	Use apostrophes only to show possession, to mark expressions of time or measurement, or to show plurality of numbers and letters. Do not use an apostrophe to form a plural.
	Error: ✗ I'm sorry, but your essay had too many error's in it.
	Correction: I'm sorry, but your essay had too many ~~error's~~ *errors* in it.

Review Test

Unit Six

review

Correct all errors in the following paragraphs using the first correction as a model. The number in parentheses at the end of each paragraph indicates how many errors you should find.

Americans'
~~American's~~ attitude toward flying has changed since the industry

was deregulated. In the day's when fares and routes were strictly

regulated, airlines could compete with each other only in terms of each air-

lines service and convenience. Customers preference for airlines

was often decided by the quality of meal service. I can remember their

serving three-course meals with free wine on linen tablecloths to coach

customer's. Coach passengers meals on international flights were often

rather elegant, more like first-class passengers meals today. Many

airplanes on international flights had a passengers lounge with armchairs,

couches, and an open bar for everyones use. (8)

In the world of todays deregulated industry, things are very

different. Deregulations main effect was to force airlines into direct,

open competition. Since airlines revenue is highly sensitive to passenger

load (the average percentage of seats' occupied on each flight), airlines began cutting prices to ensure that every planes seating capacity was maximized. The more people on a flight, the more profitable it was. Airlines concerns about passengers leg room quickly became a thing of the past. Attracting passengers by offering the lowest fare means that airlines have to cut costs at every turn. One of the fare wars first casualties was meal service. Southwest Airlines even jokes about it's "two-course" meals—peanuts and pretzels. (9)

Unit Six

review

Using Other Punctuation and Capitalizing Words

OVERVIEW

The Nuts and Bolts of Other Punctuation and Capitalization

This unit covers capitalization and the remaining marks of punctuation most likely to cause problems for writers.

Lesson 23 shows you how to use periods, commas, semicolons, and other punctuation with quotation marks.

> Example: ✗ The instructor warned, "This next test will be harder than the last one".
>
> Correction: The instructor warned, "This next test will be
> *one."*
> harder than the last ~~one".~~
> ^

Lesson 24 shows you how to use semicolons correctly in your writing. Semicolons have the same function as periods: Both are used to signal the end of a complete sentence. Semicolons, however, are sometimes confused with colons.

> Example: ✗ Soy sauce contains the following ingredients; water, extract of soya beans, wheat flour, and salt.
>
> Correction: Soy sauce contains the following ingredients ⫶ water, extract of soya beans, wheat flour, and salt. ^

Lesson 25 shows you how to use colons correctly in your writing. The most common use of a colon is to introduce a list. A frequent mistake is to use a colon to introduce a list that is actually a required part of the sentence. In this case, the colon is incorrect.

> Example: ✗ To remove this wallpaper, I will need: a sponge, a bucket of warm water, a commercial stripping solution, and a 4-inch putty knife.

Correction: To remove this wallpaper, I will need⫽ a sponge,
              a bucket of warm water, a commercial stripping solution,
              and a 4-inch putty knife.

Lesson 26 gives you some guidelines for capitalizing certain words. **Proper nouns** and **proper adjectives** are capitalized to show that they are the official names of specific, individual persons, places, or institutions. Other special capitalization rules govern, for example, names of ethnic groups, languages, and certain academic courses.

Example: ✗ Gustavo barra, my Professor, has taught english and
             french in brazil, bolivia, and los Angeles.

                        Barra   professor   English
Correction: Gustavo ~~barra~~, my ~~Professor~~, has taught ~~english~~
                        French   Brazil Bolivia   Los
              and ~~french~~ in ~~brazil~~, ~~bolivia~~, and ~~los~~ Angeles.

Quotation Marks with Other Punctuation

EXAMPLE 1

Error: ✗ Edgar Allan Poe wrote "The Raven", "Annabel Lee", and "The Bells".

Correction: Edgar Allan Poe wrote "The Raven,"/ "Annabel Lee,"/ and "The Bells."/

EXAMPLE 2

Error: ✗ Bjorg asked, "Do you want to play tennis"?

Correction: Bjorg asked, "Do you want to play tennis?"/

What's the Problem?

American punctuation style has a number of rules that govern where periods, commas, colons, semicolons, question marks, and exclamation points should go when they are used together with quotation marks. Some of these rules make sense, but others seem arbitrary. It might help you remember these conventions if you think of them as the "Rule of Two." *Two* punctuation marks (periods and commas) go inside the quotation marks, *two* other marks (colons and semicolons) go outside, and *two* others (question marks and exclamation points) can go either place depending on the meaning of the sentence.

- **Two Go Inside**

  Period: "I know what you mean."

  Comma: The band played "Satin Doll," "Take the 'A' Train," and "Misty."

- **Two Go Outside**

  Semicolon: I didn't like "Satin Doll"; the tempo was too slow.

  Colon: All three horn players soloed during "Misty": the trumpeter, the trombonist, and the saxophonist.

- **Two Can Go Either Place, Depending on Meaning**

Question mark (inside):   She asked me, "Do you like jazz?"

Question mark (outside):   What didn't you like about "Satin Doll"?

Exclamation point (inside):   Someone yelled, "Encore!"

Exclamation point (outside):   I want to hear "Autumn Leaves"!

Now you should be able to see what went wrong in the two example sentences. In Example 1, the commas are outside the quotation marks, where they should never be. In Example 2, the question mark is in the wrong place. What is being quoted (*"Do you want to play tennis"*) is a question. Therefore, the question mark should go *inside* the quotation marks along with the rest of the question.

Diagnostic Exercise

CORRECTED SENTENCES APPEAR ON PAGE 481.

Using the Rule of Two as a guide, correct any misplaced punctuation in the following sentences. If a sentence is correct as written, write *OK*.

Example: The British singer Adele had one of her biggest hits with "Rolling in the Deep**.**"**/**

1. She described this song as a "dark bluesy gospel disco tune".

2. Are you still writing a paper about Langston Hughes's poem "I, Too, Sing America?"

3. Someone screamed, "Watch out for that tree!"

4. The sign read, "Keep Out", but I asked myself, "Who would mind if I went in"?

5. I have a hard time understanding the plot of the story "An Occurrence at Owl Creek Bridge," yet my paper on it is due soon.

Fixing This Problem in Your Writing

Knowing where to place periods, commas, semicolons, and colons with quotation marks is simply a matter of memorizing the "Rule of Two": periods and commas go *inside* the quotation marks; semicolons and colons go *outside* the quotation marks. So far, so good.

However, the placement of question marks and exclamation points is more complicated because their placement depends on the meaning of the sentence. The following tip will help you decide where to put question marks and exclamation points used with quotations.

> **UNQUOTE TIP**   Take whatever is inside the quotation marks out of the sentence and out of the quotation marks. Now, how would you punctuate this new sentence? If you would use a question mark or an exclamation point, then this same punctuation belongs *inside* the closing quotation mark in the original sentence.

Let's apply this tip to Example 2, taking what is inside the quotation marks out of the sentence and out of quotation marks:

> Example 2:   ✗ Bjorg asked, "Do you want to play tennis"?
>
> Tip applied: Do you want to play tennis?

As you can see, the quoted material, *Do you want to play tennis*, is a question, so we correct the sentence by placing the question mark inside the closing quotation mark as follows:

> Correction: Bjorg asked, "Do you want to play tennis?"

Here is an example in which the question mark belongs outside the quotation mark:

> Example: ✗ Have you read Edgar Allan Poe's poem "The Raven?"
>
> Tip applied: The Raven
>
> *The Raven* is not a question, so the question mark belongs outside the closing quotation mark.
>
> Correction: Have you read Edgar Allan Poe's poem "The Raven"?

Here is an especially tricky case in which the quoted material is a question, but, in addition, the whole sentence is also a question:

> Example: Who said, "May we leave early"

Does the question mark belong inside or outside the quotation marks? The Unquote Tip works even here. Because *May we leave early* is a question, the question mark belongs inside the closing quotation mark:

> Tip applied: May we leave early?
>
> Correction: Who said, "May we leave early?"

Lesson 23

" "

Keep in mind this one final rule of thumb. Only one closing punctuation mark (period, question mark, or exclamation point) can ever appear after the last word in a sentence. In other words, you can't have one closing punctuation mark inside the quotation mark and another one outside.

Error: ✗ Who said, "May we leave early?"?

Correction: Who said, "May we leave early?"~~?~~

✳ *Putting It All Together*

Identify Errors in Using Quotation Marks with Other Punctuation

_____ Anytime you use quotation marks, check to see whether you have used other punctuation marks correctly.

Correct Errors in Using Quotation Marks with Other Punctuation

_____ Place periods and commas *inside* quotation marks.

_____ Place semicolons and colons *outside* quotation marks.

_____ For question marks and exclamation points, use the Unquote Tip to determine whether the material inside the quotation marks needs a question mark or an exclamation point. If it does, then the quotation mark or exclamation point goes *inside* the quotation mark. Otherwise, the quotation mark or exclamation point goes *outside* the quotation mark.

Sentence Practice 1

CORRECTED SENTENCES APPEAR ON PAGE 481.

For each sentence, take the material that is inside quotation marks out of quotation marks. Using the Unquote Tip, correct any sentence that has punctuation errors. Write *OK* if the sentence is correct.

Letter from Birmingham Jail

Example: Who wrote "Letter from Birmingham Jail~~?~~"?
                                                              ^

1. Gage asked, "When can we eat"?

2. My least favorite Black Eyed Peas' song is "Where Is the Love?"

3. The coach yelled at the top of her lungs, "Quit goofing off!"

4. The title of my poem is "Are You Ready to Rumble?"

5. Charlene responded, "Why are you following me"?

 For more practice using quotation marks, go to **Exercise Central** at
bedfordstmartins.com/commonsense

Sentence Practice 2

CORRECTED SENTENCES APPEAR ON PAGE 481.

For each sentence, take the material that is inside quotation marks out of
quotation marks. Using the Unquote Tip, correct any sentence that has punctuation errors. Write *OK* if the sentence is correct.

> **Example:** Can you tell me the meaning of the word
> *alliteration*
> "alliteration̸"?̸
> ^

1. Did she say, "The store opens at noon?"

2. Didn't we read the essay entitled "A Modest Proposal"?

3. Do you know the opening lyrics to "Are You Lonesome Tonight?"

4. The angry customer screamed, "Don't walk away from me"!

5. Do you know who asked, "Can we have an open-book test?"

Lesson 23

" "

Sentence Practice 3

Combine the following sentences by using the title or quotation in the second
sentence in place of *IT* in the first sentence.

> **Example:** They danced to IT. "Isn't She Lovely?"
>
> **Answer:** *They danced to "Isn't She Lovely?"*

1. On last night's *American Idol,* someone badly sang IT. "What's My
   Name?"

2. The sergeant shouted IT. "Get in formation!"

3. The annoying child kept asking IT. "Are we there yet?"

4. My boss asked IT. "Are you late again?"

5. Somebody yelled IT. "Watch out!"

Editing Practice 1

CORRECTED SENTENCES APPEAR ON PAGE 481.

Correct all errors in the following passage using the first correction as a model. The number in parentheses at the end of the passage indicates how many errors you should find.

My girlfriend sleepily asked, "Why are you calling me so late?"/ It

was 2:00 A.M., and I apparently had awakened her.

"Sorry," I muttered, realizing the time. "I've been studying all night

and needed a break". This apparently wasn't the right answer.

She yelled, "I was sound asleep"! After another moment, she added,

"Do you think I stayed up just in case you needed to call someone"?

"Well, I guess this is a bad time to call," I meekly suggested. "I'll

let you go back to sleep". She hung up before I could say anything else.

I decided that cramming all night before a test was a bad idea for several

reasons. (4)

Editing Practice 2

Correct all errors in the following paragraph using the first correction as a model. The number in parentheses at the end of the paragraph indicates how many errors you should find.

Many conflicts have given rise to what might be called "war songs."/

Each war, it seems, becomes the subject of popular music. World War I,

for example, had its protest songs, such as "I Didn't Raise My Boy to Be

a Soldier". This song captured many Americans' desire to stay out of the

war. Once the United States entered the war, though, many songs served

to rally the troops and the general public. One of the most famous is "Over

There". All good American parents and "sweethearts," according to this

song, should be proud and eager to send their loved ones to fight in the war.

George M. Cohan received a Congressional Medal of Honor for

composing this immensely popular song. In Irving Berlin's "Oh, How I Hate to Get Up in the Morning", however, the singer is less enthusiastic about fighting in the trenches, taking a lighthearted view of military life but still celebrating victory. (3)

Applying What You Know

Write a hypothetical conversation between you and a friend in which you discuss a movie that you have seen recently. Use quotation marks to represent dialogue. After you finish, check to see if you used other punctuation correctly with the quotation marks.

The Bottom Line	Remember this: "Periods and commas always go inside quotation marks. Colons and semicolons always go outside quotation marks."

Lesson 23

" "

Semicolons

EXAMPLE 1   *Semicolon Used Instead of Colon*

Error: ✗ Li brought the drinks; lemonade, cola, and iced tea.

Correction: Li brought the drinks:/ lemonade, cola, and iced tea.
                                  ^

EXAMPLE 2   *Semicolon Used Instead of Comma*

Error: ✗ He forgot water; which is what I want.

Correction: He forgot water,;/ which was what I want.
                            ^

What's the Problem?

A **semicolon** is easier to use than you might think; however, a misused semi-colon can be particularly distracting. Sometimes, writers confuse semicolons with colons (as in Example 1) and incorrectly use a semicolon to introduce a list. (See Lesson 25 on correctly using colons to begin lists.) Other times, semicolons are mistakenly used when a comma is needed (as in Example 2).

Many people don't understand the function of a semicolon. Its main use is to separate two related **independent clauses**—two groups of words that could be separated by a period. For example:

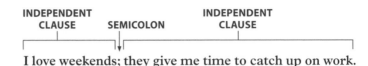

| INDEPENDENT CLAUSE | SEMICOLON | INDEPENDENT CLAUSE |

Example: I love weekends; they give me time to catch up on work.

Diagnostic Exercise

CORRECTED SENTENCES APPEAR ON PAGE 481.

Correct all semicolon errors in the following sentences. If there are no errors, write *OK* above the sentence.

Example: Human evolution occurred when food choices were far
            fewer than they are today;, and far lower in fat and sugar.
                                     ^

1. Natural selection resulted in humans having excellent mechanisms to defend against weight loss; but poor mechanisms for preventing obesity.

2. As a person's weight increases, so do the chances of him or her developing several major health problems; diabetes, heart disease, stroke, and even some types of cancer.

3. To measure obesity, the World Health Organization uses body mass index; this is defined as body weight in kilograms divided by the square of a person's height.

4. In the United States, obesity is overtaking smoking as the major cause of death; a trend that is unlikely to change soon.

5. Obesity depends largely on genetic factors; for instance, adopted children's weight is more likely to match that of their biological, rather than their adoptive, parents.

Fixing This Problem in Your Writing

The following tip can help you determine whether you have correctly used a semicolon to join two independent clauses.

Lesson 24

;

IMAGINARY PERIOD TIP Can you replace the semicolon with a period? If there is a complete sentence on both sides of the imaginary period, the semicolon is correct.

Let's apply this tip to a correct example:

Example: **Baby giraffes are tall; their average height is six feet.**

INDEPENDENT CLAUSE   INDEPENDENT CLAUSE

Tip applied: **Baby giraffes are tall. Their average height is six feet.**

Changing semicolon to period = two complete sentences = correct use of semicolon

In contrast, the Imaginary Period Tip reveals that Example 1 is an error because what comes after the new period is a **fragment**. (See Lesson 1 on fragments.) *Lemonade, cola, and iced tea* cannot stand alone as a sentence, so there is an error in Example 1:

Example 1: **✗ Li brought the drinks; lemonade, cola, and iced tea.**

INDEPENDENT
CLAUSE   FRAGMENT

Tip applied: Li brought the drinks. **X** Lemonade, cola, and iced tea.

Changing semicolon to period = fragment = semicolon error

If you know the rule for using colons (see Lesson 25), it is easy to correct Example 1:

Correction: Li brought the drinks:/ lemonade, cola, and iced tea.

Do not change a semicolon to a colon unless you understand the rules for colons. If you are unsure, reword the original sentence so that it has a structure you know how to punctuate. For instance, another correction of Example 1 is *Li brought lemonade, cola, and iced tea.*

The Imaginary Period Tip also reveals the error in Example 2. As usual, it is the second part of the example that becomes a fragment when we apply the Imaginary Period Tip.

Example 2:   **X** He forgot water; which is what I want.

INDEPENDENT
CLAUSE   FRAGMENT

Tip applied: He forgot water. **X** Which is what I want.

Changing semicolon to period = fragment = semicolon error

To correct the error, use a comma instead of a semicolon.

Correction: He forgot water,/ which is what I want.

Avoid combining just any two ideas with a semicolon; join ideas that are very closely connected. Semicolons are typically used to show the following kinds of relationships.

- **Cause-and-effect** relation between two ideas:

  The attic had not been cleaned in years; it smelled of dust and mold.

- **Generalization-and-example** relation between two ideas:

  Telephone solicitors always call at dinnertime; last night, we were interrupted twice during our meal.

- **Statement-and-comment** relation between two ideas:

  My wife considers *The Three Stooges* to be utterly moronic; I still think they are pretty funny.

In addition, semicolons are often used with **transitional terms** (words like *however, thus, nevertheless, therefore*) to help the reader see how the idea in the second part of the sentence relates to the idea in the first part. When using a transitional term right after a semicolon, put a comma after the term. (See Lesson 14 on transitional terms.)

✳ *Putting It All Together*

Identify Semicolon Errors in Your Writing

_____ Most semicolons are used to join two independent clauses that are closely related. To confirm that you have correctly used a semicolon in this way, pretend to replace the semicolon with a period. If this imaginary period produces two complete sentences, the semicolon is correct.

_____ If you are left with a fragment on either side of the imaginary period, the semicolon is incorrect.

Correct Semicolon Errors in Your Writing

_____ You can usually fix semicolon errors by replacing the semicolon with a colon or a comma. If you are not sure which replacement is correct, reword the original to make a more familiar sentence structure for you to punctuate.

Lesson 24

;

Sentence Practice 1

CORRECTED SENTENCES APPEAR ON PAGE 482.

Using the Imaginary Period Tip, examine the part of the sentence before the semicolon and the part after the semicolon. If one part can stand alone as a complete sentence, write *OK* above it. If the other part cannot stand alone as a complete sentence, write *X* above it. If either part cannot stand alone, correct the semicolon error.

Example:	David wanted to borrow my book; the one about home improvement.
	OK *X*
Tip applied:	David wanted to borrow my book. The one about home improvement.
Answer:	David wanted to borrow my book̸, the one about home improvement.

1. Next week, we will have a major test; one that will be difficult.

2. Delaware's nickname is First State; it was the first state to ratify the Constitution.

3. My car is too loud; I think it needs a new muffler.

4. Allyson and I went to the same high school; Pine Tree High School.

5. Ken brought several items; napkins, glasses, and forks.

 For more practice using semicolons, go to **Exercise Central** at **bedfordstmartins.com/commonsense**

Sentence Practice 2

CORRECTED SENTENCES APPEAR ON PAGE 482.

Using the Imaginary Period Tip, examine the part of the sentence before the semicolon and the part after the semicolon. If one part can stand alone as a complete sentence, write *OK* above it. If the other part cannot stand alone as a complete sentence, write *X* above it. If either part cannot stand alone, correct the semicolon error.

Lesson 24

;

Example: I hate three things; soggy pancakes, runny eggs, and burnt toast.

                                   OK   *X*

Tip applied: I hate three things. Soggy pancakes, runny eggs, and burnt toast.

Answer: I hate three things**;** soggy pancakes, runny eggs, and burnt toast.   ^

1. Her truck failed to start; because the battery was dead.

2. I read an article about Ralph Bunche; the first African American to win the Nobel Peace Prize.

3. Annie ordered a parfait; a dessert made of ice cream, fruit, and syrup.

4. Actor Spencer Tracy was asked to play the Penguin on the TV show *Batman*; he declined when he was told he could not kill Batman.

5. I need to go to the store; which is only about one mile away.

Sentence Practice 3

Use a semicolon to combine each sentence below with a closely related idea. Make sure your new idea could stand alone as a separate sentence.

Example: The song "I'd Like to Teach the World to Sing" originated as a Coca-Cola ad.

Answer: *The song "I'd Like to Teach the World to Sing" originated as a Coca-Cola ad; the song was a major hit in 1972.*

1. My physics teacher was late again.
2. This physics book cost more than I expected.
3. Pineapples were first discovered in South America.
4. This dorm still does not have wireless Internet service.
5. Blue M&M candies replaced tan ones in 1995.
6. A cell phone went off during a test in my calculus class.
7. James Buchanan is the only American president who never married.
8. Australia is the only continent without glaciers.
9. A popular topping for pizza in Australia is eggs.
10. My laptop computer is not working as well as I expected.

Editing Practice 1

CORRECTED SENTENCES APPEAR ON PAGE 482.

Correct all errors in the following paragraphs using the first correction as a model. The number in parentheses at the end of each paragraph indicates how many errors you should find.

Langston Hughes is one of the best-known African American poets**;** his fame having begun in 1915, when he was thirteen. At that time, he was elected poet of his graduating class; an unusual selection not merely because he was one of only two African American students in his class but because he had never written any poems. Hughes explained that nobody else in the class had written any poetry either. His classmates elected him; however, because they assumed that poetry requires rhythm and that he must have rhythm because of his ethnicity. (2)

Even though such reasoning had an element of stereotyping, Hughes was inspired; and wrote a graduation poem that the teachers and students

Lesson 24

;

enthusiastically received. He went on to publish many types of writing;
poems, plays, short stories, children's books, histories, and song lyrics, just
to name a few. (2)

Editing Practice 2

CORRECTED SENTENCES APPEAR ON PAGE 482.

Correct all errors in the following paragraph using the first correction as a
model. The number in parentheses at the end of the paragraph indicates how
many errors you should find.

Something needs to change at my apartment/ because I cannot cope
with the mess any longer. Six months ago, it seemed like living with two
high school friends would be great; we liked hanging around each other and
shared the same interests. What I did not fully understand was that they
were (and are) slobs. One likes cooking; which I think is a great hobby. It's
not so great, however, when he doesn't clean up the mess that he makes.
My other roommate leaves clothes all over the house; even in our one
bathroom. One time, I counted what seemed like half of his entire wardrobe
on the bathroom floor; four pairs of jeans, three pairs of dress pants, ten
T-shirts, and five dress shirts. Neither of my roommates is bothered by the
messiness of our apartment; they seem to thrive in such conditions. I am
not a fanatic about cleanliness; however, I cannot stand it when people seem
to expect other people to clean up after the mess they make. (3)

Editing Practice 3

Correct all errors in the following paragraphs using the first correction as a
model. The number in parentheses at the end of each paragraph indicates
how many errors you should find.

Our basketball team has a new coach this year/, Carl McFarlane.
The previous coach was offered a position at Utah State University; after

they made an offer he could not refuse. Fans here were disappointed when the old coach left, but Coach McFarlane has proven to be a popular choice. He had eight winning seasons in a row when coaching at the University of Georgia; in addition, his teams were usually ranked in the top twenty. (1)

There was some controversy about his salary; Coach McFarlane earns more than anyone else on the university payroll. He also receives several opportunities for bonuses; especially if his team wins the conference title. At first, I thought he was overpaid, but I have changed my thinking. For one thing; 60 percent of his salary comes from money donated to the athletic program. Contrary to what some people think, no funds are taken from academics to pay the coach's salary. A record number of season tickets have already been sold; maybe that indicates the school will be able to recoup some of the money spent on Coach McFarlane's salary. (2)

Lesson 24

;

Applying What You Know

Write a paragraph describing a sports team you like or dislike (or a paragraph explaining why you do not have a favorite sports team). Do not use semicolons just yet. Trade your draft with a partner. In your partner's draft, look for two places where you could use a semicolon to combine ideas that are very closely connected and worth emphasizing. (Add a transitional term after the semicolon, if you wish.) See if your partner agrees with your choices or has other ideas about where semicolons could best be used.

The Bottom Line	What comes *before* a semicolon should be able to stand alone; what comes *afterward* should also be able to stand alone.

Colons

EXAMPLE 1

Error: ✗ Liliana bought: milk, cereal, and sugar.

Correction: Liliana bought⁄ milk, cereal, and sugar.

EXAMPLE 2

Error: ✗ For our trip, be sure to bring items such as: books,
              clothes, and lots of money.

Correction: For our trip, be sure to bring items such as⁄ books,
              clothes, and lots of money.

What's the Problem?

A **colon** has several functions. One is to introduce a quotation. Another common but often misunderstood function of the colon is to introduce *certain types* of lists. This lesson focuses on colons used with lists because they account for many writers' errors with colons.

   A colon is used to introduce a list that is *not* needed for the sentence to be grammatically correct. In the following example, the colon is used correctly because the sentence would be complete even if you left out the list following the colon:

                        COMPLETE SENTENCE
                 ┌──────────────┴──────────────┐
Example: I called three friends: Jose, Tyrone, and Mark.

              The part before the colon is a complete sentence, so the colon
              is OK.

A colon *cannot* introduce a list if the list is needed for the sentence to be complete. For instance, the lists in Examples 1 and 2 are needed for the sentence to be complete. Leaving them out would create **fragments** (see Lesson 1). Therefore, these lists should *not* be introduced by a colon.

One reason this error occurs is that many people mistakenly associate colons with *any* type of list. But remember, you should use a colon only when you could delete the list and still have a grammatical sentence.

Diagnostic Exercise

CORRECTED SENTENCES APPEAR ON PAGE 482.

Correct all colon errors in the following sentences. If there are no errors, write *OK* above the sentence.

> Example: The recipe calls for several ingredients we lack,
> including/ yeast, cornmeal, and beer.

1. It is almost impossible to find English words that rhyme with these four terms: *purple, month, orange,* and *silver.*

2. Please remember to pack toiletry essentials such as: toothpaste, a toothbrush, deodorant, and shampoo.

3. You can probably guess that some of the most common surnames in the United States are: Smith, Johnson, Williams, Jones, and Brown.

4. The Rocky Mountain states are comprised of the following: Idaho, Wyoming, Montana, Nevada, Utah, Colorado, New Mexico, and Arizona.

5. Nicole suggested that you immediately contact several people, such as: Maria, Paul, Denise, and Stephanie.

Lesson 25

Fixing This Problem in Your Writing

Here is a tip that can help you determine whether a colon is correctly used with a list.

> **IMAGINARY PERIOD TIP**   If you replace the colon with a period, would the part *before* the period be a *complete* sentence? If so, the colon is probably correct.

Why does this tip work? It reveals whether the list is a necessary part of a grammatical sentence. If the list is necessary, *do not* use a colon:

Grammatically complete sentence + Colon = **Correct**

Fragment + Colon = **Incorrect**

The Imaginary Period Tip reveals that the colon is incorrect in Example 1 because *Liliana bought* is not a complete sentence.

Example 1:   ✗ Liliana bought: milk, cereal, and sugar.

FRAGMENT   More words needed here

Tip applied: ✗ Liliana bought.

Fragment + Colon = Incorrect

Correction: Liliana bought⁄ milk, cereal, and sugar.

Delete the colon to correct the sentence.

When we apply the Imaginary Period Tip to Example 2, we see that what comes before the colon again cannot stand alone as a grammatical sentence (words are obviously missing):

Example 2:   ✗ For our trip, be sure to bring items such as: books, clothes, and lots of money.

FRAGMENT   More words needed here

Tip applied: ✗ For our trip, be sure to bring items such as.

Fragment + Colon = Incorrect

Correction: For our trip, be sure to bring items such as⁄ books, clothes, and lots of money.

When you see an error like this, the correction is usually simple: Delete the colon. Rarely, in fact, is any punctuation needed at all.

Note how the Imaginary Period Tip can confirm that a colon is used correctly:

Example: Chris took two science courses: Physics 101 and Biology 210.

COMPLETE SENTENCE

Tip applied: Chris took two science courses.

Grammatically complete sentence + Colon = Correct

In fact, leaving out the colon in the above example would be an error. Most students, however, create colon errors by using them too often, rather than not often enough.

Lesson 25

MORE EXAMPLES

Lists with Colons

My roommate has two pets: an iguana and a poodle.

We found three items under the couch: a candy bar, my reading glasses, and a beer bottle.

Lists without Colons

Simón Bolivar liberated five South American countries, including Bolivia, Colombia, and Peru.

For this course, you need to bring a calculator, graph paper, two textbooks, and several erasers.

✳ *Putting It All Together*

Identify Colon Errors

____ Each time you use a colon to introduce a list, see whether what comes *before* the colon could stand alone as a complete, grammatical sentence.

Correct Colon Errors

____ If what comes before the colon *cannot* stand alone, do not use a colon to introduce the list.

____ If what comes before the colon *can* stand alone, you can use a colon to introduce the list.

Lesson 25

:

Sentence Practice 1

CORRECTED SENTENCES APPEAR ON PAGE 482.

Determine whether the colon is correct by applying the Imaginary Period Tip. Write *OK* above colons that are used correctly. Correct any colons that are used incorrectly.

Example: To mend your pants, I will need: scissors, thread, a needle, and gratitude.

Tip applied: *To mend your pants, I will need.*

Correction: To mend your pants, I will need/ scissors, thread, a needle, and gratitude.

1. Use the proper form to order ordinary supplies such as: pens, paper, and paperclips.

2. My friend Kamilah has lived in several countries, including: Mexico, Brazil, and Ireland.

3. This literature course has two prerequisites: English 101 and English 102.

4. Jeremy said that he has two conflicting desires: to have his cake and to eat it, too.

5. In fall, I am enrolling in: Biology 101, History 101, English 102, and Math 220.

 For more practice using colons, go to **Exercise Central** at
bedfordstmartins.com/commonsense

Sentence Practice 2

CORRECTED SENTENCES APPEAR ON PAGE 482.

Lesson 25

Determine whether the colon is correct by applying the Imaginary Period Tip. Write *OK* above colons that are used correctly. Correct any colons that are used incorrectly.

Example: The subjects I like to read about are: Chinese history, dog breeding, and finance.

Tip applied: *The subjects I like to read about are.*

Correction: The subjects I like to read about are/ Chinese history, dog breeding, and finance.

1. Some famous people had dyslexia, such as: Leonardo da Vinci, Winston Churchill, Albert Einstein, and George Patton.

2. Remember to buy everything we need to clean the apartment: soap, sponges, and a mop.

3. Native Americans added many words to English: *totem, tomahawk, hickory, raccoon,* and other common terms.

4. Many languages have contributed to English, especially: French, Latin, and German.

5. New words in English arise from many sources, including: gang culture, popular music, and the computer industry.

Sentence Practice 3

Combine the sentences by using a colon and deleting unnecessary words.

> **Example:**   The ice cream came in three flavors. The flavors were chocolate, strawberry, and vanilla.
>
> **Answer:**   *The ice cream came in three flavors: chocolate, strawberry, and vanilla.*

1. The poems you should read for tomorrow are as follows. The poems are "Wishes for Sons," "The Big Heart," and "Expect Nothing."

2. I dislike three professional football teams. These teams are the Giants, the Bears, and the Chargers.

3. You need to remember two things. These two things are to e-mail me often and to be careful with your money.

4. My boss said that I can work more hours during three months. These three months are November, December, and May.

5. In my last essay, I somehow misused three different types of punctuation. These three types were colons, semicolons, and quotation marks.

Editing Practice 1

CORRECTED SENTENCES APPEAR ON PAGE 483.

Correct all errors in the following paragraphs using the first correction as a model. The number in parentheses at the end of each paragraph indicates how many errors you should find.

My college sponsors various trips for students, including/ rafting, skiing, and hiking trips. This fall, I am going on one of the hiking trips. There is a fee involved, but it is still an affordable trip. I have to supply my own: water container, snacks, and backpack. However, the school provides several things: water, lunch, first-aid kits, and even insect repellent. Some items I definitely plan to leave at home are: my cell phone, my MP3 player, and my credit cards. (2)

I wanted a few of my friends to come, such as: my roommate, his brother, and two guys who work with me at the grocery store. They declined. I myself love to go on long walks. Last year, I hiked in several places: northern Alabama, southern Kentucky, and along the coastline in Georgia. Sure, hiking can be a little tedious at times, and you have to be fit to walk several hours a day. However, the rewards include: getting away from the noise of the city, strengthening your leg muscles, and spending time with people who also love hiking. Compared to other hobbies and activities, it's also pretty cheap. (2)

Editing Practice 2

Correct all errors in the following paragraph using the first correction as a model. The number in parentheses at the end of the paragraph indicates how many errors you should find.

Two professions that seem unlikely to overlap are/ acting and politics. However, an actor's political experience can sometimes help his or her acting career. For example, though many people know him from his role as District Attorney Arthur Branch on *Law & Order*, Fred Dalton Thompson served as a United States Senator from 1994 through 2003. Thompson has also been involved with political groups such as: the International Security Advisory Board, the American Enterprise Institute, and the Council on Foreign Relations. Casting directors must appreciate Thompson's background in politics because he is often chosen to play governmental figures. In addition to playing a D.A. on television, many of Thompson's movie roles have been political: F.B.I. agent, director of the C.I.A., major general, senator, and White House Chief of Staff. Thompson is not the only person in the entertainment industry with political experience, though. Some other actors who have also been involved in politics include: Clint Eastwood, Al Franken, Jerry Springer, Jesse Ventura, and Kal Penn.

Lesson 25

Applying What You Know

Colons have various functions. See what sorts of colons you find in a magazine article or newspaper. For your next class meeting, bring examples of at least three uses of a colon. Be ready to explain to the class the function of each example—what the colon is doing in the sentence.

The Bottom Line	When using a colon to introduce a list, remember these two steps: replace the colon with a period and see whether what comes before the period is a complete sentence.

Capitalization

EXAMPLE 1   *Capitalization Needed*

Error: ✗ My english teacher asked us to read stories by
                Flannery O'Connor and other writers from the south.

                                English
Correction: My ~~english~~ teacher asked us to read stories by
                    ^
                                                        South
                Flannery O'Connor and other writers from the ~~south~~.
                                                                ^

EXAMPLE 2   *Unnecessary Capitalization*

Error: ✗ How hard were your Math classes in High School?

                                    math   *high school*
Correction: How hard were your ~~Math~~ classes in ~~High School~~?
                                      ^   ^

What's the Problem?

Some words (**proper nouns** and **proper adjectives**) should be capitalized
to show they are the official names or nicknames of specific persons, places,
things, or events. In addition, many words are capitalized because they are derived from official names. In Example 1, *English* must be capitalized because
it is derived from the name of a country (England). Also, *South* should be
capitalized since people widely recognize it as the name of a specific region.

More general words are not capitalized. In Example 2, *math* is a **common noun** that should *not* be capitalized because it is a general term for a
type of class. Similarly, *high school* is a general term, *not* the name of a specific
school. Compare these common nouns with the proper nouns *Calculus I* and
Lewis and Clark High School.

Capitalization is not an issue in speech, so the rules can be difficult to
learn. Compounding the problem is the fact that capitalization varies according to how words are used in a sentence (compare *My uncle is here* with *I saw
Uncle Brett there*). You must be careful because errors in capitalization can

confuse readers by sending the wrong message about whether a word is the specific name of somebody (or something) or whether the word is merely a general description.

Diagnostic Exercise

CORRECTED SENTENCES APPEAR ON PAGE 483.

Correct all errors in the following paragraph using the first correction as a model. The number in parentheses at the end of the paragraph indicates how many errors you should find.

> *Tecumseh*
> The name ~~tecumseh~~ translates as "Shooting Star." This is a fitting
> ^
> name for the shawnee leader who reached great fame among Indians dur-
> ing Thomas Jefferson's Presidency. From Canada to Georgia and West to
> the Mississippi, Tecumseh was considered a charismatic Chief. He was a
> gifted and natural Commander, equal parts politician and warrior. (5)

Fixing This Problem in Your Writing

Lesson 26

cap

Because some capitalization guidelines vary according to the writer's profession or field of study, always consult the handbook, style guide, or dictionary suggested by your teacher or readers for capitalization guidelines. The following are a few tips that are valid no matter what class, profession, or reader you might have.

> **PERSON TIP**   Capitalize a person's title or a family term when (1) it is followed by a proper name or (2) it is used in *place* of the person's name.

A person's title would be something like *Senator*, *Associate Dean*, or *General*. A family term might be *Uncle* or *Mother*. These words are not always capitalized—just when they are used before a proper name or as if they are the person's name. First, then, you have to see how these words are used in the sentence, as in the following correct example:

> No cap: *Not* used in place of a person's real name or followed by a name
>
> Tip applied: Is Mother ready to meet the detective and Professor Xavier?
>
> Cap: Used in place of person's real name   Cap: Followed by a name

Here is another way to think of the Person Tip: If you can replace the person's title or family term with a first name, you need to capitalize the title or family term. Below we have replaced the titles and family terms in the previous example with proper names to see whether the words should be capitalized:

Replacement does *not* work, so *detective* is *not* a proper noun.
↓

Juanita   ✗ Sally   Chuck

Tip applied: Is ~~Mother~~ ready to meet the ~~detective~~ and ~~Professor~~ Xavier?
↑   ↑
Replacement works, so both *Mother* and *Professor* are proper nouns.

Take a close look at the instance when a proper noun sounds truly peculiar. You would not say *the Sally*. Thus, *detective* cannot be replaced by a real name. This proves *detective* is not a proper noun and should not be capitalized, at least not in this sentence.

> **GROUP TIP**   Capitalize any term that a group of people accept as describing their culture, language, nationality, religion, or ethnic background.

Lesson 26

> **PLACE TIP**   Capitalize any name you could find on a map or that is widely recognized as a *distinct* place or region. Do not capitalize general directions or general locations.

cap

Place names that might be capitalized include *Rocky Mountains, Pacific Ocean, New England, Dixie,* and the *West.* If you merely told a person to *head west* or *drive to the ocean*, these terms would not be capitalized since they are just directions, not places.

Often, the decision to capitalize depends on whether your readers consider a word to be a specific name. Many Texans capitalize *East Texas* because they know it is a specific area, but readers from other parts of the country might not recognize this as a distinct region—just a vague reference (hence, *east Texas* would be fine for them).

Example 1 illustrates these two tips:

Group Tip: *English* is derived from the name of a group of people, so it needs a cap.
↓

Example 1:   ✗ My english teacher asked us to read stories by
Flannery O'Connor and other writers from the south.
↑
Place Tip: *South* is the name of a specific region, so it needs a cap.

English
Correction: My ~~english~~ teacher asked us to read stories by Flannery
                          ^
                                                                    South
O'Connor and other writers from the ~~south~~.
                                                              ^

> **SCHOOL TIP** Capitalize the official name of a specific school or course. Do *not* capitalize general references to a school, course, or field of study.

Many writers err by habitually capitalizing schools, subjects, and informal names of courses. However, only specific and formal names should be capitalized, as in the following examples:

Proper nouns: Math 101, Department of History, BA in Communication Studies, Kilgore Community College, English Composition II, Longview High School

Common nouns: math class, history, a communications degree, the community college, my composition course, high school

Let's apply the School Tip to Example 2:

Example 2:   ✗ How hard were your <u>Math</u> classes in <u>High School</u>?

School Tip: *Math* and *high school* are both general references, not specific titles, so no caps are needed.

                                      math   *high school*
Correction: How hard were your ~~Math~~ classes in ~~High School~~?
                                                ^   ^

Lesson 26

cap

MORE EXAMPLES

Person Terms

Are you voting, **Governor**? **Press Secretary Jones** said you are.

I asked **Dad** not to call me at work, and so did **Aunt Tammie**.

The **governor** didn't answer; neither did her **press secretary**.

My **dad** can be nosy at times, as my **aunt** often points out.

Group Terms

Most of the **New Englanders** I met on my trip were **Boston Red Sox** fans.

Yesterday, members of the **English Honors Organization** read five poems written by **African Americans**.

Many people along the **eastern coast** are fans of other **professional baseball teams**.

The club will also discuss poetry by other **ethnic minorities**.

Place Terms

I am visiting the **Grand Canyon** this summer.

The **West** is identified with rugged individualism.

The **canyon** is huge.

We traveled **west** all the way to **San Francisco**.

School Terms

I will take **History 110** this fall and obtain my **BA** in **History** by spring.

My neighbor teaches **Oceanography I** at **Gulfport High School**.

I am a **history** major working on a **bachelor's degree**.

The **high school** I went to didn't have courses in **oceanography**.

Lesson 26

cap **✳ Putting It All Together**

Identify Capitalization Errors in Your Writing

_____ Proofread your writing for references to individuals, groups, schools, courses, subjects, and places.

Correct Capitalization Errors in Your Writing

_____ Capitalize proper nouns and proper adjectives — official names and titles of specific people, cultures, and locations. Do not capitalize general references.

_____ Use the four tips in this lesson to help you decide whether terms are proper nouns or adjectives that require capitalization. The tips can be summarized as follows:

Capitalize	Example
Family Term + Name	**U**ncle **M**arty called.
Family Term Used as a Name	Did **M**other arrive?

Capitalize	Example
Title + Name	Is **D**octor **C**hang in?
Title Used as a Name	I am here, **S**enator.
Name Accepted by Group	She is a **B**aptist.
Name Found on Map	**G**ulf of **M**exico
Recognized Name of Region	**P**acific **N**orthwest
Name of Specific School	**M**artin **L**uther **K**ing **H**igh **S**chool
Name of Specific Course	**M**ath 110; **A**dvanced **A**lgebra
Name of Specific Degree	**A**ssociate's **D**egree in **L**iberal **A**rts

Sentence Practice 1

CORRECTED SENTENCES APPEAR ON PAGE 483.

If the underlined word is correct in terms of capitalization, write *OK* over it. Correct any error, and refer to one of the four tips to explain why there is an error.

Lesson 26

cap

> *General*   *OK*   *OK*
> **Example:**   Yes, ~~general~~, your <u>uncle</u> called from <u>Boston</u> today.
>
> **Tip applied:**   *Person Tip: "General" is a title that could be replaced by a name.*

1. My <u>father</u> has a job teaching <u>Biology</u> in eastern <u>Delaware</u>.

2. Theodore Roosevelt was once <u>governor</u> of <u>New York</u>.

3. Much of the <u>southwestern</u> United States was once <u>Mexican</u> territory.

4. Students write in almost every class at this <u>University</u>, even <u>Physical Education</u> courses.

5. Tenskwatawa was a <u>native american</u> leader who encouraged his people to give up alcohol along with <u>european</u> clothing and tools.

 For more practice using capitalization, go to **Exercise Central** at **bedfordstmartins.com/commonsense**

Sentence Practice 2

CORRECTED SENTENCES APPEAR ON PAGE 483.

If the underlined word is correct in terms of capitalization, write *OK* over it. Correct any error, and refer to one of the four tips to explain why there is an error.

> *geology*
> Example: I have to take my ~~Geology~~ class again.
>   ^
> Tip applied: *School Tip: The term geology is not the name of a specific class (the word my in front indicates a general term).*

1. In the 1860s, Montana's present Capital, Helena, was named Last Chance Gulch.

2. The university president spoke at graduation this year.

3. Did you say that aunt Iva is arriving today?

4. The rhone river and the rhine river both rise out of the Alps of Switzerland.

5. My Grandmother believes she can meet with the Pope during our visit to Rome.

Lesson 26

cap ## Sentence Practice 3

Replace *?* in each sentence with the type of word(s) indicated in the parenthesis. Capitalize according to the four tips reviewed in this lesson.

> Example: They interviewed *?*. (proper noun)
> Answer: *They interviewed Governor Whitman.*

1. I met *?* once. (proper noun)

2. My sister will graduate from *?* this spring. (proper noun)

3. Dawn learned a great deal about business by taking a course in *?*. (common noun)

4. *?* arrived late for class again. (proper noun)

5. *?* did not attend our family reunion. (common noun)

6. I enrolled in both *?* this spring. (proper nouns)

7. My roommate wants to visit *?* sometime. (proper noun)

8. I prefer a restaurant that specializes in *?* food. (proper adjective)

9. My father helped build this *?* church. (proper adjective)

10. *?* Smith sings very well. (proper noun)

Editing Practice 1

CORRECTED SENTENCES APPEAR ON PAGE 483.

Correct all errors in the following paragraphs using the first correction as a model. The number in parentheses at the end of each paragraph indicates how many errors you should find.

> *New Orleans*
> Last fall we stayed in ~~new orleans~~ for a week. We flew from newark
> ^
> in new jersey. Our trip got off to a bad start because our flight was delayed
> for two hours because of thunderstorms over the appalachians. We stayed
> in the french quarter, the oldest part of town. It and the lovely old garden
> district were not damaged by katrina, the terrible hurricane that did so
> much damage to the entire gulf coast. We really enjoyed our stay. The local
> businesses need all the support they can get. It was a pleasant change to be
> in a city that was truly grateful to see tourists. We should all support that
> lovely city in any way we can. (7)
>
> Terrible as it was, we need to bear in mind how much worse the
> loss of life could have been if not for very accurate forecasting from the
> national hurricane center and the national weather service. For example,
> compare katrina with the similar hurricane that struck galveston in 1900.
> That storm killed eight thousand people because there was no ability at the
> time to monitor off-shore weather. The storm came on shore without any
> warning at all, killing nearly everyone living along that part of texas where
> the storm hit. (5)

Lesson 26

cap

Editing Practice 2

Correct all errors in the following paragraph using the first correction as a model. The number in parentheses at the end of the paragraph indicates how many errors you should find.

college
All of us when we first start ~~College~~ or University struggle with the
^
decision of what to major in. Some people have a very clear idea of what
profession they want to enter from the very moment they start school,
and so they know exactly what to major in. That certainly was not the
case with me. I didn't have a clue what I wanted to do after I got my
Bachelor's Degree. As a result I kind of floundered around changing from
one Program to another. Some majors in the Humanities, like History,
English, or Philosophy, give people a really good, well-rounded education
that makes them able to deal with complicated ideas and write well. The
problem, of course, is that these programs do not lead directly to any
career path. For example, one of my classmates got a rhodes scholarship,
one of the most prestigious academic awards in the world, and ended up
scooping twenty-nine flavors of ice cream when he got back from oxford. In the long run, however, people with good humanistic educations
do very well—better, in fact, than people with more immediately useful
degrees like Accounting and Finance. People with only narrow professional
educations tend to stall out at midcareer. By the way, my friend with the
Scholarship ended up being a highly successful Lawyer, but there is no
denying that he had a hard time for a while after he graduated. (12)

Lesson 26

cap

Applying What You Know

Write a paragraph describing the three most helpful courses you have taken
in college or high school, and indicate why these might help you as you work
toward a particular major or profession. Use the four tips we have discussed
(especially the School Tip) to make sure you have capitalized words correctly.

The Bottom Line	According to rules of formal English, official names, titles, and nicknames are capitalized.

Using Other Punctuation and Capitalizing Words

REVIEW

Punctuation marks and capitalization form an important part of written English. The following chart sums up the tips that will help you avoid four problems writers encounter in using punctuation marks and capitalization.

TIPS	QUICK FIXES AND EXAMPLES
Lesson 23. Quotation Marks with Other Punctuation	
The Unquote Tip (p. 233) helps you determine whether quotation marks and exclamation points should go inside or outside closing quotation marks.	Periods and commas always go inside quotation marks. Semicolons and colons always go outside quotation marks. Question marks and exclamation points go *inside* if they are part of the quotation and *outside* if they are part of the entire surrounding sentence. Error: ✗ Tim said, "You need to leave". Correction: Tim said, "You need to leave."/
Lesson 24. Semicolons	
The Imaginary Period Tip (p. 239) helps you determine whether a semicolon is correctly joining two independent clauses.	If replacing a semicolon with an imaginary period results in a fragment on either side, the semicolon is incorrect. Try replacing it with a colon or a comma. Error: ✗ My parents walked into my dorm room; not even bothering to knock first. Correction: My parents walked into my dorm room/, not even bothering to knock first.
Lesson 25. Colons	
The Imaginary Period Tip (p. 247) helps you make sure that a colon is correctly used to introduce a list.	If what comes before a colon and list *cannot* stand alone as a sentence, the colon is incorrect and should be deleted. Error: ✗ My roommate enjoys: jogging, swimming, and playing video games. Correction: My roommate enjoys/ jogging, swimming, and playing video games.

TIPS	QUICK FIXES AND EXAMPLES
Lesson 26. Capitalization	

The Person Tip (p. 255), Group Tip (p. 256), Place Tip (p. 256), and School Tip (p. 257) help you know when to capitalize these types of words.	Capitalize official names or nicknames of specific people or places. Capitalize cultural, national, religious, ethnic, or language groups. Also capitalize specific school or course names.
	
	Error: **✗** My spanish instructor asked us to read a book written by a catholic priest.
	
	            Spanish
	Correction: My ~~spanish~~ instructor asked us to
	        ^ *Catholic*
	read a book written by a ~~catholic~~ priest.
	                       ^

Review Test

Correct all errors in the following paragraph using the first correction as a model. The number in parentheses at the end of the paragraph indicates how many errors you should find.

Unit Seven

review

        roommate

My ~~Roommate~~ Troy invited me to visit his hometown, College
  ^

Station, Texas, over Christmas break. I had never been to the south before,

much less to Texas. Since I had grown up in new England, the prospect of

visiting a new part of the Country was pretty exciting. Troy said that we

would have to drive West for twelve hours to reach College Station; which is

in the Central part of the state. College Station is really just a college town,

but it also has: cotton, retail, and cattle. (7)

Writing Clear Sentences

OVERVIEW

The Nuts and Bolts of Writing Clear Sentences

This unit covers three topics that can make your writing unclear: faulty parallelism, the passive voice, and dangling modifiers.

Lesson 27 shows you how to create parallel sentences. **Parallelism** refers to a series of two or more identical grammatical structures joined by a **coordinating conjunction** (usually *and* or *or*). The most common parallelism errors involve verb forms that either end in *-ing* (**gerunds**) or appear after *to* (**infinitives**). **Faulty parallelism** results when items in a series are not all in the same grammatical form.

Example: ✗ Sylvia likes <u>reading</u> poetry, <u>listening</u> to music, and <u>to</u> <u>collect</u> spiders.

Correction: Sylvia likes reading poetry, listening to music, and
                       collecting
                       ~~to collect~~ spiders.
                       ^

Lesson 28 shows you how to revise passive-voice sentences. In most sentences, the subject of the sentence performs the action of the verb. This type of sentence is said to be in the **active voice**. In the **passive voice**, the subject of the sentence does not perform the action; instead, it *receives* the action of the verb. Although passive-voice sentences are not grammatically incorrect, active-voice sentences are clearer and stronger.

Example (passive voice):   The new parking rule was criticized by the students.

                                             students criticized the
Correction (active voice):   The new parking rule. ~~was criticized by the~~
                                             ^   ^
                                             ~~students.~~

265

Lesson 29 will help you identify and correct **dangling modifiers**. Certain modifiers can be moved outside the main sentence to provide background information and clarity. If these modifiers are not clearly connected to the words they describe, the meaning may be misunderstood. These unconnected modifiers are called dangling modifiers because they are not properly attached to the main sentence.

Example: ✗ While still a student, Microsoft recruited my sister for a job as a programmer.

The dangling modifier *while still a student* makes it sound like Microsoft is a student.

Correction: While still a student, Microsoft recruited ~~my sister~~ for a job as a programmer.

(with insertion above "my sister": my sister was)
(with insertion above strikethrough: her)

Parallelism

EXAMPLE 1

Error: ✗ Mickey likes <u>to bike</u>, <u>swim</u>, and <u>to go</u> on long walks.

                                  to

Correction 1:   Mickey likes to bike, swim, and to go on long walks.

Correction 2:   Mickey likes to bike, swim, and ~~to~~ go on long walks.

EXAMPLE 2

Error: ✗ He also loves <u>eating</u> pizza and to <u>watch</u> reruns of *Baywatch*.

                                        watching

Correction 1:   He also loves eating pizza and ~~to watch~~ reruns of *Baywatch*.

                           to eat

Correction 2:   He also loves ~~eating~~ pizza and to watch reruns of *Baywatch*.

What's the Problem?

The term **parallelism** refers to a series of two or more grammatical elements of the same type joined by *and* (or sometimes by *or*). For example, the following sentence has parallel verb forms:

    <u>Eat</u>, <u>drink</u>, and <u>be</u> merry.

When one of the elements breaks the pattern set by the other element(s), the resulting error is called **faulty parallelism**. The most common type of faulty parallelism involves the inconsistent use of verb forms. In Example 1, for instance, *to* is used with the first and third verbs (*to bike* and *to go*), but not with the second verb (*swim*).

    In Example 2, *eating* is the *-ing* form of the verb *eat*, but the second verb, *to watch*, is not the *-ing* form. Either one is grammatical by itself:

He also loves <u>eating</u> pizza.

He also loves <u>to watch</u> reruns of *Baywatch*.

However, when they are joined together by the coordinating conjunction *and*, they create an ungrammatical sentence with faulty parallelism.

Diagnostic Exercise

CORRECTED SENTENCES APPEAR ON PAGE 484.

Correct all errors in the following paragraph using the first correction as a model. The number in parentheses at the end of the paragraph indicates how many errors you should find.

We all go to college for different reasons: to get an education, meet new people, and ~~to~~ gain the skills for a job. The best programs are ones that reach several of these goals at the same time. I like to take courses that interest me and building skills that will lead to a job. For example, it is great to read about something in a class and then applying it in a practical situation. That is why I am doing an internship program. I have the opportunity to get credits, develop professional skills, and to make important contacts. The internship will be worthwhile, even if I have to go to school an extra semester to earn all the credits I need to graduate. (3)

Lesson 27

//

Fixing This Problem in Your Writing

Faulty parallelism happens when we lose track of exactly which elements are supposed to be parallel. Use the following tip to proofread your writing for this problem.

> **THE PARALLELISM STACK TIP**   Whenever you use an **infinitive** (the *to* form of a verb) or a **gerund** (the *-ing* form of a verb) after an *and* or an *or*, arrange the elements that should be parallel in a "parallelism stack." Placing parallel elements in a column makes it easy to see whether these elements have exactly the same form.

Let's apply the Parallelism Stack Tip to the first example:

Example 1:   ✗ Mickey likes <u>to bike</u>, <u>swim</u>, and <u>to go</u> on long walks.

Tip applied: ✗ Mickey likes   <u>to bike</u>
                                <u>swim</u>, and
                                <u>to go</u> on long walks.

The Parallelism Stack Tip shows us at a glance where the parallelism derails: the infinitives *to bike* and *to go* are not parallel to the base form *swim*. (Base forms are simply infinitive verbs without the *to*.)

To correct the error in Example 1, we can use *to* with each of the verbs:

                                        to
Correction 1:   Mickey likes to bike, swim, and to go on long walks.
                                        ^

When we apply the Parallelism Stack Tip now, we see that the verbs in the sentence are indeed parallel:

Confirmation: Mickey likes   <u>to bike</u>,
                                <u>to swim</u>, and
                                <u>to go</u> on long walks.

We can also correct the sentence by using only one initial *to* plus the base form of each verb (without the *to*):

Correction 2:   Mickey likes to bike, swim, and ~~to~~ go on long walks.

When we apply the Parallelism Stack Tip, we again see that the verbs in the sentence are indeed parallel:

Confirmation: Mickey likes to   <u>bike</u>,
                                <u>swim</u>, and
                                <u>go</u> on long walks.

Notice that when we use only a single *to*, it is no longer part of the parallelism stack because *to* is not repeated as part of the parallelism. The parallel elements now are just the base forms *bike*, *swim*, and *go*.

Let's apply the Parallelism Stack Tip to Example 2:

Example 2:   ✗ He also loves <u>eating</u> pizza and <u>to watch</u> reruns of *Baywatch.*

Tip applied: ✗ He also loves   <u>eating</u> pizza and
                                <u>to watch</u> reruns of *Baywatch.*

We can see at a glance that *eating* and *to watch* are not parallel. Here are the parallelism stacks for the three possible corrections. In this first correction, there are two parallel gerunds (*-ing* verbs):

watching

Correction 1:   He also loves eating pizza and ~~to watch~~ reruns of
              Baywatch.
              ^

Confirmation: He also loves   eating pizza and
                              watching reruns of *Baywatch.*

In the second correction, we use two parallel infinitives (*to* verbs):

to eat

Correction 2:   He also loves ~~eating~~ pizza and to watch reruns of
              Baywatch.
              ^

Confirmation: He also loves   to eat pizza and
                              to watch reruns of *Baywatch.*

Finally, we can also correct the error by using just one *to* plus the base
form of each verb:

to eat

Correction 3:   He also loves ~~eating~~ pizza and ~~to~~ watch reruns of
              Baywatch.
              ^

Confirmation: He also loves to   eat pizza and
                              watch reruns of *Baywatch.*

As Example 2 illustrates, there are a number of ways to fix faulty parallelism.
The main problem is spotting the faulty parallelism to begin with.

✳ *Putting It All Together*

Identify Faulty Parallelism

_____ When you use a coordinating conjunction (*and*, *or*), use the Parallelism Stack Tip to make sure that the parallel elements on both sides
are in the same grammatical form. Be especially careful with infinitives (verbs with *to*) since they are the most common source of faulty
parallelism.

Correct Faulty Parallelism

_____ Rewrite the faulty element to make it match the other elements in
the series. Use all gerunds (*-ing* verbs), all infinitives (*to* forms), or a
single initial *to* followed by all base forms (verbs without *to*).

Sentence Practice 1

CORRECTED SENTENCES APPEAR ON PAGE 484.

Create parallelism stacks for the parallel elements in the following sentences. Underline all the verbs that are used in forming the parallel structure. Mark with an *X* any nonparallel elements, and rewrite the sentence to correct the faulty parallelism.

> Example: I want to improve my computer skills, go online, and to surf the Internet.
>
> I want   <u>to improve</u> my skills,
> **X** <u>go</u> online, and
> <u>to surf</u> the Internet.
>
>   *to*
> Correction: I want to improve my computer skills, go online, and to surf the Internet.   ^

1. My boss said that I need to work faster, work harder, and to stop taking long breaks.

2. A new federal program gives me the chance to take several classes this summer and getting my degree within two years.

3. Dr. Sanchez helped me to write more clearly, to avoid grammatical errors, and turn in my papers on time.

4. A common approach to writing a lab report is to begin with the materials needed and to end with a summary of the findings.

5. My chemistry teacher said that we also need to state the purpose of the experiment, to explain the procedures, and explain the shortcomings of the experiment.

Lesson 27

//

 For more practice using parallelism, go to **Exercise Central** at **bedfordstmartins.com/commonsense**

Sentence Practice 2

CORRECTED SENTENCES APPEAR ON PAGE 484.

Create parallelism stacks for the parallel elements in the following sentences. Underline all the verbs that are used in forming the parallel structure, and rewrite the sentence to correct faulty parallelism errors. Write *OK* above any sentences that do not contain faulty parallelism.

Example: It is hard to admit a mistake and starting over again.

It is hard   to admit a mistake and
            starting over again.

            admitting
Correction: It is hard ~~to admit~~ a mistake and starting over again.
                        ^

1. The porters began sorting the baggage and clearing a space for us to assemble.

2. I have to put the cat out, water the plants, and to leave a house key with a friend.

3. This semester, I started working at home in the mornings and to do my schoolwork later in the afternoons.

4. I do not want you to lose the directions and becoming lost.

5. I remembered filling out the form, handing it to the clerk, and asking her to check it.

Sentence Practice 3

Combine each of the following groups of sentences. Use parallel forms of the verbs in parentheses.

Example: The children are eager (open) their presents.
            The children are eager (play) with their toys.
            The children are eager (show) them off.

Answer: *The children are eager to open their presents, play with their toys, and show them off.*

1. My boss is eager (get) the costs for the new product. My boss is eager (begin) selling it. My boss is eager (see) profits.

2. (Brush) your teeth correctly is important. (Floss) regularly is important. (Visit) a dentist twice a year is important.

3. I cannot stand it when friends (make) complicated plans. I cannot stand it when friends (call) me at the last second. I cannot stand it when friends (expect) me to be ready on time.

4. Texas Slim likes (drink) Lone Star Beer. Texas Slim likes (eat) barbecue. Texas Slim likes (watch) Martha Stewart on TV.

5. You should try (prepare) nutritious meals. You should try (watch) your weight. You should try (get) enough sleep.

Editing Practice 1

CORRECTED SENTENCES APPEAR ON PAGE 484.

Correct all parallelism errors in the following paragraph using the first correction as a model. The number in parentheses at the end of the paragraph indicates how many errors you should find.

> My boyfriend, Matt, loves talking on his cell phone and ~~to play~~ *playing* video games. In fact, he seems to do little else. He spends hours doing both at the same time. I talk on my cell and play video games sometimes, but I also like meeting people face to face, going out with friends, and to have a little variation in what I do. Just last weekend, I had an opportunity to participate in a blood drive and going to a baseball game. During that entire time, Matt managed to run up two hundred minutes on his cell phone and to complete Half-Life 2 for the tenth time. This weekend, I plan to watch a movie with our friends, go for a long walk around the park, and to work in my garden. If I can't get him to join me with at least one of these activities, I might have to find someone who is more compatible with my interests. (3)

Editing Practice 2

Correct all parallelism errors in the following paragraph using the first correction as a model. The number in parentheses at the end of the paragraph indicates how many errors you should find.

> Ms. Astin, my supervisor, asked me yesterday to stay late, file reports, and ~~to~~ photocopy a dozen spreadsheets. Normally, I would not mind, but my day was already hectic. I hated to start three new assignments and falling even further behind with my regular duties. Arguing with Ms. Astin, however, was pointless. She ordered me to stop my other work, start on her assignments, and to stay in the office until the work was done. On the positive side, I have worked a great deal of overtime lately, so my

Lesson 27

//

next paycheck should be larger than usual. I normally enjoy working in our office and to give extra help when needed. I just need a little more notice next time before my boss assigns extra work. (3)

Applying What You Know

On your own paper, write a short essay listing the kinds of skills you think you will need in future jobs. In your writing, try to use several parallel verb forms. When you are finished, switch papers with a partner and use the Putting It All Together checklist to make sure that your partner's writing does not contain faulty parallelism.

The Bottom Line	Make verb forms parallel by **using** the Parallelism Stack Tip and **checking** to see that each verb has exactly the same form.

Lesson 27

//

LESSON 28

Passive Voice

EXAMPLE 1

Error: ✗ A plane <u>was taken</u> to Chicago by our family.

Correction: *Our family took a plane to Chicago.*
~~A plane was taken to Chicago by our family.~~
                  ^

EXAMPLE 2

Error: ✗ A report <u>was written</u>.

Correction: *Somebody wrote a report.*
~~A report was written.~~
                  ^

What's the Problem?

All action verbs occur in one of two **voices**: **active** or **passive**. In an active-voice sentence, the subject performs the action and is the main focus of the sentence. In a passive-voice sentence, however, the focus is on what happened *to* something. In other words, the subject of a passive-voice sentence *receives* the action. For example, compare the following sentences:

Active: <u>Arnold</u> <u>kicked</u> the ball.

               The subject (*Arnold*) performs the action.

Passive: The <u>ball</u> <u>was kicked</u> by Arnold.

               The subject (*ball*) receives the action.

Using the passive voice is not a grammatical error. However, the passive voice can lead to a dull style because it does not stress action (see Example 1). Also, it can "hide" the person or thing doing an action. For instance, Example 2 does not indicate *who* wrote the report.

Sometimes people use the passive-voice to be polite. (For example, compare *Mistakes were made* with *You made mistakes*.) However, writers should avoid using the passive voice unless they have a good reason to do so.

Diagnostic Exercise

CORRECTED SENTENCES APPEAR ON PAGE 484.

Change all passive-voice verbs to the active voice using the first correction as a model. The number in parentheses at the end of the paragraph indicates how many errors you should find.

> *Matt's apartment manager called him, wanting*
> ~~Matt was called by his apartment manager, who wanted~~ to know
>   ^
> why he played his music so loudly. Matt was surprised by the phone call;
> he didn't think his music was loud. He apologized, but he said his radio
> was playing at only a fourth of its potential volume. Apparently, the man-
> ager was satisfied by this response. Matt was told by her that she would
> speak with the people who complained. I have heard that they have a
> history of complaining. (3)

Fixing This Problem in Your Writing

Identifying the Passive Voice

To recognize the passive voice in your writing, use the following tip.

Lesson 28

pass

> **TO BE + PAST PARTICIPLE TIP**   The passive voice follows a consistent formula: a form of the verb *to be* as a helping verb + a past participle form of another verb.

Let's look at some examples:

Subject	To Be	+	Past Participle
The contract	is		signed.
The game	was		played.
The burgers	were		eaten.
The contest	had been		won.

Most past participles end in *-ed* (*borrowed, played*). Some irregular verbs, however, form the past participle with *-en* (*eaten, taken, written*), while others form it by changing a vowel (*sing-sung, ring-rung, win-won*).

Using the Active Voice

Once you have identified the passive voice in your writing, test it against its active-voice counterpart to see which sounds better. Unless there is a good reason to use the passive voice, you should generally use the active voice. To make a passive sentence active, use the following tip.

> **FLIP-FLOP TIP** Turn passive-voice sentences into active-voice sentences by flip-flopping what comes before and after the passive verb, forcing the subject of the new sentence to perform the action. (If nothing comes after the passive verb, then the new subject in the active-voice sentence will usually be *somebody* or *something*.)

Here is the Flip-Flop Tip applied to Example 1:

	SUBJECT
Example 1:	✗ A plane was taken to Chicago by our family.

	NEW SUBJECT		
Tip applied:	Our family	took	a plane to Chicago.

The subject (*family*) now performs the action (*took*).

Important: The flip-flop requires that you eliminate the helping verb form of *to be* (*was*), changing *was taken* to *took*.

Here is the Flip-Flop Tip applied to Example 2:

	SUBJECT
Example 2:	✗ A report was written. [by somebody]

	NEW SUBJECT
Tip applied:	Somebody wrote a report.

In this revision, we added the subject *Somebody* because the original sentence did not specify who wrote the report.

✳ *Putting It All Together*

Identify the Passive Voice

_____ Use the *To Be* + Past Participle Tip to identify passive voice in your writing. ➤

Lesson 28

pass

> ### *Eliminate Instances of Unnecessary Passive Voice*
>
> _____ Turn passive-voice sentences into active-voice sentences by using the Flip-Flop Tip to make the subject in the new sentence perform the action.
>
> _____ Delete the helping verb form of *to be* to make the active sentence grammatically correct.
>
> _____ Use the active form unless there is a compelling reason to use the passive.

Sentence Practice 1

CORRECTED SENTENCES APPEAR ON PAGE 484.

In each of the following sentences, underline the *to be* verb and the past participle verb that follows it. Then change the passive-voice sentence into an active-voice one by flip-flopping what comes before and after the verbs you've underlined.

Example:

The gardener carelessly left a rake in the yard.

A rake <u>was</u> carelessly <u>left</u> in the yard by the gardener.

1. This computer was used by me.

2. Supper was prepared by Jim.

3. In Japan, only major streets are provided with names by cities.

4. Until 2008, the sale of the energy drink Red Bull was prohibited by France.

5. Television advertisements for wine are banned by France's government.

Lesson 28

pass

> For more practice using the active voice, go to **Exercise Central** at
> **bedfordstmartins.com/commonsense**

Sentence Practice 2

CORRECTED SENTENCES APPEAR ON PAGE 484.

In each of the following sentences, underline the *to be* verb and the past participle verb that follows it. Then change the passive-voice sentence into an active-voice one by flip-flopping what comes before and after the verbs you've underlined.

	The famous chef Jamie Oliver presented a cooking demonstration.
Example:	A cooking demonstration <u>was presented</u> by the famous chef Jamie Oliver.

1. The tuition increase was announced by the college president.

2. On Tuesday, a dormitory was destroyed by a massive fire.

3. Everyone has been affected by the recession.

4. In 1993, the rapper LL Cool J was invited by President Clinton to perform at the presidential inaugural gala.

5. In a 1940 edition of *Look* magazine, winter sportswear was modeled by future president Gerald Ford.

Sentence Practice 3

Each item below contains two nouns. Use the first noun as the subject of an active-voice sentence; then use the second noun as the subject of a passive-voice sentence.

Example:	the Senate/the bill	
Answer:	*Active:*	*The Senate passed the bill.*
	Passive:	*The bill was passed by the Senate.*

1. Dr. Bailey/required

2. she/kicked

3. my pet snake/eats

4. I/fixed

5. my English teacher/graded

Lesson 28

pass

Editing Practice 1

CORRECTED SENTENCES APPEAR ON PAGE 484.

Change every passive-voice sentence in the following paragraph to an active-voice sentence using the first correction as a model. The number in parentheses at the end of the paragraph indicates how many errors you should find.

More and more students have chosen urban campuses
~~Urban campuses have been chosen by more and more students~~
   ^

in the past few years. At my school, like many others, parking and

transportation have become big issues for many students. Riding the bus is encouraged by the school, but that is not practical for everybody. Only a few bus routes can be used by riders. In addition, evening classes are taken by nearly everybody. Bad as the buses are during the day, at night they are impossible. Only one route is covered by the night buses. And that route has only one bus every hour. If the last bus were missed, you would be stuck for the night in the middle of a nearly deserted campus. This is not a pretty thought. (5)

Editing Practice 2

CORRECTED SENTENCES APPEAR ON PAGE 485.

Change every passive-voice sentence in the following paragraph to an active-voice sentence using the first correction as a model. The number in parentheses at the end of the paragraph indicates how many errors you should find.

> *The student council has proposed a new plan.*
> ~~A new plan has been proposed by the student council.~~ Their idea is
>   ^

that several buses could be chartered by the school. These buses would shuttle between the campus and the central bus station downtown. Nearly all the bus routes can be accessed by passengers from the central station. I think this idea would be supported by a lot of students. This plan is being put forward by the council. A committee is being formed by the council to see how many students would be interested in this plan. If a reasonable number of students can be persuaded by us to sign a petition, I think we can actually pull it off. (6)

Editing Practice 3

Change every passive-voice sentence in the following paragraph to an active-voice sentence using the first correction as a model. The number in parentheses at the end of the paragraph indicates how many errors you should find.

> *About half of the students actually use buses.*
> ~~Buses are actually used by about half of the students.~~ Cars are
>   ^

used by the other half. The problem for these students is parking. Over the

Lesson 28

pass

years, several of the larger parking lots have been replaced by classrooms. We needed the classrooms, but student parking needs were not considered by the administration. A big part of the problem is that parking is needed by everybody during the late afternoon. Plenty of parking meters have been installed by the city, but they are limited to one hour. Even if a student is taking only one class, one hour is not long enough to get back to feed the meter. As a result, students are being overwhelmed by parking tickets. (6)

Applying What You Know

Compare several paragraphs of a daily newspaper and a textbook (keep the overall length of the paragraphs from each source about the same). Count the number of times passive voice is used. Share your findings with a small group, and discuss whether textbooks or newspapers seem to use the passive voice more often. Why do you think this is the case?

The Bottom Line	In active-voice sentences, the **subject performs** the action.

Lesson 28

pass

Dangling Modifiers

EXAMPLE 1 *Introductory Modifier Not Followed by Word It Describes*

Error: ✗ <u>Damaged beyond repair</u>, <u>Nina</u> threw her watch away.

Nina's watch had to be thrown away.

Correction: Damaged beyond repair, ~~Nina threw her watch away~~.
^

EXAMPLE 2 *No Word in Sentence for Introductory Modifier to Describe*

Error: ✗ <u>While waiting for my bus</u>, it began to snow.

I noticed that it had begun to snow.

Correction: While waiting for my bus, ~~it began to snow~~.
^

What's the Problem?

Modifiers are words that describe other words. Some modifiers are simple. For example, *big* is a modifier (or an **adjective**) describing *house* in *big house*. Other modifiers are complex and involve several words that together function as a modifier. Consider this sentence: *Suddenly feeling sick, Barry went home.* In this example, *Suddenly feeling sick* is a modifier that describes *Barry*.

Sometimes, these complex modifiers are not placed close enough to the words they describe (Example 1), or there is *nothing* in the sentence they can correctly modify (Example 2). Such errors are called **dangling modifiers**. Dangling modifiers tend to occur because on first glance they might seem to be correctly modifying a word in the sentence, but in fact they are not.

We will discuss the problem in more detail, but first let's consider a correct example of a complex modifier. Here, the modifier *Working all day* is indeed right next to the word it modifies (*Jody*):

Working all day, Jody finished her essay on time.

Introductory modifier describes a nearby noun.

282

This example is correct because there is no confusion about what the modifier is describing. In contrast, dangling modifiers either lack something to modify or are not sufficiently close to what they are supposed to describe.

The most common errors with modifiers occur when the modifier is at the beginning of a sentence, so this lesson focuses on this situation.

Diagnostic Exercise

CORRECTED SENTENCES APPEAR ON PAGE 485.

Correct all errors using the first correction as a model. The number in parentheses at the end of the paragraph indicates how many dangling modifier errors you should find.

Studying for hours, ~~my eyes grew tired~~. *I felt my eyes grow tired.* I walked to the snack bar for a cup of coffee. Upon arriving, the place was closed. Deciding against walking a mile to another place, the thought crossed my mind that maybe I should quit for a while and get some sleep. I returned to my room and tried to decide what to do. Torn between the need to sleep and the need to study, the alarm clock went off and made me realize it was time for class. After struggling to stay awake in class, my decision was to get some sleep and then get back to work. (4)

Fixing This Problem in Your Writing

Lesson 29

dm

As we mentioned above, most dangling modifiers occur at the beginning of a sentence, right before the main subject and verb. Not all introductory modifiers are "dangling," so how do you know which ones are? Here is a tip that will help you identify dangling modifiers.

ILLOGICAL ACTION TIP Look for introductory elements that involve an *action* and check to see whether these elements are making illogical claims about the nearest noun or pronoun. If so, the introductory element is a dangling modifier.

Let's apply this tip to a sentence that uses a complex modifier correctly:

> <u>After leaving the theater, Makayla</u> stopped by my apartment.
>
> The introductory modifier includes an action, and the noun immediately follows the action.

As you can see, this introductory element contains an action that is making a *logical* claim about the noun right after it. The structure makes this claim:

<u>After leaving the theater, Makayla</u> . . . = Makayla left the theater

The sentence is correct because it implies that Makayla left the theater—a logical action.

Consider Example 1 that began the lesson, however. Here, too, the introductory element includes an action, but the claim made about the noun is not logical.

Example 1:   ✗ <u>Damaged beyond repair, Nina</u> threw her watch away.

> The introductory element includes an action, and the noun immediately follows the introduction.

Tip applied: ✗ <u>Damaged beyond repair, Nina</u> . . . = Nina was damaged beyond repair?

Actually, Nina's *watch* was damaged beyond repair—not Nina. You can correct such an error in many ways. In the correction below, we leave the introductory element as it was but change the noun that follows it to the correct one (*watch*). Below the correction you see the logical claim the revised sentence makes.

Correction: Damaged beyond repair, ~~Nina threw her watch away.~~
                                       Nina's watch had to be thrown away.

Verification: <u>Damaged beyond repair, Nina's watch</u> . . . = Nina's watch was damaged beyond repair

Now let's look at Example 2:

Example 2:   ✗ <u>While waiting for my bus, it</u> began to snow.

> The introductory element includes an action, and the pronoun immediately follows the introduction.

Tip applied: ✗ <u>While waiting for my bus, it</u> . . . = it waited for my bus?

To correct this error, we can add an appropriate word (*I*) for the introductory modifier to describe.

Correction: While waiting for my bus, ~~it began to snow.~~
                                         I noticed that it had begun to snow.

We can also revise the modifier itself to correct the sentence.

Correction: *I was*
While waiting for my bus, it began to snow.
    ^

Because we added *I was*, the introduction is no longer making a claim about *it*, meaning there is no chance of a dangling modifier:

Verification: While I was waiting for my bus, it began . . . = No claim made about *it*

MORE EXAMPLES

Error: ✗ Pulling as hard as he could, the rope broke in Rodney's hand.

Correction: *Rodney felt the rope break in his hand.*
Pulling as hard as he could, ~~the rope broke in Rodney's hand~~.
    ^

Error: ✗ When hearing the cars collide, my heart skipped a beat.

Correction: *When I heard the cars collide,*
~~When hearing the cars collide~~, my heart skipped a beat.
    ^

*Error: ✗ After eating at a restaurant, Haley's stomach became upset.

Correction: *After she ate at a restaurant,*
~~After eating at a restaurant~~, Haley's stomach
    ^
became upset.

*This example illustrates a common misunderstanding. The sentence might *seem* fine because readers can figure out that Haley is at a restaurant. Grammatically, though, there is an error because the word *Haley's* is an adjective (modifying *stomach*). An adjective cannot eat at a restaurant—only nouns or pronouns can perform an action. The nearest noun is *stomach*, but a stomach cannot eat out either.

Lesson 29

dm

✻ *Putting It All Together*

Identify Dangling Modifiers

____ Look for groups of words that describe something else in a sentence. Dangling modifiers occur when the group of words is not close enough to what it describes *or* when there is nothing in the sentence for it to describe.
    ➤

_____ In particular, look for introductory elements that involve an action and check to see whether these elements are making illogical claims about the noun (or pronoun) that directly follows them. If the action implies something illogical about the noun (or pronoun) right after the introduction, you have identified a dangling modifier.

Correct Dangling Modifiers

_____ You can correct many dangling modifiers by adding a subject to the introductory element. For example, you would change *While waiting for my bus, it began to snow* to *While I was waiting for my bus, it began to snow.*

_____ To correct other dangling modifiers, leave the introductory element alone and instead revise the *rest* of the sentence so the noun (or pronoun) immediately following the introductory element is the subject actually performing the action described. For example, you would change *Damaged beyond repair, Nina threw her watch away* to *Damaged beyond repair, Nina's watch had to be thrown away.*

Sentence Practice 1

CORRECTED SENTENCES APPEAR ON PAGE 485.

Lesson 29

dm

Underline the modifying phrase once and the noun or pronoun that immediately follows it twice. Is it logical for the underlined phase to modify the noun or pronoun? If logical, write *OK*. If illogical, rewrite the sentence.

Example: ✗ After recovering from the flu, my first priority was to find a new job.

Answer: <u>After recovering from the flu,</u> <u>my first priority</u> was to find a new job.

Correction: *After I recovered from the flu, my first priority was finding a new job.*

1. Being well prepared, passing the test was easy for me.

2. While sleeping on the couch, my back began to hurt.

3. Since arriving at this school, Jeff's study habits have changed dramatically.

4. Hurrying to answer the phone, her knee hit the table.

5. Understanding the importance of outlining, I developed a plan for writing the next paper.

For more practice with dangling modifiers, go to **Exercise Central** at
bedfordstmartins.com/commonsense

Sentence Practice 2

CORRECTED SENTENCES APPEAR ON PAGE 485.

Underline the modifying phrase once and the noun or pronoun that immediately follows it twice. Is it logical for the underlined phase to modify the noun or pronoun? If logical, write *OK*. If illogical, rewrite the sentence.

Example: ✗ After hearing the bad news, the dinner party was called off.

Answer: <u>After hearing the bad news</u>, the <u><u>dinner party</u></u> was called off.

Correction: *After hearing the bad news, we called off the dinner party.*

1. While riding a bike to school, Michael was almost hit by a car.

2. While reading a book on a Kindle, the battery went dead.

3. Wanting to finish the book, I found a copy at the library.

4. After eating a huge lunch, a little rest is the only thing I want.

5. Realizing we were late, our only choice was to take a taxi.

Sentence Practice 3

Combine the two short sentences by making the second sentence into a phrase or clause that can be moved in front of the underlined subject. Punctuate appropriately, and avoid dangling modifiers.

Example: The <u>chicken</u> was injured by a speeding truck. The chicken was crossing the road.

Answer: *While crossing the road, the chicken was injured by a speeding truck.*

1. The <u>cat</u> seemed nervous. The cat heard the panting of a dog.

2. <u>We</u> left the party early. We were disgusted by the obnoxious behavior of the host.

3. <u>Carlos</u> easily jumped over the barricade. Carlos was in excellent shape.

Lesson 29

dm

4. The <u>chicken</u> looked both ways. The chicken was concerned about the heavy traffic.

5. The <u>chicken</u> decided never to cross the road again. The chicken was frightened by her near-death experience.

Editing Practice 1

CORRECTED SENTENCES APPEAR ON PAGE 485.

Correct all errors in the following paragraphs using the first correction as a model. The number in parentheses at the end of each paragraph indicates how many errors you should find.

Last summer I flew from Seattle to New York. Not having flown for a while, ~~the trip was quite an eye-opener~~. On the positive side, it really is
  _∧ *I had an eye-opening experience*
much easier than it used to be to compare rates and schedules. Spending a few minutes (well, quite a few minutes actually) on the computer, the best choice was obvious. That's it for the good news. Everything else was downhill from there. Knowing that I needed to get to the airport in plenty of time, my plan was to get there an hour and a half before departure time. Even then, I very nearly missed my flight. What I hadn't bargained on was how much longer it would take to get through security. Taking off my coat, jacket, and shoes and unpacking my laptop were awkward enough. The real problem was trying to get my shoes back on while juggling all my clothes and my computer. Balancing on one foot and then the other, my shoes proved almost impossible to wedge onto my feet one-handed. (3)

The flight itself was uneventful, though not very pleasant. Seated in the middle seat, it seemed like the flight lasted forever. One thing that had changed since the last time I have flown was the lack of leg room. Even being of only average height, my legs did not fit into the space. I thought

Lesson 29

dm

that was pretty bad; then the person in front of me reclined his seat to the maximum. The top of his seat was about 12 inches from my face. I quickly discovered that I could not read. Holding my book so close to my face, my eyes could not focus on the page. Nevertheless, I lived to tell the tale and even survived the return flight. (3)

Editing Practice 2

Correct all errors in the following paragraphs using the first correction as a model. The number in parentheses at the end of each paragraph indicates how many errors you should find.

      Annoyed by the swarm of students trying to buy textbooks, *Jacquita was not having a good day* ~~it was not a good day for Jacquita~~. While trying to register for classes earlier in the week, a computer glitch occurred. As a result, she had to register for new classes. Unable to take the classes she had originally wanted, replacements were necessary, and Jacquita had to return her old books to buy new ones. (2)

      Now, she was back in the bookstore along with dozens of other students. Searching for used textbooks, Jacquita had to compete with other students wanting the same books. Her new classes also required more books. After finding all of the books she needed, a long line of students waiting at the register confronted Jacquita. Frustrated by the slow pace, another register opened up, but a dozen students stepped in front of her as she moved to the new line. Jacquita decided that next semester she would register earlier in case another computer glitch occurred. (2)

Lesson 29

dm

Applying What You Know

Introductory elements can always be deleted because they are not grammatically necessary. However, they are commonly used because they add useful information. Write a paragraph describing an awkward or embarrassing classroom experience. Try to write it without using introductory elements. Now, go back and add useful information in the form of introductory elements. Add at least three, and put a comma after each one. Use the Illogical Action Tip to make sure you avoid dangling modifiers.

The Bottom Line	**Using a little caution,** you can avoid dangling modifiers.

Lesson 29

dm

Writing Clear Sentences

REVIEW

This unit presents sentence structures that can be misused (in the case of faulty parallelism and dangling modifiers) or inappropriately used (in the case of passive voice). The following chart sums up tips that will help you avoid three problems writers encounter: creating faulty parallelism, overusing the passive voice, and creating dangling modifiers.

TIPS	QUICK FIXES AND EXAMPLES
Lesson 27. Parallelism	
The Parallelism Stack Tip (p. 268) helps you spot faulty parallelism in your writing.	When using a series of verbs joined by *and* (or sometimes by *or*), use all *-ing* forms, all *to* forms, or a single *to* followed by all base forms. Error: **X** She prefers dancing, working on her computer, and to spend time with friends. Correction: She prefers dancing, working on her computer, and ~~to spend~~ *spending* time with friends.
Lesson 28. Passive Voice	
The *To Be* + Past Participle Tip (p. 276) helps you recognize passive-voice sentences. The Flip-Flop Tip (p. 277) helps you convert passive-voice sentences into active-voice ones.	Revise passive-voice sentences by flip-flopping what comes before with what comes after the passive verb, making the subject of the new sentences perform the action. Passive: The test was taken three times by me. Active: I took the test three times.
Lesson 29. Dangling Modifiers	
The Illogical Action Tip (p. 283) helps you identify dangling modifiers.	If an introductory element makes an illogical claim about the noun or pronoun that follows it, the sentence probably needs to be revised. Error: **X** Confused by the question, my answer was wildly off the mark. Correction: Confused by the question, *I gave an answer that* ~~my answer~~ was wildly off the mark.

Review Test

Correct all errors in the following paragraphs using the first correction as a model. The number in parentheses at the end of each paragraph indicates how many errors you should find.

This summer, I took a bowling class and learned how to select a comfortable ball, ~~to~~ be consistent in my approach, and aim the ball. I have always liked to bowl or watching my friends bowl. Since I had to take a PE course anyway, the requirement was satisfied by a bowling course. Most of my bad habits were corrected by this course. (3)

Some of my worst habits were to vary my approach almost every time I bowled and throwing the ball with all my strength. I was shown by my instructor that I did not need to hurl the ball at the pins. The pins can easily be knocked down by a slower, more controlled release. Amazingly, it takes just a little effort to knock a pin over and starting a chain reaction that can knock them all down. My scores have been greatly improved by my more deliberate approach. (5)

Unit Eight

review

Choosing the Right Article

OVERVIEW

The Nuts and Bolts of Choosing the Right Article

ESL

One of the most complicated and confusing aspects of English for non-native speakers is the use of **articles**. There are two types of articles, **definite** (*the*) and **indefinite** (*a* and *an*, together with *some*, which behaves like an indefinite article). The choice among these articles—and the additional option of using no article at all—is determined by the nature of the noun the article modifies. This unit will examine how both the form of nouns and the meaning of nouns affect the choice of articles.

There are two main groups of nouns: proper nouns and common nouns. **Proper nouns** name particular people, places, and institutions and are usually capitalized. Most categories of proper nouns do not involve the use of articles. For example:

People:	Ms. Chin, Martin Luther King Jr., Oprah Winfrey
Places:	Chicago, State Street, Niagara Falls, China, Mexico City
Institutions:	General Motors, Apple Computer, Columbia University

However, some proper nouns are used with the definite article *the*. While many such uses do not follow a particular rule, some uses of *the* do. Just for fun, see whether you can figure out the rules for using *the* with certain classes of proper nouns, based on the following examples. (*Hint:* Think about the difference in meaning between the nouns that don't use articles and the ones that use *the*.) **(ANSWERS APPEAR ON PAGE 486.)**

No Article	Used with *the*
Mt. Everest, Mt. McKinley, Pikes Peak, Mt. Hood, Mt. Washington	the Alps, the Rockies, the Sierra Nevadas, the Andes, the Himalayas
Lake Como, Golden Pond, Lake Ontario, Walden Pond	the Atlantic, the Mediterranean Sea, the Pacific, the Indian Ocean

This unit focuses on the other type of nouns —common nouns. **Common nouns** are not capitalized and are not the names of particular people, places, or institutions. For example, *Ms. Chin* is the name of a particular person, but the common noun *woman* is not. The choice of which article to use with a common noun (or whether to use any article at all) depends on three questions, each of which is discussed in its own lesson.

Lesson 30 helps you answer the question *What is the form of the noun?* The choice of which article to use depends, in part, on whether the noun is singular or plural and whether it is a count noun or a noncount noun.

> Example: ✗ Our team manager loaded all the equipments onto the bus before the game.
>
> Correction: Our team manager loaded all the equipment~~s~~ onto the bus before the game.

Lesson 31 helps you answer the question *Does the reader know which specific noun I am referring to?* The choice of which article to use depends, in part, on whether the writer is referring to a specific person, place, or thing that is known to the reader.

> Example: ✗ Let's go to a coffee shop at the corner of Main Street and Maple.
>
>   *the*
> Correction: Let's go to ~~a~~ coffee shop at the corner of Main Street and Maple.   ^

Lesson 32 helps you answer the question *Am I using the noun to make a generalization?* The choice of which article to use depends, in part, on whether the noun is being used to make a generalization—a broad statement or conclusion—about something.

> Example: ✗ The nutritionists now believe that eating soybeans may help stop calcium loss and prevent osteoporosis.
>
>   *Nutritionists*
> Correction: ~~The nutritionists~~ now believe that eating soybeans may
>   ^
>   help stop calcium loss and prevent osteoporosis.

This unit is somewhat different from other units in the book. In the other units, the lessons are loosely connected. Usually, you can do one lesson in a unit without doing any other lessons first. In this unit, however, that is not the case; the three lessons are tightly connected. You should do all three lessons in order. They work together to support the *article decision tree*, a technique that helps you decide which article (if any) to use with a given common noun. This technique is discussed in the Unit Nine Review.

Unit Nine

overview
ESL

Incorrect Plurals and Indefinite Articles with Noncount Nouns

---

EXAMPLE 1   *Noncount Noun Incorrectly Used with Plural Ending*

Error: ✗ There have been many studies about the effect of television <u>violences</u> on children.

Correction: There have been many studies about the effect of
                     violence
television ~~violences~~ on children.
           ^

EXAMPLE 2   *Noncount Noun Incorrectly Used with Indefinite Article (a/an)*

Error: ✗ A customs agent might ask to see <u>a luggage</u>.

Correction: A customs agent might ask to see ~~a~~ luggage.

What's the Problem?

A large number of nouns in English cannot be used in the plural (like ✗ *violences* in Example 1). These nouns are called **noncount nouns** because they cannot be counted with number words like *one, two, three*. That is, we cannot say the following:

     ✗ one violence, two violences, three violences . . .

     ✗ one luggage, two luggages, three luggages . . .

Another peculiarity of this group of nouns is that they cannot be used with the indefinite article *a* or *an* (like ✗ *a luggage* in Example 2). The article *a/an* comes from the number word *one*; because we cannot say *one luggage*, we also cannot say *a luggage* or *a violence*. (Note that the indefinite article has two forms: *a* before words beginning with a consonant sound and *an* before words beginning with a vowel sound. For example, <u>*a*</u> *banana* but <u>*an*</u> *apple*.)

Diagnostic Exercise

CORRECTED SENTENCES APPEAR ON PAGE 486.

Correct all errors in the following paragraph using the first correction as a model. The number in parentheses at the end of the paragraph indicates how many errors you should find.

        modernization

    The ~~modernizations~~ of agriculture has meant a huge increase

in just a few crops—wheats and rices for a human consumption, corns

for an animal consumption, and cottons for industrial productions. This

specialization in a few crops is called a *monoculture*. A monoculture has

some disadvantages: It reduces a biodiversity and requires huge amounts

of energies and fertilizer. (11)

Fixing This Problem in Your Writing

Noncount nouns are hard to characterize. Nevertheless, the following tips will help you make good guesses about which nouns are noncountable.

> **GENERAL CATEGORIES TIP**   Most noncount nouns are generic names for categories of things.

For example, the noncount noun *luggage* is a generic or collective term that refers to an entire category of things we carry with us. In contrast, the names of *specific types* of luggage, like *suitcase*, *backpack*, and *briefcase* are all countable:

    one suitcase, two suitcases

    one backpack, two backpacks

    one briefcase, two briefcases

Lesson 30

art
ESL

> **OTHER NONCOUNT CATEGORIES TIP**   Most noncount nouns fall in to the following categories: abstractions, academic fields, food, gerunds (words ending in *-ing* used as nouns), languages, liquids and gases, materials, natural phenomena, sports and games, and weather words.

Here are examples of the main categories of noncount nouns:

Abstractions: hope, faith, charity, beauty, luck, knowledge, reliability

Academic fields: anthropology, chemistry, literature, physics

Food: butter, rice, cheese, meat, chicken, salt, sugar

Gerunds (words ending in *-ing* used as nouns): smiling, wishing, walking

Languages: English, Chinese, Spanish, Russian

Liquids and gases: water, coffee, tea, wine, blood, air, oxygen, gasoline

Materials: gold, paper, wood, silk, glass, sand, plastic

Natural phenomena: gravity, electricity, space, matter

Sports and games: tennis, soccer, baseball, chess, poker

Weather words: fog, snow, rain, pollution, wind

Let's see how the two tips can be applied to the example sentences.

Example 1:   ✗ There have been many studies about the effect of television <u>violences</u> on children.

Tip applied: violence = abstraction

Correction: There have been many studies about the effect of
                              violence
                television ~~violences~~ on children.
                              ^

Lesson 30

art

ESL

The Other Noncount Categories Tip helps us identify *violence* as an abstraction; you cannot point to it, touch it, or weigh it. Unless you know otherwise, you should assume that an abstraction is a noncount noun and cannot be made plural.

Example 2:   ✗ A customs agent might ask to see <u>a luggage</u>.

Tip applied: luggage = general category

The General Categories Tip helps us see that *luggage* is a noncount noun because it is a generic category of countable nouns: suitcases, cartons, boxes, backpacks, etc. Because it is a noncount noun, it should not be used with the article *a*:

Correction: A customs agent might ask to see ~~a~~ luggage.

✳ Putting It All Together

Identify Noncount Noun Errors

_____ Determine which nouns in your writing refer to general categories of things (like *luggage* or *equipment*) or abstract ideas (like *violence* or *knowledge*). Use the Other Noncount Categories Tip to identify other types of noncount nouns in your writing. These words cannot be made plural and cannot be used with *a* or *an.*

Correct Noncount Noun Errors

_____ Edit noncount nouns by removing the plural *-s* ending or removing the indefinite article *a* or *an.*

Sentence Practice 1

CORRECTED SENTENCES APPEAR ON PAGE 486.

In the following sentences, correct all noncount nouns that have been incorrectly used in the plural or with the article *a* or *an.*

> Example: I hate it when the wind blows. The ~~dusts~~ *dust* gets everywhere.

1. There is never enough times to get my works done!
2. It is amazing how much efforts go into routine maintenances.
3. I have never seen a weather like this.
4. I am sure they did it for our benefits.
5. The smokes from the fires was really bothering my visions.

 For more practice with noncount nouns, go to **Exercise Central** at **bedfordstmartins.com/commonsense**

Lesson 30

art
ESL

Sentence Practice 2

CORRECTED SENTENCES APPEAR ON PAGE 486.

In the following sentences, underline and correct all noncount nouns that have been incorrectly used in the plural or with the article *a* or *an.*

Example: We need to develop our ~~understandings~~ of the
                                              understanding
                                                    ^
              ~~environments~~.
              environment
                  ^

1. The children could hardly stand the excitements of going to Disneyland.

2. The company is trying to stockpile basic commodities such as coals and timbers.

3. Most nonprofit organizations are dedicated to the betterments of all humankinds.

4. In many states, grocery stores can sell beers and wines but not hard liquors.

5. We really appreciated his advices and guidances.

Sentence Practice 3

Below are other nouns that can be used either as noncount or as count nouns, though often with considerably different meanings. Use each noun in two different sentences—once as a noncount noun and once as a plural count noun. Explain the difference in meaning.

Example: paper

Answer:

Noncount: *The book is printed on very cheap <u>paper</u>. [<u>Paper</u> is a raw material.]*

Count: *I read two <u>papers</u> this morning. [<u>Papers</u> means "newspapers" or "essays."]*

1. Baseball

2. Coffee

3. Bridge

4. Iron

5. Nickel

Lesson 30

art
ESL

Editing Practice 1

CORRECTED SENTENCES APPEAR ON PAGE 486.

Correct all errors involving noncount nouns in the following paragraph using the first correction as a model. The number in parentheses at the end of the paragraph indicates how many errors you should find.

people
There is almost nothing more important to ~~peoples~~ than meals and
^
eatings. Every culture has elaborate rituals connected with foods. After all,

we are all interested in the natures of the food we eat. Every culture has its

own ideas about what a good nutrition is. For example, in some parts of

Asia, food is divided into two groups—"cooling" and "warming." In Japan,

for example, eels are eaten during warm weathers because eels are be-

lieved to help cool the bloods. (6)

Editing Practice 2

Correct all errors involving noncount nouns in the following paragraph using the first correction as a model. Also make whatever other changes are necessary for the corrected sentences to be grammatically correct. The number in parentheses at the end of the paragraph indicates how many errors you should find.

knowledge is
In the United States, despite what scientific ~~knowledges are~~ telling us
^
about food and healths, our eating habits are about the worst in the world.

One of the things that strikes most foreign visitors is how much obesi-

ties they see. Researches show that Americans are consuming about 200

calories a day more than they did ten years ago. It is interesting that while

overeatings have increased in the last decade, nearly every other health

factor has shown a great deal of improvement. Americans now smoke

many fewer cigarettes than they used to, and Americans drink less alcohols

than they used to. Automobile safeties have also improved greatly. Death

due to drunk drivings has declined dramatically. Given how health- and

Lesson 30

art
ESL

safety-conscious we Americans are, it is hard to see why we cannot get our

eating problem under control. (7)

Applying What You Know

Examine several paragraphs of a newspaper. How many noncount nouns can you find? Using the list provided in this lesson (on page 298), identify which categories these noncount nouns fall in to.

The Bottom Line	**Count nouns** can be made plural, but noncount nouns cannot.

Using *A/An, Some,* and *The*

ESL

EXAMPLE 1 *Definite Article (the) Used Instead of Indefinite Article (a)*

Error: ✗ Masanori had <u>the good idea</u>.

Correction: Masanori had ~~the~~ *a* good idea.

EXAMPLE 2 *Indefinite Article (a) Used Instead of Definite Article (the)*

Error: ✗ Effie stepped into a telephone booth and picked up <u>a phone</u>.

Correction: Effie stepped into a telephone booth and picked up ~~a~~ *the* phone.

What's the Problem?

English has two different types of articles used with nouns: **definite** and **indefinite**:

- The **definite article** is always *the,* which is used with all types of **common nouns** (singular and plural, **count** and **noncount**).

- Using **indefinite articles** is more complicated. The indefinite articles *a* and *an* are used *only* with singular count nouns (*a truck, an apple*). *Some* is used with plural count nouns (*some trucks, some apples*) and all noncount nouns (*some violence, some water*).

The family of articles is represented in this diagram:

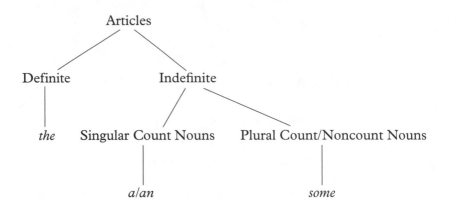

Every time you use a common noun, you must decide which type of article to use. Use the definite article *the* if BOTH of the following statements are true about the noun: (1) you have a specific person, place, thing, or idea in mind, and (2) you can reasonably assume that the reader will know *which* specific noun you mean. Use the indefinite articles *a/an* and *some* when EITHER (1) you do not have a particular person, place, thing, or idea in mind or (2) you have a particular noun in mind, but you do not assume that the reader can identify *which* one you are talking about.

Diagnostic Exercise

CORRECTED SENTENCES APPEAR ON PAGE 486.

Lesson 31

art
ESL

Correct all errors in the following paragraph using the first correction as a model. The number in parentheses at the end of the paragraph indicates how many errors you should find.

Doctors have long known that we need to have iron in our diets.
                                                          a
Recently, however, ~~the~~ new study has revealed that we may be getting too
                    ^
much iron. The human body keeps all an iron it digests. An only way we
lose stored iron in a body is through bleeding. John Murray, the researcher
at the University of Minnesota, discovered that people who live on the
very low iron diet may have the greatly reduced risk of the heart attack.
Another study found that diets high in meat have the strong correlation

with a high risk of heart disease. Apparently, when people have the high level of iron, excess iron may worsen the effect of cholesterol. (10)

Fixing This Problem in Your Writing

Here are four tips that will help you decide which article to use.

PREVIOUS-MENTION TIP   Use the definite article *the* if you have already mentioned the noun.

Suppose Example 1 occurred in the following context:

Masanori was working on his newest book. ✗ He couldn't think of a title, but then he had <u>the good idea</u>.

Because Masanori's good idea has not been mentioned previously, the sentence should use the indefinite article *a* instead of the definite article *the*:

a

Tip applied: . . . but then he had ~~the~~ good idea.

^

Now suppose that this was the next sentence in the example:

He thought that the idea for the title was promising.

When we apply the Previous-Mention Tip to this sentence, we see that the definite article *the* is correct because the noun *idea* has already been mentioned in the previous sentence.

DEFINED-BY-MODIFIERS TIP   Use the definite article *the* if the noun is followed by a word or words that uniquely identify the noun.

Some nouns are followed by *restrictive modifiers*, words that specifically identify the particular noun in question. As a result, the reader can tell which specific noun the writer is referring to, so these nouns require a definite article *even if the noun has not been mentioned previously.* Here are some nouns defined by restrictive modifiers. All of these nouns, even when mentioned for the first time, require the definite article *the*:

DEFINITE
ARTICLE   NOUN   +   RESTRICTIVE MODIFIER

The cat on our porch belongs to a neighbor.

Lesson 31

art
ESL

DEFINITE
ARTICLE   NOUN   +   RESTRICTIVE MODIFIER

The cat sitting on the porch belongs to a neighbor.

DEFINITE
ARTICLE   NOUN   +   RESTRICTIVE MODIFIER

The cat that was sitting on the porch belongs to a neighbor.

> **NORMAL-EXPECTATIONS TIP**   Use the definite article *the* if the noun meets our normal expectations about the way things work.

Let's apply this tip to Example 2:

Example 2:   ✗ Effie went into a telephone booth and picked up **a phone.**

Even though the noun *phone* has not been mentioned, the writer should have used the definite article *the* because the reader expects telephone booths to contain phones:

Tip applied: ✗ Effie went into a telephone booth and picked up
the
~~a~~ phone.
^

> **UNIQUENESS TIP**   Use the definite article *the* if the noun is unique and everybody would be expected to know about it.

Lesson 31

art
ESL

Tip applied: The sun was beginning to rise above the horizon.

Unless you are writing a science-fiction novel, our planet has only one sun and one horizon, and everybody already knows about them. Even though *sun* and *horizon* have not been mentioned before, it would be wrong to use the indefinite article with these two nouns (✗ *A sun was beginning to rise above a horizon*) because it would incorrectly imply that there are multiple suns and multiple horizons.

✳ Putting It All Together

Identify Errors in Using Definite and Indefinite Articles

_____ As you proofread your paper, ask yourself the following questions about the common nouns you are using:

- Have you already mentioned the noun?
- Is the noun followed by a restrictive modifier?
- Does the noun meet normal expectations about how things work?
- Is the noun something unique (such as the sun) that everybody already knows about?

Correct Errors in Using Definite and Indefinite Articles

_____ If you answer *yes* to ANY of the questions above, use the definite article *the*.

_____ If you answer *no* to ALL of the questions above, use the indefinite articles *a/an* or *some*. Use *a/an* with singular count nouns and use *some* with plural count nouns and all noncount nouns.

Sentence Practice 1

CORRECTED SENTENCES APPEAR ON PAGE 486.

The following sentences contain one or more correct uses of the definite article *the* (underlined). Assume that there is no previous mention of the noun that *the* modifies. For each underlined *the*, indicate which tip provides the best explanation for using *the*: the Defined-by-Modifiers Tip, the Normal-Expectations Tip, or the Uniqueness Tip.

Example: The pumpkin pie you made for Thanksgiving was really good.

Answer: *Defined-by-Modifiers Tip*

1. A lunar eclipse happens when the earth's shadow falls on the moon.

2. You will be given ten questions, and you need to find the answers as soon as possible.

3. The lesson that we covered yesterday will be on the next exam.

4. The evening stars were just visible in the east.

5. You're right. The idea that I had would never have worked.

Lesson 31

art
ESL

For more practice using articles, go to **Exercise Central** at
bedfordstmartins.com/commonsense

Sentence Practice 2

CORRECTED SENTENCES APPEAR ON PAGE 486.

The following sentences contain one or more correct uses of the definite article *the* (underlined). Assume that there is no previous mention of the noun that *the* modifies. For each underlined *the*, indicate which tip provides the best explanation for using *the*: the Defined-by-Modifiers Tip, the Normal-Expectations Tip, or the Uniqueness Tip.

> Example: When you are going out in a boat, always check <u>the</u> weather first.
>
> Answer: *Uniqueness Tip*

1. <u>The</u> present I got for Louise came from a little boutique downtown.

2. When we got to Symphony Hall, <u>the</u> orchestra was just tuning up.

3. It was as clear as <u>the</u> nose on your face. (saying)

4. <u>The</u> big bang happened about 13.7 billion years ago.

5. Fortunately, none of <u>the</u> dire predictions made about the year 2000 ever came about.

Sentence Practice 3

Fill in the blanks with the correct article: *the* or *a/an*.

> Example: I took _____*a*_____ picture of _____*the*_____ New York skyline.

Lesson 31

art
ESL

1. We got _____ city map and found _____ location of _____ restaurant we were going to.

2. I made _____ mistake on _____ first question on _____ exam in chemistry.

3. When they got to _____ airport in Denver, they had to wait _____ hour.

4. There was _____ truck parked in _____ parking lot next to Safeway.

5. After I got home, I went into _____ kitchen and fixed myself _____ sandwich.

Editing Practice 1

CORRECTED SENTENCES APPEAR ON PAGE 487.

Correct all the errors involving definite and indefinite articles in the following paragraph using the first correction as a model. The number in parentheses at the end of the paragraph indicates how many errors you should find.

      Like many young people just out of school, I recently moved into ~~the~~ *an* apartment. I was on my own for the first time. I rented the unfurnished apartment because it was a lot cheaper than getting one already furnished. As is normally the case in the United States, an apartment came already furnished with the stove and refrigerator. (This is not the case in Europe. The friends of mine rented the apartment in Rome for the semester abroad program. The unfurnished apartment there did not even have the sink, let alone any kitchen appliances.) I decided that a kitchen had to be my highest priority. I bought the set of dishes and the pots and pans at the big chain store. My parents gave me the old set of kitchen utensils. I went to Goodwill and got the really cheap kitchen table and four wobbly chairs. With that plus my sleeping bag and air mattress, I was ready to move in. (14)

Editing Practice 2

Correct all the errors involving definite and indefinite articles in the following paragraph using the first correction as a model. The number in parentheses at the end of the paragraph indicates how many errors you should find.

      Eventually, of course, I needed a lot more stuff. I could get along without ~~the~~ *a* desk since I could always use a kitchen table for writing. I had no comfortable place to sit down, so I had to get the living room furniture. I decided against getting the couch because it would take up too much space; instead I got the armchairs on sale. I could arrange some armchairs any way I needed to use them. I thought about buying the TV, but the new

Lesson 31

art
ESL

plasma screens are so expensive that I finally decided to borrow just the unused TV set from my parents. Eventually I would like to get the real bed, but that will have to wait until I get a few more paychecks. After seeing what happened to the friends of mine who got into financial trouble by furnishing their new apartment with credit cards, I decided that if I couldn't pay cash for furniture, I could get along without it. (9)

Applying What You Know

Photocopy a couple of paragraphs from something you are reading. Go through the copy and cross out every article so that you can no longer tell what the article was. Set the text aside for a while and then see if you can replace all the articles correctly.

The Bottom Line	Use *the* only when readers will know what noun *the* refers to.

Lesson 31

art
ESL

Making Generalizations without Articles

ESL

EXAMPLE 1

Error: ✗ The barn is always full of some mice.

Correction: The barn is always full of ~~some~~ mice.

EXAMPLE 2

Error: ✗ Our family usually has the fish for dinner on Fridays.

Correction: Our family usually has ~~the~~ fish for dinner on Fridays.

What's the Problem?

Generally speaking, common nouns in English must be preceded by an **article** (*a/an, some,* or *the*) or a **modifier** like a number or a possessive pronoun (*his, her, your, their, our*). However, there is one major exception to this rule: To make a generalization about something, we must use a noun without any articles.

For instance, in Example 1, the writer is not talking about any specific mice. Rather, the writer is making a generalization about the *category* of animals that live in the barn. Therefore, the writer should use *mice* by itself, without any article.

In Example 2, the writer makes a generalization about the family's typical meal on Fridays. Therefore, the writer should have used *fish* by itself, without any article.

Diagnostic Exercise

CORRECTED SENTENCES APPEAR ON PAGE 487.

Correct all errors in the following paragraph using the first correction as a model. The number in parentheses at the end of the paragraph indicates how many errors you should find.

               Scientists
~~The scientists~~ have long known that the honeybees are somehow able
         ^
to tell some other bees where to look for some food. In the 1940s, Karl von
Frisch of the University of Munich discovered that the type of the dance
that the bees make when they return to their beehive is significant. It
seems that the honeybees are able to signal both the direction of the food
that they found and its approximate distance from their hive to the bees
who had remained at the hive. (6)

Fixing This Problem in Your Writing

Anytime you use a **noncount noun** or a plural **count noun**, check to see
whether you are using that noun as part of a generalization. If so, then you
should not use an article.

    Following are some tips that will help you recognize the kinds of sentences in which noncount or plural count nouns are being used to make a
generalization and therefore do not require an article in front of them.

> **ADVERB-OF-FREQUENCY TIP**   Look for adverbs of frequency such as *always*,
> *often*, *generally*, *frequently*, or *usually*. Adverbs of frequency are often used in
> sentences that describe habitual or repeated actions — typically a sign of a
> generalization.

Lesson 32

art
ESL

Notice that both of the example sentences contain adverbs of frequency, a
signal that the sentences are making a generalization about a noun and therefore should not use an article:

Tip applied: The barn is <u>always</u> full of ~~some~~ mice.

Tip applied: Our family <u>usually</u> has ~~the~~ fish for dinner on Fridays.

> **PRESENT TENSE TIP**   Sentences used for making generalizations are normally
> written in the present tense.

Writers usually use the present tense to make generalizations, so be especially
sure to check noncount nouns and plural count nouns in sentences that use
the present tense to see whether these nouns are being used to make gener-

alizations. Notice, for instance, that both of the example sentences are in the present tense. This is a signal that the sentence might be making a generalization about a noun and therefore should not use an article with that noun.

Example 1:   The barn is always full of ~~some~~ mice.

Example 2:   Our family usually has ~~the~~ fish for dinner on Fridays.

> **NO-MODIFIERS TIP**   A noun used for making a generalization is not usually restricted by any modifiers that follow the noun.

Modifiers after a noun usually restrict the meaning of the noun so that it is not a generalization about a whole category of things. Compare the following two sentences:

No post-noun modifier: Cheese is very crumbly.

Post-noun modifier: The cheese in the refrigerator is crumbly.

The first sentence is an unrestricted generalization about all cheese; therefore, the noun *cheese* does not use an article. The second sentence is talking only about the cheese that is *in the refrigerator*. Since the writer is referring to a particular piece of cheese (and not making a generalization about all cheeses), the definite article *the* is needed in this sentence.

> **MOST TIP**   A noun that can be modified by the word *most* is probably being used to make a generalization.

For example, you can modify the noun *classes* in the following sentence with the word *most* to confirm that you are using *classes* as a generalization:

Example: Classes are held in the mornings.

Tip applied: Most classes are held in the mornings.

Classes therefore should be used without any article.

Lesson 32

art
ESL

✳ *Putting It All Together*

Identify Errors in Using Articles

_____   When you use a noncount noun or a plural count noun, check to see whether you are using that noun to make a generalization by asking yourself the following questions: ➤

- Are there adverbs of frequency in the sentence?
- Is the sentence in the present tense?
- Is the noun in question free from following modifiers?
- Can you put *most* in front of the noun in question?

Correct Errors in Using Articles

____ If the answer to one or more of the above questions is *yes*, then it is likely that the noun is being used to make a generalization, and thus no article should be used.

Sentence Practice 1

CORRECTED SENTENCES APPEAR ON PAGE 487.

The following sentences make generalizations, and their underlined nouns are used without articles. For each underlined noun, identify which tip helps you determine that the noun is part of a generalization: the Adverb-of-Frequency Tip, the Present Tense Tip, the No-Modifiers Tip, or the *Most* Tip. *Note:* There may be multiple acceptable answers.

Example: Typically, <u>employers</u> look for trained and motivated <u>workers.</u>

Answer: *Adverb-of-Frequency Tip (typically), Present Tense Tip, No-Modifiers Tip (employers)*

1. <u>Twins</u> usually run in <u>families.</u>
2. <u>Filling stations</u> are not normally able to do extensive <u>automotive</u> <u>repairs.</u>
3. <u>Laughter</u> is the best medicine. [saying]
4. Most <u>people</u> who live off the electric grid have <u>generators.</u>
5. <u>Bees</u> are absolutely essential for <u>agriculture.</u>

Lesson 32

art
ESL

 For more practice using nouns, go to **Exercise Central** at **bedfordstmartins.com/commonsense**

Sentence Practice 2

CORRECTED SENTENCES APPEAR ON PAGE 487.

In the following sentences, underline any noncount nouns and plural count nouns that are used for making generalizations. Cross out any articles incorrectly used with these nouns. Assume that there is no previous context that these sentences refer to.

> **Example:** You can usually get the prescriptions filled at the grocery stores.
>
> **Answer:** You can usually get ~~the~~ prescriptions filled at ~~the~~ grocery stores.

1. Most countries tax the cigarettes and the alcohol heavily.

2. His company represents the authors, the playwrights, and the other creative artists.

3. The disease, the poverty, and the malnutrition are closely linked.

4. The prices of the glass, the steel, and the cement have actually dropped because of the decline in the construction.

5. Due to the global warming, the winters may actually get much colder in some places.

Sentence Practice 3

Combine the following sentences by adding the underlined information in the second sentence to the underlined noun in the first sentence. The added modification restricts the noun so that it is no longer a generalization. Make the necessary changes in articles.

> **Example:** Pianos are pretty expensive.
> They are used in public performances.
>
> **Answer:** *The pianos used in public performances are pretty expensive.*

1. Seniors are excused from class.
   They are in the school play.

2. Clouds were threatening rain.
   They were in the west.

3. Disputes are hard to resolve.
   They were involved in property rights cases.

4. Tea comes from Japan.
   They serve it in this restaurant.

5. Malls are now too small.
   They were built in the '70s and '80s.

Lesson 32

art
ESL

Editing Practice 1

CORRECTED SENTENCES APPEAR ON PAGE 487.

Correct all the errors involving articles in the following paragraph using the first correction as a model. The number in parentheses at the end of the paragraph indicates how many errors you should find.

Deborah Tannen has written extensively about the different conversational styles of ~~the~~ men and women. Males and females use the casual language in quite different ways, especially when the men are talking to men and the women are talking to women. When the groups of men are in a conversation, each speaker tries to control the topic. The most important tool in gaining and keeping the control is the humor. The humor is usually directed at others in the group, often in the form of the teasing. However, the teasing cannot go too far; it cannot be seen as actually insulting. Being able to be teased without getting angry and then responding in kind is a valued skill. The verbal competition among groups of young men is a near cultural universal. (8)

Editing Practice 2

Correct all the errors involving articles in the following paragraph using the first correction as a model. The number in parentheses at the end of the paragraph indicates how many errors you should find.

Young
~~The young~~ women usually behave quite differently. They are very careful about taking the turns. Even in the animated conversations, women are less likely to interrupt than men are. When they do interrupt, the interruptions that they make are supportive rather than confrontational. For example, interruptions will often provide the examples that confirm what the speaker is saying. Women are generally very careful to avoid the confrontations and even the controversial topics. Typically, the

group is careful to make sure that everyone has plenty of the opportunity

to participate. The entire dynamic of their conversation is to build the

group solidarity. (7)

Applying What You Know

On a separate sheet of paper, write a paragraph or two in which you generalize about the differences in male and female language that you have observed. Do you think Dr. Tannen's generalizations are true? (See Editing Practices 1–2, which discuss Dr. Tannen's theories.) Identify every noncount noun and plural count noun in your essay. Then trade papers with a partner and use the Putting It All Together checklist on page 313 to make sure your partner has not incorrectly used articles with generalizations.

The Bottom Line	**Nouns** that are used to make **generalizations** are not used with **articles**.

Lesson 32

art
ESL

Choosing the Right Article

REVIEW

Every time you use a common noun, you must decide whether or not you need to use an article; if you do need to use an article, you must choose which one it should be. Your choice should be governed by four decisions:

- Decision 1: *Generalization?* Is the noun (whether a noncount noun or a plural count noun) being used to make a generalization (see Lesson 32)? If the answer is *yes*, use No article at all. If the answer is *no*, then you must make the following decision.

- Decision 2: *Known or New?* Is your intended meaning of the noun "known" to the reader or is it "new" (see Lesson 31)? If the intended meaning is known to the reader, use the definite article *the*. If the meaning will be new, use an indefinite article: *a, an,* or *some*. The choice of indefinite article is determined by the next two decisions.

- Decision 3: *Plural or Singular?* If the new noun is plural, then you must use *some*. If the new noun is singular, then you must decide whether it is a count or a noncount noun. That brings you to the final decision.

- Decision 4: *Count or Noncount?* If the singular noun is a count noun, then you must use the indefinite article *a* or *an*. If the singular noun is a noncount noun, use *some* (see Lesson 30).

Use one or more of these tips to help you make Decision 1:

ADVERB-OF-FREQUENCY TIP Look for adverbs of frequency such as *always, often, generally, frequently,* or *usually*. Adverbs of frequency are often used in sentences that describe habitual or repeated actions — typically a sign of a generalization.

PRESENT TENSE TIP Sentences used for making generalizations are normally written in the present tense.

NO-MODIFIERS TIP A noun used for making a generalization is not usually restricted by any modifiers that follow the noun.

MOST TIP   A noun that can be modified by the word *most* is probably being used to make a generalization.

Use one or more of these tips to help you make Decision 2:

PREVIOUS-MENTION TIP   Use the definite article *the* if you have already mentioned the noun.

DEFINED-BY-MODIFIERS TIP   Use the definite article *the* if the noun is followed by a word or words that uniquely identify the noun.

NORMAL-EXPECTATIONS TIP   Use the definite article *the* if the noun meets our normal expectations about the way things work.

UNIQUENESS TIP   Use the definite article *the* if the noun is unique and everybody would be expected to know about it.

Use these tips to help you make Decisions 3 and 4:

GENERAL CATEGORIES TIP   Most noncount nouns are generic names for categories of things.

OTHER NONCOUNT CATEGORIES TIP   Most noncount nouns fall into the following categories: abstractions, academic fields, food, gerunds (words ending in *-ing* used as nouns), languages, liquids and gases, materials, natural phenomena, sports and games, and weather words.

Unit Nine

review
ESL

Use a decision tree to help you choose the right article

The decision tree on the next page maps out a process for choosing the right article for each common noun in your writing. Using this tool, you can proceed step by step from Decision 1 to Decision 4.

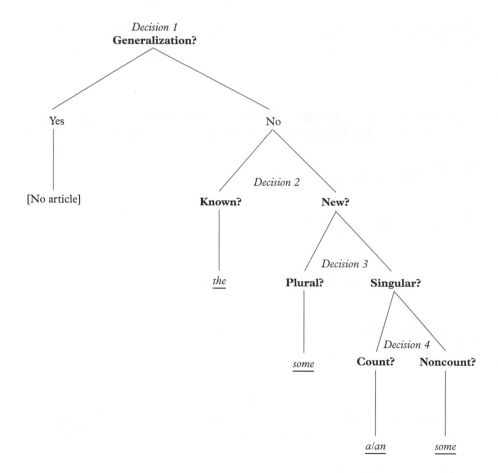

Review Test

The decision tree above shows you how these four sets of decisions flow step by step from Decision 1 to Decision 4. Use the decision tree to edit the following paragraphs for correct use of articles. The number in parentheses at the end of each paragraph indicates how many errors you should find.

Some cellular phones can certainly come in handy in a emergency. If the driver witnesses an accident or is involved in an accident, he or she can call a State Police without having to waste crucial time. In the event of the flat tire or dead battery, a driver can call tow truck without having to walk a mile or two—or more—to a phone. Wireless technology has allowed the family members to reach loved ones in an emergency, even if the person whom they are trying to reach is at the business meeting or a baseball game. (9)

For me, a beauty of having the cell phone is being able to maximize my time. I like having a flexibility to make the important phone calls either when I'm home or as I'm driving home. (4)

Using Verbs Correctly

OVERVIEW

The Nuts and Bolts of Verbs

ESL

All of the lessons in this unit deal with various aspects of **verb** use that are likely to be troublesome for non-native speakers.

Lesson 33 shows you how to use the **progressive tenses**, which are made with the helping verb *be* (in some form) followed by a verb in the *-ing* form. The progressive tense signals that an action was, is, or will be in progress at some specific moment in time (*Rina is watching TV now*). Some writers do not use the progressive tense when they should (or use it when they shouldn't). Others mistakenly use certain verbs in the progressive tense when they shouldn't. Here is an example of the first kind of mistake.

Example:　　Dr. Hernandez can't see you right now. ✗ She talks with another patient.

　　　　　　　　　　　　　　　　　　　　　　　　　　　　　is talking
Correction:　Dr. Hernandez can't see you right now. She ~~talks~~
　　　　　　with another patient.　　　　　　　　　　　　^

Lesson 34 shows you how to use **two-word verbs**. When a two-word verb (or phrasal verb) is made with an adverb, it is called a **separable two-word verb** because the adverb can be separated from the verb. That is, it can be moved after the object (*Jamie looked up the word / Jamie looked the word up*). When the compound is made with a preposition, it is called an **inseparable two-word verb** because the preposition can never be moved away from the verb (*Ben depended on Maria / ✗ Ben depended Maria on*). Sometimes writers confuse the two types of two-word verbs and don't move adverbs when they should, or they move prepositions when they shouldn't.

Example:　　✗ I didn't know her phone number, so I looked up it.

　　　　　　　　　　　　　　　　　　　　　　　looked it up
Correction:　I didn't know her phone number, so I ~~looked up it~~.
　　　　　　　　　　　　　　　　　　　　　　　　^

Lesson 35 shows you how to check for the proper word order in **informa-tion questions**. Information questions are questions that begin with words that require a detailed response like *who*, *where*, and *why* (as opposed to simple questions that can be answered with *yes* or *no*). Sometimes non-native speakers fail to invert the helping verb and the subject word when forming information questions.

Example: ✗ Where you want to go after class?

                     do you want
Correction: Where ~~you want~~ to go after class?
                    ^

Lesson 36 shows you how you can avoid the reverse mistake of inverting the helping verb and the subject, which is appropriate for information ques-tions, when you are creating certain types of **noun clauses**.

Example: ✗ We found out where should we go after class.

                                we should go
Correction: We found out where ~~should we go~~ after class.
                             ^

The Progressive Tenses

EXAMPLE 1	*Present Tense Used Instead of Progressive Tense*
Error:	✗ I can't talk to you right now. I <u>study</u> for my exams.
Correction:	I can't talk to you right now. I <s>study</s> *am studying* for my exams.
EXAMPLE 2	*Progressive Tense Used Incorrectly*
Error:	✗ Ms. Higa <u>was owning</u> a house in San Francisco then.
Correction:	Ms. Higa <s>was owning</s> *owned* a house in San Francisco then.

What's the Problem?

The **progressive tenses** are created by using some form of the helping verb *be* with a **present participle** (a verb form ending in *-ing*). The progressive tenses are used to indicate continuous activity. There are three forms of progressive verbs:

- The *present progressive tense* uses the helping verb *be* in one of its three present tense forms (*am, are, is*); for example: *I <u>am</u> smiling. They <u>are</u> smiling. She <u>is</u> smiling.*

- The *past progressive tense* uses the helping verb *be* in one of its two past tense forms (*was, were*); for example: *He <u>was</u> smiling. They <u>were</u> smiling.*

- The *future progressive tense* uses *will* with the helping verb *be*; for example: *They <u>will be</u> smiling.*

There are two common mistakes writers make when using the progressive tense. The first is mistakenly using the present tense when the present progressive tense should be used or vice versa. In Example 1, for instance, the writer incorrectly used the present tense *study* instead of the present progressive tense *am studying*.

The second mistake is using any of the progressive tenses with certain verbs that cannot logically take a progressive form because they do not describe an action that occurs over a definite moment of time. We call these verbs **steady-state verbs**. The verb *own* in Example 2 is an example of a steady-state verb that cannot be used in the progressive tense. We'll discuss such steady-state verbs in more detail later in the lesson.

Diagnostic Exercise

CORRECTED SENTENCES APPEAR ON PAGE 487.

Correct all errors in the following paragraph using the first correction as a model. The number in parentheses at the end of the paragraph indicates how many errors you should find.

Every weekday morning at 6 A.M., my alarm ~~is going~~ *goes* off. By 6:15, the breakfast dishes are on the table, and the coffee brews. I always am getting the children up next. It is very hard for them to get going. On Mondays, they are resembling bears coming out of hibernation. While they take their showers with their eyes still closed, I get everyone's clothes ready. Since the youngest child still is needing a lot of help getting dressed, I usually am spending some extra time with her talking about the day's events. By 7 A.M., we all sit at the table for breakfast. The children are loving pancakes and waffles, but there just isn't time to make them except on weekends. Breakfast goes by quickly, unless somebody is spilling the milk or juice. I am wishing we had more time in the morning, but every morning I am being amazed when I am looking back and realizing that we got it all done again. (13)

Lesson 33

vt
ESL

Fixing This Problem in Your Writing

To avoid progressive verb mistakes, we first need to understand the basic difference in meaning between the present tense and the present progressive tense.

We saw in Lesson 6 that the main function of the present tense in English is to make "timeless" statements or generalizations about events that happen all the time. The present progressive tense is used to talk about what is happening at the exact present moment of time. Compare the following sentences:

> Present tense: I <u>study</u> English every day.
>
> Present progressive: I <u>am studying</u> English right now.

Both sentences are grammatical, but they mean different things. The present tense sentence is a generalization about the speaker's study habits (he or she studies every day), but it does not tell us what the speaker is actually doing at this moment. For all we know, the speaker is out watching a kung-fu movie with a friend.

The present progressive tense sentence, however, tells us what the speaker is in the process of doing *at the present moment* (he or she is studying English). The sentence tells us nothing about the speaker's study habits. This may be the first and last time that the speaker will ever study English.

As you might guess, the future progressive is used to describe an action that will be in progress at some future point in time, for example:

> Future progressive: I <u>will be working</u> on my paper all next weekend.

Likewise, the past progressive is used to describe an action that was in progress at some past moment of time, for example:

> Past progressive: I <u>was working</u> on my paper when you called.

Here is a tip to help you remember when to use the progressive tenses.

THE PROGRESSIVE TIP   If an action is in <u>progress</u> at some moment of time, use a progressive (-*ing*) form of the verb.

As you saw in Example 2 at the beginning of the lesson, some verbs cannot be used in a progressive form. These steady-state verbs are used to describe conditions or states that are unchanging over a long period of time. The unchanging nature of these verbs makes them incompatible with the in-progress, "right now" nature of the progressive tense. For example, compare the following progressive sentences:

Maria is **studying** for the exam.

✗ Maria is **knowing** the answer.

The progressive tense is grammatical in the first sentence but not in the second. *Studying* is an action that progresses—it starts, goes on for a while, and then ends. The progressive tense correctly conveys this meaning. *Knowing* something, however, is a state of being. It is not an action that occurs over a definite period of time, so it cannot form the progressive tense.

Here is a tip that will help you identify steady-state verbs.

> **STEADY-STATE VERB TIP** Verbs that refer to unchanging, steady-state conditions cannot form the progressive tense. Most steady-state verbs fall into three broad categories: mental activity, emotional condition, and possession.

Here are some examples of steady-state verbs:

- **Mental activity:** *believe, doubt, forget, imagine, know, mean*
- **Emotional condition:** *appreciate, care, dislike, envy, fear, hate, like, love, need, prefer, want*
- **Possession:** *belong, consist of, contain, own, possess*

This list is far from complete. Moreover, some verbs on this list cannot be used with progressive tenses when they have one meaning but can be used with progressive tenses when they have another meaning. For example, verbs of sense perception cannot be used in the progressive when they describe something:

✗ The soup <u>is tasting</u> too salty.

However, the same verb *can* be used in the progressive when a person physically performs the action of the verb:

The cook <u>is tasting</u> the soup to see if it needs more salt.

Additional examples of steady-state verbs follow.

MORE EXAMPLES

Mental Activity

Error: ✗ I <u>am thinking</u> that you are right.

Correction: I ~~am thinking~~ that you are right.
                  think ^

Emotional Condition

Error: ✗ Hiroshi <u>is loving</u> his new job.

Correction: Hiroshi ~~is loving~~ his new job.
                   loves ^

Possession

Error: ✗ Juan is belonging to the student union.

Correction: Juan ~~is belonging~~ to the student union.
          belongs

✳ *Putting It All Together*

Identify Errors in Using the Progressive Tenses

____ Check to see whether a verb is describing a continuous, "in-progress" action — an action that progressed, is progressing, or will progress over some particular moment of time.

Correct Errors in Using the Progressive Tenses

____ If you are describing an action that progressed, is progressing, or will progress over some particular moment of time, use the appropriate progressive tense (form of *be* + a verb ending in *-ing*).

____ If the verb describes an unchanging condition or state of being, check to see whether the meaning of the verb is a mental activity, emotional condition, or possession. If it does have one of these meanings, then do *not* use the progressive tense.

Sentence Practice 1

CORRECTED SENTENCES APPEAR ON PAGE 488.

The underlined verbs in the following sentences are in the progressive tense. In some sentences the progressive tense is used correctly, but in others it is incorrect because it is applied to a steady-state verb. Correct any instances of the progressive tense that use steady-state verbs.

Example: We ~~are doubting~~ that they will be playing outside in such
         doubt
         bad weather.

1. The offer is including free installation and service for the first year.

2. No one was noticing how poorly they were maintaining their records.

3. I am hating it when people are disagreeing about such trivial matters.

4. We are needing more help while we <u>are hosting</u> the conference.

5. It <u>isn't seeming</u> to <u>be getting</u> any better.

 For more practice with verb tense, go to **Exercise Central** at
bedfordstmartins.com/commonsense

Sentence Practice 2

CORRECTED SENTENCES APPEAR ON PAGE 488.

The underlined verbs in the following sentences are in the progressive tense. In some sentences, the progressive tense is used correctly, but in others it is incorrect because it is applied to a steady-state verb. Correct any instances of the progressive tense that use steady-state verbs.

Example: I <s>am seeing</s> *see* what you meant when you <u>were complaining</u> about their food.

1. She <u>is running</u> some errands right now, but she <u>will be calling</u> you back as soon as she <u>is getting</u> home.

2. She certainly <u>is resembling</u> her mother.

3. I <u>am promising</u> that I will <u>be considering</u> it seriously.

4. He <u>is belonging</u> to all the civic organizations in town.

5. I <u>am hating</u> that our school <u>is having</u> such a restrictive policy on using computers.

Sentence Practice 3

Combine the following sentences by adding the underlined information in the second sentence to the first sentence. Change the past tense of the first sentence to the appropriate progressive tense.

Example: **I flew to Chicago.**

             It will be <u>this time tomorrow</u>.

Answer: *I will be flying to Chicago this time tomorrow.*

1. I'm sorry. She met with another client.
   It is <u>now</u>.

2. She met with another client.
   It was <u>when you called</u>.

Lesson 33

vt
ESL

3. We painted the garage.
    We did it <u>when the rain storm hit</u>.

4. I slept soundly.
    I did it <u>when the alarm went off</u>.

5. I took my last exam.
    It will happen <u>when you get here</u>.

Editing Practice 1

CORRECTED SENTENCES APPEAR ON PAGE 488.

Correct all errors involving the progressive tenses in the following paragraph using the first correction as a model. The number in parentheses at the end of the paragraph indicates how many errors you should find.

        think

I ~~am thinking~~ that I would go crazy if I tried to write the way

my husband does. I am spending just as much time on my papers as he

does, but I am writing in a completely different way. I am spending much

of my time thinking through what I am going to say before I ever put a

word down on paper. When I am feeling that I really know what I want to

say, I sit down and write a complete draft. Then I make an outline for what

I have written. Often this outline is showing me where I need to go back

and expand an idea or rearrange something. But, on the whole, I am not

needing to make a lot of changes. My husband is thinking that I am a lazy

writer, but he is wrong. Just because I don't sit at my computer for hours

on end doesn't mean I am not working. (7)

Lesson 33

vt
ESL

Editing Practice 2

Correct all errors involving the progressive tenses in the following paragraphs using the first correction as a model. The number in parentheses at the end of each paragraph indicates how many errors you should find.

        compose

Despite the fact that we ~~are composing~~ our papers in totally

different ways, we end up at the same point—papers that are needing to be proofread. We have both learned the hard way that neither one of us is very good at catching our own mistakes. My husband is an especially bad speller. He is relying a lot (too much, in my opinion) on his computer's spell-checker. The spell-checker is wonderful, but it can be a bit of a trap. He is believing that once he has run the spell-checker, he can forget about spelling errors. Well, he is wrong. He is having the tendency to make mistakes with little words. For example, he is often typing *and* for *an* or *as*, *the* for *they*, and *your* for *you*. The trouble is that the spell-checker doesn't see these little word substitutions as mistakes, so it is never correcting them. (6)

   I tell him it is impossible to read for meaning and read for mechanical errors at the same time. The best way to catch mistakes in grammar, spelling, and punctuation is to proofread each other's papers. Even then, we are needing to read very slowly. One trick that is seeming to work is to proofread backward. That is, we are starting at the last sentence in each paragraph. We proofread it. Then we read the next-to-last sentence, and so on, working our way to the beginning of the paragraph. This is very tedious, but it seems to work because we are being able to concentrate just on mechanics without getting distracted by the meaning of the paper. (4)

Applying What You Know

On your own paper, write a paragraph or two about your own writing process. Use the Putting It All Together checklist on page 328 to make sure that you have used the present and progressive tenses correctly.

Lesson 33

vt
ESL

The Bottom Line	The progressive tenses are used for events that **are taking** place at a particular moment of time.

LESSON 34

ESL **Two-Word Verbs**

[*Note:* See pages 461–463 for a glossary of one hundred commonly used separable two-word verbs.]

EXAMPLE 1

Error: ✗ Roland <u>called up her.</u>

Correction: Roland called ~~up~~ *up* her.

EXAMPLE 2

Error: ✗ Misako <u>turned down them.</u>

Correction: Misako turned ~~down~~ *down* them.

What's the Problem?

Most **verbs** in English can be combined with an **adverb** or a **preposition** to form a **two-word verb** (also known as a *phrasal verb*). Two-word verbs are very common in English but can pose problems for non-native speakers. One problem is that it is difficult to determine the meaning of a two-word verb based on the meanings of its individual words. Consider the expression *come by*:

How did you <u>come by</u> that picture?

Come by means to "get" or "obtain," but you couldn't know that just by looking at the words *come* and *by*.

Another problem with two-word verbs is a grammatical one. There are two types of two-word verbs: *separable* and *inseparable*:

- **Separable Two-Word Verb = Verb + Adverb**

  VERB ADVERB

  The prince <u>turned</u> <u>down</u> the king.

  Turned down = rejected

- **Inseparable Two-Word Verb = Verb + Preposition**

  VERB PREPOSITION

  The prince <u>turned</u> <u>against</u> the king.

  Turned against = became an enemy of

When we use a **separable two-word verb**, the adverb can be separated from the verb (thus the term *separable*) and moved to a position immediately *after* the object. Here is an example:

Before: The prince <u>turned</u> <u>down</u> the king.

After: The prince <u>turned</u> (down) the king.
            [The prince <u>turned</u> the king <u>down</u>.]

When the object is a noun, as in the example above, the two-word verb is correct whether it is separated or not. However, if the object is a **pronoun**, the adverb MUST be moved after the pronoun:

Before: ✗ The prince <u>turned</u> <u>down</u> him.

After: The prince <u>turned</u> (down) him.
            [The prince <u>turned</u> him <u>down</u>.]

When we use an **inseparable two-word verb**, the preposition *cannot* be separated from the verb (thus the term *inseparable*). Here is an example:

Before: The prince <u>turned</u> <u>against</u> the king.

After: ✗ The prince <u>turned</u> (against) the king.
            [✗ The prince <u>turned</u> the king <u>against</u>.]

Lesson 34

vf
ESL

The problem that non-native speakers face is telling separable and inseparable two-word verbs apart. Later in the lesson, we'll offer some tips you can use to help you differentiate between the two.

Diagnostic Exercise

CORRECTED SENTENCES APPEAR ON PAGE 488.

Correct all two-word verb errors in the following paragraph using the first correction as a model. The number in parentheses at the end of the paragraph indicates how many errors you should find.

It used to be that making a plane reservation was a simple matter.
You found a travel agency and ~~called up it~~ *called it up*. Since the agency didn't work

for any airlines, it looked for the best fare and found out it. There was no

direct cost to you since the airlines paid the commission; they built in it

to the price of your ticket. After the airlines were deregulated, however, this

system began to fall apart. Faced with much greater competition,

airlines identified commission costs as an unnecessary expense, and they

cut down them by reducing the commission they paid agencies. Some

airlines, like Southwest, even cut out them entirely. As a result, most travel

agencies stopped selling tickets for those airlines. If you want to know

about their fares, you must deal with each of the airlines separately. The

catch, of course, is that if you call one of them, its representative can talk

only about its fares, and you have no way to check out it to see if you have

the best bargain. (5)

Fixing This Problem in Your Writing

Lesson 34

vf
ESL

Here are the ten most common adverbs used in *separable* two-word verbs:

apart	away	down	out	together
around	back	off	over	up

When you see one of these words in a two-word verb, you can be fairly sure that the verb and adverb are separable. The point to keep in mind is that when a separable two-word verb is followed by a *noun*, you have the option of separating the verb and the adverb. However, when the two-word verb is followed by a *pronoun*, then you MUST separate the verb and the adverb.

Look at the following examples of separable two-word verbs. Notice the difference in the position of the adverb when it is followed by a *noun* and when it is followed by a *pronoun*. The first sentence in each pair has a noun object, and the second in each pair has a pronoun object.

SEPARABLE TWO-WORD VERBS

Verb + Adverb	Meaning	Example
take apart	disassemble	We **took apart** the bicycle. We **took** it **apart**.
show around	give a tour to	We **showed around** the visitors. We **showed** them **around**.
throw away	discard	We **threw away** the boxes. We **threw** them **away**.
put back	replace	We **put back** the books. We **put** them **back**.
break down	categorize	We **broke down** the addresses by zip code. We **broke** them **down** by zip code.
call off	cancel	We **called off** the meeting. We **called** it **off**.
find out	discover	We **found out** the truth. We **found** it **out**.
talk over	discuss	We **talked over** the situation. We **talked** it **over**.
keep together	group/bunch	We **kept together** all the loose papers. We **kept** them **together**.
hang up	disconnect	We **hung up** the phone. We **hung** it **up**.

Lesson 34

vf
ESL

Probably the most useful way to distinguish between *separable* and *inseparable* two-word verbs is to see if the word following the two-word verb can be used in a **prepositional phrase**. If it can, it is a preposition and can't be separated from the verb it is next to. Use the following tip to determine whether the second word in a two-word verb is a preposition.

> **THE MOVIES TIP** If the second word in a two-word verb can be used to form a prepositional phrase with *the movies*, it is a preposition and thus inseparable from the verb. If it does not work with *the movies*, it is an adverb and thus separable from the verb.

Let's apply *The Movies* Tip to the first example:

Example 1: ✗ Roland <u>called up</u> her.

Tip applied: ✗ <u>up</u> the movies

Because *up the movies* does not make sense, we know that *up* is not a preposition. Thus, *up* is an adverb and is separable from the verb. Because the object in this sentence is a pronoun (*her*), *up* MUST be separated from the verb:

Correction: Roland called u̶p̶ ^up^ her.

Now let's apply *The Movies* Tip to the second example sentence:

Example 2: ✗ Misako <u>turned down</u> them.

Tip applied: ✗ <u>down</u> the movies

Once again, when we apply *The Movies* Tip we see that *down the movies* does not make sense, so we know that *down* is not a preposition. Thus, *down* is an adverb and MUST be moved *after* the object since the object is a pronoun:

Correction: Misako turned d̶o̶w̶n̶ ^down^ them.

Here is an example with an inseparable two-word verb:

Example: We <u>stopped at</u> a fast-food restaurant for lunch.

Tip applied: at the movies

Since *at* makes sense with *the movies* as an object, we can reasonably predict that *stop at* is an inseparable two-word verb. If we replaced the noun phrase *a fast-food restaurant* with the pronoun *it*, we would not move the preposition:

Example: We <u>stopped at</u> it for lunch.

Two additional words—*in* and *on*—are commonly used in two-word verbs, either as adverbs in separable two-word verbs or as prepositions in inseparable two-word verbs. Here are some examples.

IN AND *ON* AS ADVERBS (SEPARABLE)

Verb + Adverb	Meaning	Example
turn in	submit	We **turned in** our papers.
		We **turned** them **in**.
turn on	activate	We **turned on** the radio.
		We **turned** it **on**.

IN AND *ON* AS PREPOSITIONS (INSEPARABLE)

Verb + Adverb	Meaning	Example
look into	investigate	The FBI will **look into** the bombing.
		The FBI will **look into** it.
call on	visit	We **called on** some friends.
		We **called on** them.

Unfortunately, *The Movies* Tip does not help with two-word verbs that use *in* or *on* since these words can be either adverbs or prepositions. By listening to native speakers use these words and by using them in your own speaking and writing, you will soon learn the correct uses of two-word verbs with *in* and *on*.

✳ *Putting It All Together*

Identify Two-Word Verb Errors

_____ Use *The Movies* Tip to help distinguish between separable (verb + adverb) and inseparable (verb + preposition) two-word verbs.

Correct Two-Word Verb Errors

_____ If a separable two-word verb is followed by an object noun, you have the option of placing the adverb before or after the noun.

_____ If a separable two-word verb is followed by an object pronoun, you *must* move the adverb to follow the pronoun.

_____ Inseparable two-word verbs must *never* be separated by nouns or pronouns.

Lesson 34

vf
ESL

Sentence Practice 1

CORRECTED SENTENCES APPEAR ON PAGE 488.

Correct the errors in the underlined two-word verbs. If the sentence is correct as is, write *OK* above it. Use *The Movies* Tip to confirm your answer.

> *check them out*
>
> Example: I took my books to the desk to ~~check out them~~.
>   ^
> Confirmation: *out the movies (adverb = separable)*

1. You must be careful to <u>guard it against</u>.

2. The policeman <u>straightened out them</u> when they crossed the street while the light was green.

3. Finally, I can <u>cross it off</u> my list of things to do.

4. You need to <u>hurry up them</u> because it is getting dark.

5. We <u>searched after it</u> all afternoon.

 For more practice using two-word verbs, go to **Exercise Central** at **bedfordstmartins.com/commonsense**

Sentence Practice 2

CORRECTED SENTENCES APPEAR ON PAGE 488.

Correct the errors in the underlined two-word verbs. If the sentence is correct as is, write *OK* above it. Use *The Movies* Tip to confirm your answer.

> *OK*
> Example: It never <u>occurred to me</u>.
>
> Confirmation: *to the movies (preposition = inseparable)*

1. I will <u>fill in you</u> on what happened during the meeting.

2. The milk had expired, so I <u>threw away it</u>.

3. John finished his algebra homework and asked his tutor to <u>check over it</u>.

4. When Jodie heard the joke, it <u>cracked up her</u>.

5. The analyst's associates were helpful. They <u>backed up him</u>.

Sentence Practice 3

Replace the underlined objects with an appropriate pronoun. If the pronoun follows a separable two-word verb (verb + adverb), then move the adverb to follow the pronoun. If the pronoun follows an inseparable two-word verb (verb + preposition), do not move it.

Lesson 34

vf
ESL

Example: Round up <u>the usual suspects</u>.

Answer: *Round them up.*

1. I was finished, so I put away <u>my books</u>.
2. I went for a walk to break in <u>my sneakers</u>.
3. I really couldn't figure out <u>the problem</u>.
4. Did you back up <u>your computer file</u>?
5. The teacher was just passing out <u>the assignment</u>.

Editing Practice 1

CORRECTED SENTENCES APPEAR ON PAGE 489.

Correct all errors involving separable two-word verbs in the following paragraph using the first correction as a model. The number in parentheses at the end of the paragraph indicates how many errors you should find.

I have two papers due this week, but I can't just ~~dash off them~~ *dash them off*

like some people (my wife, for example) can. I really have to take my time

and plan out them. I need to get a bunch of ideas together and then write

down them. Then, I have to work up them into some kind of logical order.

Sometimes, when I am trying to work out the relationship of a number of

half-formed ideas, I find it helps to copy out them onto 3″ × 5″ cards. Then

I can sort out them in a number of different ways until I get a clear picture

of what I am trying to say. Then I put my key ideas into a few short sen-

tences so that I can sum up them simply and clearly. If I can't summarize

my ideas for myself, I certainly can't get across them to my readers. (7)

Editing Practice 2

Correct all errors involving separable two-word verbs in the following paragraphs using the first correction as a model. The number in parentheses at
the end of each paragraph indicates how many errors you should find.

Ideally, at this point I would like to ~~put away it~~ *put it away* for a day or two, so

that I could come back and look at my ideas with fresh eyes. Unfortunately,

Lesson 34

vf
ESL

I never seem to have time to put off it for more than a couple of hours, at best. Even then, putting aside it for a little while seems to help me organize my ideas and to lay out them in an effective manner. (3)

The next step is to actually start writing the paper. I think of a good way to get started, and then I try out it. If I have a good beginning, the paper almost seems to write itself. If I keep getting stuck, then I know that I have to go back and think over it again because something is wrong. Often when I am stuck, I find that I have confused two ideas or have somehow mixed up them. Writer's block, at least in my case, is usually not a writing problem but a thinking problem. When I know what I want to say, it is (relatively) easy to write down it. (4)

Applying What You Know

On a separate piece of paper, write a paragraph or two describing your writing process. What steps do you follow when you write a paper? Try to use several separable and inseparable two-word verbs. When you are done, use the Putting It All Together checklist on page 337 to make sure that your placement of nouns and pronouns with the two-word verbs is correct.

The Bottom Line	Adverbs in separable verb phrases are unique. We can **move** them **around**.

Lesson 34

vf
ESL

Information Questions

ESL

EXAMPLE 1	***Helping Verb in Wrong Place***
Error:	✗ Where we <u>can</u> park?
Correction:	*can* Where we ~~can~~ park? ‸
EXAMPLE 2	***Missing Form of Do Following Question Word***
Error:	✗ What he wants to see?
Correction:	*does he want* What ~~he wants~~ to see? ‸

What's the Problem?

Information questions begin with *question words.* The most common question words are *who(m), what, where, why, when,* plus the compound question words *how often, whose* + noun, and *which* + noun/pronoun. Question words are ALWAYS followed immediately by a verb, and sometimes this verb is a **helping verb**. The following are the seven helping verbs (in their various forms):

be (am, is, are, was, were)

have (have, has, had)

can/could

may/might

must

shall/should

will/would

Helping verbs normally come after the subject of a sentence (*You will order*). In a question, however, the helping verb must come immediately after the question word (and thus *before* the subject). For example, we turn the statement *You will order* into a question by moving the helping verb (*will*) to the spot that directly follows the question word (*What*).

Statement: You <u>will</u> order.

Question: What <u>will</u> you order?

When there is no helping verb available, a form of the verb *do* must be added after the question word. For example, the information question *Where did you go?* is formed by inserting the appropriate form of *do* right after the question word:

Statement: You walked.

Question: Where <u>did</u> you walk?

Sometimes non-native speakers form information questions incorrectly by either (a) failing to move a helping verb to a position right after the information question (as in Example 1: ✗ *Where we can park?*) or (b) failing to insert some form of *do* (*do, does, did*) right after the question word when there is no other helping verb in the sentence (as in Example 2: ✗ *What he wants to see?*). Information questions are especially difficult for non-native speakers because many languages form information questions by merely putting the question word at the front of the sentence without moving the verb around.

Diagnostic Exercise

CORRECTED SENTENCES APPEAR ON PAGE 489.

Correct all errors in the following dialogue using the first correction as a model. The number in parentheses at the end of the dialogue indicates how many errors you should find.

Lesson 35

info ?s
ESL

Anna: When ~~your flight leave~~? *does your flight leave*

Maria: At 6:15. Why are so you worried? We're not going to be late, are we?

Anna: I don't think so, but how long it takes to get to the airport?

Maria: It depends on the traffic. If the roads are crowded, it will take an hour.

Anna: How soon you will be ready to leave?

Maria: Don't get upset. I'm nearly done packing now. Have you seen my alarm clock?

Anna:	I don't know where it is. When you used it last?
Maria:	For my interview, two days ago. Here it is in the dresser drawer.
Anna:	Where I left the car keys?
Maria:	Come on! Now you're the one who is going to make us late. Why we didn't get started sooner? (6)

Fixing This Problem in Your Writing

Correcting information question errors involves two steps: (1) check to see whether there is a verb after the question word, and (2) supply the correct verb if one is missing. The following two tips will help you follow these steps.

QUESTION WORD + VERB TIP Whenever you ask an information question, check to see that there is a verb after the question word. If the question word is not followed by a verb, you must supply one (see the next tip).

MISSING VERB TIP If there is no verb following an information question, supply one by either (1) moving a helping verb (some form of *be, have, can/could, may/might, must, shall/should,* or *will/would*) or (2) inserting the appropriate form of *do* if there is no helping verb available to be moved.

When we apply the Question Word + Verb Tip to the two example sentences, we see that both sentences contain errors:

Example 1:	✗ Where we can park?
Tip applied:	✗ Where _____ we can park?
	MISSING VERB

Example 2:	✗ What he wants to see?
Tip applied:	✗ What _____ he wants to see?
	MISSING VERB

Now let's apply the Missing Verb Tip to the two examples:

Tip applied: Where we can park?

> Identify the helping verb *can* and move it to follow the question word.

can
Correction: Where we ~~can~~ park?
                  ^

Lesson 35

info ?s
ESL

Tip applied: ✗ What he wants to see?

There is no helping verb to move, so add a form of *do*.

                                does he want
Correction: What ~~he wants~~ to see?
                        ^

Notice that when we add *does* to the above example, the verb *wants* changes to *want*.

So far, we have looked only at examples in which the helping verb *immediately* follows the question word. Sometimes, the question word will be part of a larger group of words such as *how much time*, *who else*, or *which one*. In these cases, the helping verb or the form of *do* will not immediately follow the question word (*how* or *who*, in these cases) but will follow the question phrase.

How much time <u>do</u> we have?

Who else <u>is</u> going to the party?

Which one <u>are</u> you wearing?

MORE EXAMPLES

Correctly Formed Question	*Incorrectly Formed Question*
Helping Verb Correctly Placed	Helping Verb Incorrectly Placed
Whom <u>have</u> they chosen?	✗ Whom they <u>have</u> chosen?
Where <u>should</u> I go?	✗ Where I <u>should</u> go?
When <u>will</u> the meeting start?	✗ When the meeting <u>will</u> start?
Form of *Do* Correctly Placed	Form of *Do* Missing
What <u>do</u> they want?	✗ What they want?
Why <u>did</u> they say that?	✗ Why they said that?
Which one <u>does</u> he want?	✗ Which one he wants?

Lesson 35

info ?s
ESL

✳ *Putting It All Together*

Identify Information Question Errors

_____ When you write information questions, look at the word immediately following the question word. If it is not a verb, then the information question is probably incorrectly formed.

Correct Information Question Errors

_____ To correct the error, you must place a verb after the question word.

_____ If the sentence contains a helping verb, move that verb so that it follows the question word.

_____ If the sentence does not contain a helping verb, add the appropriate form of the verb *do*, and change the main verb if necessary.

Sentence Practice 1

CORRECTED SENTENCES APPEAR ON PAGE 489.

The following sentences contain helping verbs. Underline the word or phrase after the initial question word. If the underlined word is a verb, write *OK*. If the underlined word is not a verb, find the helping verb and move it immediately after the initial question word.

Example: ✗ Who you can trust to give good advice?

Correction: Who you ~~can~~ trust to give good advice?
                         can
                         ^

1. How soon dinner will be ready?

2. Where are the children going to school next year?

3. Why your company won't open a branch in Hong Kong?

4. How long your parents have been living in California?

5. When the people you work with will know about your new job?

 For more practice with information questions, go to **Exercise Central** at **bedfordstmartins.com/commonsense**

Lesson 35

info ?s
ESL

Sentence Practice 2

CORRECTED SENTENCES APPEAR ON PAGE 489.

The following sentences contain incorrectly formed information questions. Find the helping verb and move it immediately after the question word. If there is no helping verb that can be moved, use the appropriate form of the verb *do* and place it after the question word.

Example: ✗ Why they think there is a mistake in the order?

                    do/did

Correction: Why they think there is a mistake in the order?
                     ^

1. Where you hide all the Christmas presents?
2. What they are laughing at?
3. How much you think I should pay for it?
4. How far we can drive before we need to get gas?
5. How long we should wait for them?

Sentence Practice 3

Turn the following statements into information questions by moving the underlined question word to the beginning of the sentence and making the necessary changes to the verb.

Example: ✗ The Weather Channel predicted rain <u>when</u>.

Answer: *When did the Weather Channel predict rain?*

1. The chicken crossed the road <u>why</u>.
2. The mechanic changes the oil <u>how often</u>.
3. You wanted to see <u>who(m)</u>.
4. They picked <u>which one</u>.
5. They can't come <u>why</u>.

Editing Practice 1

CORRECTED SENTENCES APPEAR ON PAGE 489.

Lesson 35

info ?s
ESL

Correct all errors involving information questions in the following dialogue using the first correction as a model. The number in parentheses at the end of the dialogue indicates how many errors you should find.

                will

Anna: What you ~~will~~ do when you get back home?
         ^

Maria: The usual things. Why you want to know?

Anna: No reason. I'm just asking.

Maria: I think that I will spend most of my time catching up on my writing assignments.

Anna: What you have to work on?

Maria: I have to write a paper for my linguistics class.

Anna: What it is about?

Maria: How children acquire language.

Anna: Who you are going to see?

Maria: Nobody. Why you keep asking?

Anna: I called home last night.

Maria: Oh, who you talked to?

Anna: I talked to Aunt Josie. Guess what she said?

Maria: I don't know. Anyway, why I should care what she said?

Anna: She said Roberto is coming over for dinner. (7)

Editing Practice 2

Correct all errors involving information questions in the following dialogue using the first correction as a model. The number in parentheses at the end of the dialogue indicates how many errors you should find.

Maria: What time it is̶?   *is*

Anna: Why you ^ not tell me about Roberto?

Maria: It's no big deal.

Anna: Oh, then why you are keeping it a big secret?

Maria: It is not a secret. Aunt Josie just asked him over, that's all.

Anna: Uh-huh. When he is coming over?

Maria: I don't know. Maybe Wednesday night.

Anna: Who else Aunt Josie invited over?

Maria: How I should know? Maybe nobody else.

Anna: Uh-huh.

Maria: Look. It's time to go.

Anna: Why you are so anxious to change the subject?

Lesson 35

info ?s
ESL

Maria: Why you not mind your own business?

Anna: Because your business is much more interesting! (7)

Applying What You Know

On a separate piece of paper, work with a partner to write a short dialogue about two friends asking each other about their plans for the weekend. Use as many information questions as possible. Use the Putting It All Together checklist on page 344 to make sure that your questions are formed correctly.

The Bottom Line	Where **should** the helping verb go in information questions?

Lesson 35

info ?s
ESL

Word Order in Noun Clauses

ESL

EXAMPLE 1

Error: ✗ I know where <u>can</u> you get it.

Correction: I know where ~~can~~ you get it.
                          can ^

EXAMPLE 2

Error: ✗ What <u>does</u> he want is anybody's guess.

Correction: What ~~does~~ he ~~want~~ is anybody's guess.
                          wants ^

What's the Problem?

A **noun clause** is a group of words that, like a noun, can function as a subject, object of a verb, or object of a preposition. Here is an example of a noun clause in each of these roles:

Subject: <u>What they said</u> is none of your business.

Object of a verb: We know <u>how you feel about it</u>.

Object of a preposition: I asked them about <u>where we could eat</u>.

As you can see from these examples, noun clauses usually begin with one of the following words: *who(m)*, *what*, *when*, *where*, *why*, *how*, *which* + noun, or *whose* + noun/pronoun. Sometimes non-native speakers (and occasionally native speakers too) mistakenly use a helping verb or a form of *do* immediately after the introductory word as they would in an **information question** (see Lesson 35). This is what happened in the two example sentences above.

In Example 1, the helping verb *can* is incorrectly placed right after the introductory word *where*:

Example 1:   ✗ I know where <u>can</u> you get it.

349

In Example 2, *does* is incorrectly inserted after the introductory word *what*:

Example 2:   ✗ What <u>does</u> he want is anybody's guess.

The cause of this problem is easy to identify. As we saw in Lesson 35, we create information questions by moving the helping verb from its normal place between the subject and the main verb to a new position right after the question word. Or, we add some form of *do* after the question word. Because information questions are more common than noun clauses, nonnative speakers often mistakenly apply this Question Word + Helping Verb or Question Word + *Do* pattern of information questions to noun clauses. In noun clauses, however, this word order is incorrect:

QUESTION WORD + HELPING VERB

Question (correct):   <u>Where</u> <u>could</u> we go?

Noun clause (incorrect):   ✗ I wondered <u>where</u> <u>could</u> we go.

Since the sentence with a noun clause is not a question, the Question Word + Helping Verb word order is incorrect. We must put the helping verb *could* back in its normal place between the subject and the main verb:

could

Corrected noun clause: I wondered where ~~could~~ we go.

Diagnostic Exercise

CORRECTED SENTENCES APPEAR ON PAGE 490.

Correct all noun clause errors in the following paragraph using the first correction as a model. The number in parentheses at the end of the paragraph indicates how many errors you should find.

Lesson 36

w.o.
ESL

Many non-Americans ask why ~~is~~ *is* the American court system so cumbersome. To understand that, you need to know something about where did it come from and how did it evolve. Until the Revolutionary War, the American legal system was exactly what was the British legal system. Despite the many advantages of the British legal system, colonial Americans felt that the British had used the powers of the government to override the rights of individual citizens. This deep distrust of the ability of the government to use its power fairly explains why is the American system so heavily weighted in favor of the defendant. Often court cases in the United States are fought on the ground of what is admissible government evidence. (5)

Fixing This Problem in Your Writing

The key to using correct word order in noun clauses is to avoid the habit of automatically including a helping verb or some form of *do* immediately after such introductory words as *who(m)*, *what*, *when*, *where*, and the like. These introductory words function in two completely different ways:

- If you are asking an information question, a helping verb or an added form of *do* belongs right after the question word.

- If you are *not* asking an information question, then the word group is a noun clause. In noun clauses, a helping verb or an added form of *do* should *not* come right after the introductory word.

Use the following tip to determine whether your sentence actually contains an information question.

> **QUESTION MARK TIP** Anytime you use *who(m)*, *what*, *when*, *where*, *why*, *how*, *which* + noun, or *whose* + noun/pronoun, ask yourself whether it makes sense to punctuate the sentence with a question mark. If you can, the sentence is an information question, and the Question Word + Helping Verb or Question Word + *Do* word order is correct. If you cannot use a question mark, then you are dealing with a noun clause and may need to move the helping verb to its normal position or delete the added *do*.

Here is the Question Mark Tip applied to an example:

Tip applied: Where can I get the bus?

Since this is a valid information question, we know that the Question Word + Helping Verb order (*Where can*) is correct.

Now here is the Question Mark Tip applied to Example 1:

Example 1:   ✗ I know where can you get it.

Tip applied: ✗ I know where can you get it?

Since the question makes no sense, we know that this example is not a valid information question. Instead, it contains a noun clause, which we must restore to its normal statement form. In this case, we move the helping verb

Lesson 36

w.o.
ESL

can to its normal position between the subject and the main verb of the noun clause.

Correction: I know where *can* ~~can~~ you get it.

Now let's look at Example 2:

Example 2:   ✗ What does he want is anybody's guess.

Tip applied: What does he want is anybody's guess?

Again, the question makes no sense, so we know that we cannot use the Question Word + *Do* word order. To restore the noun clause to its normal statement form, we delete *does*. (Note that when you delete a form of *do*, you must make sure the main verb is in the appropriate form.)

Correction: What ~~does~~ he *wants* ~~want~~ is anybody's guess.

The Question Mark Tip is an easy way to remind yourself that every time you use introductory words like *who(m)*, *what*, *why*, or *how*, you should make sure you don't use the inverted information question word order in noun clauses.

✳ Putting It All Together

Identify Noun Clause Errors

_____ Whenever you use introductory question words such as *who(m)*, *what*, *when*, *where*, *why*, *how*, *which* + noun, and *whose* + noun/pronoun, check whether you have asked an information question by seeing if a question mark is appropriate.

_____ If the resulting question does not make sense, then you have not asked a real information question in your sentence. Instead, the sentence contains a noun clause, and you should not use the Question Word + Helping Verb or Question Word + *Do* word order.

Correct Noun Clause Errors

_____ If the noun clause contains a helping verb right after the subject, move that verb back to its normal place between the subject and the main verb.

_____ If the noun clause has an added *do* (in any form) right after the subject, delete it and make the appropriate change in the main verb of the noun clause.

Lesson 36

W.O.
ESL

Sentence Practice 1

CORRECTED SENTENCES APPEAR ON PAGE 490.

The following sentences may contain incorrectly formed noun clauses. Underline the noun clauses and restore any incorrectly formed noun clauses to their proper forms. If the noun clause is formed correctly, write *OK*.

> Example: ✗ It all depends on how do you feel about it.
>
> Correction: It all depends on <u>how d̶o̶ you feel about it</u>.

1. You can get what will you need for school there.

2. What did they decide to do is entirely their own business.

3. I don't understand why they did such a foolish thing.

4. How often were they right proved what were they doing was on the right track.

5. What have most people learned only reflects what have they been taught.

 For more practice with word order, go to **Exercise Central** at **bedfordstmartins.com/commonsense**

Sentence Practice 2

CORRECTED SENTENCES APPEAR ON PAGE 490.

Underline all the noun clauses in the following sentences. If the underlined clause is NOT in question word order, write *OK*. If the underlined clause asks a question, rewrite the clause as a statement, making whatever verb changes are necessary.

> Example: ✗ May I remind you of what did you promise to do?
>
> Correction: May I remind you of <u>what d̶i̶d̶ you p̶r̶o̶m̶i̶s̶e̶ *promised* to</u> do? *Question*

1. What were they offering attracted a lot of customers.

2. What happened illustrated how easily can anybody make a mistake.

3. You should never ignore how much will something cost in the long run.

4. I have no idea where did they go.

5. We are meeting to discuss what should we do about the problem.

Lesson 36

W.O.
ESL

Sentence Practice 3

Turn the following information questions into noun clauses, and insert them in place of the *IT* in the statements after the questions.

Example: Where did you go? Tell me IT.

Answer: *Tell me where you went.*

1. Why were you late? I wondered IT.
2. What did the sign say? I couldn't make out IT.
3. How did Hermione do it? Henry finally figured out IT.
4. Who is the guilty party? It is up to the court to determine IT.
5. Where did we go wrong? IT is obvious to us now.

Editing Practice 1

CORRECTED SENTENCES APPEAR ON PAGE 490.

Correct all errors involving noun clauses in the following paragraph using the first correction as a model. The number in parentheses at the end of the paragraph indicates how many errors you should find.

One of the many big changes in ~~how can we teach writing~~ has
how we can teach writing
been to look at writing as a topic in its own right. For more than a decade now, there has been substantial research on how do students learn to write and what is the difference between the way good and poor writers go about the process of writing. Perhaps the most helpful finding is that good writers go through a definite two-step process. What do they write first is an exploration of the topic. Often it starts as a crude draft that wouldn't make much sense to anybody but the writer. But apparently it is how are we able to think through what do we want to say. It is really important to get to the point where can the writer boil down the key ideas in a few sentences. This first step in the cycle results in a draft that has all the key ideas worked out. The second step in the cycle is a semifinal draft that is very sensitive to how will the paper make sense to the audience. Here is where is an outline critical to make sure the paper will make sense to the reader. (8)

Lesson 36

W.O.
ESL

Editing Practice 2

Correct all errors involving noun clauses in the following paragraph using the first correction as a model. The number in parentheses at the end of the paragraph indicates how many errors you should find.

One of the problems that students in writing classes have is that
they never know ~~who are they~~ *who they are* writing to. In other words, they never have

a real subject or a real audience to write for. If you have no real subject,

how can you tell how well have you written about it? The response to this

concern has been another big change in how do we teach writing called

"writing across the curriculum." The key idea is that writing should

also be taught outside the English classroom. For example, students in a

history class are asked to write a paper imagining what was it like to live

in a different time. Science classes are natural places for writing across

the curriculum because nearly all steps in the scientific process lend

themselves to writing. For example, students can write what did they

observe in an experiment and what did they conclude from the experi-

ment. An effective use of writing in math classes is asking students to

explain how did they arrive at their answers. (6)

Applying What You Know

On a separate piece of paper, write a short essay about how you were taught writing. What were the most important things you learned in class? What things did you have to learn on your own? Use the Putting It All Together checklist on page 352 to make sure that you have formed noun clauses correctly.

Lesson 36

w.o.
ESL

The Bottom Line	You should know **how noun clauses are different** from information questions.

Using Verbs Correctly

REVIEW

This unit presented various aspects of verb use that non-native speakers find particularly troublesome. The following chart sums up the tips that will help you avoid these problems.

TIPS	QUICK FIXES AND EXAMPLES
Lesson 33. The Progressive Tenses	
The Progressive Tip (p. 326) helps you know when to use the progressive tense. The Steady-State Verb Tip (p. 327) reminds you which verbs cannot form the progressive tense.	Use the progressive tense for verbs that describe actions in progress at some point in time, not for verbs that describe mental activities, emotional conditions, or possession. Error: Could you be a little more quiet? ✗ I talk on the telephone. Correction: Could you be a little more quiet? *am talking* I ~~talk~~ on the telephone. ^
Lesson 34. Two-Word Verbs	
The Movies Tip (p. 336) helps you distinguish between separable and inseparable two-word verbs.	If a separable two-word verb is followed by a noun, you *can* separate the verb (*take out the trash* / *take the trash out*); if it is followed by a pronoun, you must separate the verb (*take it out*). Error: ✗ We fought it about all evening. *fought about it* Correction: We ~~fought it about~~ all evening. ^
Lesson 35. Information Questions	
The Question Word + Verb Tip (p. 343) and the Missing Verb Tip (p. 343) help you follow the correct word order when forming an information question.	If a question word is not followed by a helping verb or some form of *do*, move the helping verb there (if there is one) or add the appropriate form of *do*. Error: ✗ How much time it will take? *will* Correction: How much time it ~~will~~ take? ^

TIPS	QUICK FIXES AND EXAMPLES
Lesson 36. Word Order in Noun Clauses	
The Question Mark Tip (p. 351) helps you determine whether a sentence is an information question or a statement that includes a noun clause.	In noun clauses, do *not* place the helping verb immediately after the word that introduces the clause (*who(m)*, *what*, *when*, and so on). Instead, the helping verb must go in its normal place between the subject and the main verb.
	Error: ✗ I know how difficult will it be for you to do that.
	will Correction: I know how difficult ~~will~~ it be for ^ you to do that.

Review Test

Correct the verb errors in the following paragraphs using the first correction as a model. The number in parentheses at the end of each paragraph indicates how many errors you should find.

quickly learn

    When people visit Venice they ~~are quickly learning~~ about how many
                          ^
problems does the modern city face. The most publicized problem is flooding. Several times every year, the water is rising to flood parts of the city in several feet of water. Even the famous Piazza San Marco must be closed because water covers up it. The flooding is caused by a variety of factors. What most people think is the main cause? You get a different answer from nearly every expert you are asking. What do many people believe is that the canals no longer drain properly because people have filled in them. As a result, rainwater and the water from rivers flowing into the top of the lagoon are blocked; the islands have dammed up them. (8)

    Another problem that everybody is recognizing is that parts of the city are simply sinking into the lagoon under their own weight. For example, consider the Piazza San Marco. In this square are two absolutely enormous stone buildings: the Basilica of San Marco, one of the most

Unit Ten

review
ESL

amazing churches in the world, and the Ducal Palace. How many hundreds of thousands of tons you think they each weigh? When you look closely at the Ducal Palace, you will notice something odd about the proportions of the stone columns on the ground floor. They are too short. It looks like something has worn down them. In fact, just the opposite is the case. Over the centuries the palace has sunk about five feet, and the ground has been filled them around. What do you see in paintings of the Ducal Palace made two hundred years ago is that the columns are noticeably taller than they are today. (5)

Unit Ten

review
ESL

Documenting Sources and Avoiding Plagiarism

OVERVIEW

The Nuts and Bolts of Documentation and Plagiarism

This unit provides basic information on documenting sources and avoiding plagiarism. If you follow the rules of proper documentation, readers will know when you use someone else's ideas or wording in your paper. Plagiarism occurs when those rules are not followed. Intentional plagiarism is considered a form of cheating, but plagiarism can also result when writers do not fully cite a source or document a source incorrectly.

Citation and documentation styles can be complex, and a comprehensive explanation might easily fill dozens of pages. Unfortunately, writers are often so overwhelmed by the details that they do not understand the most important rules. Thus, to avoid adding to the confusion, this unit focuses on the fundamental concepts: direct quotation, paraphrase, citation, and documentation on the Works Cited page. It also provides information on citing print books and magazines using the documentation system known as MLA (which stands for Modern Language Association). More detail on the MLA and APA (American Psychological Association) citation systems can be found in Appendices A and B.

While these lessons do not provide an exhaustive guide to all research rules and tips, they do concentrate on the basic issues that students must understand for practically every researched essay they write.

Lesson 37 discusses the difference between a direct quotation (repeating word for word what a source says) and a paraphrase (putting someone's ideas into your own words). This lesson also discusses the blended paraphrase, a paraphrase that uses some of the distinct wording from the original source. To avoid plagiarism, it is important to follow the guidelines developed for each way of using a source. Here, for instance, is an example of how to correct a direct quotation that lacks quotation marks.

Example: **✗** The author writes, the economy can be improved only by lowering taxes for corporations (Gomez 23).

Correction: The author writes, "The economy can be improved only by lowering taxes for corporations " (Gomez 23).

Lesson 38 covers two other major elements of MLA documentation: parenthetical citation and the Works Cited page. To avoid plagiarism, you must do more than use quotation marks correctly. Each time you use someone else's ideas or wording, you must identify the source with a brief notation that includes the source author's last name in parentheses at the end of the appropriate sentence (along with a page number, if provided). In addition, at the end of your paper you should include a Works Cited page where you list (in alphabetical order) all your sources—regardless of whether you used a direct quote, paraphrase, or blended paraphrase.

The paraphrase in the example below is technically plagiarism because it does not have a citation.

Example: **✗** One study found that surgeons who regularly played video games made 37 percent fewer operating errors than non-gamer surgeons.

To correct this error, you would add a citation, along with a Works Cited entry that would appear on the last page of the paper.

Correction: One study found that surgeons who regularly played video games made 37 percent fewer operating errors than non-gamer surgeons./ *(Johnson 41-42).*

Works Cited entry: Johnson, Steven. "Your Brain on Video Games." *Discover* July 2005: 39-43. Print.

Using Direct Quotations and Paraphrases

EXAMPLE 1   *Direct Quotation with Missing Quotation Marks*

Error: ✗ As one book states, like Gregorian chant, Islamic chanting has developed a wide variety of approaches and styles (Kerman and Tomlinson 74).

Correction: As one book states, ~~like~~ *"Like* Gregorian chant, Islamic chanting has developed a wide variety of approaches and styles *"* (Kerman and Tomlinson 74).

EXAMPLE 2   *Direct Quotation with Unnecessary* **That**

Error: ✗ Darth Vader said that "No, I am your father."

Correction: Darth Vader said ~~that~~, "No, I am your father."

What's the Problem?

A researched essay draws on the words and ideas of others, usually what they have written in print or online. Although your essay might refer to the overall ideas found in a source, you will likely refer to specific sentences. No matter the source or how you use it, you must follow specific guidelines so readers will know exactly (1) which ideas or words are taken from sources, (2) what sources you used, and (3) where those sources can be found, in case readers want to read or evaluate them.

This lesson focuses on techniques for correctly using specific statements from a source incorporated into one sentence rather than used as an extract. In particular, this lesson helps you understand the difference between direct quotes and paraphrases—and how to properly indicate which of these you use.

Although it does deal with commas and quotation marks, this lesson goes beyond the "grammatical" to help you learn to avoid **plagiarism**. Definitions vary, but plagiarizing is essentially failing to fully indicate that certain ideas or groups of words are taken from another source. Plagiarism typically occurs because either (1) a writer did not fully understand how he or she used a source or (2) a writer meant to deceive readers by claiming ideas or wording as his or her own. The first case is largely accidental, while the second amounts to cheating. Unfortunately, readers cannot always determine a writer's intentions and may assume the worst: that the offense is deliberate.

We believe plagiarism often occurs because students do not fully understand how to quote or cite a source. For example, it is not enough to put the source author's name in parentheses at the end of the sentence. Technically, a sentence that ends with a citation is still plagiarized if it fails to show that significant portions are taken *word for word* from the source. Many people (not just English teachers) evaluate your writing based on your language choices; if you appear to claim someone else's wording as yours, a reader might impose a harsh penalty, even if you did not intend to plagiarize.

Thus, it is crucial to understand the difference between a **direct quotation** and a **paraphrase** (also called an **indirect quotation**). This distinction governs the punctuation and wording choices that let readers know when you are and are not using someone else's language.

A direct quote is *exactly* what another person has written or said. An alternative is a paraphrase, in which you put another writer's material in your own words. One reason writers commit errors when trying to use a source is that they both paraphrase and quote directly in one sentence but do not follow proper citation guidelines. When a paraphrase uses a notable portion of the exact language of a source (more than just a few scattered words), we refer to it as a **blended paraphrase**—a paraphrase that uses quotation marks to show that certain portions are taken word for word. This approach is fine as long as you make it clear what wording or ideas are not yours.

Diagnostic Exercise

CORRECTED SENTENCES APPEAR ON PAGE 490.

Correct any quotation errors in the following sentences. If a sentence is correct, write *OK* above it.

Lesson 37

doc

Example: The book states, "It it is only a slight exaggeration to say that seventeenth-century New England was governed by Puritans for Puritanism" (Roark et al. 83).

1. One book suggests that New England of the 1600s was in large part governed by Puritans for Puritanism (Roark et al. 83).

2. As the authors write, "The charter of the Massachusetts Bay Company empowered the company's stockholders, known as freemen, to meet as a body known as the General Court and make the laws needed to govern the company's affairs" (Roark et al. 83).

3. According to one book, the stockholders of the Massachusetts Bay Company could establish the laws for governing the company's business (Roark et al. 83).

4. These historians also write that "The colonists transformed this arrangement for running a joint-stock company into a structure for governing the colony" (Roark et al. 83).

5. These historians also write, "The colonists transformed this arrangement for running a joint-stock company into a structure for governing the colony" (Roark et al. 83).

Fixing This Problem in Your Writing

In a paraphrase, you take someone else's ideas and put them in your own words without changing the meaning of the original source. A true paraphrase does not use quotation marks because it uses little, if any, of the source's actual phrasing. However, paraphrases as well as direct quotations normally must give credit to the source in the form of a citation, such as the author's last name in parentheses (see Lesson 38).

Let's begin with a summary of the three major approaches to using a source and the role of quotation marks in each:

Direct Quotation = Stated *Exactly* as Said/Written = Quotes

Paraphrase = Restated in Your Words = No Quotes

Blended Paraphrase = Mostly Your Own = Quotes around Source's Wording

A direct quotation typically follows a standard formula.

DIRECT QUOTE TIP   If the material you directly quote is a complete sentence, begin your sentence with a tag, followed by a comma, and then the source material (capitalize the first word) with quotation marks around it. End your sentence with a citation and the final punctuation (usually a period).

Lesson 37

doc

A *tag* is a brief statement that sets up the quote (such as *According to President Obama* or *The author states*). At times, the punctuation after this tag can be a colon, but we suggest the more common approach of using a comma.

Here is a visual representation of the tip, followed by an example:

TAG + COMMA + "QUOTE" + (CITATION) + FINAL PUNCTUATION

She wrote, "They lost the war" (Greene 3).

Example 1 at the beginning of the lesson fails to follow this formula.

Example: ✗ As one book states, like Gregorian chant, Islamic chanting has developed a wide variety of approaches and styles (Kerman and Tomlinson 74).

It correctly uses a tag and a comma (*As one book states,*). However, this direct quote lacks quotation marks and capitalization. Even with a tag and citation, the writer claims the wording as his or her own. To correct this problem, add quotation marks and capitalize the first word of the quote.

"Like

Tip applied: As one book states, ~~like~~ Gregorian chant, Islamic
                         ^
chanting has developed a wide variety of approaches and styles *"* (Kerman and Tomlinson 74).
                ^

If you paraphrase the material, be sure your own language makes up the majority of the wording. The trick is that you usually have to repeat at least some of the same words. Many people mistakenly believe there is a paraphrasing "rule" saying that you have to change a certain number of words. Others believe that just changing a word "here and there" results in a paraphrase that requires no quotation marks. In truth, neither paraphrasing nor plagiarizing depends on a specific number of new or old words. Instead, to help you craft an acceptable paraphrase, remember this tip:

> **PUT IT AWAY TIP**   When you paraphrase, put the source aside, and then write your version. Afterward, revise for accuracy by looking at the source.

Lesson 37

doc

To paraphrase without "peeking," closely read your source at least twice (without memorizing it). By putting this source material away, you greatly increase the chance you are truly paraphrasing. Afterward, it is equally important to look at the source while you edit, making sure you did not change its meaning or accidentally repeat key phrases. No doubt, you and the source will use a *few* of the same words, but usually they represent major ideas that cannot be changed without altering the meaning of the original source. By using the Put It Away Tip, you are much more likely to incorporate such words into a very different type of sentence and thus to create a true paraphrase.

Let's compare the example and the first sentence from the Diagnostic Exercise (p. 362). The example sentence, which is corrected below, follows the formula found in the Direct Quote Tip: tag, comma, source material (enclosed by quotation marks), citation, and final punctuation (which comes after, not before, the citation).

> **Correct direct quote:**   The book states, "It is only a slight exaggeration to say that seventeenth-century New England was governed by Puritans for Puritanism" (Roark et al. 83).

The sentence below, however, starts off as a paraphrase but incorrectly ends with an unattributed exact phrase from the source (we added the underlining).

> **Incorrect paraphrase:**   ✗ One book suggests that New England of the 1600s was in large part <u>governed by Puritans for Puritanism</u> (Roark et al. 83).

A citation is used in both versions, yet the so-called paraphrase includes several words from the original. Using *New England* and *was* is fine. It would be awkward to change *New England* to anything else, and *was* by itself is too common a word to worry about. But the last few words are also in the original text. The major clue that the wording is plagiarized is that the underlined phrase is *not* an ordinary way of putting the idea. Instead, the ending—even if it's just a few words—is so distinct that you cannot claim it as your own. One correction would be as follows:

> One book suggests that New England of the 1600s was in large part run by Puritans who wanted to preserve Puritanism (Roark et al. 83).

What happens if your paraphrase doesn't sound right and needs to keep several key words? One suitable option is the blended paraphrase. Using this approach, you can easily correct the paraphrasing error by adding quotation marks around the final phrase.

> One book suggests that New England of the 1600s was in large part "governed by Puritans for Puritanism" (Roark et al. 83).

Lesson 37

doc

BLENDED PARAPHRASE TIP   If your paraphrase keeps phrases that are not yours, use quotation marks around this part. If in doubt, use too many quotation marks in your essay rather than too few.

With a blended paraphrase, quotation marks and a citation are essential. As a paraphrase, its sentence structure is essentially "yours," but the reader cannot tell which phrases are someone else's—unless you use quotation marks followed by a citation.

As seen in the blended paraphrase on the previous page, you can still use a tag, as you normally would with a direct quote. But with any paraphrase blended or not, you can dispense with the tag and let the citation and the rest of the sentence identify your source. For instance, another revision of the flawed paraphrase could omit the tag:

> ~~One book suggests that~~ New England of the 1600s was in large part "governed by Puritans for Puritanism" (Roark et al. 83).

Still, a tag followed by *that* is a handy way to begin a paraphrase. It helps you avoid confusing a direct quotation with a paraphrase. Here, then, is a fourth tip.

> **THAT PARAPHRASE TIP** To begin a paraphrase, use *that* to separate a tag from the material taken from a source. However, avoid introducing a direct quote with *that*.

Example 2 below fails to follow this tip. As a result, *that* incorrectly indicates what comes after will be a paraphrase; in reality, the remainder of the sentence is a direct quote.

Example 2: ✗ Darth Vader said that "No, I am your father."

To correct this error and restore order, simply remove *that*, making sure the next word is quoted material that begins with a capital letter. These steps result in a direct quote in Correction 1.

Correction 1: Darth Vader said, "No, I am your father."

If you prefer a paraphrase, use the *That* Paraphrase Tip and rely on your own words, as seen in Correction 2.

Correction 2: Darth Vader said that he was Luke's father.

Note: A citation was omitted in Example 2 and the corrections because the quotation is a famous line from a well-known movie. Except in such rare instances, always provide a citation for direct quotations, paraphrases, and blended paraphrases.

Lesson 37

doc

✳ *Putting It All Together*

Identify Errors in Direct Quotations and Paraphrases

_____ Look for instances in which you use the wording of a source without using quotation marks.

_____ Determine if you lack a citation when you use either the ideas or wording of a source.

Correct Errors in Direct Quotations and Paraphrases

_____ Use the Direct Quote Tip when using the exact wording of an entire sentence: Use a tag, a comma, an initial capital in and quotation marks around the source material, a citation, and then the final punctuation.

_____ Avoid looking at the source while you draft a paraphrase.

_____ If you use any of the source's distinctive wording in your paraphrase, make it a blended paraphrase: Put quotation marks around the source's wording.

_____ Use *that* to introduce paraphrased material. Avoid an introductory *that* for direct quotes.

_____ Use a citation whenever you paraphrase or quote directly.

Sentence Practice 1

CORRECTED SENTENCES APPEAR ON PAGE 490.

Use each of the following statements as a direct quotation in a sentence of your own. (Additional contextual information is in brackets.) Then turn the direct quotation into a paraphrase starting with *that*. Do not worry about citations for the purpose of this exercise.

Example:
> *Thomas Paine once wrote, "These*
> ~~These~~ **are the times that try men's souls. "**
>   ^   ^
> [Thomas Paine, writing about the need to fight the British in 1776]

Paraphrase: *Thomas Paine believed that circumstances in his day tested people's convictions.*

1. I want to seize fate by the throat. [Composer Ludwig van Beethoven, in a letter he wrote in 1801]

Lesson 37

doc

2. From where the sun now stands, I will fight no more forever. [Chief Joseph, speaking to his Nez Percé tribe]

3. The covers of this book are too far apart. [Ambrose Bierce, in a review of another writer's book]

4. I beheld the wretch—the miserable monster whom I had created. [Mary Wollstonecraft Shelley, in her 1818 novel, *Frankenstein*]

5. Talk low, talk slow, and don't say too much. [John Wayne, giving acting advice]

> For more practice using direct quotations and paraphrases, go to **Exercise Central** at **bedfordstmartins.com/commonsense**

Sentence Practice 2

CORRECTED SENTENCES APPEAR ON PAGE 491.

Use each of the following statements as a direct quotation in a sentence of your own. (Additional contextual information is in brackets.) Then turn the direct quotation into a paraphrase starting with *that*. Do not worry about citations for the purpose of this exercise.

Example: *The poet Robert Frost once remarked, "The* ~~The~~ brain is a wonderful organ. It starts working the moment you get up and does not stop until you get into the office. *"* [Poet Robert Frost]

Paraphrase: *The poet Robert Frost said sarcastically that the brain, though functioning constantly, seems to shut down when a person gets to work.*

1. The reason I'm going ahead with this attempt now is because I just cannot wait any longer to impress you. [From a letter by John Hinckley to actress Jodie Foster, on the day he shot President Reagan]

2. The trouble with some women is they get all excited about nothing, and then they marry him. [Cher, singer and actress]

3. My life had its beginning in the midst of the most miserable, desolate, and discouraging surroundings. [Former slave Booker T. Washington, writing in 1901 about the effects of slavery]

4. When I'm good, I'm very good, but when I'm bad, I'm better. [Actress Mae West, in the movie *I'm No Angel*]

Lesson 37

doc

5. I see one-third of a nation ill-housed, ill-clad, ill-nourished. [Franklin Roosevelt, referring to the Great Depression in 1937]

Sentence Practice 3

Create a blended paraphrase by replacing *IT* in each sentence with a paraphrase of the direct quotation that follows. Do not worry about citations for the purposes of this exercise.

Example: **Winston Churchill said IT. "A joke is a very serious thing."**

Answer: *Winston Churchill said that making a joke is actually a serious matter.*

1. Sharon said IT. "I have to leave soon."
2. The coaches claimed IT. "We are pleased with the team's performance."
3. Dominique loudly announced IT. "This book is the best I have ever read!"
4. Mark Twain supposedly said IT. "Everybody talks about the weather, but nobody does anything about it."
5. Cal said IT. "The sky is falling!"
6. Right before he died, President Franklin Roosevelt said IT. "I have a terrific headache."
7. The last words of actor Humphrey Bogart were IT. "I should never have switched from scotch to martinis."
8. My father called and asked IT. "Did you remember to pay your tuition this semester?"
9. The mayor stated IT. "This year, the city will have to hire a dozen more firefighters."
10. My biology teacher explained IT. "A bat's leg bones are so tiny that no bat is able to use its legs to walk."

Editing Practice 1

CORRECTED SENTENCES APPEAR ON PAGE 491.

Correct all errors involving quotation marks in the following paragraph, using the first correction as a model. The number in parentheses at the end of

Lesson 37

doc

the paragraph indicates how many errors you should find. Count a pair of quotation marks as one error.

that she

My mother told me ~~that, "She~~ believed every marriage was a
^
compromise. For example, my brother Pete has had a lot of trouble

quitting smoking. He likes to quote Mark Twain, who said "quitting

smoking is easy. I've done it dozens of times." After my brother got mar-

ried, his wife told him that "he could not keep smoking inside the house."

She wants him to quit, but she knows how hard it will be for him to do it.

She told me that "her uncle, who had been a heavy smoker, had died

from lung disease." Naturally, she is very concerned about Pete. Last

night, Pete told us I am going to try nicotine patches. We all hope that

they will work. (4)

Editing Practice 2

Correct all errors involving quotation marks in the following paragraph, using the first correction as a model. The number in parentheses at the end of
the paragraph indicates how many errors you should find. Count a pair of
quotation marks as one error.

Many traditional sayings emphasize the virtues of saving things. My
, "Waste
mother always said ~~waste~~ not, want not. " That may be true, but my wife
^   ^
and I have some real differences on saving things. At least once a week

my wife asks me honey, do you really want to keep THIS? It doesn't make

much difference what the THIS is, but my answer will probably be the

same sure I do. I think that every marriage is doomed to have one person

who is a saver and one person who is a thrower-away. The saver in me is

always saying but I might need that someday. My wife's response is sure,

but you will never find it in all the junk you have accumulated. Of course, I

would never actually say that to my wife. (4)

Lesson 37

doc

Applying What You Know

Write a short essay about a disagreement between you and someone close to you. Include several real or hypothetical conversations that employ both direct quotation and paraphrase. Exchange essays with a partner, and check each other's writing for correctly used direct quotes and paraphrases.

The Bottom Line	As suggested in this lesson, "Be sure to use quotation marks in direct quotations and blended paraphrases."

Lesson 37

doc

Citing Sources Correctly

EXAMPLE 1   *Incorrect Parenthetical Citation*

Error: ✗ One book explains that jazz musician Louis Armstrong endured great poverty as he grew up in New Orleans (Kerman and Tomlinson).

Correction: One book explains that jazz musician Louis Armstrong endured great poverty as he grew up in New Orleans
401
(Kerman and Tomlinson).
                                                    ^

EXAMPLE 2   *Incorrect Works Cited Entry*

Error: ✗ Kerman, Joseph, and Gary Tomlinson. *Listen*. 6th ed. p. 401.

Correction: Kerman, Joseph, and Gary Tomlinson. *Listen*. 6th ed. ~~p. 401.~~ *Boston: Bedford/St. Martin's, 2008. Print.*

What's the Problem?

The previous lesson covered using quotations and paraphrases. But the writer of a researched essay must take other steps to correctly document sources and avoid **plagiarism**. As discussed in Lesson 37, plagiarism results from failing to fully indicate that certain ideas or groups of words are taken from another source. Once you understand the difference between direct quotes, paraphrases, and blended paraphrases (and how to create each), you must then follow the appropriate rules for identifying their sources, a process referred to as **documentation**.

One reason documentation errors occur is that there are hundreds of documentation guidelines and rules, and their number has grown along with the diversity of online sources. In fact, there are entirely different systems of documentation, although two are more common in college writing: MLA (Modern Language Association) guidelines and APA (American Psychological Association) guidelines. In this lesson we focus on MLA, the system used most often in English courses.

It would take an entire book to cover all the possible scenarios and details of MLA citation. The good news is that most documentation rules come down to two basic elements: individual citations within the research paper plus a page that lists all sources used (MLA calls this a Works Cited page, though it is also referred to as a Bibliography or References page) at the end of your paper. To help you understand these two essential elements, this lesson focuses on the most common types of sources: books and magazine articles. These sources are often used in research and are relatively straightforward in terms of formatting for both an in-text citation and a Works Cited page. (Appendices A and B offer brief guides for citing and documenting other types of sources and for implementing the other widely used documentation system, APA.)

A common mistake writers make is not providing a correct citation in a sentence that uses an outside source. Another error is not having the correct Works Cited entry that matches the in-text citation. Again, such mistakes are construed as plagiarism, whether the lapse was intentional or not.

In an attempt to avoid these problems, many students use "online citation generators" that claim to produce a correct MLA entry for whatever source is typed in to the database. These programs are notoriously inaccurate, and at the college level in particular, the resulting mistakes can hurt your grade. Put your grade in your own hands—learn MLA citation and documentation so you will be able to detect when these software programs are wrong.

Diagnostic Exercise

CORRECTED SENTENCES APPEAR ON PAGE 491.

Correct citation and documentation errors in the following direct quotes and bracketed Works Cited entries. Evaluate each item separately; don't assume that another sentence in the research paper would provide missing information. If a sentence or a Works Cited entry is correct, write *OK* above it.

Example: According to one scholar, "Military technologies made few advances during the centuries following the fall of Rome**/**" *(Volti 257)*.

OK

[Volti, Rudi. *Society and Technological Change*. 6th ed. New York: Worth, 2010. Print.]

1.   "But in the sixth century, a new technology emerged that added a new dimension to warfare" (p. 257).
     [Volti, Rudi. *Society and Technological Change*, 2010]

Lesson 38

doc

2. One source states, "The device was the stirrup, an invention of Chinese origin that had diffused to Europe by the ninth century" (Volti 257). [Volti, Rudi. *Society and Technological Change*. 6th ed. New York: Worth, 2010. Print.]

3. The scholar S. A. Nigosian explains, "As a young man Muhammad joined the merchant caravans, and at the age of twenty-five he entered the service of a wealthy widow, Khadijah." [Page 415. Nigosian, S. A. *World Religions: A Historical Approach*. 4th ed. Boston: Bedford/St. Martin's, 2008. Print.]

4. As one textbook states, "According to tradition, Muhammad experienced at the age of forty his first unexpected divine communication with the Angel Gabriel" (Nigosian 415). [*World Religions: A Historical Approach*. 4th ed. Boston: Bedford/St. Martin's, 2008. Print.]

5. Nigosian writes, "Like Abraham, Moses, Samuel, and Jesus, Muhammad heard a divine voice" (415). [No Works Cited entry. Provide one based on above information.]

Fixing This Problem in Your Writing

Whether you paraphrase or quote directly, you must include information on where the material originally appeared. Provide this information in the correct format, but before worrying about the formatting details, consider this first tip, which works well for a basic quote or paraphrase.

> **THREE-PART TIP** Each time you use a source, assume it has three matching parts: (1) the quote or paraphrase, (2) a matching parenthetical citation, and (3) a corresponding entry on a Works Cited page.

These interrelated parts are represented in the following hypothetical example. Parts 1 and 2 share a block because in your paper they usually appear together in one sentence, while Part 3 appears on a separate Works Cited page.

Lesson 38

doc

PART 1		PART 2		PART 3
Quote	+	Citation	+	Works Cited
One candidate claimed, "I actually won the election"		(Greene 17).		Greene, Al. *Political Careers*. New York: Global, 2011. Print.

Using a Parenthetical Citation

The Three-Part Tip offers a starting place: identifying and using the three essential elements for incorporating, citing, and documenting a source. Lesson 37 explains the first element (using a direct quote or a paraphrase). The next tip covers the second element.

> **CITATION TIP** At the end of a sentence that uses a source, provide a parenthetical citation. The normal format is (*author's last name + page number*).

Such a citation is often called a parenthetical citation or an in-text citation because it appears in parentheses and in the text (body) of your paper. Each sentence that uses a source should identify it, and a citation at the end of the sentence is the most common approach.

In the example below, the Citation Tip rounds out the first two parts of the Three-Part Tip. The formatting identifies the student's own writing, material from a source, the source author's last name, and the page number where this material appears in the source.

| STUDENT'S TAG | BORROWED MATERIAL | CITATION |
| | | AUTHOR'S NAME   PAGE |

One candidate claimed, "I actually won the election" (Greene 17).

Note: Use only the author's last name, give just a page number (not an abbreviation for *page*), and place the period after the citation (not before).

There are exceptions to the Citation Tip, especially when you use successive sentences from a single source or when your tag supplies everything that would go in parentheses. Again, this lesson does not delve into exceptions. The important concept to understand first is that you should identify any ideas or wording you borrow by putting the author's last name in parentheses.

To avoid plagiarism, remember that the Citation Tip applies to paraphrases as well as to quotations. If you put someone's ideas into your own words (a paraphrase), a citation is still essential. Example 1 at the beginning of this lesson largely abides by this rule, for there is a citation.

Example 1: ✗ One book explains that jazz musician Louis Armstrong endured great poverty as he grew up in New Orleans (Kerman and Tomlinson).

However, the writer omitted the page where this idea appears in the authors' book. To fix this problem, supply the page number.

Lesson 38

doc

Tip applied: **One book explains that jazz musician Louis Armstrong**
endured great poverty as he grew up in New Orleans
401
(Kerman and Tomlinson).
^

Creating a Works Cited Page

A citation is merely a clue about the source. An author's last name and a page number offer too little information to find the source. Therefore, a researched essay should end with a list of all the sources you quoted directly or paraphrased. (You should omit from this list any sources you read but did not use.) On this Works Cited page, readers should find all the information needed to find each source you cite. The works cited are listed in alphabetical order, with the second and subsequent lines of each entry indented and the entire page double-spaced.

Make sure your paper follows the Three-Part Tip: Every citation should have a matching Works Cited entry, and anything listed on the Works Cited page should conspicuously be used in your paper and cited (either in the text or in parentheses).

Keep this next tip in mind when composing this list of sources.

WORKS CITED TIP   The Works Cited page should supply everything necessary to locate each source. The typical pattern is *author's name + name of publication + publication details.*

Properly formatting a parenthetical citation is simple compared to formatting a Works Cited entry. The Citation Tip applies to almost any source having an author and a page number. As the Works Cited Tip suggests, however, the details for a Works Cited entry will vary depending on the type of source used. A reader needs certain details to find a magazine article and others to track down a book or blog.

Consider the previous example. After quoting Al Greene, we provide a citation at the end of the sentence: *(Greene 17)*. Even if we use only one source, a Works Cited page is needed.

Lesson 38

doc

Works Cited

Greene, Al. *Political Careers.* New York: Global, 2011. Print.

As reflected in the example and outlined in the following tip, there is a starting point for correctly formatting an entry for a book.

> **BOOK ENTRY TIP** For each book entry, start with the following pattern — including the punctuation, italicization, and capitalization:
>
> Last Name, First Name. *Complete Name of Book.* City of Publication:
>   Abbreviated Name of Publisher, Most Recent Year of Publication. Print.

This pattern follows the formula of the Works Cited Tip, but it also provides the details helpful for finding a particular book.

When using the Book Entry Tip, you should also provide any extra information a reader needs to find the book (see Appendix A). For instance, Example 2 is a coauthored book in its sixth edition.

Example 2:   ✗ Kerman, Joseph, and Gary Tomlinson. *Listen.* 6th ed.
              p. 401.

Example 2 correctly gives that information, yet it leaves out the publisher data at the end of the entry. To correct this error, follow the Book Entry Tip, but be sure to keep any additional information needed (in this case the second author's name and edition number) even if it does not exactly fit the tip's formula.

Tip applied: **Kerman, Joseph, and Gary Tomlinson.** *Listen.* **6th ed.**
               ~~p. 401.~~ *Boston: Bedford/St. Martin's, 2008. Print.*

The correction keeps the information about the two authors and the sixth edition, but we added the publisher information that the Book Entry Tip requires.

We deleted the page number because, as the tip indicates, this information is not needed on the Works Cited page. The citation within the paper itself already provided the page number.

An entry for a magazine article shares the overall pattern indicated in the Works Cited Tip (*author's name* + *name of publication* + *publication details*), but this pattern is tailored so your readers can find the specific issue you used.

Lesson 38

doc

> **MAGAZINE ENTRY TIP** For each magazine entry, start with the following pattern — including the punctuation, italicization, and capitalization:
>
> Last Name, First Name. "Title of Article." *Magazine Name* Date of Publication:
>   Page range of entire article. Print.

Each of the following two examples gives full names of the author, article, and magazine. Both include the range of page numbers for the *entire* article. Both also end with the word *Print*, letting readers know this is a hardcopy source, not an online one.

> O'Connell-Rodwell, Caitlin. "Male Bonding." *Smithsonian* Sept. 2010: 50-59. Print.

> Scherer, Michael. "The Odd Couple." *Time* 10 Jan. 2011: 36-41. Print.

The entries have only one difference in terms of format: The first one does not include the day of the month, while the second does. Because *Smithsonian* appears only once a month (at most), there is no specific day listed.

✳ *Putting It All Together*

Identify Errors in Citations and Works Cited Entries

_____ Look for paraphrases and direct quotes that require a parenthetical citation.

_____ Make sure that more detailed information is given on your Works Cited page for every source identified in a parenthetical citation.

Correct Errors in Citations and Works Cited Entries

_____ Using the Citation Tip, put a parenthetical citation at the end of a sentence to identify any outside source it uses: (*author's name + page number*).

_____ On your Works Cited page, provide a full citation for every source you cited in parentheses.

_____ Follow the specific citation guidelines of the documentation system you use. Each type of source requires its own particular format, as indicated by the Book Entry Tip and Magazine Entry Tip.

Lesson 38

doc

Sentence Practice 1

CORRECTED SENTENCES APPEAR ON PAGE 492.

Provide a parenthetical citation at the end of each direct quotation, and then provide a works cited entry based on the information given for each book. Refer to Appendix A if necessary.

Example: According to one book, "Social Darwinists equated wealth and power with 'fitness' and believed that the unfit should be allowed to die off to advance the progress of humanity."

Page 447 of *The American Promise: A Compact History*. Roark, James L., et al. Print. Boston. 2010. Bedford/ St. Martin's

Correction: According to one book, "Social Darwinists equated wealth and power with 'fitness' and believed that the unfit should be allowed to die off to advance the progress of humanity/" *(Roark et al. 447).*

Roark, James L., et al. *The American Promise: A Compact History*. Boston: Bedford/St. Martin's, 2010. Print.

1. As the authors state, "The railroad boom of the 1850s signaled the growing industrial might of the American economy."

 The American Promise: A Compact History, by James L. Roark et al. Bedford/St. Martin's, located in Boston. Published in 2010. Print. Page 283.

2. According to the author, "Modern philosophy has never recovered from its false starts."

 Adler, Mortimer J. Page 200 of *Ten Philosophical Mistakes*. Published by Macmillan in 1985, New York City. Print.

3. One textbook explains, "In 1972 the FCC mandated access channels in the nation's top one hundred TV markets, requiring cable systems to carry their own original programming."

 Page 189 of *Media and Culture: An Introduction to Mass Communication*. Campbell, Richard, Christopher R. Martin, and Bettina Fabos. 2011. Print. Boston. Bedford/St. Martin's.

4. The story ends with the line, "In the deep glens where they lived all things were older than man and they hummed of mystery."

 The Road, by Cormac McCarthy. Published in New York City by Vintage, 2006. Page 287. Print.

5. One scholar explains, "Math has many branches because it focuses on different sorts of relationships."

 Page 236 of *The Ape That Spoke: Language and the Evolution of the Human Mind*. By John McCrone. Published by William Morrow and Company in New York City, 1991. Print.

Lesson 38

doc

For more practice documenting sources, go to **Exercise Central** at **bedfordstmartins.com/commonsense**

Sentence Practice 2

CORRECTED SENTENCES APPEAR ON PAGE 492.

Provide a parenthetical citation at the end of each paraphrase, and then provide a works cited entry based on the general information given for each magazine. Refer to Appendix A if necessary.

Example: One writer claims, "As for gun control, a fever of excess has overtaken the country during the past twenty years."

One-page article (p. 25) by Joe Klein: "Arms and the Unbalanced" in *Time*. Jan. 24, 2011. Print.

Correction: One writer claims, "As for gun control, a fever of excess has overtaken the country during the past twenty years/" *(Klein 25).*

Klein, Joe. "Arms and the Unbalanced." *Time* 24 Jan. 2011: 25. Print.

1. In the same issue, another writer suggests, "Like them or not, guns are as American as covered wagons and the infield-fly rule."

    Michael Grunwald's article "Fire Away" in *Time*. January 24, 2011. Print. Appears on page 37 of pages 37-39.

2. As one writer puts it, "To human eyes, the night sky is a confetti of stars."

    Abigail Tucker. "Invisible Glory" in *Smithsonian*, Feb. 2011. Appears on page 74 of pages 74-79. Print.

3. One historian writes, "The Soviet commander in Cuba, General Issa Pliyev, was also preparing for war."

    Dobbs, Michael. "The End Was Near." Appears on page 28 of pages 26-33 of *Military History*, November 2010. Print.

4. The author writes, "I want to use my phone as a modem for my laptop, and I don't want to pay a fortune."

    One-page article (p. 154) by Stephen Manes. "Where's Wireless Data for the Rest of Us?" *PC World*, June 2006. Print.

5. The article states, "If some see the building as a tribute to terrorists, of course they are enraged."

    Nancy Gibbs. One-page article (p. 76). "Sacred Spaces." *Time* Aug. 30, 2010. Print.

Lesson 38

doc

Sentence Practice 3

Using one book or magazine article, complete each sentence with either a direct quote or a paraphrase as indicated. Provide a parenthetical citation for each sentence. Provide a works cited entry after your first sentence; for this exercise, that one entry will cover the other four sentences.

Example:	One source states, [direct quotation]
Answer:	One source states, *"Speculation about mental associations goes back at least to the time of Aristotle"* (Gray 335).
Works Cited entry:	Gray, Peter. *Psychology*. 6th ed. Boston: Worth, 2011. Print.

1. One source states, [direct quotation]

2. This source goes on to claim that [paraphrase]

3. A sentence I find interesting is one in which the source states that [paraphrase]

4. According to this source, [direct quotation]

5. Some people might not realize that [paraphrase]

Editing Practice 1

CORRECTED SENTENCES APPEAR ON PAGE 492.

Correct all errors in the Works Cited page below using the first correction as a model. The names are correct, but there are other problems with punctuation, order, or unnecessary information. Some entries might have no errors; others might have more than one. The number in parentheses at the end of the list indicates how many errors you should correct.

Works Cited

Brood, Bob.
What We Really Value: Beyond Rubrics in Teaching and Assessing Writing.
^
    Logan, Utah: Utah State UP, 2003. ~~Bob Brood.~~ Print.

Style in Rhetoric and Composition: A Critical Sourcebook. By Paul Butler.

    Boston: Bedford/St. Martin's, 2010. Print.

Haussamen, Brock, *Grammar Alive: A Guide for Teachers*. Urbana: NCTE,

    2003. Page 33. Print.

Lesson 38

doc

Phelps, Louise Weatherbee. *Composition as a Human Science.* New York: Oxford UP, 1988. Print.

Shaugnessy, Mina P. *Errors and Expectations: A Guide for the Teacher of Basic Writing.* New York, Oxford UP, 1977. Print.

Sheridan, Daniel. *Teaching Secondary English: Readings and Applications.* 2nd ed. Published by Lawrence Erlbaum, in Mahwah, in 2001. Print.

(7)

Editing Practice 2

CORRECTED SENTENCES APPEAR ON PAGE 492.

Correct all errors in the Works Cited page below using the first correction as a model. The names are correct, but there are problems with punctuation, order, or unnecessary information. Some entries might have no errors; others might have more than one. The number in parentheses at the end of the list indicates how many errors you should correct.

Works Cited

Brinkley, Douglas. "Frontier Prophets." *Audubon* Nov./Dec. 2010*/:* 74-77. Print.

Casares, Oscar. "Grass Roots." *Texas Monthly* Dec. 2008: 116-23. Print.

Doreen Cubie. "Welcoming Travelers and Wildlife." *National Wildlife* Feb./March 2011: pages 16-19. Print.

Tucker, Abigail. "Snow Phantom." *Smithsonian* Feb. 2011: 36-43. Print.

Walsh, Bryan. "Going Green." *Time* July 19, 2010: 45. Print.

Weintraub, Arlene. Break That Hovering Habit Early. *U.S. News and World Report* Sept. 2010: 42-43. Print.

Lesson 38

doc

(4)

Applying What You Know

Find either a book or a magazine article on a topic with which you are familiar. Use a direct quotation and a paraphrase in a paragraph in which you describe the book or article. Add a Works Cited page.

The Bottom Line	As two authors explain, "If you follow the rules for proper documentation, readers will know when you use someone else's ideas or wording in your paper" (Beason and Lester 359). Beason, Larry, and Mark Lester. *A Commonsense Guide to Grammar and Usage*. 6th ed. Boston: Bedford/St. Martin's, 2012. Print.

Lesson 38

doc

Documenting Sources and Avoiding Plagiarism

REVIEW

To avoid plagiarism and give readers the information they need to determine when you use a source, your paper should reflect the appropriate rules for using quotation marks, providing citations, and including a Works Cited page listing all the sources you quoted or paraphrased. The following tips will help you avoid common problems in documenting sources.

TIPS	QUICK FIXES AND EXAMPLES
Lesson 37. Using Direct Quotations and Paraphrases	
The Direct Quote Tip (p. 363) offers a reliable way to structure a direct quotation. The Put It Away Tip (p. 364), Blended Paraphrase Tip (p. 365), and *That* Paraphrase Tip (p. 366) help you correctly paraphrase.	Error: ✗ One writer explains, mystics of nearly every faith, including all five of the world's major religions, have long told tales of astral projection. *"Mystics* Correction: One writer explains, ~~mystics~~ of nearly every faith, including all five of the world's major religions, have long told tales of astral projection**/**" *(Kotler 62).*
Lesson 38. Citing Sources Correctly	

The Three-Part Tip (p. 374) describes the major elements of correct documentation. The Citation Tip (p. 375) and Works Cited Tip (p. 376) explain general requirements, while the Book Entry Tip (p. 377) and Magazine Entry Tip (p. 377) cover the details.	Error: ✗ One book argues that rock music has seen a revival in the past thirty years (Kerman and Tomlinson).
	
	Kerman, Joseph, and Gary Tomlinson. *Listen.* 6th ed. p. 420.
	
	Correction: One book argues that rock music has seen a revival in the past thirty years
	                    420
	(Kerman and Tomlinson).
	                              ^
	
	Kerman, Joseph, and Gary Tomlinson. *Listen.* 6th ed. ~~p. 420.~~ *Boston: Bedford/ St. Martin's, 2008. Print.*

REVIEW TEST

Each item below consists of (1) a sentence from a source, (2) a sentence that attempts to use and document this source, and (3) a works cited entry. Correct the quotation, citation, and documentation errors. The number in brackets at the end of the item is the number of errors you should correct.

Example: ***Source:*** "If you really want to fight poverty, fuel growth, and combat extremism, try girl power."

Use: According to one writer, ~~if~~ "If you really want to fight poverty, fuel growth, and combat extremism, try girl power/" (Gibbs 64).

Works Cited: Gibbs, Nancy. "The Best Investment." *Time* 14 Feb. 2011: ~~page~~ 64.
[5]

1. ***Source:*** "English is, in short, one of the world's great growth industries."

   Use: One author claims that the English language is one of the world's great growth industries (Bryson 13).

   Works Cited: Bill Bryson. *The Mother Tongue: English and How It Got That Way*. New York: Perennial, 1990.
   [3]

2. ***Source:*** "The Celts associated squares with permanence, stability, and earthly matters."

   Use: According to one writer, "The Celts associated squares with permanence, stability, and earthly matters." (Parry page 62)

   Works Cited: Parry, Susan. The Sacred Nature of Celtic Art. *Renaissance* Jan. 2006: 60-64.
   [4]

3. ***Source:*** "The earliest Scottish fortifications date back to the Iron Age."

   Use: One book indicates that "The oldest Scottish forts date back to the Iron Age" (5).

   Works Cited: Gambaro, Cristina. *Castles of Scotland: Past and Present.* New York: Barnes and Noble, 2005.
   [3]

4. ***Source:*** "Perhaps the best known dog in World War I was Stubby, the first formally trained military dog in U.S. service."

Unit Eleven

review

Use: According to one account, the most famous dog during World War I was Stubby, a dog credited as the first formally trained military dog in U.S. service (27).

Works Cited: O'Connell, Libby H. "Putting the 'Service' in Service Dogs." *History Channel Magazine* Nov./Dec. 2006. 26-28. [3]

A Commonsense Writing Guide

OVERVIEW

Understanding grammar and usage is an important part of learning how to write correctly. However, correct grammar and usage are not the *only* parts of successful writing. Unit Eleven covers the basics of avoiding plagiarism and documenting sources, which are integral in research writing, and this final unit offers a concise guide to reading and to writing a paper, additional skills to be mastered by the successful writer.

Here are two points you should know:

- This unit emphasizes an often overlooked fact: Teachers have expectations that affect how they respond to what student writers do. A writer's situation always affects his or her choices, and teachers are a normal part of a student writer's situation.

- This section offers no formulas for writing. Instead, we encourage you to develop questions to ask yourself, your teacher, or anyone giving you feedback about your writing. Asking yourself critical questions throughout your writing process is one of the most important steps you can take toward improving your writing.

What Readers Look For

Since writing is meant to be read, begin by thinking about what readers typically expect. Though definitions of "good writing" differ from culture to culture, the chart on the next page presents five *basic standards* that readers in the United States use to evaluate writing. Keep in mind that you might have to adjust these standards based on your own specific situation, audience, and assignment.

The remainder of this unit offers strategies you can use so your papers reflect these five standards. Because the main part of this book focuses on style and mechanics, this unit concentrates on purpose, support, and organization.

✳ *Basic Standards for Evaluating Writing*

Purpose: Readers expect a paper to be focused, based on a clear and appropriate purpose. A focused paper

- stays on one subject
- makes a specific point about this subject
- considers its audience
- is narrow enough to fulfill its purpose within the assignment's page-length requirements

Support: Readers expect a paper to contain enough supporting detail to fulfill its purpose. A well-supported paper

- gives readers a clear understanding of the paper's subject matter
- explains or proves the paper's one main point with details, examples, and evidence
- offers in-depth thinking, not just obvious or superficial generalizations

Organization: Readers expect a paper to have a sense of order. This typically means that

- the paper has an introduction, a body, and a conclusion
- each paragraph has one major point
- paragraphs are arranged so they clearly build on one another
- individual sentences flow from one to another

Style: Readers expect writers to use words and sentence patterns that suit their purpose and topic. For most college papers, style means that

- the writing is *either* formal *or* informal, depending on the paper's purpose
- sentences should not be too choppy or too awkward
- writers choose the words that most clearly and precisely convey ideas to a particular audience

Mechanics: Readers expect that writers follow the conventions and rules of standard English (see Units One through Ten). If a writer uses outside sources, readers will expect those sources to be documented properly (see Unit Eleven).

Unit Twelve

overview

What Writers Do

Reading and writing: What is the connection?   Reading is more closely connected to writing than you might assume. Both writing and reading involve processes—evolving steps you go through to understand and create information. Reading as well as writing depends on your situation. For example, you do not read a physics textbook the same way you read an e-mail from a friend. Nor do you follow the same steps to create a grocery list as you would a research paper. Writing depends on reading (and vice versa), and both are shaped by specific processes and situations. Thus, the next four lessons discuss how to read and write more effectively by considering certain situations, especially those common in higher education, and processes. You already know how to read and write, but these lessons will help you read and write better in college.

This unit begins with a discussion of reading because many (perhaps most) writing assignments in college are closely connected with reading material that you either are assigned or must find yourself. Even if your reading skills are strong, we encourage you to study Lesson 39 so you will better understand concepts of and tips for reading that also relate to writing.

What is a *writing process*?   At one time or another, most of us have written a paper in one sitting. Sometimes, the result was acceptable or even good; other times, the paper didn't reflect our best thinking. For most people, their "best thinking" isn't what comes off the top of their heads. Rather, it is the result of a process. Using a *process* in writing means coming up with good ideas, developing plans, trying out your best ideas, making improvements, and sharing your ideas with readers. There is no one right way to proceed, and the route can even be messy. It would be convenient if there were a formula, but the truth is that each writer, situation, purpose, and audience requires a unique approach. You can, however, think about three general stages.

Planning ⟶ Drafting ⟶ Revising

Writing is not always a neat step-by-step process. When you revise a paragraph to make it descriptive, for instance, you might also do more planning. Keep in mind as well that writing is not just drafting. You need to plan, write, rewrite, and make improvements. You can consider editing as the final stage, using the other parts of this book to guide you.

What is a *writing situation*?   Your exact writing process will depend on your situation. A writer's situation is a combination of everything that directly affects a given piece of writing. Here are the basic elements:

Unit Twelve

overview

assignment, purpose, readers (audience), deadline, tools for writing, and physical environment. Your writing situation will change with every assignment. For example, some assignments may require research. Others may require that you consider a community or a corporate (rather than an academic) audience. Some writing assignments begin and end in the classroom during an exam. Others may be long-term and require several trips to the library or computer lab. How you prepare to write is affected by your overall writing situation.

Unit Twelve

overview

Reading

Writing depends on reading. At the very least, you yourself read everything you write, and your teacher and classmates frequently read your writing as well. One way to improve your writing ability is to read, read, read.

There is one other reason to consider the connections between reading and writing. Many college teachers base their writing assignments on something they will ask you to read— such as a textbook, a novel, a journal article, or an item from the Internet. College requires you to read a range of items— from textbooks to literature to government documents (to name just a few). There are also different ways to write about these diverse reading selections. Thus, this lesson offers *general* strategies for reading and writing about what you read. Later lessons focus more on the actual process of writing and on specific types of college assignments.

Types of Assignments

College teachers often make writing assignments such as the following, although they might call these assignments by different names:

- **Objective Summary.** This is a brief description of what a reading selection covers—its most important ideas. Your own opinions about the selection and its topic are kept out as much as possible.

- **Evaluative Summary.** This also is a brief description of what an author covers in a reading selection, but you are allowed to offer more of your own opinions and reflections about the selection or the topic.

- **Critique (or Review).** This is not always brief, nor is your specific purpose to summarize. Instead, your purpose is to evaluate a reading selection. Your paper would describe the selection's strengths or weaknesses (or both) and then provide reasons to support your evaluation. The goal is to convince your readers that your evaluation is valid and reasonable.

- **Reflection.** Like a critique, the purpose is not to summarize. Compared to a critique, a reflection is less formal and does not focus on convincing readers. The reflection is a more personal response that makes a connection between you and what the author writes. For instance, you might discuss what you learned from the reading selection or how it relates to your own experiences.

- **Explanation (or Analysis).** This assignment is most often used when the reading selection is a work of fiction or literature—such as a poem, short story, or novel. Your purpose is to offer an explanation about the meaning of the reading selection. This type of writing is particularly broad, covering many specific forms. One common form involves answering a particular question about the author's work; this question could be one you develop or one the teacher assigns. Another common form is describing the overall point or theme of a work of literature.

- **Research Paper.** Although many teachers avoid this particular name, the so-called research paper requires you to use books, magazines, newspapers, or the Internet to find material about a topic. Then, you select the best sources and use them to support your own point or position, being sure to cite and document them. Some papers might use two or three sources, while others might require a dozen or more.

Lesson 40 describes how to determine your general purpose in writing a paper. When an assignment asks you to write about something you've read, usually the purpose fits one of the above categories.

> **COMMONSENSE TIP**   Do not overlook this first step of identifying the purpose of the assignment. Many students seem to think that all "writing about reading" assignments are the same, but it is a critical mistake to write, for example, a reflective essay when the teacher expects a research paper.

Understanding What You Read

No matter what the assignment is, you need to read something well if you are to write about it. College students face challenging, complex reading selections, and while just skimming or casually reading an article or a book will work well in some situations, college requires you to have a better understanding of what you read. Keep in mind that "reading" something does not simply mean being able to sound out the words. Reading means *understanding* what is written. Here are four practical suggestions for helping you read (and understand) more effectively.

Lesson 39

read

Tip #1: Do not worry about reading quickly.   Many people think they are poor readers because they do not read quickly, and such an attitude typically lowers their confidence (and, thus, their ability to read well). In truth, many of your professors read slowly, taking time to consider fully what they are reading. Many people "read" quickly but are unable to understand the material, so have they really read it at all?

Certainly, there are occasions when time is essential, and college students usually feel a shortage of time. Avoid thinking that every situation calls for a quick reading. Indeed, reading too quickly can eventually take more time if it results in such a poor understanding that you are unable to write. In sum, find time—ample time—to devote to reading.

Tip #2: Preview what you are going to read.   Research has shown that if you have an idea of what is coming up next in a reading selection, you will better understand what you read. Take a few moments or more to look through the reading material for these "signposts" that indicate what is coming up next in the reading selection:

- An introductory paragraph in which the author indicates his or her purpose

- Information indicating where and when the selection originally appeared (knowing this information can provide useful background for what you are about to read)

- Preface (an overview or a description of the reading selection)

- Headings and subheadings (these often indicate what the author considers to be important topics)

- Visual cues, such as pictures, diagrams, and lists

- Words or phrases that are emphasized (boldfaced, underlined, italicized, capitalized)

- A conclusion or summary

- Review or discussion questions at the end (these often point you to what you should know after finishing, so look for the answers to them *as* you read)

Tip #3: Don't skip the introduction; don't focus just on the ending.   Some authors recognize that readers need to understand what is coming up next in a reading selection. Consequently, authors often explicitly provide a preview in the introduction of, say, a particular chapter. Avoid the temptation to skip this preview, even if it seems dull. The author is basically

Lesson 39

read

doing the readers' work for them by providing a preview, and the author's own evaluation of what is important in the selection is, indeed, likely to be important.

In contrast, some readers assume that the summary or conclusion is basically all they need to know, and they skim (or skip) everything else. Even the best-written summary is just a *general* description of an author's ideas, and many college teachers—realizing what the conclusion does not cover—want students to understand the important details, not just the simple basics.

Tip #4: Use writing to reinforce your reading. Researchers who study reading and writing have found that people who write *as* they read (or soon afterward) better understand what they read. Here are a few strategies to try:

- **Highlighting.** This technique is "writing" in the sense that you produce markings to indicate a type of meaning (even if you are just emphasizing somebody else's ideas). Highlighting not only helps you identify important portions of a text but also keeps you more active during the reading process, making you more alert and receptive.

  Many students, however, rely on just this one simple strategy. Although helpful, it can be a bit superficial in terms of engaging the reader in understanding, interpreting, and critiquing a text. Other strategies, such as those below, require more work but usually result in a better understanding.

- **Note taking.** For many students, one of the most useful strategies is taking notes while they read—brief comments, questions, definitions, explanations, or evaluations. Use notes to clarify what you read or help you identify problematic portions. Notes can even make connections to what the teacher or others have said (especially if there is disagreement). Such notes can be put in the margin (if it's your book), on cards, on paper, or on the computer.

COMMONSENSE TIP Many students buy used textbooks in which another student has written notes or highlighted. Do *not* assume the previous owner of the book was accurate or logical in terms of his or her highlighting or note taking! In addition, relying on somebody else's markings or notes does little to increase your own active involvement in reading.

Lesson 39

read

- **Summarizing.** A study conducted several years ago found that students in a psychology course received better test scores when they wrote summaries of chapters assigned from their psychology textbook. Even if you are not required to write an objective summary (a type of writing described earlier in this lesson), writing a brief, straightforward summary will help you understand whatever you summarize. In doing so, you will likely reread the selection, which alone helps you better understand the material.

Be selective about what you summarize. This strategy can be a time-consuming way to improve your comprehension of what you read, and you cannot use it for every reading situation. If it is not practical to write a summary, at least consider an oral summary—summarizing aloud, perhaps in a study group.

- **Rereading and Reviewing.** As you read, you will naturally find yourself not truly understanding some parts. Whether your attention is drifting or whether you just don't follow what the author is writing, don't continue until you have reread the troublesome sentence, passage, or page.

  What happens if rereading does not help? In such cases, it is best to backtrack to earlier portions that might have set up the troublesome portion of the text. If that does not help, *then* you should proceed in hopes that the subsequent sections will clarify the author's message.

  Many people consider their reading done when they reach the last words of a text. In some situations, though, the act of reading—of really understanding the text—has only begun at that point. Making sense of a reading selection means understanding, evaluating, and questioning the material, and these acts can best be done *after* an initial reading of the text. Reviewing might mean, in fact, rereading some or all of the selection, or it might mean taking notes or highlighting significant portions. The important point to remember is that reading often means taking time to reflect on what you read—time to absorb, critique, and reconsider the message.

✳ Critical Questions for Reading

You might be confused about what you should do to "reflect" on something you read. Reflection is a highly individualistic activity that depends on what you read, why you are reading it, and who you are. However, we wish to end this lesson by noting questions you can use to help you understand, evaluate, and write about a reading selection.

Topic and Purpose

- What does the author's purpose seem to be? What is his or her thesis, claim, or position?

- Who do you think the author's intended audience is? Where was the selection published?
- Do you agree with the author's major point? Do you think most people would?

Relevance

- Can you think of something current or historical that is relevant to the major topic of this passage?
- How does this reading selection relate to your life? That is, is it relevant to your past, present, or future?
- What about other people — is the selection relevant to most people? For whom is it not?
- Is there something else you have read (or heard or seen) that supports or contradicts this reading selection?

Support

- What does the selection fail to include even though it is related to the topic, and was it reasonable for the author to leave out this material?
- If the reading selection involves a story, consider the characters, setting, and actions. How do all or any of these contribute to a particular interpretation of the story?
- Find two or three sentences you found memorable, insightful, or interesting. Why are these notable or important to you?
- If the author is making an argument or a recommendation, what would be the results if society were to accept it? What is needed to turn the author's ideas into something concrete and useful?

Organization

- Consider how the reading selection is organized — what comes first and last, and how it can otherwise be divided into different sections. How well does the author's arrangement work?
- Is the introduction successful in pulling the reader in? Does the conclusion merely summarize, or does it make a more important point?

Style and Tone

- Consider the author's word choice and the way he or she puts sentences together. Are these effective choices?

Lesson 39

read

- What sort of person does the author appear to be? Consider the author's tone, his or her word choice, and the types of reasons or information provided to readers.
- Could some readers find the selection offensive?
- Whether you agree or disagree with the author, why do you respect or not respect the way he or she writes?

For additional questions, consider those suggested in Lesson 40 for dealing with purpose and standards. Although intended for writers, those questions are also relevant for readers.

Above all, do not merely accept what another person has put down in writing. College readers should not only understand a reading selection but also question and evaluate it.

Applying What You Know

Find a brief article from a magazine or Web site. Bring it to class and be ready to discuss the article in terms of any of the questions listed in the Critical Questions for Reading. End your discussion by stating why you did or did not enjoy reading this particular article.

Planning

Whether you are assigned an in-class essay or a long-term research project, start by determining your purpose. Determining your purpose means more than completing the sentence, "What I want to do in this paper is . . ." It also involves answering these questions:

- What effect do I want to have on readers?
- What do I want to get out of this paper—besides a good grade?
- How will my paper reflect the task that the teacher assigned?
- What does the teacher want me to learn from doing this task?

Working your way through questions like these can be overwhelming, so we suggest first thinking about purpose in two ways: Your *general purpose* is the basic goal of the paper according to the assignment. Your *specific purpose* is the general purpose plus your narrowed topic and the point you want to make.

Determine Your General Purpose

Your first step in the planning stage is determining your general purpose— what you are required to do with the subject or topic.

> **COMMONSENSE TIP** Don't assume that your paper meets the assignment simply because it is "on topic." In this early stage of writing, many people mistakenly place more emphasis on staying on the topic than on making sure they understand the general purpose of the assignment.

Rarely will teachers say simply, "Write a paper about the pyramids." Although some teachers will assign just a subject, most teachers have additional expectations about what you should do with this subject. Most college writing has one of three general purposes: to express yourself, to inform readers, or to persuade readers.

- **Expressing Yourself.** The goal is to express your personal reactions and feelings. The emphasis is on you and your individual response to a subject. A personal narrative, a paper describing an event in your life of special significance, is a common type of expressive writing assignment. For a paper on the pyramids, your teacher might ask the following: What relevance does this story about a woman's trip to see the pyramids have to your life?

- **Informing Readers.** The goal is to explain or describe something in a clear, accurate, thorough way. Usually you should try to be objective and keep your personal feelings out of the assignment. Like a reporter, you focus on the subject and provide information that would be new to readers. For example, you might be asked to write a paper that explains the origins of the pyramids.

- **Persuading Readers.** The goal is to convince readers to accept your claim or position. In most persuasive writing you do in college, you should concentrate on logic, not emotions. The desired effect of persuasion is to convince readers to agree with you. A persuasive assignment might ask the following: Should the pyramids be preserved? Take a stand.

> **COMMONSENSE TIP** If you believe your teacher has given you a wide-open assignment, you might be able to pick any subject or general purpose, but double-check to see if this is *really* the case. Usually teachers (like most readers) have some expectations about a written assignment.

Suppose your teacher has assigned a paper that asks you to summarize the plot of a novel. This paper is likely to have an informative purpose. But suppose your paper winds up describing how you personally reacted to the book (expression), or it argues that the main character is a horrible person (persuasion). Your paper might fail because it does not achieve the general purpose your teacher assigned—to inform.

BUT WHAT HAPPENS IF . . . ?

"I still cannot determine what my general purpose should be." Your best approach is to ask the teacher. Avoid putting it this way, though: "What do you want in this paper?" That is too general and may suggest that you just want a formula. Instead, ask a specific question: For instance, "Is the general purpose to express myself, to provide information, or to support a claim?"

"But asking the teacher isn't practical, and I really, really don't know what the general purpose is!" You might consult someone else in the class, but if all else fails, we suggest you assume that the general purpose is to

Lesson 40

plan

persuade. Persuasion is one of the most common types of writing in college.

"The assignment allows me to write almost anything I want." Again, be sure to confirm this interpretation, preferably by trying out a sample approach with the teacher to see if there are restrictions. Even if there are none, do not assume that your paper can wander from one purpose to another. Having a wide-open assignment does not give you license to say everything; it gives you the added responsibility of determining a clear purpose.

Determine Your Specific Purpose

The second part of determining your purpose is adding your own narrowed topic, which leads to your *specific purpose*. In other words, your specific purpose is your own particular approach to the general assignment—your paper's focus.

The following chart will help you see the difference between an assignment's general purpose and a writer's specific purpose.

If Your General Purpose Is . . .	Your Specific Purpose Might Be . . .
To express your feelings about a holiday or celebration	To express your discomfort with school-sponsored celebrations of Halloween
To inform others about a holiday or celebration	To inform others about the ancient origins of Halloween
To make an argument about a holiday or celebration	To argue that Halloween should not be celebrated in public schools

Understand Your Audience

When you are narrowing your subject and purpose, you should consider your audience. Are you writing for just your teacher, a larger public, or a specific group? Once you make this determination, there are many additional questions to ask. We suggest you start with the following:

Lesson 40

- What should I assume readers already know about the subject?
- What information would readers consider new, necessary, and insightful?

plan

- Will they care about the subject and have strong opinions about it?
- Will they resist any of my ideas?

Suppose your nursing instructor asks you to present a proposal for improving response time in a hospital emergency room and tells you that your audience is a group of local hospital administrators. Your *general purpose* will be to persuade your readers, and your *specific purpose* will be to argue for your idea about how to solve the problem. In planning, you would keep in mind that administrators often think of the hospital's bottom-line financial situation first, so solutions that require an increase in staff without an increase in revenue will meet with resistance. If, on the other hand, your audience is fellow nurses committed to quality care, you may have to work harder to propose that ER staff spend less time with each patient. What's certain is that your proposal will be strengthened by careful consideration of your audience's point of view.

> **COMMONSENSE TIP**   It can be frustrating to second-guess an audience's view, especially if it is one you find intimidating. However, at least consider an audience's general level of expertise and attitude about your subject. If it is distracting to try to define your audience exactly, wait until later. But determine at least a *basic* idea of how your audience might react to what you have to say.

Connecting Purpose and Audience

Let's consider another student's planning choices. The first assignment in Stephanie's writing class was to explain why she chose to go to college. Her initial impulse was to list several general reasons explaining why most people go to college; however, Stephanie decided to consider her writing situation more carefully. First, she took out the assignment sheet (often called a *prompt*) and highlighted the words that indicated the purpose of the paper (general or specific purpose) and the audience.

> Write an **explanation** of **why** you decided to attend college. This **information** will help **me understand** you better as both a **person** and a **writer**. Keep your response to one paragraph of 250 to 300 words, and bring it to our next class meeting.

Obviously, the teacher would be the audience for this paper (the word *me* emphasized this fact). The words *explanation*, *information*, and *understand* made it clear to Stephanie that the general purpose of this short paper would

Lesson 40

plan

be to inform—to tell this teacher something new and useful. Stephanie's specific purpose seemed merely to explain why she went to college. As straightforward as this prompt seemed, the more Stephanie thought about it, the more she questioned her plan of listing several reasons why most people attend college. She thought about two planning issues more carefully: her specific purpose and how her audience might react to various options.

Stephanie correctly assumed her teacher would not be really informed if all Stephanie did was briefly cover a number of reasons why most people go to college. First, this teacher had probably heard the same general reasons already, and it is difficult to inform someone in such a position by providing only basic, commonplace explanations. In addition, Stephanie saw that the prompt indicated that the teacher wanted to know the students better as *individuals*, so Stephanie had to think about reasons why *she* in particular went to college—not why people in general go.

Thus, Stephanie's first major decision during the planning stage was to approach her explanation in a way that would not be generic or ordinary, for she indeed had her own special experiences that influenced her choice of attending college. After reflecting on these experiences, she developed a more specific purpose that she eventually turned into the first sentence of her paragraph. Below is a draft, with this "purpose sentence" underlined.

> <u>Like many people, I decided to go to college because I want job</u>
> <u>opportunities, but I am also here because I want to avoid the problems</u>
> <u>my brothers now face.</u> In some ways, I am like other students you have
> encountered. I am in college because a college degree will give me the skills
> employers want. What I hope you will understand about me, however, is that
> I am also in college because I have seen people close to me jump into major
> responsibilities right after high school, and I have seen how college can often
> take a backseat to other things. My two brothers, Carl and Tom, had all sorts
> of plans about what they would do with a college degree, but they postponed
> these so they could marry and have full-time jobs. I know people are able to
> go back to college in situations such as theirs, but Carl and Tom are now so
> caught up with their jobs and families that they do not know when, if ever,
> they will return to college. Are they happy? I think so. Will a college degree
> guarantee happiness? I know it does not. However, I decided to go to college
> before taking on major responsibilities and to make sure I have the opportu-
> nity to find out if college is for me. It is still early to tell, but I am glad I can
> take time to determine what I want to do in life.

Lesson 40

plan

Everything in this paragraph goes back to a unique specific purpose that arose when Stephanie took time to plan her response based on both purpose and audience. Later, we will discuss in detail why writers revise drafts, but it isn't too early to stress that writers must consider how to alter their plans. Stephanie worried that her teacher might find the paragraph *too* personal or might assume Stephanie was making massive generalizations about the chances of older adults going to college. Stephanie decided she would stay with her true feelings since these did indeed account for why she chose college, but she decided to delete the last sentence of her draft and add the following:

> *Perhaps my brothers can find out one day if college would make them happier, for I see many older, married students at this college. However, I decided to find out now if college is for me, rather than waiting for "one day" that might never happen.*

In sum, this student started to do what many writers do when first given an assignment: write about the first ideas that come to mind, and cover each idea very quickly. Only after considering a purpose that her audience might appreciate more did this particular student begin writing a paragraph that avoids these common problems.

Explore Your Subject and Develop Support

For your paper to be effective, you must narrow your topic to something you can manage within the boundaries of the assignment. For example, a three- to five-page essay would hardly cover the broad subject of *nutrition*. But if you spend some time exploring aspects of the topic that most interest you and are appropriate to your purpose and your audience, you might come up with a narrower, more manageable subject like *the importance of folic acid in a pregnant woman's diet*. Here are two prewriting strategies to help you narrow your subject and decide what you might use as supporting information.

The idea behind these prewriting strategies is to narrow a topic and explore ideas without worrying about correct spelling or grammar at this early stage. If English is not your first language, you may find it easier to freewrite or cluster in your native language.

ESL

Freewriting. This technique is helpful for people whose thinking is often spontaneous and creative (which would include most of us some of the time). Here are some guidelines:

- **Start writing** on the assigned subject or task without worrying about where you are headed. Just do a "mind spill," spontaneously writing whatever comes to mind about the subject and/or your purpose.

Lesson 40

plan

- **Write quickly** and legibly, but avoid thinking too long about what you should say next. Just keep pen or fingers moving. Do not worry about spelling, grammar, wording, or anything that slows your thinking. You are writing to generate ideas for yourself, not for others.

- **Keep writing** whatever comes to mind. There is no magic time limit, but write long enough so that new ideas develop and the words come more easily.

- **Ask questions** if you are running into writer's block. Don't talk yourself into believing you have nothing to say. If all else fails, explain why you think you have nothing to say, or answer one of these questions: "How has this subject affected me personally?" or "Why has it never mattered?"

- **Reflect** on what you have written after you are done. Reread your freewriting and look for something that interests you or your readers. Circle these parts.

Clustering.   Instead of sentences, use words and brief phrases to explore a subject. Clustering has a visual aspect that appeals to many writers. Here are the basic steps:

- **Write down your subject** in the middle of a blank page. Circle it.

- **Start branching** off this central idea. That is, write down related words that come to mind. Circle each new idea. Draw lines to connect related ideas.

- **Continue branching** as related ideas cross your mind. Don't expect that every idea will have the same number of branches. Your point is to explore ideas, not to draw a tidy diagram.

- **Develop several layers** for at least a couple of topics. If you don't have many layers, you could wind up with ordinary, rather superficial ideas.

- **Reflect** on what you have written after you are done. Then examine the connections you have made and continue to draw lines between groups of ideas. Doing so allows you to consider how ideas support one another.

The next page shows a cluster for an assignment on ways to enhance safety. One writer, as part of his planning, decided that he needed to narrow the broad topic of "safety" to something more focused and manageable. Notice that this writer developed some ideas more than others.

Lesson 40

Think about what clustering does. You come up with not only a more specific subject but also major ideas to bring to your writing. If this writer decided to write on "road rage," the cluster diagram offers supporting ideas, such as "ways to control temper" and "relaxation techniques."

plan

COMMONSENSE TIP   Use these planning techniques whenever you need to develop ideas. In this section, we focus on clustering and other techniques to help you narrow your subject and come up with major ideas, but you can use these techniques earlier in the process to choose a subject and determine your audience and purpose. These techniques also help you to find and group supporting ideas.

Write a Thesis Sentence

Once you have explored possible topics and purposes, you should write an initial thesis sentence. This sentence expresses the point you want to make in your paper. It may change as you think more about your assignment, but it helps to have a *working thesis* at this point. In most college writing, a thesis sentence has these characteristics:

- It states the writer's single main point.

- It is clear and specific.

- It is placed in the opening paragraph (generally, it is the first or last sentence).

- It prepares readers for the rest of the paper.

Here are some sample thesis sentences based on the general and specific purposes described on page 400.

Thesis Sentence for Expressive Writing
Halloween might seem a casual, fun holiday for some, but for me it was offensive and uncomfortable when I felt forced to celebrate it in school.

Thesis Sentence for Informative Writing
If you think Halloween is just a "kids' night," you might be surprised to know that this holiday has ancient religious origins.

Thesis Sentence for Persuasive Writing
Halloween should not be celebrated in public schools.

> **COMMONSENSE TIP** See pages 412–413 for a list of different types of topic sentences that indicate the purpose of a single paragraph. Read through these categories to get an idea of the various ways to create a thesis sentence.

 ESL In some cultures, writers avoid making points directly. In English, however, readers appreciate writing that has a clear, direct point. Start by drafting a thesis sentence. You can revise it to make it more straightforward later.

Plan Your Paper's Organization

Once you have some idea about what you want to say, consider how to organize, or arrange, these ideas. Sometimes, deciding how to arrange ideas helps writers come up with a better purpose or better support, so be willing to make changes.

Think of your paper as needing these distinct parts:

Lesson 40

1. an **introduction:** a way to announce your subject, draw your readers' attention and interest, and indicate your specific purpose and main point

plan

2. a **body:** the section in which you provide major ideas and supporting ideas to achieve your purpose
3. a **conclusion:** the place where your readers feel a sense of completion

The first step of planning your paper's organization is to remind yourself of your purpose.

COMMONSENSE TIP If you are still not sure how to word your thesis sentence, try to phrase it in the most direct way possible: "In this paper, my primary purpose is to . . ." Later, you can revise this sentence to be less formulaic.

The next step is to answer this question: *Does the teacher expect a particular type of organization?* You must determine how much flexibility you have in organizing your paper. Look at the assignment's wording, ask classmates, ask your teacher, or reread any material covered in class about organization. Teachers often expect writers to use a particular organizing structure. Sometimes, they are direct about this expectation by using certain "tip off" words: *arrange, develop, form, format, method of development, mode, order, organize, pattern, scheme, shape,* or *structure.*

Your writing instructor may name the type of writing you are to do (such as a business letter, a lab report, or a book review) and expect you to use the organization associated with this type of writing. Most common assignments, however, require you to organize your writing in whatever way best suits your purpose, audience, and subject. In a personal narrative, you might present events in chronological (time) order. In an informative essay, you might explain a process by proceeding through the steps in the process. Finally, you might develop a persuasive essay by presenting your ideas in order of importance, from strong to strongest. No matter what the assignment, you can think further about your organization by writing an informal outline.

Write an Informal Outline. Think of an outline as a *tentative plan* for arranging your ideas. Some students remember so many formal *dos* and *don't*s about writing an outline that they forget its real purpose. We suggest you develop an outline that is more than rough notes, but not so formal that it distracts you from your writing process. That is, develop an outline that would be clear to someone else (especially if you want feedback), but avoid becoming frustrated by formatting issues, such as "Do I indent three or five spaces?" or "Do I use a Roman numeral here?" Even if you are given formal rules to follow, it is more manageable to start with an informal outline that focuses on ideas, not technical details. You can revise it later.

Lesson 40

plan

Write an informal outline that indicates the following:

- your thesis statement (the point of your paper)
- your major support
- some minor ideas that support the major ones

An outline should also reflect the type of organization that readers expect or the type you have selected.

Here is an outline of one writer's effort to persuade her company's benefits manager to endorse a tuition reimbursement program for employees. The assignment did not specify a type of organization, so the writer decided to give background information, anticipate any opposition, and then base the major body paragraphs on the reasons supporting her thesis.

Thesis: As part of the general employee benefits package, the company should provide tuition reimbursement.

Introduction

—Discuss the company's history of poor employee retention.

—Discuss recent news about the value of adult education.

—State thesis.

Body

(Anticipate possible opposition) A tuition reimbursement program is unnecessary.

—Tuition reimbursement is too expensive.

—The company's training department sufficiently meets the needs of the company.

(Major support point) A tuition reimbursement fund is not wasted money.

—Tuition reimbursement offsets the costs of advertising for, recruiting, and training new employees.

—Tuition reimbursement as part of a comprehensive benefits package attracts quality job candidates and retains good employees.

(Major support point) Tuition reimbursement builds employee confidence and job satisfaction.

—This kind of program helps employees build job-relevant skills.

—Increased job satisfaction means a decrease in employee turnover.

(Major support point) Tuition reimbursement programs enhance a company's internal training function.

—Employee education is strengthened by a team approach; company trainers still assess employees' needs and then inform employees about local schools and programs that meet those needs.

Lesson 40

plan

—*The company's internal training staff is free from repeated new-employee training; staff can focus on developing more customized programs.*

Conclusion

—*Summarize benefits of thesis.*

— *Emphasize that a tuition reimbursement program can help the company fulfill its mission: to develop quality products and honor quality employees.*

COMMONSENSE TIP Use question marks, bullets, indentation, or numbered lists to remind you where you have questions or to indicate which ideas are more important than others. The appearance of an outline can help you see how ideas connect. Don't obsess over making your outline look neat and orderly, though.

BUT WHAT HAPPENS IF . . . ?

"I don't know how many paragraphs I should have—especially in the middle part of my paper." There is no magic number of paragraphs a paper needs, but you should consider any number indicated in the assignment, the length requirements of the paper, and how much you need to say to achieve your specific purpose. Unless the assignment calls for a very short paper, you need more than one paragraph in the body. At the same time, be careful not to have too many. For example, more than ten paragraphs in a three-page paper may mean that your paragraphs are too short to be clear, convincing, or interesting.

"I can sketch out major ideas, but I don't know what to put under them." You may find it helpful to do more freewriting or clustering (see pp. 403–404). Then you could add more to your outline.

✳ *Critical Questions for Planning*

Write down your general purpose, specific purpose, and possible audience. Next, answer the set of questions that best relates to your general purpose.

If your assignment is . . .	*Answer these questions . . .*
Expressive	What could you say about your own experiences with this subject that would also matter to your readers?

	Do you have personal experience with this subject that are so unusual that your readers would be intrigued?
	What strong feelings do you have about this subject? Can you write about them in a way that your readers will understand these feelings?
Informative	What questions might your readers already have about this subject?
	What do they need to know to be fully informed?
	If readers are somehow going to use this information in their lives, what should they know?
Persuasive	What controversies already exist in regard to your subject?
	How would you defend your position against specific objections raised by readers?
	What additional information or evidence could you provide that would change their minds?

Applying What You Know

In college and the workforce, you cannot always pick what you will write about, but often you can find a way to work in a subject you know well or enjoy. Make a list of five topics, controversies, or things you know well or enjoy. Share these in a small-group discussion, and explain why you listed them. Your teacher will likely want to know what topics the class finds intriguing, so be prepared to share these with the entire class.

Lesson 40

plan

Drafting

As you begin to draft, you should have a clear plan for your paper based on the following checklist. If there is an item on this list that you have not considered, you may want to do some more planning.

_____ I have determined the assignment's *general purpose*: expressive, informative, or persuasive.

_____ I have determined my *specific purpose*: what I specifically want to express, inform readers about, or persuade them to believe (my narrowed topic).

_____ I have considered my *audience* and have an idea of who will (or should) read my paper, their background in the subject, and their attitude toward it.

_____ I have written a working *thesis sentence*: a clear and specific statement of the point of my paper.

_____ I have developed major *support* for my specific purpose: the main explanations, information, evidence, or events that will help me make my overall point.

_____ I have written an *organizational plan*: the way I will arrange at least the major ideas.

Now you should write a draft, modifying your plan or discarding it if necessary. The key to successful drafting is *flexibility*. We suggest you start with a basic introduction that includes your specific purpose and thesis statement and prepares your reader for the rest of your paper, and then proceed by drafting according to your informal outline.

> **COMMONSENSE TIP** Don't spend a huge amount of time on the introduction while you are drafting. If drafting the paper causes you to modify your specific purpose and thesis, you'll need to revise the introduction anyway.

Pay most attention to presenting the point of your paper (purpose), to developing your ideas (support), and to connecting these ideas to each other (organization). Pay less attention to stylistic and mechanical matters covered in the first part of this book. You can address these matters in the revision stage.

Write Topic Sentences and Paragraphs

Begin writing your paper by drafting paragraphs. Keep in mind that each paragraph should include just one main topic. If your paragraph rambles or covers too many topics, you run the risk of confusing your readers.

One way writers help readers is by using topic sentences. A topic sentence is usually a one-sentence statement that indicates the purpose, subject, or point of a paragraph. It might help you to think of the topic sentence as the controlling idea for a paragraph. Just as a thesis sentence presents the controlling idea for a paper, a topic sentence presents the controlling idea for each paragraph in the body of your paper. Sometimes, in fact, you might be assigned to write just a paragraph, not an entire essay. In this case, your topic sentence becomes your contract with your readers. (See p. 414 for guidelines on completing the single-paragraph assignment.)

There is no law that requires the topic sentence to be the first sentence of a paragraph, but we suggest you start each paragraph in the body of your paper with a topic sentence to give you something to refer to while developing the paragraph, to remind you of the point. You can always alter your use of topic sentences in the revision stage, keeping in mind that those topic sentences help readers identify your major ideas.

> **COMMONSENSE TIP**   One exception to the important role of topic sentences is in narration, or telling a story (often called a "personal narrative"). When relating an experience, you might not use topic sentences often, though you would still divide the story into paragraphs. Instead of using topic sentences, you would rely on chronological order (telling events as they happened) and careful transitions.

Topic sentences vary in how they convey the main idea of a paragraph. Try different approaches. If you use a question for every topic sentence in a paper, for example, your readers might find your paper predictable and boring.

Lesson 41

COMMON TYPES OF TOPIC SENTENCES

The Direct Approach explicitly announces the purpose of the paragraph.

draft

In this paragraph, I will explain why the school would lose money with a football team.

The purpose of this paragraph is to define a few important terms.

The Question indicates the paragraph's purpose by posing a question it will answer.

Why should we debate this issue anyway?

Where does lava come from?

The Nutshell states the major idea—not the purpose—of the paragraph, usually in just one sentence. (This is probably the most common type of topic sentence in college writing.)

A second reason for impeaching the governor is that she received illegal contributions.

Before long, I realized my aunt was sick.

Addressing the Reader anticipates what readers might be wondering about or doubting. The paragraph provides a response.

You might be wondering why it is necessary to build a new stadium.

My opponents would reasonably question my statistics, but the figures are accurate.

Connecting to the Previous Paragraph makes a clear link with the preceding ideas.

In contrast, however, the African swallow flies at a much faster rate.

After you complete the third step, proceed to the next: applying the varnish.

Let me offer one example of this concept.

The Alert calls special attention to a point the paragraph will cover. Readers should understand the importance of the paragraph.

It would be a mistake to assume that students do not care about racism.

If our leaders do not change this law, there will be a terrible price to pay.

Nothing will ever make me forget what I felt when I heard about Juan's death.

Lesson 41

With a topic sentence to guide you as well as your readers, you can now provide the details needed to clarify, support, or expand the paragraph's point.

draft

> **COMMONSENSE TIP** Be careful about being too direct when you write a topic sentence. Although useful for complex or highly formal papers, it often strikes readers as dull and contrived. However, the direct approach can be useful in a draft to clarify what you should focus on. You could revise it later into something less direct.

Strategies for Writing a Single-Paragraph Assignment

Suppose your assignment is to write a single paragraph. Fortunately, almost everything covered in this writing guide applies to writing paragraphs. When planning, drafting, and revising a paragraph, you still have to consider basic standards for effective writing (like those outlined on p. 388). Here is a checklist for completing the single-paragraph assignment.

✳ *Checklist: Writing a Paragraph*

_____ Determine your purpose. See page 398.
- Determine the general purpose of the assignment (to express, to inform, or to persuade).
- Determine your specific purpose.

_____ Consider your audience. See page 400.
- Ask yourself questions about your readers' knowledge of and attitudes about your subject.

_____ Use a prewriting strategy (freewriting, clustering) to narrow your subject. See page 403.

_____ Write a topic sentence that states the main point of your paragraph. See page 405.

_____ Based on what you considered while prewriting, choose the details, examples, and evidence that best support your topic sentence. See page 406.

_____ Consider how you will organize these supporting ideas so that they clearly build on one another. See pages 406–409.
- Arrange these ideas in a brief informal outline of your paragraph.
- Plan a paragraph that is clearly structured. See page 412. In college writing, a paragraph often has the following parts:

  a *topic sentence* that states the main point of your paragraph

Lesson 41

draft

a *body* made up of several sentences that support, explain, or prove your topic sentence

a *concluding sentence* that takes readers back to the main idea of the paragraph

___ Write a draft of your paragraph based on your planning. See page 411.

___ Revise your paragraph. Consider what steps you might take to improve it. See page 422.

- Ask your teacher and other students for feedback.
- Ask yourself revision questions based on your purpose.
- Ask yourself revision questions based on the five basic standards.

___ Edit your paragraph by eliminating errors in grammar, punctuation, mechanics, and word use. Follow the specific guidelines given in Units One through Ten of this book.

Consider how the following paragraph, written as part of an economics exam, reflects some of the steps in the checklist above.

Example assignment: **Explain the difference between a country's gross national product (GNP) and its gross domestic product (GDP).**

EXAMPLE PARAGRAPH RESPONSE

Though they are both important indicators of a country's economic well-being, GNP and GDP are not the same. The GNP is the total market value of all goods and services produced by a country's labor force and capital anywhere in the world. For example, the market value of clothing produced and sold by The Gap, regardless of store and factory location, would figure into the United States' GNP. The GNP would include profits earned from Canadian and European stores, as well as from stores in places like Boston, Atlanta, and Los Angeles. The GDP, on the other hand, is the total market value of goods and services produced by a country's labor force and capital within a country's borders. Profits earned by The Gap in places other than the United States would not count toward the country's GDP. Each of these figures is a separate but equally valuable way to measure a country's economic health.

As the topic sentence indicates, the paragraph will focus on differences between GNP and GDP, and every sentence afterward explains at least one of these two concepts. Because this is a complex paragraph with technical information, the paragraph ends by reminding us of the overall point.

Lesson 41

draft

Put More Support into Paragraphs

Drafting involves arranging and developing the major ideas you sketched out in your outline. You should present each major idea in a paragraph. Then, within each paragraph, you have to provide additional details and support for the major idea. Avoid simply rewording your topic sentence; support it by adding new information, evidence, or ideas in each paragraph. To do this, ask yourself questions based on your purpose and audience.

GENERAL PURPOSE: *TO EXPRESS*

- If my subject involves an experience, what details can I include to bring this experience to life? How do I make clear to my audience how this experience affected me?

- If I am writing about a more abstract subject (such as something I read or a feeling I have about an idea), what details should I include to describe this subject and, more important, my personal reaction to it?

GENERAL PURPOSE: *TO INFORM*

- Considering limits on the paper's length, what should I tell my audience about the subject? What details, examples, or explanations will they need?

- Have I defined important terms, especially those that have a special meaning?

- To help readers understand the subject, can I compare it to something more familiar? Have I fully described the parts or functions of my subject?

- What information could I add that would be new to readers?

GENERAL PURPOSE: *TO PERSUADE*

- What are the major reasons why readers should accept the claim I am making?

- To prove my point, can I draw on what other writers have said?

- Can I give real or hypothetical examples to support my argument?

- If readers have doubts about my facts, can I convince them that my information is accurate?

- Have I carefully considered any objections or criticisms my readers might raise?

Lesson 41

draft

COMMONSENSE TIP   If your paragraph becomes too long, divide it into two or more paragraphs. You should avoid having more than one purpose or point in a single paragraph, but you certainly can have two or more paragraphs that deal with a similar idea in different ways.

One Student's Draft

To better understand your choices as you write, take a look at one student's draft. Daniel was given the following assignment:

> *Take a position on a controversy that involves some form of recreation or sport. Convince readers to accept your position. Use your own ideas and experiences, rather than drawing on outside research.*

Daniel adapted the processes described in this lesson but did not follow a formula. Here are the basic steps of the drafting process and how he went through them.

Step 1: Determine the general purpose of the assignment.
Three words in the assignment were especially important for Daniel: *controversy*, *convince*, and *position*. These words made it clear the teacher wanted a persuasive essay. Thus, Daniel knew he was not supposed to merely write about his opinion. He realized the real goal was to write an essay that would compel readers to agree with him on a controversial subject. From the wording of the assignment, he also knew he had to write about a specific type of recreation or sport. Daniel immediately thought of two sports he knew and enjoyed: hunting and water skiing. He liked water skiing the most but knew hunting was a much more controversial topic that would lend itself to an argumentative essay.

Step 2: Consider how the audience might affect the essay.
The teacher's assignment did not say much about the audience for the paper, except that writers would need to convince them. For a brief time, Daniel considered writing the paper for fellow hunters. But why write an argument to people who already agreed with him? He thus assumed he would aim his argument at people who disliked hunting or who did not consider it a true sport. He knew they might never become hunters no matter how well he wrote, but he could attempt to persuade them to respect hunting as a sport.

Step 3: Narrow the topic to determine a specific purpose.
Daniel freewrote for five minutes and discovered how many types of hunting

Lesson 41

draft

(and hunters) there were—all the way from shark hunting to hunting with a bow and arrow. He focused on the type he knew best: deer hunting. He decided to defend the sport against criticisms he had heard from friends and acquaintances.

Step 4: Consider possible support and develop an informal outline.

Daniel recalled all the complaints he had heard about hunting and wasn't certain what his exact thesis would be. He decided that, for this draft, he would use a broad thesis sentence and revise it later if need be. Once he had that matter settled, he decided on the major points he most wanted to bring up, based on the arguments he had heard before about why deer hunting is "wrong." He listed all the arguments (for and against) that he had encountered. Then, he made an outline that covered some of these points—the ones he considered the most persuasive. Here is his outline:

> <u>Thesis statement</u>: *In this paper, I will argue why deer hunting is a true sport.*
>
> <u>Introduction</u>:
> * *Give personal experience about some people's misconceptions about hunting.*
> * *Indicate my position (my thesis statement).*
> * *(Separate paragraph?) Explain what I mean by "hunting" and "sport."*
>
> <u>Reason #1</u>:
> * *Deer hunting is a true sport because*
>   * *-- it is competitive because the deer has its own advantages in the contest*
>   * *-- it takes special skills*
>
> <u>Conclusion</u>:
> * *Point out my experience with enjoying people and wildlife through hunting.*

Step 5: Write a draft.

With this basic plan, Daniel began writing. He was worried about how many paragraphs he should have but decided the goal for draft one was just to write down his major ideas. He knew he could revise the essay later for any organizational problems.

Before you read Daniel's draft, consider the basic guidelines below for writing an argument. We tailored the basic standards from page 388 to cover this particular type of writing. Consider how these guidelines might have helped Daniel as he drafted—as well as helped him consider what to change once he completed a draft.

Lesson 41

draft

GUIDELINES FOR WRITING AN ARGUMENT

Purpose: The thesis must be controversial. That is, someone must be able to disagree with it if the claim is truly argumentative.

Support: You usually can't cover every possible reason for and against your thesis. Focus on the reasons most likely to convince the majority of people who disagree with your position.

Organization: There is no rule about where to put your most important reason. What is essential is that you avoid the temptation to list a bunch of reasons—especially in just one paragraph. Focus each paragraph on thoroughly explaining one major reason that supports your thesis.

Style: Your goal is to make your readers accept your claim. Therefore, avoid a rude or confrontational tone. You rarely win over an audience by insulting them.

Mechanics: Right or not, many people will judge your argument by how well you follow conventions of formal English. Mechanical errors can affect your overall credibility. However, the revising stage will allow you to correct any such problems. For now, focus on getting your best ideas onto paper.

Here is Daniel's draft. He adhered to his informal outline for the most part, but then changed his mind about a few things (such as the conclusion). How well does this draft reflect the guidelines listed above? Remember: This is a work in progress, and the writer has time to revise. (Daniel's revision is not included in this lesson. You will have the opportunity to revise his draft in Lesson 42.)

DANIEL'S FIRST DRAFT

Deer Hunting as a True Sport

Not long ago, a girl I work with asked me what I was doing over the weekend, and I told her I was going deer hunting. She immediately said, "Why do you want to murder deer? What challenge is there in blasting harmless animals with a high-powered rifle?" She became upset and walked away before I could even explain why I enjoy this sport. My friend might never read this paper, but I want to explain to others why deer hunting is a true sport.

First, I should explain what I mean by "sport" and "hunting." I know all too well that some people say they're going deer hunting when all they do is camp out, get drunk, and drive through the woods trying to shoot deer. I don't consider that hunting. True hunting involves a serious attempt to carefully find your prey and then kill the deer with one accurate shot. The word

Lesson 41

draft

"sport" refers to any recreational activity where mental and physical talent is needed to achieve a difficult goal, and hunting meets this definition.

Hunting deer requires a good deal of talent if the hunter is to compete against a deer. You might think the unarmed deer has no advantages in this contest. However, the truth is that the deer has natural defenses that give it the advantage. Deer move silently if they move at all. Many learn to stay hidden in thick bushes during deer season. When they do come out, they are well camouflaged and hard to detect. Another advantage the deer has is its speed. These are not stupid animals. They seem to know when they are being hunted, and the slightest sound can make them bolt away so fast that even an expert sharpshooter would miss. They usually travel in a herd and use special signs to warn each other. If a deer hears something suspicious, it will raise its tail as a warning to others. If one deer hears or sees you, then in seconds they will all know. Their sense of smell, sight, and hearing are superb, so it is not common for you to be in their presence long without their knowing it.

A hunter has to be skilled to compete against this adversary. Successful hunters have to wait patiently while remaining still and quiet in a spot where they suspect the deer might come. Not just anyone can pick out fresh deer trails or remain out of sight, especially at 6:00 in the morning when the temperature is below freezing.

Another talent the hunter needs is the ability to shoot well. I myself have had to shoot a deer from one hundred yards away. Even with a scope, it can be a difficult shot because you do not want to merely wound the deer. A steady hand and patience are just as important as having good eyesight or a high-powered scope.

Many people will never give deer hunting a try. I understand it is not a sport for everyone. But too many people criticize deer hunters without really understanding the sport. I might not have persuaded you to become a hunter, but I hope to have proven that deer hunting is not a mindless activity that pits a human against a helpless opponent.

✳ Critical Questions for Drafting

Whether you are writing a single paragraph or an essay, these questions can assist you, especially toward the end of the drafting stage.

Purpose and Audience

- Have you changed your mind about your topic since you began your draft? If so, start thinking about the changes your draft will need in order to be consistent.

Lesson 41

draft

- Now that you have examined your topic more carefully, who is the best audience for this draft? If you have changed your mind about your audience, you might also need to reconsider some of what you have written thus far.

Support

- What ideas need clarification? Adding details is one of the important parts of the drafting stage. Add too much detail rather than too little. Later, you can decide what to delete, if anything.
- What claims need more support or proof? If you are trying to persuade readers, you cannot just express yourself. You must convince them. Consider their possible objections and respond to them.

Organization

- Does each paragraph focus on one main idea? It's very common for paragraphs to ramble a bit while the writer explores ideas. You can fix such problems later, but at least be aware that some paragraphs might need to be tightened and revised for coherence.
- Is there an introduction and a conclusion to your essay? During the drafting stage, these sections are often far from complete, but you need to recognize these potential problems so you can address them later.

Applying What You Know

Once you have completed a draft of an essay, make an outline that effectively summarizes its major points. If you cannot do so, the draft will likely need to be revised later for organization.

Lesson 41

draft

LESSON 42

Revising

If your deadline allows, put your draft aside and return later to revise it. You might make small changes here and there as you draft, but don't consider your writing complete simply because you have put your ideas onto paper. Now it is time to consider how to improve your draft. You will get the most out of this stage of writing if you understand one of the most often-overlooked principles of writing.

> **COMMONSENSE TIP** Revision is *more* than looking for problems with individual words and sentences. It means looking for ways to improve your overall purpose, support, and organization. You revise your paper to make it clearer and stronger.

Too often, writers look only at individual sentences and words when they revise. These are important, of course; that is why we wrote this book. However, a grammatically correct paper can be useless if it lacks ideas or is unorganized. This lesson will help you revise your paper on a deeper level.

Ask Questions as You Revise

Many writers are confused about what to revise. As one student put it, "If I knew what had to be revised, I would have done it when I drafted the paper!" But even experienced writers cannot keep track of all the questions they could ask themselves to improve their papers as they write. Revising, therefore, means looking for opportunities for improvement that perhaps did not occur to you in the midst of putting your ideas into words, sentences, and paragraphs.

In college, you are usually writing not just for yourself but for others, so it is useful to obtain feedback from at least one other person. It might be helpful to write down specific questions for this person to consider. Developing a habit of asking yourself such questions will also help you understand what to revise when feedback isn't practical. There are two sets of questions to ask of your draft:

422

Questions based on your *general purpose*

Questions based on *basic standards* that apply to most college writing

These questions overlap, but each set presents a different way of thinking about revision. Tailor these to fit your own specific purpose and situation.

Ask Questions about *General Purpose*. We began this writing guide by telling you to start your writing process by determining your purpose. You should also make a habit of rethinking your purpose at the revision stage. Here are some more questions to ask yourself as you revise.

GENERAL PURPOSE: *TO EXPRESS*

- What is the point of my story? Is that point clear?
- Does this paper give an account of how I really feel?
- What details could I add to help show how I feel or think about my subject?
- Have I brought my subject to life for my readers?
- Are the events in my narrative arranged in an order that makes sense for my purpose and audience?

GENERAL PURPOSE: *TO INFORM*

- What is the point of my paper? Is that point clear?
- What information have I left out? Would readers expect me to cover this material?
- Have I told my readers something that is new or not widely known? Have I provided enough examples or explanations?
- Have I gone beyond the basic idea and given my readers a deeper understanding of the subject?
- Can I add more facts, details, or examples, perhaps based on research?
- Are my details and examples arranged in an order that makes sense for my purpose and audience?

GENERAL PURPOSE: *TO PERSUADE*

- What is the point of my paper? Is that point clear?
- Is my claim really arguable? Did I mistakenly word it in a way that nobody could disagree with?
- Where is my strongest support? How can I make it stronger? Where is my weakest support? Should I keep it? If I keep it, how can I strengthen it?

Lesson 42

rev

- What criticisms will I face from readers with an opposing viewpoint? What can I do to gain their support?

- Do my supporting ideas follow each other in an order that makes the most sense for my purpose and audience?

Some of these questions are similar to those you asked when you developed paragraphs and topic sentences (pp. 405, 412). It is not unusual for writers to ask themselves similar questions from the beginning to the end of the writing process. After all, if you had to ask completely new questions, you might end up writing a new paper.

Ask Questions Based on *Basic Standards*.

Another way to approach revision is to think about how readers evaluate writing. Practically everything we have discussed so far goes back to the basic standards for good writing that we presented in the Unit Twelve Overview: purpose, support, organization, style, and mechanics (see p. 388). If readers indeed use these criteria to evaluate writing, then one way to revise is to ask yourself questions about these criteria. Consider how these questions might be tailored to suit both your general and your specific purposes.

BASIC STANDARD: *PURPOSE*

- Is my specific purpose clear?

- Does my thesis control the paper? Do my topic sentences help my paragraphs show, explain, or prove my thesis?

- Have I delivered on my thesis? That is, did I do everything it indicated I would do? If not, should I continue to narrow my specific purpose?

- If my paper does not deliver on my thesis, should I add more to my paper so that it does everything I indicated I would do?

COMMONSENSE TIP While you were planning and drafting, your thesis sentence was something to start you off, but at this stage, think of it as a contract. In one sense you are promising readers that your paper will achieve whatever purpose you have indicated in your thesis sentence. Make sure the wording is exactly what it should be to match your paper.

BASIC STANDARD: *SUPPORT*

- Where can I add more details, examples, or facts so readers will understand my point? On the other hand, should I delete some specifics because they do not clearly support my point?

- Do I give the most support to the paragraphs that are most important for my purpose?

- In each paragraph, what would my readers possibly disagree with? What could I delete, add, or change to make my argument more convincing?

- Is my support too general or vague as a whole or within paragraphs? What can I do to be more specific?

- Are my details, examples, and evidence too common or obvious?

BASIC STANDARD: *ORGANIZATION*

- Do I have an introduction that alerts readers to my specific purpose and my thesis?

- Does each paragraph revolve around one point?

- Do my paragraphs build on each other? Does each have a clear connection to the one before and after it? If not, can I rearrange paragraphs, add words or sentences to clarify connections, or delete paragraphs that do not fit?

- Within paragraphs, does each sentence relate to the one before and after it?

- Does the conclusion merely summarize? If so, what else could I do to give a sense of closure?

COMMONSENSE TIP To help you clarify the connections between sentences, consider using transitional words and phrases like these:

also	for example	in fact
as a matter of fact	for instance	in short
as a result	furthermore	indeed
as I said earlier	however	nevertheless
consequently	in addition	next
finally	in brief	therefore
first	in comparison	to sum up

Be careful not to overuse these terms; use them only when they express a true relationship. (See Lesson 14 for guidance in punctuating transitional terms.)

BASIC STANDARD: *STYLE*

- Considering my audience and my purpose, is my paper too formal? Too informal? Do I use too much slang? Too many stuffy words? Do I seem too "chummy" or relaxed with readers? Too impersonal?

Lesson 42

rev

- Can I combine sentences for more variety? What sentences seem too choppy or too awkward?

- What clearer or more precise words could I use?

BASIC STANDARD: *MECHANICS*

- Have I followed the guidelines in Units One through Ten of this book?

- If my paper uses outside sources, have I followed the guidelines in Unit Eleven of this book?

You must decide how to answer these questions. We wish we could give the answers as easily as we pose the questions, but your own opinions and writing situation will determine how you will respond.

Below is an example of one student's revision process using such questions to examine her draft.

Using Questions

Consider how one student, Maria, asked a few questions to help revise a short paper. Here is the assignment:

> *Write a paragraph (about 250 words) that explains your position about a controversy in a town or city you know well. This is a brief argument, so focus on important reasons.*

After freewriting, Maria chose a problem involving her hometown of Marshall, Texas: whether to have a curfew for minors. Maria realized that she needed to take a stance and decided she was against the proposed curfew. Thus, she developed a thesis sentence that would serve as a topic sentence for her paragraph: *"Marshall should not have a curfew for minors."* Using clustering, she considered several reasons supporting her position. (These prewriting and drafting techniques are discussed in the previous two lessons.) Maria then wrote the following draft.

> *Marshall should not have a curfew for minors. First, it's not fair to have a curfew for just minors. Second, how can it be enforced? There are not enough police officers working at night to help with real crimes. Third, a curfew punishes all teenagers just because a few have caused trouble lately after midnight. Finally, the real troublemakers are going to cause trouble no matter what the curfew is. How would a curfew cut down, for instance, on teenagers who sell illegal drugs? This proposed curfew is completely illogical and will not accomplish anything.*

This paragraph was far shorter than what the teacher required. Maria was not sure how to revise the paragraph to make it longer, for the paragraph seemed to express her feelings on the topic. To help her not only with the length but also with detecting other problems, Maria looked at the questions dealing with her general purpose.

She considered the assignment again and noticed several important terms from the prompt: "your position," "controversy," "argument," and "important reasons." She realized that her general purpose was not just to express her opinion but to *convince* readers to accept her position. This perspective led Maria to consider one set of questions especially important for persuasive writing:

> *Where is my strongest support, and how can I make it even stronger?*
>
> *Where is my weakest support, and should I keep it? If so, how can I make it strong?*

Maria's first draft was, unfortunately, a "shotgun" approach. She tossed in as many reasons as she could without concentrating on any of them, hoping that at least one reason would work. She also did not make her reasons strong from a reader's perspective. Maria realized she had merely given a list of reasons without really trying to convince people. To improve this draft as well as to make it meet the word requirement, she decided to focus on what she thought to be the two most convincing reasons: the first and third reasons from the draft.

Maria was not sure how to make these reasons stronger, so she next considered questions dealing with basic standards. Rather than answering all these questions, she focused on the ones dealing with support, since these are designed to help writers add and improve reasons that strengthen their claims. She thought two in particular would help her add useful support:

> *Where can I add more details, examples, or facts so readers will understand my point?*
>
> *What would my readers disagree with?*

After considering these questions, Maria realized she did not have a single specific example (or any sort of specifics at all) in her draft. Nor had she considered why people might disagree with any of her reasons. The two questions above helped her realize her paragraph would be clearer and more convincing if she (1) gave concrete, realistic details and (2) explained why her reasons are valid despite potential criticism from some readers.

She used her hometown newspaper to provide her with specifics. To deal with potential criticisms, she talked with a friend who supported the idea of a curfew. Her revised paragraph focused on doing a good job with two reasons, rather than superficially covering four vague reasons.

> *Marshall should not have a curfew for minors. First, it is not fair to have a curfew for just minors. I examined the Marshall newspaper for the last three days. There were sixteen crimes described in the paper, and the reporters gave ages for suspects in twelve of the crimes. Only four of the twelve suspects were minors, and only two of these crimes occurred late at night. If the curfew is designed to cut down on crime, should it not be applied to the people who actually commit the most crimes? I do not believe there is enough evidence to prove that minors commit the majority of crimes, so they should not be singled out. In addition, a curfew punishes all teenagers just because a few have caused trouble after midnight. Some people might say that a curfew is not a real punishment at all. They say that minors could stay at home for entertainment, go to a friend's home, or be accompanied by an adult after the curfew. However, keeping people from enjoying themselves in public is a punishment. Some movies, for example, end after the curfew, and many people like to enjoy a late-night meal at a restaurant after seeing a show or dancing. Furthermore, not all parents are willing or able to hang out with their children at night. Forbidding people to enjoy a harmless but enjoyable activity is a punishment, and it is an unfair punishment because teenagers who do not break the law should not suffer simply because a few teenagers are guilty.*

The more Maria thought about specific information and how people might respond to her reasons, the more she realized she could add to even this much longer paragraph. Thus, she added two final sentences not only to give a sense of closure to the paragraph but also to let people know that even more could be said.

> *The idea of a curfew is complex and controversial. I have covered only two reasons, but many issues need to be considered before Marshall adopts a curfew.*

BUT WHAT HAPPENS IF . . . ?

"I now see a need to revise but am not sure how." Suppose you see a problem with your logic in one paragraph. We suggest you go back to the prewriting techniques suggested earlier (see p. 403)—or to whatever critical thinking strategies you use to come up with ideas or solve a problem. Don't underestimate the value of using the *basic standards* on page 388 as your own personal revision checklist, though.

"I'm not sure if my revision made the paper any better." We have to be truthful: There are times when revisions hurt rather than help. If you are unsure, it is time to have someone read your draft and give you an honest reaction. Try to get feedback from at least two people.

COMMONSENSE TIP When you ask for help, avoid explaining the reason behind a revision or at least wait until your reader has finished reading and responding. Otherwise, you are basically saying, "Here's why I did this. Tell me I'm right."

"My paper is a total mess. I'm not sure where to start revising." Don't overlook this option: Maybe your draft has done the job of helping you explore ideas. Now put it away and start over. This is undoubtedly the hardest thing a writer can do—admit that a draft isn't working. Many people, in fact, cannot bring themselves to start over. But consider it an option.

COMMONSENSE TIP One last time before you're ready to turn in the assignment, look back at the wording the teacher used in giving the assignment. Too many students get so caught up in their writing process that they overlook specific requirements.

The bottom line? Writing is a process that is never 100 percent complete. There is no such thing as a perfect draft. If you go about your writing believing that the goal is perfection, you might get discouraged. Instead, think of it this way: The goal is to produce writing that is *as effective as you can make it*, given your deadline.

✳ *Critical Questions for Revising*

Lesson 42 has focused on questions you should ask yourself while revising. It's nearly impossible to remember them all, so we end this lesson by noting what we believe are the most important questions you should ask as you revise your writing.

Purpose and Audience

- What is the overall purpose of your draft?

Lesson 42

rev

- Where might readers think that you have drifted away from this purpose?
- Does your draft fulfill all your teacher's requirements? (Check the written assignment, if one was given to you.)

Support

- What details can you add to help readers fully understand what your draft is saying?
- What additional logic or evidence can you add to persuade readers to accept anything you have said that might be debatable?

Organization

- What is the purpose of each paragraph? Do paragraphs ramble, or is there a controlling idea that will be clear to your readers?
- Have you made the connections between sentences clear?

Style, Grammar, and Usage

- What words could you change to make your meaning more clear or more specific?
- Are there any sentences that seem too long or awkward?
- Do you have any doubts about particular punctuation choices you made? (Look at your use of commas and apostrophes in particular.)

Applying What You Know

Reread Daniel's draft presented at the end of Lesson 41. Use the questions listed above to describe at least five specific changes you think Daniel should consider. Make sure at least a couple go beyond merely changing particular words or punctuation marks to address deeper revision issues.

APPENDIX A

Brief Documentation Guide for MLA

In college, it is particularly important that writers let readers know which words or ideas were borrowed and from where. Known as documentation, this identification process properly and clearly indicates the use of other people's words and ideas. Improper or incomplete documentation can lead to plagiarism, a serious offense normally considered a form of cheating or fraud.

When writers document sources, they must follow specific rules for citing the research materials they use. This brief guide provides the basic rules of what is called the MLA (Modern Language Association) system of documentation, which is the most common system for composition courses. This guide is not intended to cover all possible types of sources you might use, just some of the more common ones. For more information on correctly using other people's ideas, see Lessons 37 and 38, or go to *Research and Documentation Online* at hackerhandbooks.com/resdoc.

MLA Format for In-Text Citations

Provide an in-text citation every time you quote, paraphrase, or summarize a source (see Lesson 37). Your citation, which usually includes both source and page number, should appear after sentences that refer to a source. Follow the models below for examples.

ONE AUTHOR

"Every day, around thirty-four new food products alone are introduced. The dizzying array of new items reflects a micro-splitting of problems to create more 'must-have' new solutions" (Hammerslough 14).

Hammerslough points out that "[e]very day, around thirty-four new food products alone are introduced. The dizzying array of new items reflects a micro-splitting of problems to create more 'must-have' new solutions" (14).

TWO OR THREE AUTHORS

More than 90 percent of the hazardous waste produced in the United States comes from seven major industries, all energy-intensive (Romm and Curtis 70).

FOUR OR MORE AUTHORS

Boys tend to get called on in the classroom more often than girls (Oesterling et al. 243).

CORPORATE AUTHOR OR GOVERNMENT PUBLICATION

Physical activity has been shown to protect against certain forms of cancer "either by balancing caloric intake with energy expenditure or by other mechanisms" (American Cancer Society 43).

UNKNOWN AUTHOR

According to a recent study, drivers are 42 percent more likely to get into an accident if they are using a wireless phone while driving ("Driving Dangerously" 32).

RELIGIOUS WORK

Consider the words of Solomon: "If your enemies are hungry, give them bread to eat; and if they are thirsty, give them water to drink" (*New Revised Standard Bible*, Prov. 25.21).

SOURCE WITHOUT PAGE NUMBERS

"There is no definitive correlation between benign breast tumors and breast cancer" (Pratt).

INDIRECT SOURCE

In discussing the baby mania trend, *Time* writers claimed, "Career women are opting for pregnancy and they are doing it in style" (qtd. in Faludi 106).

MLA Format for a List of Works Cited

At the end of your paper, you must provide a list of the sources from which you quoted, paraphrased, or summarized. Put the entire list in alphabetical order using the author's last name first and the title as it appears on the title page of the source. If your source has no author, alphabetize it by the first main word of the title. Double-space your Works Cited page. Begin each entry at the left margin and indent the subsequent lines five spaces.

Books

ONE AUTHOR

Hammerslough, Jane. *Dematerializing: Taming the Power of Possessions.* Cambridge Perseus, 2001. Print.

TWO OR THREE AUTHORS

Douglas, Susan J., and Meredith W. Michaels. *The Mommy Myth: The Idealization of Motherhood and How It Has Undermined Women.* New York: Free P, 2004. Print.

FOUR OR MORE AUTHORS

Foster, Hal, et al. *Art Since 1900.* New York: Thames, 2005. Print.

UNKNOWN AUTHOR

National Geographic Atlas of the World. 9th ed. Washington, DC: Nat. Geographic, 2010. Print.

EDITOR OR COMPILER

Byrne, Patrick H., ed. *Dialogue Between Science and Religion.* Scranton: U of Scranton P, 2005. Print.

EDITOR AND AUTHOR

Ellison, Ralph. *Living with Music: Ralph Ellison's Jazz Writings.* Ed. Robert G. O'Meally. New York: Modern, 2002. Print.

EDITION NUMBERS

Honderich, Ted, ed. *The Oxford Companion to Philosophy.* 2nd ed. Oxford: Oxford UP, 2005. Print.

ANTHOLOGY

Singer, Peter, and Renata Singer, eds. *The Moral of the Story: An Anthology of Ethics Through Literature.* Oxford: Blackwell, 2005. Print.

A WORK IN AN ANTHOLOGY

Roberts, Deborah. "Unmasking Step-Motherhood." *Rise Up Singing: Black Women Writers on Motherhood.* Ed. Cecelie S. Berry. New York: Doubleday, 2004. 127–32. Print.

SIGNED ARTICLE IN A REFERENCE BOOK

Cheney, Ralph Holt. "Coffee." *Collier's Encyclopedia.* 2004 ed. Print.

UNSIGNED ARTICLE IN A REFERENCE BOOK

"Sonata." *The American Heritage Dictionary of the English Language.* 4th ed. 2000. Print.

Periodicals

ARTICLE IN A MONTHLY MAGAZINE

Stone, Richard. "Dinosaurs' Living Descendants." *Smithsonian* Dec. 2010: 54-62. Print.

ARTICLE IN A WEEKLY MAGAZINE

Luscombe, Belinda. "The Myth of the Slippery Bachelor." *Time* 14 Dec. 2011: 51-53. Print.

ARTICLE IN A JOURNAL

Shaw, Adrienne. "What Is Video Game Culture? Cultural Studies and Game Studies." *Games and Culture* 5 (2010): 403-24. Print.

ARTICLE IN A NEWSPAPER

Northington, Hope. "Literary Capital Draws Visitors." *Mobile Press-Register* 7 Feb. 2011: C1. Print.

UNKNOWN AUTHOR

"Consumer Confidence Suffers Sharper Fall Than Expected." Associated Press. *New York Times* 31 July 2002: C6. Print.

EDITORIAL

"Terry Schiavo's Affliction." Editorial. *Boston Globe* 5 Apr. 2005: A14. Print.

LETTER TO THE EDITOR

Levy, Ronald. "Distorted View of Israel." Letter. *Boston Globe* 1 Aug. 2002: A18. Print.

Electronic Sources

PROFESSIONAL SITE: ENTIRE WEB SITE

United States Government. *The White House*. U.S. Govt., n.d. Web. 15 Jan. 2011.

PROFESSIONAL SITE: SPECIFIC PAGE

United States Government. "Educate to Innovate." *The White House*. U.S. Govt., n.d. Web. 6 April 2011.

"Disability Services Online." *Stephen F. Austin State University*. SFASU, 2008. Web. 8 June 2011.

PERSONAL WEB SITE

Kilbourne, Jean. Home page. Jean Kilbourne, 9 Sept. 2007. Web.
10 Nov. 2010.

ARTICLE FROM AN ONLINE MAGAZINE OR NEWSPAPER

Greenwald, Glenn. "The Art of Neoconservative Innuendo." *Salon
.com*. Salon Media Group, 20 Sept. 2007. Web. 22 Sept. 2010.

ONLINE BOOK

Wharton, Edith. *The Age of Innocence*. New York: Windsor, 1920. *Google
Books*. Web. 8 Nov. 2011

ARTICLE FROM AN ONLINE DATABASE

Rice, Raymond J. "Cannibalism and the Act of Revenge in Tudor-
Stuart Drama." *Studies in English Literature, 1500–1900* 44.2
(2004): 297-317. *Expanded Academic ASAP*. Web. 9 Jan. 2009.

E-MAIL MESSAGE

Balbert, Peter. "Re: The Hemingway Hero." Message to the author.
15 Mar. 2009. E-mail.

POSTING TO AN ONLINE DISCUSSION

Ponterio, Bob. "Re: European Constitution." *Foreign Language
Teaching Forum*. University at Buffalo, 7 Apr. 2005. Web. 9 Apr.
2010.

Other Sources

ADVERTISEMENT

Nike. Advertisement. *Vogue* Nov. 2001: 94-95. Print.

INTERVIEW

Dole, Bob. Interview by Terry Gross. *Fresh Air*. Natl. Public Radio.
WBUR, Boston. 12 Apr. 2005. Radio.

PAMPHLET

Administrative Office of the United States Courts. *Bankruptcy Basics*.
Washington: GPO, 2006. Print.

FILM OR DVD

The King's Speech. Dir. Tom Hooper. Perf. Colin Firth, Helena
Bonham Carter, Geoffrey Rush, and Guy Pearce. Weinstein/
Anchor Bay, 2010. DVD.

SOUND RECORDING

Palmer, Keke. "The Game Song." *So Uncool*. Atlantic, 2007. CD.

TELEVISION OR RADIO PROGRAM

Lawrence of Arabia: The Battle for the Arab World. PBS. WSRE, Pensacola, FL. 20 Sept. 2007. Television.

PUBLISHED INTERVIEW

Gould, Stephen Jay. "Life's Work: Questions for Stephen Jay Gould." *New York Times Magazine* 2 June 2002: 18. Print.

APPENDIX B

Brief Documentation Guide for APA

As discussed in Appendix A, writers must let readers know which words or ideas they take from another source. This appendix provides the basic rules of the APA (American Psychological Association) system of documentation. This guide is not intended to cover all types of sources, just some of the more common. For more information on citing and documenting sources using APA, visit *Research and Documentation Online* at hackerhandbooks.com/ resdoc. (See also Lessons 37 and 38 for general principles of documentation, although those focus on the MLA system.)

APA Format for In-Text Citations

Provide an in-text citation when you quote, paraphrase, or summarize a source. With the APA system, this parenthetical citation includes the last name of the source's author(s) and the year it was published. A page number is required for a direct quotation and is recommended but not required for a paraphrase. If your sentence refers only to larger ideas of a source, a page number is not needed in the citation.

ONE AUTHOR

"Every day, around thirty-four new food products alone are introduced. The dizzying array of new items reflects a micro-splitting of problems to create more 'must-have' new solutions" (Hammerslough, 2001, p. 14).

TWO AUTHORS

More than 90 percent of the hazardous waste produced in the United States comes from seven major industries, all energy-intensive (Romm & Curtis, 2005).

CORPORATE AUTHOR OR GOVERNMENT PUBLICATION

Physical activity has been shown to protect against certain forms of cancer "either by balancing caloric intake with energy expenditure or by other mechanisms" (American Cancer Society, 2009, p. 4).

INDIRECT SOURCES

In discussing the baby mania trend, *Time* writers claimed, "Career women are opting for pregnancy and they are doing it in style" (as cited in Faludi, 2008, p. 106).

APA Format for References

At the end of your paper, provide a list of all sources from which you quoted, paraphrased, or summarized. Use "References" as the title. Arrange the list in alphabetical order using the author's last name. If a source has no author, alphabetize it by the first main word of the title. Double-space throughout, begin each entry at the left margin, and indent subsequent lines.

Books

ONE AUTHOR

Hammerslough, J. (2001). *Dematerializing: Taming the power of possessions*. Cambridge, MA: Perseus.

MULTIPLE AUTHORS

Douglas, S. J., & Michaels, M. W. (2004). *The mommy myth: The idealization of motherhood and how it has undermined women*. New York, NY: Free Press.

UNKNOWN AUTHOR

National Geographic atlas of the world (9th ed.). (2010). Washington, DC: National Geographic.

EDITION NUMBERS

Honderich, T. (Ed.). (2005). *The Oxford companion to philosophy* (2nd ed.). Oxford, England: Oxford University Press.

ANTHOLOGY

Singer, P., & Singer, R. (Eds.). (2005). *The moral of the story: An anthology of ethics through literature*. Oxford, England: Blackwell.

A WORK IN AN ANTHOLOGY

Roberts, D. (2004). Unmasking step-motherhood. In C. S. Berry (Ed.), *Rise up singing: Black women writers on motherhood* (pp. 127-132). New York, NY: Doubleday.

SIGNED ARTICLE IN A REFERENCE BOOK

Cheney, R. H. (1998). Coffee. In *Collier's encyclopedia* (pp. 143-145). New York, NY: Collier's.

UNSIGNED ARTICLE IN A REFERENCE BOOK

Sonata. (2000). *The American heritage dictionary of the English language* (p. 658, 4th ed.). Boston, MA: Houghton Mifflin.

Periodicals

ARTICLE IN A MONTHLY MAGAZINE

Stone, R. (2010, December). Dinosaurs' living descendants. *Smithsonian, 41,* 54–62.

ARTICLE IN A WEEKLY MAGAZINE

Luscombe, B. (2001, December 14). The myth of the slippery bachelor. *Time, 177,* 51–53.

ARTICLE IN A JOURNAL

Shaw, A. (2010). What is video game culture? Cultural studies and game studies. *Games and Culture, 5,* 403–424.

ARTICLE IN A NEWSPAPER

Northington, H. (2011, February 7). Literary capital draws visitors. *Mobile Press-Register,* p. C1.

UNKNOWN AUTHOR

Consumer confidence suffers sharper fall than expected. (2002, July 31). *New York Times,* p. C6.

LETTER TO THE EDITOR

Levy, R. (2002, August 1). Distorted view of Israel [Letter to the editor]. *Boston Globe,* p. A18.

Electronic Sources

DOCUMENT FROM A WEB SITE

United States Government. *Educate to innovate.* (n.d.). *The White House.* Retrieved April 6, 2011, from http://www.whitehouse.gov/issues/education/educate-innovate.

ARTICLE FROM AN ONLINE MAGAZINE OR NEWSPAPER

Greenwald, G. (2007, September 20). The art of neoconservative innuendo. *Salon.com.* Retrieved from http://www.salon.com/news/opinion/glenn_greenwald/2007/09/20/ledeen.

ONLINE BOOK

Wharton, E. (1920). *The age of innocence.* New York, NY: Windsor. Retrieved from http://books.google.com/books?id=3PcYAAAAYAAJ&printsec=frontcover&dq=inauthor:%22Edith+Wharton%22&hl=en&ei=6X5QTeDVFNS_tgf8waC3AQ&sa=X&oi=book_result&ct=result&resnum=3&ved=0CDgQ6AEwAjgK#v=onepage&q&f=false.

ARTICLE FROM ONLINE DATABASE

Rice, R. J. (2004). Cannibalism and the act of revenge in Tudor-Stuart drama. *Studies in English Literature, 1500–1900*, 44, 297-317. Retrieved from http://www.gale.cengage.com/PeriodicalSolutions/academicAsap.htm.

ONLINE POSTING

Ponterio, B. (2005, April 7). Re: European constitution [Electronic mailing list message]. Retrieved from http://listserv.buffalo.edu/cgi-bin/wa?A2=ind0504&L=flteach&T=0&P=248.

Other Sources

PAMPHLET

Administrative Office of the United States Courts. (2006). *Bankruptcy basics* [Brochure]. Washington, DC: Government Printing Office.

FILM OR VIDEO

Hooper, T. (Director), & Seidler, D. (Writer). (2010). *The king's speech* [Motion picture]. United States: The Weinstein Company/Anchor Bay Entertainment.

Wikileaks release 1.0. [Video file]. (2009, December 30). Retrieved from http://www.youtube.com/watch?v=0i39Vs-h4XM.

TELEVISION OR RADIO PROGRAM

Weddle, D., & Thompson, B. (Writers). Rymer, M. (Director). (2008). He that believeth in me [Television series episode]. *Battlestar Galactica*. New York, NY: Syfy.

APPENDIX C

Guide to Grammar Terminology

This guide is an alphabetical listing of all the grammar terms used in this book. Each term is defined with an example. For some grammar terms, there are also helpful hints and suggestions. Anytime you encounter a grammar term you are unsure about, look it up in this guide.

> **NOTE** Examples of the term being defined are in ***bold italic*** type. References to important related terms are underlined. Ungrammatical phrases or sentences are indicated by an **✗**.

Action verb Verbs are divided into two grammatical classes: action verbs and linking verbs. All verbs are action verbs unless they belong to a small class of special verbs called linking verbs that can be followed by adjectives. The term action verb is confusing because many action verbs do not actually express any action. For example, the verb *miss* in the sentence *I **missed** my bus* is an action verb though it does not express any action. *Miss* is an action verb because the verb *miss* is not followed by an adjective and therefore cannot be classified as a linking verb. Any verb that is not a linking verb is, by default, an action verb. Also see linking verb.

Active The term *active* or *active voice* refers to sentences in which the subject plays the role of the actor, or the "doer" of the action, as opposed to passive sentences, in which the subject is the person or thing *receiving* the action of the verb. For example, in the active sentence ***Sandy saw Pat***, the subject *Sandy* is doing the seeing, whereas in the passive sentence ***Pat was seen by Sandy***, *Pat* is the person being seen. Also see passive.

Adjective Adjectives play two different roles: (1) they modify the nouns that they precede (*a **large** tree*); or (2) after certain verbs like *be, seem,* and *become,* adjectives describe the subject of the sentence. For example, in the sentence *The tree is **green**,* the adjective *green* describes the subject *tree.* Also see article and proper adjective.

Adjective clause An adjective clause (also called a relative clause) always modifies the noun it follows. In the sentence *The tree **that we planted** is getting leaves,* the adjective clause *that we planted* modifies the noun *tree.* An adjective clause begins with a relative pronoun (*that* in the example sentence is a relative pronoun). There are two types of adjective clauses. Depending on the relation of the adjective clause to the noun it modifies, the clause is either an essential adjective clause or a nonessential adjective clause.

Adjective prepositional phrase Prepositional phrases are modifiers. If they modify nouns, they play the role of adjectives and, accordingly, they are called adjective prepositional phrases. For example, in the sentence *The light **in the hall closet** has burned out*, the prepositional phrase *in the hall closet* is an adjective preposition phrase because it modifies the noun *light*.

Adverb An adverb modifies a verb (*walked **briskly***), an adjective (***pretty** tall*), another adverb (***very** badly*), or a sentence (***Truthfully**, I do not know the answer*). Adverbs that modify verbs give *when, where, why, how*, or *to what degree* information. Such adverbs normally occur at the end of a sentence but can usually be moved to the beginning; for example: *I got a ticket **yesterday**. **Yesterday**, I got a ticket*. An adverb prepositional phrase or an adverb clause also modifies a verb and may move to the beginning of the sentence.

Adverb clause An adverb clause modifies a verb, giving *when, where, why*, or *how* information. Adverb clauses are easily moved to the beginning of the independent clause from their normal position after the main clause; for example: *I was at the office **when you called**. **When you called**, I was at the office*.

Adverb prepositional phrase Prepositional phrases are modifiers. If they modify verbs, adjectives, or other adverbs, they play the role of adverbs and, accordingly, they are called adverb prepositional phrases. For example, in the sentence *We cleaned out the garage **over the weekend***, the prepositional phrase *over the weekend* is an adverb prepositional phrase because it modifies the verb *cleaned out* and tells us when the action of the verb took place.

Agreement Some words in a sentence are so closely related that the form of one determines the form of another. When such words are correctly chosen in relation to one another, they are in *agreement*. A pronoun should agree with its antecedent in terms of gender and number (*The **boy** ate **his** food*), and a subject should agree with its verb in terms of number (***He was** hungry*). Also see subject-verb agreement.

Antecedent See pronoun antecedent.

Appositive An appositive is a noun (or a noun and its modifiers) that renames (further identifies) a preceding noun. For example, in *My English teacher, **Ms. Rodriguez**, also teaches Spanish, Ms. Rodriguez* is an appositive that renames (further identifies) the noun *teacher*. Usually, two commas set off the appositive from the rest of the sentence, as in the example here.

Article Articles are a special kind of adjective that come before all other types of adjectives. For example, in the phrase **the** *tall trees*, the article *the* must come before the adjective *tall*; that is, we cannot say ✗ *tall the trees*. There are two types of articles: definite (*the*) and indefinite (*a* and *an*).

Blended paraphrase A blended paraphrase combines elements of a direct and an indirect quotation. Like a paraphrase, it puts someone else's ideas into your own words for the most part, but you put quotation marks around distinctive wording that is also found in the original source. This source must be properly attributed in your paper and documented in your list of works cited or references.

Clause A clause contains at least one subject and one verb. A clause that stands alone as a complete thought is called an independent clause or a main clause. All sentences must contain at least one main clause. For types of clauses that cannot stand alone, see dependent clause.

Colon The colon (:) is frequently used to introduce lists. The part of the sentence before the colon should be able to stand alone as an independent clause, for example, ***These are the three most common flavors of ice cream: vanilla, chocolate, and strawberry***. Do not break up an independent clause with a colon. A common error is adding a colon after the verb, for example, *✗ The three most common flavors of ice cream are: vanilla, chocolate, and strawberry.*

Comma splice A comma splice is the incorrect use of a comma to join two sentences or two independent clauses (***✗ Angela answered the phone, she was the only person in the office***). Also see fused sentence and run-on sentence.

Common noun A common noun refers to categories of people, places, things, and ideas, in contrast to a proper noun, which names particular individual people or places. For example, *reporter* is a common noun, but *Lois Lane* is a proper noun. Common nouns can be identified by their use of the definite article *the*. For example, *replace* and *replacement* are related words, but you can tell that ***replacement*** is a common noun because you can say *the replacement*. *Replace* is not a common noun because you cannot say *✗ the replace.*

Complement A complement is a noun, a pronoun, or an adjective required by a verb to make a valid sentence. For example, in the sentence *Scrooge became **rich***, the adjective *rich* is the complement of the verb *became*. If the complement is omitted, the sentence is no longer valid: *✗ Scrooge became.* In traditional grammar, the complement must refer back to and describe the subject. In our example sentence, *rich* describes the subject *Scrooge*.

Complete sentence A complete sentence is an independent clause that can be correctly punctuated with a terminal punctuation mark, such as a period, a question mark, or an exclamation point. The opposite of a complete sentence is a fragment, which is only part of a sentence and which cannot be punctuated correctly with a terminal punctuation mark.

Compound A compound consists of two or more grammatical units of the same type joined by *and* or another coordinating conjunction. For example, in the sentence *Donald is **rich** and **famous**, rich* and *famous* are compound adjectives. For more examples, see compound verb, compound sentence, and compound subject.

Compound sentence When two or more sentences (independent clauses) are combined into one, the result is a compound sentence. A compound sentence is usually created by inserting a <u>coordinating conjunction</u> between the two "former" sentences, as in *I left the party early,* **but** *Angie refused to leave.*

Compound subject Compound subjects are two (or more) <u>subjects</u> joined by a <u>coordinating conjunction</u>. For example, the sentence ***My next-door neighbor*** *and **I** usually carpool to work,* contains two subjects (*neighbor* and *I*) joined by the coordinating conjunction *and.*

Compound verb Compound verbs are two verbs (more accurately, two <u>predicates</u>) joined by a <u>coordinating conjunction</u>. For example, in the sentence *Batman **went** to his bat cave and **called** his butler,* the verbs *went* and *called* are compound verbs joined by the coordinating conjunction *and.*

Conjunction The term *conjunction* means "join together." Conjunctions are words that join grammatical elements together. There are two types of conjunctions: (1) <u>coordinating conjunctions</u>—words like ***and, but***, and ***or***—and (2) <u>subordinating conjunctions</u>—words like ***when, since, because***, and ***if***, which begin adverb clauses.

Conjunctive adverb See <u>transitional term</u>.

Contraction A contraction is the shortened form of a word that results from leaving out some letters or sounds. In writing, the missing letters in contractions are indicated by an apostrophe ('); for example, ***I'll*** is the contracted form of *I will.* This use of the apostrophe in contractions is different from its use to indicate possession; see <u>possessive apostrophe</u>.

Coordinating conjunction A coordinating conjunction joins grammatical units of the same type, creating a <u>compound</u>. There are seven coordinating conjunctions, which can be remembered by the acronym *FANBOYS:* ***for, and, nor, but, or, yet, so***.

Count noun A count noun is a <u>common noun</u> that can be counted: ***one cat/ two cats***. Nouns that have irregular plural forms—such as ***one child/two children, one goose/two geese,*** and ***one deer/two deer***—are also count nouns. For nouns that cannot be counted, see <u>noncount noun</u>.

Dangling modifier A dangling modifier is a noun modifier (usually a <u>participial phrase</u>) that does not actually modify the noun it is intended to modify. The modifier is said to be "dangling" because the noun it is supposed to modify is not in the sentence. For example, in the sentence ***Based on the evidence***, *the jury acquitted the defendant,* the phrase *based on the evidence* is a dangling modifier because it does not really modify *jury.* (You cannot say that *the jury was based on the evidence.*)

Definite article The definite article is *the*, which can be used either with a singular or with a plural <u>common noun</u>. Use the definite article when referring to a specific object or thing that is also known to the reader or listener. For example, in the sentence *Please hand me **the** cup,* you can assume that the speaker is referring to a specific cup that the reader or hearer can also identify. When not referring to anything specific, or when referring to something that is *not* known to the listener, use an indefinite article: *a* or *an*.

Dependent clause A dependent clause is a clause that cannot be used as a complete sentence by itself, as opposed to an independent clause, which can stand alone. There are three types of dependent clauses: (1) an adjective clause modifies a noun (*I read the book **that you recommended***); (2) an adverb clause modifies a verb (*I was in the shower **when the telephone rang***); and (3) a noun clause plays the role of subject or object (***What you see** is **what you get***). A dependent clause is also called a subordinate clause.

Direct object Direct object is the technical term for an object required by a verb. For example, in the sentence *Donald bought a new **toupee***, the noun *toupee* is the direct object of the verb *bought*. The verb *buy* requires a direct object—when you buy, you have to buy SOMETHING.

Direct quotation A direct quotation uses quotation marks (" ") to show the reader that the words inside the marks are *exactly* what the person said or wrote; for example: *Tina said, **"I know where we can buy tickets."*** The opposite of a direct quotation is an indirect quotation, which does not use quotation marks, as in the following sentence: *Tina said that she knew where they could buy tickets.*

Elliptical adverb clause An elliptical adverb is a reduced form of an adverb clause from which the subject has been deleted and the verb changed to a participle form. For example, the adverb clause beginning the sentence ***When I looked for my hat**, I found my gloves* can be reduced to an elliptical adverb clause: ***When looking for my hat**, I found my gloves*.

Essential adjective clause Every adjective clause (also called a *relative clause*) modifies a noun, but different types of adjective clauses are related to the nouns they modify in different ways. Essential adjective clauses (also called *restrictive* adjective clauses) narrow or limit the meaning of the nouns they modify. For example, in the sentence *All the students **who miss the test** will fail the course*, the adjective clause *who miss the test* limits or defines the meaning of the noun *students*: The students threatened with failure are only those who miss the test. Essential adjective clauses are never set off with commas. An adjective clause that does not limit or define the meaning of the noun it modifies is called a nonessential adjective clause.

Faulty parallelism The term *faulty parallelism* refers to a series of two or more grammatical elements in which not all the elements are in the same grammatical form. For example, the sentence ✗ *Senator Blather is **loud, pompous**, a **fraud**, and **talks too much*** presents a series of four elements, but there is faulty parallelism because the first two elements (*loud* and *pompous*) are adjectives; the third element (*fraud*) is a noun; and the fourth element (*talks too much*) is a verb phrase.

Fragment A fragment is part of a sentence that is punctuated as though it were a complete sentence. Typically, fragments are pieces cut off from the preceding sentence; for example: *The computer lost my paper.* ✗ *Which I had worked on all night*. One way to recognize a fragment is to test it with the *I Realize* Tip. You can put the words *I realize* in front of most complete sentences and make a new grammatical sentence. However, when you put *I realize* in front of a fragment, the result will not make sense.

Fused sentence A fused sentence is a type of <u>run-on sentence</u> in which two complete sentences (or independent clauses) are joined together without any mark of punctuation. ✗ *My brother caught a cold he has been out of school for a week* is an example of a fused sentence because it consists of two complete sentences (*My brother caught a cold* and *He has been out of school for a week*) that are joined without proper punctuation. A <u>comma splice</u> is a similar type of error that incorrectly joins complete sentences with a comma.

Gender Certain third-person personal pronouns are marked for gender: *she, her,* and *hers* refer to females; *he, him,* and *his* refer to males. The third-person plural pronouns *they* and *them* are not marked for gender; that is, these pronouns can refer to males, females, or both. *They* and *them* are sometimes called "gender-neutral" or "gender-exclusive" pronouns. The third-person singular pronoun *it* refers to things that do not have gender, such as concrete objects and abstractions; so do the third-person plural pronouns *they, them,* and *their*.

Gerund A gerund is the *-ing* form of a verb (the <u>present participle</u>) that is used as a noun. For example, in the sentence *I like **taking** the bus to work, taking* is the gerund. The term *gerund* can also be used to refer to the *-ing* verb together with all the words that go with it (in what is technically called a *gerund phrase*). In the example sentence, the whole phrase ***taking the bus to work*** is a gerund phrase.

Helping verb When two or more verbs are used together in a string, the last verb in the sequence is called the <u>main verb</u>. All the other verbs that come before the main verb are called *helping verbs*. For example, in the sentence *We **should have been** tuning our instruments,* the last verb (*tuning*) is the main verb, and all the preceding verbs (*should have been*) are the helping verbs. The first helping verb in the sequence is the only verb that agrees with the subject. The most important helping verbs are ***be*** and ***have*** (in all their different forms), plus ***can, could, may, might, must, shall, should, will,*** and ***would***.

Indefinite article Indefinite articles appear in two forms, depending on the initial sound of the following word: *a* is used before words beginning with a consonant sound (***a** yellow banana*), and *an* is used before words beginning with a vowel sound (***an** old banana*). Use an indefinite article when mentioning something the reader or listener does not already know about; after that point, use the definite article *the*. For example: *I bought **an** Apple computer. The computer has **a** built-in modem. The modem is connected to my telephone line.*

Independent clause An independent clause (also called a *main clause*) can always stand alone as a <u>complete sentence</u>. Every sentence must contain at least one independent clause.

Indirect quotation An indirect quotation is a <u>paraphrase</u> of the writer's or speaker's actual, verbatim words. For example, if Mr. Lopez said, "*We are going to Florida tomorrow*," the indirect quotation might be the following: *He said **that he and his family were going to Florida the next day***. One of the distinctive features of indirect quotation is the use of *that* before the paraphrase of the writer's or speaker's words. Also notice that, unlike <u>direct quotation</u>, an indirect quotation uses no quotation marks.

Infinitive An infinitive is the form of a <u>verb</u> as it appears in the dictionary. For example, the infinitive form of *is, am, was,* and *were* is **be**. Like the *-ing* <u>present participle</u> form of verbs (<u>gerunds</u>), infinitives are often used as nouns. When serving as nouns, infinitives almost always are used with *to*; for example, *I like to eat pizza with my fingers*. As with gerunds, the term *infinitive* can also be used more broadly to include both the infinitive and the words that go with it (together called an *infinitive phrase*). In this broader sense, the infinitive in the example sentence is **to eat pizza with my fingers**.

Information question Information questions are phrases that begin with a question word, for example, *who, what, where, why, when, how often, whose* + noun, and *which* + noun or pronoun. An information question usually also contains a <u>helping verb</u> and a form of the verb *do*. For example, in "***Where did Liu go***," the verb *did* (the past tense of *do*) has been added after the question word *where*. The question word *where* seeks further specific information.

Inseparable two-word verb A <u>two-word verb</u> is a type of compound verb. When the compound is formed from a verb and a preposition, it is called an inseparable two-word verb because the preposition can never be moved away or "separated" from the verb. For example, in the sentence *The prince **turned against** the king*, the preposition *against* can never be moved away from the verb: ✗ *The prince **turned** the king **against***. However, when the two-word verb is formed with an adverb, the adverb can be moved away from the verb. A two-word verb of this type is called a <u>separable two-word verb</u>.

Introductory element An introductory element is any kind of word, phrase, or clause that has been placed at the beginning of a sentence rather than in its expected position in the middle or at the end of the sentence. Introductory elements are usually set off from the rest of the sentence by a comma (especially if the introductory element is a phrase or a clause), for example, ***Feeling a little down**, Scrooge left the party early*.

Linking verb Linking verbs are a class of verbs that can be followed by adjectives. For example, in the sentence *Jason is funny*, the verb *is* is a linking verb followed by the adjective *funny*. Linking verbs are not used to express action. Instead, linking verbs describe their subjects. In the example sentence, the adjective *funny* describes *Jason*.

Main clause See <u>independent clause</u>.

Main verb The main verb is the last verb in a string of verbs. All the verbs that precede the main verb are <u>helping verbs</u>. For example, in the sentence *Cinderella* *must have **eaten** all the chili dogs*, the main verb is *eaten*. The other two verbs (*must* and *have*) are helping verbs.

Mass noun See noncount noun.

Misplaced adverb A misplaced adverb is an adverb that does not actually modify the word that it is next to; it really modifies a word elsewhere in the sentence. For example, in the sentence ✗ *We **barely** packed enough clothes for the trip*, the adverb *barely* does not really modify *packed*. Either we packed or we didn't. The adverb *barely* really modifies *enough clothes*.

Modifier Modifiers are words that describe or give additional information about other words in a sentence. Adjectives, participles, and adjective clauses modify nouns. Adverbs and adverb clauses modify verbs, adverbs, adjectives, or whole sentences.

Noncount noun A noncount noun (also called a *mass noun*) is a common noun that cannot be used in the plural or with number words (✗ *one homework/* ✗ *two homeworks;* ✗ *one dirt/*✗ *two dirts*). A noun that can be used in the plural and with number words is called a count noun.

Nonessential adjective clause Every adjective clause (also called a *relative clause*) modifies a noun, but different types of adjective clauses have different relations with the nouns they modify. Nonessential adjective clauses (also called *nonrestrictive* adjective clauses) do not narrow or limit the meaning of the nouns they modify. Like appositives, nonessential clauses rename the nouns they modify, and, like appositives, they are set off with commas. For example, in the sentence *My mother, **who was born in Tonga**, came to the United States as a child*, the relative clause *who was born in Tonga* is nonessential because it does not narrow or define the meaning of *my mother*. My mother is still my mother no matter where she was born. A clause that defines or limits the meaning of the noun it modifies is called an essential adjective clause.

Nonrestrictive adjective clause See nonessential adjective clause.

Noun Nouns are names of people, places, things, and ideas. A noun that refers to categories (***teacher***, ***city***) is a common noun; a noun that refers to actual individual persons or places (***Mr. Smith***, ***Chicago***) is a proper noun. See also count noun, noncount noun, and noun phrase.

Noun clause A noun clause is a group of words that work together to function as a noun, as in ***Whether you go or not** is up to you*. If you look at the noun clause by itself, you will always find a word acting like a subject and a word serving as its verb. In the example above, *you* is acting like a subject, and *go* is its verb.

Noun phrase Noun phrases are groups of related words that function like single nouns. For example, in the sentence *I finally fixed **that awful crack in the bedroom ceiling**, the object of the verb *fixed* is the entire noun phrase *that awful crack in the bedroom ceiling*. The defining characteristic of noun phrases is that they can always be replaced by a pronoun. In our example, we can replace the entire noun phrase *that awful crack in the bedroom ceiling* with the pronoun *it*: I finally fixed *it* (where *it* = the noun phrase *that awful crack in the bedroom ceiling*).

Object When a noun or a pronoun follows certain verbs or any preposition, it is called an *object*. For example, in the sentence *Kermit kissed* **Miss Piggy**, the object of the verb *kissed* is *Miss Piggy*. Most pronouns have distinct object forms. Thus, to replace *Miss Piggy* with a pronoun in the example sentence, we would have to use the object form *her* rather than the subject form *she*: *Kermit kissed* **her**. Prepositional phrases consist of prepositions and their objects. For example, in the prepositional phrase *on the* **ladder**, the object of the preposition *on* is the noun *ladder*.

Parallelism The term *parallelism* refers to a series of two or more elements of the same grammatical type, usually joined by a coordinating conjunction. For example, in the sentence *I love* **to eat, to drink**, *and* **to dance** *the polka*, there are three parallel forms—all infinitives: *to eat, to drink*, and *to dance*. Failure to express parallel elements in the same grammatical form is called faulty parallelism.

Paraphrase You paraphrase when you reword what someone else has written or said. Without changing the context, you put his or her ideas into your own words, which is essential to an indirect quotation or a blended paraphrase. The source you are paraphrasing should be properly attributed with an in-text citation and end-of-paper documentation.

Participial phrase A participial phrase contains either a present or a past participle. Participial phrases modify nouns. For example, in the sentence *The workers* **repairing the roof** *found water damage, repairing the roof* is a present participial phrase modifying the noun *workers*. In the sentence *The workers* **injured in the accident** *sued the company, injured in the accident* is a past participial phrase modifying the noun *workers*.

Participle Participles are verb forms. There are two types of participles: (1) present participles (the *-ing* form of verbs such as *seeing, doing*, and *having*); and (2) past participles (for example, *seen, done*, and *had*). Both types of participles can be used as verbs (following certain helping verbs). For example, in the sentence *Michio is* **watching** *the movie*, the word *watching* is in the present participle form. In the sentence *Michio has* **watched** *the movie*, the word *watched* is in the past participle form.

Both present participles and past participles can also be used as adjectives. For example, in the saying *A* **watched** *pot never boils*, the past participle *watched* functions as an adjective modifying the noun *pot*.

Passive The term *passive* or *passive voice* describes sentences in which the subject is not the "doer" of the action but instead *receives* the action of the verb. For example, in the passive sentence *Sandy* **was seen** *by Pat*, the subject *Sandy* is not the person doing the seeing but instead is the person being seen. The passive voice can always be recognized by a unique sequence of verbs: the helping verb *be* (in some form) followed by a past participle verb form. In the example above, *was* is the past tense form of *be*, and *seen* is the past participle form of *see*. Sentences that are not in the passive voice are said to be in the <u>active voice</u>.

Past participle Past participle verb forms are used in the <u>perfect tenses</u> after the <u>helping verb</u> *have* (as in *Thelma has **seen** that movie*) or after the helping verb *be* in <u>passive</u> sentences (*That movie was **seen** by Thelma*). The past participle form of most verbs ends in *-ed*, as do most past tense forms of most verbs. How, then, can we tell a past participle from a past tense? The difference is that the past participle form of a verb always follows a helping verb. For example, in the sentence *Liam has **loved** the movies, loved* is a past participle because it follows the helping verb *has*. In the sentence *Liam **loved** the movies*, however, *loved* is a past tense verb because it does *not* follow a helping verb. Past participles can also be used as adjectives (*The car **seen** in that commercial belongs to my uncle*).

Past perfect tense See <u>perfect tenses</u>.

Past tense The past tense is used to describe an action that took place at some past time; for example, *Carlos **borrowed** my car last night*. For regular verbs, the past tense form ends in *-ed*. However, there are a large number of irregular verbs that form their past tense in different ways. The most unusual past tense is found in the verb *be*, which has two past tense forms: *was* in the singular and *were* in the plural.

Perfect tenses The perfect tenses refer to action that takes place over a period of time or is frequently repeated. There are three perfect tenses: (1) present perfect (*Niles **has seen** Daphne twice this week*); (2) past perfect (*Niles **had seen** Daphne two times last week*); and (3) future perfect (*Niles **will have seen** Daphne twice by Friday*). Notice that all the perfect tenses use *have* (in some form) as a <u>helping verb</u>, followed by a verb in the <u>past participle</u> form (*seen*, in all these examples).

Personal pronoun There are three sets of personal pronouns: (1) first-person pronouns refer to the speaker (***I, me, mine; we, us, ours***); (2) second-person pronouns refer to the hearer (***you, yours***); and (3) third-person pronouns refer to another person or thing (***he, him, his, she, her, hers, it, its; they, them, theirs***). A personal pronoun can also be categorized by the role it plays in a sentence: <u>subject</u> (*I, we, you, he, she, it, they*) or <u>object</u> (*me, us, you, him, her, them*).

Phrase In grammatical terminology, a *phrase* is a group of related words that act as a single part of speech. The most common type is the <u>prepositional phrase</u>. For example, in the sentence *Kermit kissed Miss Piggy **on the balcony***, the prepositional phrase is *on the balcony*, here acting as an <u>adverb</u>.

Plagiarism Plagiarism is a failure to appropriately indicate when your paper uses other people's ideas or wording. By following proper citation and documentation practices, you will avoid unintentional plagiarism.

Plural Referring to more than one. Plural nouns are usually formed by adding *-s* or *-es* to the singular form of the noun. Also see <u>agreement</u>; <u>subject-verb agreement</u>.

Possessive apostrophe Possessive nouns (***John's*** *book*) and possessive indefinite pronouns (***one's*** *ideas,* ***somebody's*** *book,* ***anybody's*** *guess*) are spelled with an apostrophe (') to show that the *-s* added at the end of the word is a "possessive *-s,*" as opposed to a "plural *-s.*" When an *-s* at the end of a word is both possessive *and* plural, the apostrophe goes after the *-s* (*The* ***girls'*** *dresses*). This use of the apostrophe to indicate possession is different from its use to indicate a <u>contraction</u>.

Predicate The predicate is everything in a sentence that is NOT part of the <u>subject</u>. The predicate is thus the <u>verb</u> portion of the sentence—the verb together with everything the verb controls—<u>objects</u>, <u>complements</u>, and all species of optional and obligatory <u>adverbs</u>. For example, in the sentence *Prince Charming* ***was beginning to put on a little weight***, everything except the subject *Prince Charming* is part of the predicate.

Predicate adjective Predicate adjectives are adjectives that follow <u>linking verbs</u> and describe their <u>subjects</u>. For example, in the sentence *The building was unbearably* ***hot***, the predicate adjective *hot* follows the linking verb *be* and describes its subject *the building*. Also see <u>linking verb</u>.

Predicate noun Predicate nouns are nouns that refer back to and rename, describe, or define their subjects. For example, in the sentence *Harriet became an excellent* ***tuba player***, the noun *tuba player* is a <u>predicate noun</u> because it refers back to and describes the <u>subject</u> *Harriet*.

Preposition Prepositions are words such as ***on, by, with, of, in, from, between***, and ***to***. A preposition is used with a following noun or pronoun <u>object</u> to make a <u>prepositional phrase</u>.

Prepositional phrase A prepositional phrase is a phrase consisting of a <u>preposition</u> and its object; for example: *on the beach, at noon, by Shakespeare*. Prepositional phrases function as adverbs or adjectives. For example, in the sentence *I got a message* ***at my office***, the prepositional phrase *at my office* functions as an adverb telling where I got the message. In the sentence *The chair* ***at my office*** *is not very comfortable*, the prepositional phrase *at my office* is an adjective modifying *chair*.

Present participle Present participle verb forms are used in the <u>progressive</u> <u>tenses</u> after the <u>helping verb</u> *be*, in some form. For example, in the sentence *Pranav and Liu were* ***practicing*** *their duets, were* is a form of the helping verb *be*, and *practicing* is in the present participle form. The present participle form is completely regular because it always ends in *-ing*; for example: *doing, being, seeing, helping*. Present participles can also be used as adjectives (*The car* ***turning*** *at the signal is a Buick*) or as nouns (***Seeing*** *is* ***believing***).

Present perfect tense See <u>perfect tenses</u>.

Present tense Despite its name, the most common use of the present tense is not to describe present time but, rather, to make timeless generalizations

(*The earth **is** round*) or to describe habitual, repeated actions (*I always **shop** on Saturdays*).

Present tense verb forms have an added *-s* when the subject is a third-person singular pronoun (*he, she,* or *it*) or when the subject is a noun that can be replaced with a third-person pronoun. See subject-verb agreement.

Progressive tenses Progressive tenses are used to refer to actions that are ongoing at the time of the sentence—as opposed to the present tense, which is essentially timeless. The term *progressive* refers to three related verb constructions that employ *be* (in some form) as a helping verb. If *be* is in the present tense (*am, is, are*), then the construction is called the *present progressive*; for example: *The president **is visiting** Peru now*. If *be* is in the past tense (*was, were*), then the construction is called the *past progressive*; for example: *The president **was visiting** Peru last week*. If *be* is used in the future (*will be*), then the construction is called the *future progressive*; for example: *The president **will be visiting** Peru next week*.

Pronoun A pronoun can replace a noun either as a subject or as an object. Among the many different types of pronouns, the most important is the personal pronoun. Also discussed in this book is the relative pronoun, which is the kind that begins an adjective clause. Also see gender, pronoun antecedent, and vague pronoun.

Pronoun antecedent Many pronouns refer back to a person or persons or to a thing or things mentioned earlier in the sentence or even in a previous sentence. For example, in the sentences *My **aunts** live next door. **They** are my mother's sisters*, the antecedent of the pronoun *they* is *aunts*. When a pronoun might refer to more than one antecedent, it is said to exhibit "ambiguous pronoun reference." For example, in the sentence *Aunt Sadie asked Mother where **her** keys were*, the pronoun *her* is ambiguous because it might refer either to Aunt Sadie or to Mother. A pronoun that has no real antecedent is called a vague pronoun. For example, in the sentence ***They** shouldn't allow smoking in restaurants*, the pronoun *they* is vague because it does not have any actual antecedent—it does not refer to any identified individuals.

Pronoun-antecedent agreement See agreement.

Proper adjective A proper adjective is derived from a proper noun. For example, the adjective *Jamaican* in ***Jamaican** coffee* is the adjective form of the proper noun *Jamaica*. Proper adjectives are always capitalized.

Proper noun Proper nouns are the names of specific individual persons, titles, or places. Proper nouns are always capitalized; for example: ***Queen Elizabeth, Michael Jordan, New York Times, Vancouver***. When a noun refers to a category rather than to a specific individual, it is called a common noun.

Quotation There are two types of quotation: (1) direct quotation, which uses quotation marks to report exactly what someone said, with word-for-word accuracy; and (2) indirect quotation, which paraphrases what a person said without using the writer's or speaker's exact words. Indirect quotations are not set within quotation marks.

Relative clause See adjective clause.

Relative pronoun A relative pronoun begins an adjective clause. The relative pronouns are *who, whom, whose, which,* and *that.* Relative pronouns must refer to the noun in the independent clause that the adjective clause modifies. For example, in the sentence *I got an offer **that** I can't refuse,* the relative pronoun *that* refers to *offer.* The relative pronouns *who, whom,* and *whose* are used to refer to people. For example, in the sentence *He is a man **whom** you can rely on,* the relative pronoun *whom* refers to *man.* Using *that* to refer to people is incorrect in formal writing; for example: ✗ *He is a man **that** you can rely on.*

Restrictive adjective clause See essential adjective clause.

Run-on sentence A run-on sentence consists of two or more sentences (independent clauses) that are joined together without adequate punctuation. Joining two sentences together with only a comma is called a comma splice (✗ ***My grandmother lived in Mexico when she was a girl, she moved to Texas when she was nineteen***). Joining two sentences together with no punctuation at all is called a fused sentence (✗ ***Kelsey's party is this weekend I bet she's looking forward to it***).

Semicolon The semicolon (;) is used in place of a period to join two closely related independent clauses, for example, ***A water main in the building had burst; the floors were covered with water***.

Sentence A sentence consists of at least one independent clause (with or without an accompanying dependent clause) that is punctuated with a period, an exclamation point, or a question mark.

Separable two-word verb A two-word verb is a type of compound verb. When such a compound is formed from a verb and an adverb, it is called a separable two-word verb because the adverb can be moved away or "separated" from the verb. For example, in the sentence *I **called up** my parents,* the adverb *up* can be separated from the verb by moving it after the object: *I **called** my parents **up**.* However, when the two-word verb is formed with a preposition, the preposition can never be moved away from the verb. A two-word verb of this type is called an inseparable two-word verb.

Sexist language Language that stereotypes, demeans, or unfairly excludes men or women is referred to as sexist language. One of the most common forms is the sexist or gender-exclusive use of pronouns. In this example, notice how it appears that only men vote: *Everybody should vote for **his** favorite candidate for governor.*

Singular Referring to one. Also see agreement; subject-verb agreement.

Steady-state verb Steady-state verbs describe actions or conditions that remain unchanged over a long period of time. For example, ✗ *Jennifer **is knowing***

a lot about British history is grammatically incorrect because *knowing* is a state of being, not an action that occurs over a definite period of time. The unchanging nature of steady-state verbs make them incompatible with the "right now" nature of the progressive tense. Most steady-state verbs fall into three broad categories: mental activity, emotional condition, and possession.

Subject The subject of a sentence is the doer of the action or what the sentence is about. The term *subject* has two slightly different meanings: (1) the *simple subject* is the noun or pronoun that is the doer or the topic of the sentence, and (2) the *complete subject* is the simple subject together with all its modifiers. For example, in the sentence *The **book** on the shelf belongs to my cousin*, the simple subject is *book*, and the complete subject is *the book on the shelf*.

Subject-verb agreement This term refers to the matching of the number of a present tense verb (or a present tense helping verb if there is more than one verb) with the number of the subject of that verb. Following are three examples with different subjects: (1) *Aunt Sadie **lives** in Denver.* (2) *My aunts **live** in Denver.* (3) *Aunt Sadie and Uncle Albert **live** in Denver.*

If the subject is a third-person singular personal pronoun (*he, she, it*) or if the subject is a noun that can be replaced by a third-person singular personal pronoun (as is the case with *Aunt Sadie* in example 1), then it is necessary to add an *-s* (called the *third-person singular -s*) to the present tense verb.

If the subject *cannot* be replaced by a third-person singular pronoun (as is the case in examples 2 and 3), do *not* add the third-person singular *-s* to the present tense.

Only the verb *be* has past tense forms that change to agree with the subject: *Was* is used with first-person singular and third-person singular subjects (*I **was** in Denver; Aunt Sadie **was** in Denver*); and *were* is used with all other subjects (*My aunts **were** in Denver*).

Subordinate clause See dependent clause.

Subordinating conjunction A *subordinating conjunction* (such as **when**, **since**, **because**, or **if**) begins a dependent clause.

Tense The term *tense* is used in two quite different ways. (1) It can refer to the *time* in which the action of the sentence takes place: present time, past time, and future time. (2) Usually in this book, however, the term is used in a narrower, more technical sense to mean just the *form* of the verb. In this limited sense, the term refers either to the present tense form of a verb (**see** and **sees**, for example) or to its past tense form (**saw**). There is no separate future tense form in English; we can talk about future time by using the helping verb *will*.

Tense shifting Tense shifting occurs in a piece of writing when the author shifts from one tense to another—usually from past tense to present tense or vice versa. For example, in the sentence *We **ate** at the restaurant that **is** on the pier*, the first verb (*ate*) is in the past tense, while the second verb (*is*) is in the present tense. In this particular sentence, the shifting from past tense to present tense is appropriate; sometimes, however, writers confuse readers by incorrectly shifting tenses when there is no reason to do so.

Transitional term A transitional term shows how the meaning of a second sentence is related to the meaning of the first sentence. For example, in the pair of sentences *I had planned to leave at noon.* **However***, my flight was delayed,* the transitional term *however* signals to the reader that the second sentence will contradict the first sentence in some way. Some other transitional terms are **nevertheless**, **moreover**, and **therefore**.

Two-word verb Two-word verbs are compounds (often with idiomatic meanings) formed from a verb plus either a preposition or an adverb. When the compound contains a preposition, the compound is called an inseparable two-word verb because the preposition can never be separated from the verb. When the compound contains an adverb, the adverb can be moved away from the verb; these compounds are called separable two-word verbs. Two-word verbs are also called *phrasal verbs*.

Vague pronoun A pronoun must have an antecedent to make its meaning clear. A *vague pronoun* is one that does not seem to refer to anything or anyone in particular. For example, in the sentence **They** *should do something about these terrible roads*, the pronoun *they* is a vague pronoun because it could refer to anybody—the highway department, the police, the government.

Verb A verb tells about an action in a sentence (*Alfy* **sneezed**) or describes the subject of the sentence (*Alfy* **seemed** *angry*). Only verbs can change form to show tense. That is, only verbs have present tense and past tense forms. A simple test to see whether a word is a verb is to see whether you can change it into a past tense by adding *-ed* to it.

Voice *Voice* is a technical term in grammar that refers to the relation of the subject of a sentence to the verb. If the subject is the "doer" of the action of the verb, as in the sentence **Keisha wrecked** *the car*, then the sentence is said to be in the active voice. However, if the subject is the recipient of the action of the verb, as in the sentence *The* **car was wrecked** *by Keisha*, then the sentence is said to be in the passive voice.

APPENDIX D

Glossary of Commonly Confused Words

Writers sometimes confuse certain words that sound alike but are spelled differently. Even a computer spell-checker will not catch if these words are misused because they are not misspelled. For example, *breaks* in the following sentence is incorrect:

✗ My car's **breaks** are squealing.

Because it doesn't "see" the error in meaning, a spell-check program would not suggest the correct usage:

My car's **brakes** are squealing.

Below is a list of words that are often confused with one another. (Some of these words have several meanings, but we have given only the most common usage.) Use this list of easily confused words to help you edit your writing. If you are unsure about a word that doesn't appear here, consult a dictionary.

Word	Definition	Example
accept	to approve	I **accept** your offer.
except	excluding	I kept all the receipts **except** that one.
advice	a suggestion	Can you give me investment **advice**?
advise	to recommend	I **advise** you not to go there.
affect	to influence or alter	The medication didn't **affect** Lydia at all.
effect	a result	One **effect** of this drug is drowsiness.
aisle	the space between rows	The groom fell down in the **aisle**.
isle	an island	Gilligan was bored with the **isle**.
already	previously	I have **already** eaten lunch.
all ready	completely prepared	Jan is **all ready** for the test, but I'm not.
altogether	thoroughly or generally	She was not **altogether** ready for college.
all together	in a group	The holiday brought us **all together**.
brake	a device for stopping or to stop	The **brakes** in this car are awful.
break	to destroy or divide into pieces	If you **break** the window, you'll have to pay to replace it.
breath	an inhalation or exhalation	Take a deep **breath** before diving.
breathe	to inhale or exhale	I can't **breathe** in a sauna.

Word	Definition	Example
capital	a city recognized as the home of a government	The **capital** of Texas is Austin.
capitol	the building where lawmakers meet	The **capitol** building is huge.
choose	to select	Our group will **choose** topics tomorrow.
chose	past tense of *choose*	She **chose** to make up the test.
complement	to go well with	This wine **complements** the chicken.
compliment	to praise	He **complimented** my leadership skills.
dessert	a tasty sweet	For **dessert**, we had key lime pie.
desert	a dry area	You'll need water to cross that **desert**.
device	a mechanism	This **device** will help you start a car.
devise	to arrange	Ira **devised** this meeting between us.
its	possessive form of *it*	My hamster ate all **its** food.
it's	contraction for *it is*	**It's** going to rain today, so be prepared.
later	subsequently	We ate too much. **Later,** we felt sick.
latter	the last thing mentioned	For lunch, we can have turkey or ham. I prefer the **latter**.
lead	a metallic element (noun)	They used **lead** paint on these windows.
led	past tense of verb *lead*	The guide **led** us through the canyon.
loose	not snug	Your pants are **loose** in the rear.
lose	to misplace; to fail to win	Did you **lose** the race?
maybe	perhaps	**Maybe** I'll get a raise next month.
may be	might possibly be	The project **may be** ready next week.
passed	past tense of *pass*	I **passed** her on the way to school.
past	previous time	In the **past**, I owned an IBM typewriter.
personal	private	A lot of my e-mail is **personal**.
personnel	staff	All store **personnel** should wear name tags.
principal	head of a school; most important	Report to the **principal's** office. The **principal** reason is cost.
principle	a basic truth	What **principles** would you fight for?
quiet	little or no sound	It was **quiet** in the library.
quite	very	Marc looked **quite** handsome in that suit.
set	to put	**Set** the glasses on the table, please.
sit	to be seated	The teacher wants us to **sit** in groups.
than	as compared to	My dog is smarter **than** my cat.
then	next	Fix this car. **Then** fix that car.
their	possessive of *they*	The players lost **their** final game.
there	adverb indicating place	Put the printer **there** for now.
they're	a contraction for *they are*	**They're** meeting us after work.

Word	Definition	Example
to	a preposition	Russell went **to** his algebra class.
too	very or also	He was **too** tired to work, **too**.
two	the number 2	Shannon wrote **two** papers this week.
weak	not strong	Tomás felt **weak** after the game.
week	seven days	I need a **week** off from work.
weather	the state of the atmosphere	Today's **weather** will be stormy.
whether	if	**Whether** you go or not is your decision.
whose	possessive of *who*	**Whose** turn is it now?
who's	contraction for *who is*	**Who's** ready to leave?
your	possessive of *you*	**Your** car is a mess.
you're	contraction for *you are*	If **you're** hungry, let's get lunch.

APPENDIX E

Glossary of Commonly Misspelled Words

Even in this age of automated spell-checkers, misspellings account for some of the most common, most distracting mistakes that appear in writing. One way to improve your spelling is to avoid completely relying on a spell-checker. Use this tool, but don't always trust it. As you know, spell-checkers are useless at detecting misspellings when you confuse two words, such as writing *there* when you meant *their*. Another problem with spell-checkers is you cannot always use them, such as when taking a test.

Writing and reading improve your spelling ability, but it also helps to study the correct spelling of words you misspell. Some spellings are challenging for many people, such as the words listed in this appendix and in Appendix D. Research indicates the best way to study the correct spelling of words like these is to do something active while you study, rather than just reading the words and thinking about the way they are spelled.

Here is a more active way to learn the spelling of challenging words. Say each letter aloud as you read the word. Try this at least two or three times. Then, put the correct spelling aside and try slowly to spell the word aloud, letter by letter. After that, write down what you believe to be the correct spelling, and then consult your list or book to make sure you are correct. Repeat this procedure until spelling the word becomes automatic and routine.

It can also help to prioritize the spellings you study. Focus on the troublemakers. Again, be sure to look at Appendix D for a list of commonly confused words. These account for the majority of misspellings overlooked by students using a spell-checker.

While there is little agreement about the "top ten" most common misspellings, here is a short list of frequently misspelled words in college writing (excluding the "confused words" misspellings covered in Appendix D).

Common Misspellings in College Writing

a lot (two words, not one)	February	receive
absence	misspelling	roommate
disappoint	parallel	separate
definite	perceive	sophomore
discipline	professor	writing

The previous list is a starting place for practicing your spelling, but focus on words that are challenging for you in particular. Not sure? Here is a longer list of words that are difficult to spell.

Fifty More Words That Are Frequently Misspelled

apologize	foreign	potato
arctic	grammar	privilege
arithmetic	handkerchief	probably
athlete	harass	rebellion
becoming	height	recommend
beginning	heroes	referring
believe	interest(ing)	restaurant
building	laboratory	rhythm
bureau(crat)	leisure	sandwich
calendar	maintenance	secretary
changeable	marriage	through
coming	mischievous	truly
commitment	mother	until
develop	necessary	villain
embarrass(ment)	occasion	Wednesday
existence	occurrence	yield
familiar	pastime	

APPENDIX F

Glossary of Common Two-Word Verbs

The following is an alphabetical list of one hundred common two-word verbs.

Each of the verbs on this list is a *separable* two-word verb (verb + adverb construction). Remember that if the sentence includes an object *noun*, the adverb can be placed either before or after the noun. In other words, the noun can separate the two parts of the verb. Both of these examples are correct:

Carly **turned down** the offer.

Carly **turned** the offer down.

However, when the object following the adverb is a *pronoun*, the adverb must be placed after the pronoun. In this case, the pronoun must separate the two parts of the verb.

✗ Carly **turned down** it.

Carly **turned** it **down**.

To learn more about how to identify and correct problems with two-word verbs, see Lesson 34. You may also want to consult the *Longman Phrasal Verbs Dictionary* (2001), the most complete listing of two-word verbs and their meanings.

Two-Word Verb	Meaning	Example
ask out	ask for a date	He wanted to **ask** her **out**.
ask over	invite to one's home	We **asked** them **over** for coffee.
back up	support	They **backed** our proposal **up**.
beat out	defeat, overcome	Our plan **beat out** theirs.
blow up	destroy	The bomb **blew** the building **up**.
break down	disassemble, analyze	This chart **breaks** the costs **down**.
break in	train, start	They **broke in** the new staff.
break off	discontinue, stop	We **broke off** the discussions.
bring around	convince	We'll **bring** the others **around** in time.
bring back	return	She **brought** the books **back**.
bring off	succeed in doing	They **brought** the party **off**.
bring up	mention, propose	I'll **bring** the issue **up** to my boss.
brush off	ignore, dismiss	He **brushed** their complaints **off**.
buy out	purchase	We want to **buy** the company **out**.
call off	cancel	They **called off** the meeting.
call up	telephone	Her boss **called** her **up**.
carry away	overcome objections	His idea **carried** them **away**.

Two-Word Verb	Meaning	Example
carry out	do, follow	Be sure to **carry** the orders **out**.
check out	investigate	We plan to **check** the offers **out**.
check over	test for accuracy	They **checked** the bills **over**.
cost out	price	They **cost out** the bid.
cover up	hide	They **covered up** the crime.
crack up	make someone laugh	His stories **crack** me **up**.
do in	kill, destroy	His mistakes finally **did** him **in**.
do over	repeat	I have to **do** my paper **over** again.
drag out	make longer	The boss will **drag** the meeting **out**.
dream up	create, imagine	They **dreamed** the whole thing **up**.
drop off	deliver, leave	I **dropped** the kids **off** at school.
figure out	discover	It's easy to **figure** the answer **out**.
fill in	explain something	Let's go **fill** the newcomers **in**.
fit in	schedule	I'll **fit** you **in** at one o'clock.
fix up	repair, decorate	They **fixed** the office **up** nicely.
follow up	oversee, pursue	I **followed** the plans **up**.
freeze out	exclude, keep out	We'll **freeze** the competition **out**.
get across	explain successfully	At least they **got** their ideas **across**.
give up	quit using	He **gave** junk food **up**.
hand in	submit	It is time to **hand** my paper **in**.
hang up	cause a delay	The problem really **hung** them **up**.
help out	assist	The tutor really **helped** them **out**.
hold up	restrain, delay	The accident **held** them **up**.
lay off	fire	The firm **laid** the employees **off**.
lay out	present, arrange	She wanted to **lay** the options **out**.
lead on	encourage falsely	The ads **lead** the customers **on**.
leave off	omit	I **left** my name **off** the list.
let down	disappoint	Our failure **let** them **down**.
look up	find information	We **looked** their address **up**.
make up	lie about	They **made** the whole story **up**.
mix up	confuse	Our directions **mixed** them **up**.
pass out	distribute	We **passed** the books **out**.
pass up	decline	I couldn't **pass up** chocolate cake.
pay back	repay a debt	We **paid** our loan **back**.
pay off	bribe	They **paid** the police **off**.
phase out	terminate gradually	We will **phase** the product **out** by 2014.
pick up	make happy	The news really **picked** them **up**.
point out	identify	We **pointed** the changes **out**.
polish off	finish	We **polished** the last job **off**.
pull off	succeed in doing	I **pulled** a big surprise **off**.
put back	return	She **put** the book **back** on the shelf.
put off	delay, discourage	We **put off** the decision until later.
put on	deceive, tease	You are **putting** me **on**.
rip off	cheat	The salesperson **ripped** us **off**.

Two-Word Verb	Meaning	Example
run down	criticize	They **ran** the opposition **down**.
scale back	reduce	We needed to **scale back** our plan.
seek out	search for	I **sought** the best deal **out**.
sell out	betray	He **sold** his partner **out**.
set back	delay	The rain **set** the job **back**.
set off	trigger, activate	The noise **set** the alarm **off**.
shake up	scare	The accident **shook** me **up**.
shoot down	reject	My lab group **shot** my ideas **down**.
show off	display boastingly	He **showed** his new car **off**.
shut off	stop	They **shut** the radio **off**.
shut up	silence someone	Sam **shut** his partner **up**.
smooth over	fix temporarily	He will **smooth** the situation **over**.
sound out	test one's opinion	We **sounded** them **out**.
spell out	give all details	She **spelled out** the proposal carefully.
stand up	fail to meet someone	My date **stood** me **up** twice!
straighten out	correct someone	The boss **straightened** us **out**.
string along	deceive	He was **stringing** them **along**.
sum up	summarize	My job is to **sum** the proposal **up**.
take in	deceive, trick	Their scheme really **took** us **in**.
talk over	discuss	I'd like to **talk** the plan **over**.
tear down	destroy, demolish	They **tore** the old house **down**.
tell apart	distinguish	I can't **tell** them **apart**.
think up	invent	We **thought up** a new plan.
throw away	discard	I **threw** the old papers **away**.
throw off	confuse, delay	The announcement **threw** them **off**.
track down	find	We **tracked** the book **down**.
trip up	cause a mistake	Our carelessness **tripped** us **up**.
try out	test, explore	I should **try** the new computer **out**.
tune out	ignore	I can't **tune** the distractions **out**.
turn around	change for the better	They **turned** the company **around**.
turn down	reject	She **turned** our offer **down**.
turn in	submit	I **turned** my assignment **in**.
turn off	cause to lose interest	The bad smell **turned** me **off**.
use up	use until gone	I **used** all my money **up**.
wear down	weaken gradually	Some children **wear** their parents **down**.
wear out	exhaust	The noise **wore** me **out**.
wipe out	destroy completely	The floods **wiped** the city **out**.
work up	prepare	I **worked** the new draft **up**.
write off	cancel, dismiss	They **wrote** the investment **off**.

Answer Key

LESSON 1: Fragments

Diagnostic Exercise, *page 21*

I need more money. There are only two ways to get more money, **earning** more or spending less. I am going to have to do a better job saving what money I do earn **because** there is no realistic way that I can earn more money. The first thing I did was to make a list of everything I bought, **starting** last Monday.

When I read over my list, the first thing I noticed was how much I spent on junk food, **especially** snacks and energy bars. It is really stupid to spend so much money on stuff **that** isn't even good for me. I can't just do away with snacks, though. I work long, irregular hours, and so I can't always have regular meals **like everyone else**.

The second thing I noticed was how much I was spending on drinks, **such as** coffee and bottled water. I was dropping four or five dollars every time I went to Starbucks, **which** is way more than I can afford. What really got my attention, though, was the cost of bottled water. I resolved to save some bottles and fill them from a drinking fountain. After all, you can get water for free.

Sentence Practice 1, *page 25*

1. Growers loved the Red Delicious apple variety **because** it stayed ripe for a long time. (adverb) 2. Growers kept changing the Red Delicious variety over the years, **making** the apples redder and even more long lasting. (-*ing*) 3. Unfortunately, there was a negative side effect to their changes, **taste**. (renamer) 4. OK 5. A lot of people must have agreed **because** the sales of Red Delicious slowed down. (adverb)

Sentence Practice 2, *page 26*

1. The public loves Fuji apples **because** they are sweet and crisp. (adverb) 2. Apple growers love them **since** they keep for up to six months. (adverb) 3. Apple researchers in Japan developed the Fuji apple **using** our old friend the Red Delicious. (adverb) 4. The Fuji apple is a cross between two American apples, **the** Red Delicious and the Virginia Ralls Genet. (renamer) 5. The researchers who developed the apple named it, **calling** it "Fuji" after the name of their research station. (-*ing*)

Editing Practice 1, *page 28*

Key West is a great place to visit **for** a lot of reasons. First of all, the physical setting is magnificent, **blue** sky and beautiful ocean views. Being on an island makes you much more aware of the water and the sky. Unlike the often cloudless skies on the Pacific coast, the skies in the keys often have small puffy clouds, **giving** a sense of space and depth to the sky. The color of the water is always changing **because** the coral reefs reflect the continually changing play of sun and cloud. The fact that the ocean around Key West is so shallow and so varied gives the water vibrant colors, **with** dozens of shades of green and blue everywhere you look. The beaches in California are quite drab by comparison **because** they are . . .

Editing Practice 2, *page 29*

It is interesting to compare Key West with a similar ocean-side destination in California, **Santa** Barbara, for instance. Besides being beach destinations, they share another important feature, **a** lengthy Spanish heritage. Key West today doesn't feel Spanish at all, **even** though it (and the rest of Florida) was part of the Spanish empire for nearly three hundred years. There was never any permanent Spanish settlement there **because** there was no source of fresh water on the island. Key West was a temporary home for fishermen and pirates, **a** source of much humor today. Santa Barbara, on the other hand, is overflowing with its Spanish heritage, **especially** in its architecture. Santa Barbara today looks classically Spanish, **with** its white buildings ...

LESSON 2: Run-ons: Fused Sentences and Comma Splices

Diagnostic Exercise, *page 32*

I go to school on the West Coast, but my family lives on the East Coast. My family is very close-knit; they all live within a hundred miles of each other. When I applied to college, I submitted applications to schools nearby, **and** I also submitted an application to one West Coast school. To my great surprise, I got in to the West Coast school. They had exactly the program I wanted to study, and they gave me a really good financial aid package. At first, the idea of going seemed impossible; the school just seemed so far away. My family was not at all happy; most of them said I should go to school in state. The one person who thought I should go to the West Coast was my aunt; she said I should go to the best school I could get in to no matter where it was. I am really glad that I followed her advice; I have really come to love my West Coast school.

Sentence Practice 1, *page 35*

1. I slipped on the ice going to work, **and** I wrenched my left knee. 2. The math homework is getting pretty hard, **so** I am thinking of getting a tutor. 3. Trying to sell a house in this economic climate is tough; **nobody** can get a loan. 4. Daylight saving time doesn't end until after Halloween, **so** the trick-or-treaters don't have go out in the dark. 5. Please call your mother; **she's** been trying to reach you all day.

Sentence Practice 2, *page 36*

1. Please come here; I need some help. 2. OK 3. I don't watch much TV anymore, **but** I still read *TV Guide*. 4. We are taking out the kitchen counter, **and** we are putting in a granite one. 5. OK

Editing Practice 1, *page 37*

I was late to my first class; my car broke down on the side of the highway. This is the third time this fall that I have had to pull over because of an engine problem, **and** I am not going to suffer through a fourth time. According to a mechanic, the problem has something to do with the fuel injector. I have replaced the fuse, and the mechanic has tried various other methods. Nothing has worked, **so** it does not make sense spending even more money on something that cannot be fixed. I might need a whole new fuel injector, **so** I am considering buying a new car. The one I have is only six years old, so I hate buying a new one already. It all depends on what I can afford.

Editing Practice 2, *page 38*

At my college, on-campus parking can be extremely difficult, **and** the situation will soon be worse. Currently, the college has eight parking lots for students, **but** two of them hold only about a dozen cars. During the summer, construction will begin on a new library, which we certainly need. The construction will last a year, **and** two parking lots will be closed during the construction phase. When the library opens up next year, only one of the two lots will be reopened; **the** other will have vanished because the library will cover it. Almost everyone believes we need a new library. **It** is too bad ...

UNIT TWO

LESSON 3: Nearest-Noun Agreement Errors

Diagnostic Exercise, *page 46*

The beginning of the first public schools in the United States **dates** from the early 1800s. The pressure to create public schools open to children of working-class parents **was** a direct result of the union movements in large cities. In response, state legislatures gave communities the legal right to levy local property taxes to pay for free schools open to the public. By the middle of the nineteenth century, control of the school policies and curriculum **was** in the hands of the state government. As school populations outgrew one-room schoolhouses, the design of school buildings on the East Coast **was** completely changed to accommodate separate rooms for children of different ages. Before this time, all children in a schoolhouse, regardless of age, **were** taught together . . .

Sentence Practice 1, *page 48*

1. The integration of so many different ideas **takes** a lot of time and effort. 2. The ranking of all the qualifying teams **is** always controversial. 3. Examination of the entirety of documents clearly **shows** that the defendant is innocent. 4. The losses at the start of the season **make** it hard to win the conference. 5. One of the trees in our neighborhood **has crashed** down onto the power line.

Sentence Practice 2, *page 49*

1. Any communication between the defendants and the witnesses **is** strictly prohibited. 2. During the afternoon, the temperatures inside the warehouse complex **are** unbearable. 3. The ads created by their Madison Avenue advertising firm **were** the talk of the industry. 4. status; OK 5. flights; OK

Editing Practice 1, *page 50*

Owning a pet, even the least demanding of creatures, **is** never easy. Over the years, we have had a number of cats, each of which **has** had a unique personality. Sometimes people seek out cats, and sometimes cats, instinctively knowing the house with the most defenseless owner, **choose** where to live. One of the cats that **falls** into the latter category is a big, yellow tomcat we call Ferdinand. If cats could belong to political parties, Ferdinand would be a pacifist. Absolutely nothing that happens around him **seems** to upset him. For example, every one of the cats that we had before as pets **was** terrified . . .

Editing Practice 2, *page 51*

A researcher who has studied the history of cats **believes** that the ancestor of today's domestic cats **was** a species of small wildcats native to northern Africa and southern Europe. The first evidence of cats being domesticated animals kept by humans **was** found in Egypt. An Egyptian official who oversaw large government grain storehouses **was** apparently the first to use cats to control rats and mice. In fact, in Egypt, the pet cats of an important official **were** considered sacred . . .

LESSON 4: Agreement with *There is* and *There was*

Diagnostic Exercise, *page 54*

Despite the fact that there **are** lots of movies coming out every month, there **are** surprisingly few choices open to us. Most movies are designed to fall into a few easily marketed categories. There **are** action movies for teens, romantic comedies for first dates, and slasher movies for people I don't want to even think about. Since most new movies are only in the theaters for a short period of time, there **are** only a few weeks for studios to advertise the movies. If there **were** unusual aspects or features to a new movie, the studio

wouldn't have time to find and reach an audience that falls outside the predictable categories. As a result, we get to see the same few types of movies over and over.

Sentence Practice 1, *page 55*

1. There **are** never <u>enough napkins</u> to go around. 2. After the storm ended, there **were**
<u>dozens of trees</u> down all over the city. 3. There **are** <u>a couple</u> of movies that I would like to
see. 4. You could never tell that there **were** any <u>difficulties</u> with the stage lighting. 5. OK

Sentence Practice 2, *page 56*

1. OK 2. Since it had snowed all night, there **were** only some <u>trucks</u> on the road. 3. There
are some <u>cookies and pastries</u> to go with the coffee. 4. Fortunately, there **were** a <u>flashlight</u>
<u>and</u> some <u>candles</u> in the closet. 5. There **are** <u>lots</u> of things for the children to do there.

Editing Practice 1, *page 57*

There **are** lots of reasons to visit Spain. First of all, there **are** all those wonderful, long,
sunny afternoons. Even though Spain is west of England, Spain uses the same time zone
as France and Italy, essentially giving Spain year-round daylight savings time. Moreover,
when Spain goes on daylight savings time in the summer with the rest of Europe, there
are actually two extra hours of daylight in Spain. The extra daylight in the afternoon
means that when the stores reopen after the siesta at 6 P.M., there is still plenty of daylight
when people are out and about. Most businesses and offices open at 8 or 9 in the morning
to take advantage of the fact that there **are** many hours . . .

Editing Practice 2, *page 57*

Another reason to visit Spain is to explore the art and architecture. There **are** some
of the world's greatest museums, art galleries, and churches in Spain. In Madrid, there
are half a dozen great art collections, the most famous being the Prado. The Prado has
the world's greatest collection of Spanish paintings: There **are** innumerable paintings
by Goya, Velazquez, and El Greco. The enormous wealth Spain acquired from its conquests in the New World allowed Spanish kings to purchase numerous collections of great
art masterpieces from the rest of Europe. In the Prado there **are** fantastic collections of
Dutch and Flemish paintings. For example, there **are** nearly one hundred paintings by
Rubens alone.

LESSON 5: Agreement with Compound Subjects

Diagnostic Exercise, *page 60*

I work in a busy law office. Even though we now have voice mail, answering the phone
and writing down messages **take** up a lot of my time. I am also responsible for maintaining
the law library, although most of the time I do nothing more glamorous than shelving. The
law books and reference material **are** always left scattered around the library, and some of
the lawyers even leave their dirty coffee cups on the tables. I used to have a relatively comfortable working area, but the new computer terminal and modem **have** now taken up most
of my personal space; that's progress, I guess. Despite all the stress, meeting the needs of
clients and keeping track of all the information required in a modern law office **make** it . . .

Sentence Practice 1, *page 62*

1. <u>Weekends and holidays</u> always **feel** too short. 2. <u>A runny nose and a sore throat</u> **are**
good indicators of a cold. 3. Oops! <u>The groceries and the milk</u> **are** still in the car. 4. <u>Pea-</u>
<u>nuts, pretzels, and a cookie</u> **are** about all you get to eat when you fly coach today. 5. Dur-
ing the summer, <u>the thunder and the lightning</u> in our area **are** just amazing.

Sentence Practice 2, *page 63*

1. <u>Loud drums and thunderclaps</u>; OK 2. <u>What "football" means in America and what it</u>
<u>means in the rest of the world</u> **are** totally different things. 3. <u>The light in the garage and</u>

the light over the sink **need** replacing. 4. Fortunately, <u>the captain and the crew</u> of the sunken boat **were** safe. 5. <u>The characters and the plot</u> of his latest book **are** just like those in all his other books.

Editing Practice 1, *page 64*

Many stories, plays, and even a famous opera **are** based on the legend of Don Juan. Don Juan's charm and wit supposedly **make** him utterly irresistible to women. The most famous treatment of the Don Juan legend is in Mozart's opera, *Don Giovanni (Giovanni* is the Italian form of the Spanish name *Juan*, or *John* in English). Mozart's opera is highly unusual in that comedy and villainy **are** mixed together in almost equal parts. For example, the actions and behavior of the Don constantly **keep** the audience off balance. His charm and bravery **make** him almost a hero at times. However, at other times, his aristocratic arrogance and his deliberate cruelty to women **reveal** he is far from a true hero. The delicate seduction of a willing woman and a violent rape **are** all the same to him.

UNIT THREE

LESSON 6: Present, Past, and Tense Shifting

Diagnostic Exercise, *page 70*

Last summer we took a trip to Provence, a region in the southeast corner of France, which **borders** Italy. The name *Provence* **refers** to the fact that it was the first province created by the ancient Romans outside the Italian peninsula. Today, Provence still **contains** an amazing number of well-preserved Roman ruins. While there **are** a few big towns on the coast, Provence **is** famous for its wild country and beautiful scenery. Provence **is** especially known for its abundance of wildflowers in the spring. These flowers **are** used . . .

Sentence Practice 1, *page 73*

1. Headlights that stay on all the time **have** significantly reduced automobile accidents. (Make a statement) 2. Young people **are** using their landlines less and less often. (Make a statement) 3. I **got** a very surprising phone call. (Tell a story) 4. The team's bus **had** a minor accident and they **missed** their first game. (Tell a story) 5. Halloween often **frightens** young children. (Make a statement)

Sentence Practice 2, *page 73*

1. I **left** my towel in the locker that **is** nearest the door. (Tense shifting) 2. The fact that Hawaii **does** not go on daylight savings time always **confuses** people. (No tense shifting) 3. OK (No tense shifting) 4. He **deposited** the money in an account that he **keeps** at the local credit union. (Tense shifting) 5. The accident **occurred** on a stretch of road that **has** a reputation for being dangerous. (Tense shifting)

Editing Practice 1, *page 74*

Even though Shakespeare died in 1616, performances of his plays **have** continued without interruption right up to today. I recently **attended** the Oregon Shakespeare Festival in Ashland, Oregon. In planning the performances, the director **had** to make some big decisions about how to stage plays that **are** more than 350 years old. The biggest problem for all directors today **is** whether to present Shakespearian plays in period costume or in more modern dress.

Staging the plays in modern dress **makes** the plays more interesting and often a lot more fun. For example, in a performance of *Henry IV, Part I* at Ashland a few years ago, Falstaff **came** on stage for the first time on a motor scooter with a case of beer strapped on behind. Sometimes, staging plays in different time periods **allows** the director to make political or social comments. An outstanding example of this **is** the 1995 movie version of *Richard III* with Ian McKellen in an imaginary Fascist England in the 1930s. McKellen's performance as an all-powerful, sadistic ruler in an authoritarian state **chills** the . . .

Editing Practice 2, *page 75*

Ashland's Shakespeare Festival **began** almost by accident as an outgrowth of the old Chautauqua circuit. Chautauqua **provided** entertainment to rural America before the days of radio and movies. Chautauqua **was** a mix of popular lecturers, music, and vaudeville acts—something that seems strange today. After the collapse of Chautauqua, Ashland **found** itself with a good-sized summer theater facility. After unsuccessfully trying a variety of entertainments, including boxing matches, the faculty from the local college **decided** to stage a few Shakespearian plays. The plays proved to be so successful that the Oregon Shakespeare Festival **was** born . . .

LESSON 7: The Past and the Perfect Tenses

Diagnostic Exercise, *page 78*

Unfortunately, most people **have been** involved in an automobile accident at some time. I **have been** involved in several, but my luckiest accident was one that never happened. Just after I **had gotten** my driver's license, I borrowed the family car to go to a party. Although it **had been** a very tame party, I left feeling a little hyper and silly. It was night, and there were no streetlights nearby. I **had parked** a little distance from the house, so my car was by itself. I got into the car and decided to show off a little bit by throwing the car into reverse and flooring it. I **had gone** about twenty yards backward before I thought to myself that I was doing something pretty dangerous. I slammed on the brakes in a panic. I got out of the car and found that my back bumper was about four inches from a parked car that I **had never seen**. Whenever . . .

Sentence Practice 1, *page 81*

1. I **have worked** overtime for the past six months. (Continuous) 2. The company **has bought** up empty houses since the beginning of the year. (Continuous) 3. OK (Single event) 4. It **has snowed** every day this winter since Christmas. (Continuous) 5. She **has climbed** every peak over 14,000 feet in North America. (Continuous)

Sentence Practice 2, *page 82*

1. After the book **had become** a big hit in Europe, American publishers **were** willing to take a chance on it. 2. We **decided** to cancel our trip because it **had snowed** so much during the night. 3. I **didn't** need to go through the line because I **had** already **paid** for my ticket online. 4. OK 5. After I **had finished** assembling the bike, I **found** a leftover part.

Editing Practice 1, *page 83*

The number of deaths resulting from traffic accidents **has** declined steadily over the past decade. In recent years, researchers **have cited** a number of different reasons: improved safety of vehicles, increased use of seat belts and airbags, and fewer drunk drivers. Automobile manufacturers **had been** reluctant to even talk about safety until the federal government began mandating standards in the 1980s. Over the years, manufacturers **have continued** to resist installing even inexpensive safety features. For example, manufacturers **have been** very slow to produce cars with daytime headlights, even though in recent years many Canadian researchers **have demonstrated** that this no-cost item results in significantly fewer accidents.

UNIT FOUR

LESSON 8: Pronoun Agreement

Some answers in this lesson will vary. Sample answers are shown.

Diagnostic Exercise, *page 90*

Politicians have to play a hundred different roles in meeting the expectations of their constituents. One key role for **all politicians** is to pay special attention to the concerns and problems of their constituents. The other key role is to actually participate in the process of governing. Not that long ago, there was a broad middle-of-the road consensus on most public issues. Not so today. Now, if **politicians from one party propose** anything, they are automatically attacked by politicians from the other party. In the past, **politicians** would campaign on their own ideas and agendas. Now, it is almost irrelevant for **politicians** to develop proposals to attract voters to their campaigns. What **politicians do** today is air vicious negative ads attacking their opponents, often with malicious half-truths and even outright lies. As a result, **average voters are** less and less interested in following politics, and they are even giving up casting their votes.

Sentence Practice 1, *page 93*

1. College <u>freshmen</u> **have** no idea what <u>they</u> are going to major in. 2. <u>Customers</u> **are** always right, but that doesn't mean <u>they</u> know what they are talking about. 3. <u>Students</u> who **are** late with <u>their</u> term papers will lose a full grade. 4. <u>Parents</u> **have** a responsibility to ensure that <u>their</u> children get immunized. 5. <u>Cars</u> **will** skid if you drive <u>them</u> too fast around curves.

Sentence Practice 2, *page 94*

1. Someone parked **a** car in a place where it will be towed. 2. OK 3. OK 4. Did somebody take my pen instead of **his or hers**? 5. OK (*Their* does not rename *nobody*. It renames *Becca and Alyssa*, which is plural and thus agrees with *their.*)

Editing Practice 1, *page 95*

My brother has been collecting certain cards that have been popular in the last few years. **People** might merely collect these cards, or they might actually play games with them. Many years ago, **card collectors** would have likely collected sports cards, but nowadays they . . .

At one time, Pokémon was the most popular card game. The person who created these cards must have made a great deal of money from **his or her** creations. Another Japanese-inspired game is called Yu Gi Oh, and it is still popular. In Yu Gi Oh, a player selects a card from **his or her** hand to play. The opponent likewise picks a card **to** duel with. I thought this was a mindless game until I saw how much math and strategy are involved in the dueling stage. The game is so complex that **new players** learning the game **need** all the help they can get . . .

LESSON 9: Vague Pronouns: *This, That,* and *It*

Some answers in this lesson will vary. Sample answers are shown.

Diagnostic Exercise, *page 99*

"Star Wars" was the name of a military program as well as a movie. **The program** was a large research program calling for military defense in outer space. This **plan** was initiated by President Reagan in the 1980s, and it had the official title of "Strategic Defense Initiative." The public never embraced that **name** as much as . . .

Sentence Practice 1, *page 102*

1. OK; <u>Pluto</u> 2. We did not hear about our proposal. We need to talk about **what to do next**. 3. **The fact that John slammed the door** while we were talking to him really

upset us. 4. **Students are protesting how** the budget cutback has hurt higher education. 5. **There was a lot of damage because** the weather forecast did not predict the storm.

Sentence Practice 2, *page 103*

1. **The fact that** there was an accident on the freeway causes everyone to stop and stare. 2. San Francisco is one of the most photographed cities in the world. This fame makes **the city** a natural tourist destination. 3. **The fact that** the governor and the legislature are virtually at war with each other has brought the state to its knees. 4. We need a new car, but **getting one is** not too likely in the near future. 5. Amy Brown won her election in a landslide. **That victory** came as a surprise to everyone.

Editing Practice 1, *page 104*

Some credit card companies are taking advantage of students. **This practice** is becoming increasingly common. I see salespeople from the card companies almost every week on my campus, and **their presence** seems even more common in the spring semester when students are graduating. Most students have little experience with credit companies, and the representatives know **that fact**.

The companies give away T-shirts or candy bars to get students' attention. This gimmick sparks students' interest, and then the salespeople tell students that they are "preapproved" and can get a card immediately. **The gimmick** seems to work because I always see students signing up for these cards. The salespeople often forget a small detail: That little card is going to cost an annual fee plus 21 percent interest on all charges. Most students seem to think **the offer** is still great, but they will change their minds when they see the bills adding up. Believe me, **this trick** happened to me.

Editing Practice 2, *page 104*

My college finally decided to invest in a new system for allowing students to register online without having to come to campus during registration. **The new system** is a good idea. In fact, I am surprised **this technology** has taken so long to implement here. **Online registration** has been used at other colleges in the region. **That fact** is not unusual, . . .

Under the new system, students will be given passwords allowing them to access their student accounts. Initially, **a password** will be automatically assigned to each student, but the password can be changed later. By following the onscreen directions, students can pick and choose which classes they want to take, and **their schedules** can be changed anytime up to the first day of the semester. Students can now pay tuition online as well by using their credit cards. **That payment option** is good, even though . . .

LESSON 10: Choosing the Correct Pronoun Form

Diagnostic Exercise, *page 109*

A friend and **I** visited her cousin Jim, who lives in a cabin he built from scratch. My friend asked Jim if he would mind if **she** and **I** could stay in the cabin with **him** for a few days this summer. He said that was fine if we would work with **him** building a new storeroom he wanted to add onto his cabin. My friend told him that neither **she** nor **I** had any real experience building things. Jim said that it was OK. He would work with **us**. Both my friend and **I** learned how to measure and cut lumber, pound nails, and paint without getting it all over ourselves. Jim was very good-natured about the whole thing, even though my friend and **I** were probably more trouble than we were worth.

Sentence Practice 1, *page 111*

1. They ordered it specially for <u>my mother</u> and <u>**me**</u>. 2. The manager asked <u>Harriet</u> and <u>**her**</u> to trade assignments. 3. <u>Several of their friends</u> and <u>**they**</u> are planning a vacation in Hawaii next winter. OK 4. I hesitated to ask <u>Alicia</u> and <u>**her**</u> such a big favor. 5. <u>Roberta</u> and <u>**he**</u> will graduate next spring.

Sentence Practice 2, *page 112*

1. **He** advised us that **they** had already gotten approval from her. 2. **They** were worried about how **they** had not had a chance to talk to them. 3. Did **he** ever figure out what **they** should have said to her? 4. **They** explained what **they** expected us to say about him. 5. I expected that **they** would not have time to see them.

Editing Practice 1, *page 113*

When I was in high school, my father and **I** would build a new house every other summer. My father and mother were both teachers, so **they** always had summers off. During the first summer, my father and **I** would pour the foundation and do the framing and roofing. During the school year, a contractor would supervise the plumbing, wiring, and other specialities. The following summer, my father and **I** would finish the interior work. During the next school year, my mother would take charge of all the interior decoration, and then **she** would put the house on the market.

The key to making this scheme work was having the contractor; without **him**, we could never have done it. When we first started building houses, we needed **him** for his expertise. Later on, that was not the case. We needed **him** because he could control the subcontractors.

LESSON 11: *Who, Whom,* and *That*

Diagnostic Exercise, *page 117*

An experience that we all have had is working for a bad boss. One boss **whom** we have all had is the petty tyrant, a person **who** loves to find fault with every employee **who** works in the building. It seems like the petty tyrant is more interested in finding employees **whom** he or she can belittle than in getting the job done. Even worse than the petty tyrant is a supervisor **who** is inconsistent. An inconsistent boss is a person **whom** the employees can never trust. A game that this kind of boss loves is playing favorites. One day, this boss is everyone's best buddy; the next day, the boss acts as if he or she doesn't know the name of a person **who** has worked with the company for ten years.

Sentence Practice 1, *page 120*

1. OK; shoes 2. I asked if he knew any residents **who** were interested in leasing their apartments. 3. The candidate thanked all the volunteers **who** had worked so hard on the campaign. 4. I couldn't find the clerk **who** had sold me the shirt. 5. OK; plans

Sentence Practice 2, *page 121*

1. OK; had played 2. Nobody knew the stage manager **whom** the new director had hired. 3. The people **whom** we were scheduled to meet with never showed up. 4. OK; had designed 5. You have to trust the people **whom** you have hired to do the job.

Editing Practice 1, *page 122*

My boss is someone **whom** you might consider strange. I work part time at a convenience store that is located outside the city. My boss, Ms. McDonald, is someone who wants everything exactly her way. If you ever disagree with her, she tells you to hush and then covers her ears. She is married to a man **who** sells exotic goats for a living, and he occasionally brings them to the store. Last weekend, one goat bit a customer who was buying tomatoes that the goat wanted. Ms. McDonald, **whom** the goat also tried to bite, called the police. By the time they arrived, both the goat and my boss's husband had escaped. The customer **who** was bitten said he would sue the store; Ms. McDonald simply told him to hush and covered her ears. The officers, **who** were all too familiar with her strange behavior, said she could no longer have goats in the store. It's not exactly a funny situation, but she certainly makes my job interesting.

Editing Practice 2, *page 122*

Many Americans, even those **who** are knowledgeable about different cultures, know little about many religions. One example is Buddhism. This religion was founded in India by Siddhartha Gautama, **who** is known as Buddha, and it has over 300 million followers worldwide. Another example is Confucianism. This religion is based on the teachings of Confucius, a Chinese philosopher **who** stressed . . .

Some lesser-known religions were actually founded by people **who** migrated to America. The Amish Mennonites can be traced back to the birth of the Mennonite religion in Switzerland during the 1500s. In 1693, however, the followers of Jacob Ammann broke from other Mennonites, but a great many rejoined the main group in the eighteenth century. The remainder, **who** stayed loyal to Jacob Ammann's views, migrated to Pennsylvania. These are the followers **who** became known . . .

LESSON 12: Eliminating Sexist Pronouns

Some answers in this lesson will vary. Sample answers are shown.

Diagnostic Exercise, *page 126*

My psychology teacher, Ms. Crystal, had each member of the class complete a questionnaire that would help him **or her** choose an appropriate career. I had already decided on a profession, but she said the questionnaire would offer me other options. I've always wanted to be an electrical engineer because I like to design things; **engineers spend** much of **their** time drawing designs and writing specifications. Ms. Crystal said my survey results indicated I should consider being an accountant. She also told me, however, that the survey was just one resource for choosing a career. I agree. **People have** to consider what **they know** better than anyone else: **their** own interests.

Sentence Practice 1, *page 129*

1. **Parents** should strive to make **their children** independent. 2. No **employers want their** employees to be without health-care insurance. 3. **Politicians** must choose **their** words carefully. 4. We want **all eligible voters** to cast **their ballots** in favor of the school bond. 5. **All CEOs have** to take full legal responsibility for **their** actions.

Sentence Practice 2, *page 129*

1. I never met an accountant **who didn't keep his or her office** compulsively neat. 2. Could **I get everybody's** attention please! 3. Whoever mixed the paint didn't keep good records on what proportions **were** used. 4. **Car salespeople** make it **their** business to call you by your first name at least five times in the first three minutes after **they** meet you. 5. OK [The writer is referring to a specific neighbor, who apparently is male.]

Editing Practice 1, *page 130*

In American high schools and colleges, **students** can avail **themselves** of a number of free activities open to **them**. This is completely different from European schools where **students have** virtually no extracurricular activities available to **them**. In Europe, **school-aged athletes** must find (and pay for) a private, after-school sports club that **they** can join. When European **students come** to the United States, **they are** astonished at the extracurricular activities routinely available to **them**. Often **exchange students** will single out the extracurricular activities that **they** participated in as the most enjoyable part of **their** experience in the United States. Europeans point out that one reason why test scores for the average American are so low (by international standards) is that the American **students spend** too much of **their** school day in nonacademic activities. Whether or not **American students are** well served by **their** extracurricular experience is obviously a matter of debate.

UNIT FIVE

LESSON 13: Commas with *And, But, Or,* and Other Coordinating Conjunctions

Diagnostic Exercise, *page 139*

Africa was the home of humans long before recorded history, and scientists believe humanlike creatures roamed eastern Africa at least three million years ago. Today, most archaeologists believe it was in Africa that humans became differentiated from other primates, but relatively little is known of the beginnings of African religion. Several sites include rock paintings,/ and burial remains that suggest ancient religious activity in Africa. Many objects associated with religious activity do not survive long in Africa's tropical climates, so archaeological finds are limited in terms of what they reveal about early African religion. Available finds have provided information on the development of some African religions in some areas, but little . . .

Sentence Practice 1, *page 142*

1. Soviet-made airplanes once accounted for 25 percent of the world's aircraft, but this proportion has drastically changed. 2. Someone called for you this morning,/ and left a strange message. 3. OK 4. My first class officially ends at noon, but the teacher keeps us late every day. 5. OK

Sentence Practice 2, *page 142*

1. OK 2. OK 3. My father bought an old sword in England, but the old relic is not worth much. 4. OK 5. Bahir is dropping by my place later, so I suppose I should try to clean up a bit.

Editing Practice 1, *page 144*

Writing is a form of visible language, but there is a form of writing that is not meant to be seen. Braille is written as a series of dots or bumps, and visually impaired people can "read" it with their fingers. It is written as a series of cells, and each cell contains dots that can be variously arranged. Each particular arrangement of dots has its own meaning, but what the dots represent depends on the style of Braille. There are two forms of Braille: Grade 1,/ and Grade 2. Grade 1 Braille is a system in which the dots represent letters,/ and some very short words. Grade 2 Braille is not a completely different system, but it is a shorthand version of Grade 1 that is much harder to read.

Editing Practice 2, *page 144*

The wedding ring has been around for many centuries, and its history is more complex than people might think. Ancient Greeks are often credited with inventing this tradition, but many historians believe it started with the Egyptians or Hebrews. We do know the first rings were not made of precious metals. Many of the earliest rings were made of iron,/ and did not have a gemstone. The ring was usually placed on the woman's fourth finger, for it was believed a nerve behind this finger led directly to the heart. In the United States, the ring is placed on the left hand, but it is traditionally placed on the right hand . . .

LESSON 14: Commas with Transitional Terms

Diagnostic Exercise, *page 148*

Many places around the globe have universal appeal. They are, **however,** not necessarily accessible to the general public. An international committee has designated some sites as World Heritage Sites, which are sites having international value and responsibility. In the United States, **for example,** the committee has chosen Yosemite Park and the Statue of Liberty, both of which are part of our national parks system. We tend to take our parks system for granted; **however,** it is really quite unusual. Very few developed countries have extensive public land; **consequently,** their important public sites are little more than individual buildings. The vast size of some national parks in the American West makes them unique; **therefore,** they attract visitors from every country.

Sentence Practice 1, *page 151*

1. Bill said he might be late. Indeed, he was four hours late. 2. Little is known about the Pilgrim ship *Mayflower*; we do know, however, that it weighed about 180 tons. 3. English is the predominant language in the U.S. Nevertheless, over three hundred languages are spoken within its borders. 4. none 5. A serious accident has caused major delays. In fact, some commuters have decided to stay home.

Sentence Practice 2, *page 152*

1. Sean Connery is remembered most for his James Bond movies. However, he won an Oscar for a different role in *The Untouchables*. 2. Scott Joplin wrote over sixty musical compositions. He wrote, for instance, an opera entitled *Treemonisha*. 3. none 4. The top position in the British army is field marshal. The top position in Britain's navy, in contrast, is admiral of the fleet. 5. The singer Prince has gone by more than one name. For example, his birth name is Prince Rogers Nelson.

Editing Practice 1, *page 153*

I am facing a difficult decision; **however,** it is one I have to make soon. My family would like me to help with our family business after I graduate from college. My parents own a construction company, and my major is accounting. **Consequently,** I believe that I would have a lot to offer my parents' company once I finish my degree. I could, **for example,** help them develop more precise estimates for construction projects. My plans seemed so clear and logical at one time.

I enjoy talking with my parents about different accounting methods. **Nevertheless,** I have lately been considering moving to a different part of the country and working in a different type of business. New England would be a great place to live, **for example**. **Additionally,** I am considering working as an accountant for a company that manufactures computer parts. Even though I want the family business to do well, I want to try something very different. My parents have always supported my choices; **still,** I know they will be disappointed if I do not work for them.

LESSON 15: Commas with Adverb Clauses

Diagnostic Exercise, *page 157*

After everybody was asleep Monday night, there was a fire in the dorm next door. Fortunately, a smoke detector went off/ when smoke got into the staircase. While the fire department was fighting the fire, six rooms were totally destroyed. A friend of mine in another part of the building lost her computer/ because of the smoke and water damage. If school officials close down the dorm for repairs, she will have to find a new place to stay. I heard they will make a decision today/ as soon as they receive a report from the fire inspectors.

Sentence Practice 1, *page 160*

1. When I visit my parents in New Mexico, I always bring them something from my part of the country. 2. I will go with you/ after I finish eating. 3. After Omar competed in the third basketball tournament of the season, he was not eager to travel again. 4. Because the test included over a hundred questions, I could not finish it in just fifteen minutes. 5. Stephanie wants to leave/ because she smells a strange odor in the room.

Sentence Practice 2, *page 161*

1. My roommate must not realize the word *dormitory* comes from an ancient term meaning "sleep/" because he stays up very late every night. 2. Because it always appears sleepy,

the dormouse gets its name from the same ancient term (*dorm*). 3. <u>While I was walking to my first class of the day</u>, a mouse ran across the sidewalk. 4. <u>Even though I am not fond of mice</u>, I did not let this incident delay me. 5. <u>When I awake late because of a noisy roommate who does not let me sleep</u>, I do not have time to worry about a mouse.

Editing Practice 1, *page 162*

Because I am a full-time student, my income is limited. I don't want to borrow money from my family,/ unless no other option is available. Twice, I have used a government loan to pay for my tuition, fees, and books. Without those loans, I would not have been able to attend college. Although I would prefer not to take out any more student loans, I will likely have to do so again.

My part-time job does not pay well,/ since it is a minimum-wage position. Although I can't afford any luxuries, living on this meager income is manageable. In a few years, I will likely be able to improve my standard of living greatly, so my situation is not depressing. When I graduate from college, I should be able to find a job,/ because my field is very much in demand. Until then, I will be able to get by on an occasional student loan.

LESSON 16: Commas with Introductory Elements

Diagnostic Exercise, *page 165*

Until the relatively recent development of technology, most people throughout history were largely ignorant of the world. Travelers might bring stories of distant places, but only the literate few could read about those places. For most people around the globe, information traveled slowly. For instance, the Battle of New Orleans was fought two weeks after a treaty ended the War of 1812. The combatants were unaware of the treaty's signing. Later on in the nineteenth century, the railroad and telegraph brought the world closer. Even so, coverage was still slow and spotty.

Sentence Practice 1, *page 168*

1. Although Wally Amos is best known for his brand of cookies, he was also the first African American talent agent for the William Morris Agency. 2. In France, shepherds once carried small sundials as pocket watches. 3. Even though he was best known as an actor, Jimmy Stewart was a brigadier general in the U.S. Air Force Reserve. 4. After eating, our cat likes to nap. 5. Whenever I walk, our dog likes to go with me.

Sentence Practice 2, *page 168*

1. To keep people from sneaking up on him, Wild Bill Hickok placed crumpled newspapers around his bed. 2. Before his career was suddenly ended, Jesse James robbed twelve banks and seven trains. 3. Therefore, he was a successful criminal for a time. 4. Believe it or not, the state "gem" of Washington is petrified wood. 5. When she was in a high school band, singer Dolly Parton played the snare drum.

Editing Practice 1, *page 169*

When I tried to start a student organization on campus last semester, I was surprised by the difficulties and hurdles. I wanted to establish a club for students who enjoy science fiction. After being encouraged by several friends, I contacted the school official who oversees campus organizations. She informed me I would need a faculty sponsor and had to go through an approval process that could take several weeks. Upon reading some twelve pages of forms and directions, I almost gave up. Fortunately, a couple of friends agreed to help me fill out the forms and gather signatures from students interested in the club. However, the work was still not finished. We had to arrange a schedule of events and apply for funding. It took three months before the science fiction club was approved by various committees and school administrators. Now that the club has had three successful meetings, I feel that all the work was worthwhile.

Editing Practice 2, *page 170*

Though most professional orchestras today include a pianist, the piano is a relatively new addition to the symphony. In older times when pianos were not as common as they are today, the orchestra regularly included a different keyboard instrument, the harpsichord. This older keyboard instrument is much simpler than today's piano. Nonetheless, the advantage of virtually any keyboard instrument is that it can play chords and full harmony as well as melodies. To put this concept more simply, a person can play a whole piece of music on a keyboard instrument without requiring other musicians at all. As a result of this fact, solo music . . .

LESSON 17: Commas with Adjective Clauses

Diagnostic Exercise, *page 173*

The first true clocks were built in the thirteenth century, which was an era when accurate timekeeping became increasingly important. Other timekeeping devices had been used in situations/ that were not ideal. Sundials were useless at night, when there was insufficient sunlight for casting a shadow. The wind could blow out candles, which also could be used to estimate the time. Other timekeeping devices used streams, but these could freeze in winter. By the thirteenth century, the European monastery was a major type of social organization/ that depended on precise and reliable timing . . .

Sentence Practice 1, *page 176*

1. OK [essential] 2. Bo is reading *The Silmarillion*, which was written by J. R. R. Tolkien. [nonessential] 3. OK [essential] 4. This neighborhood café, which first opened in 1939, is one of my favorite places to drink coffee. [nonessential] 5. My parents were married in the Middle Eastern country of Yemen, where a wedding feast can last three weeks. [nonessential]

Sentence Practice 2, *page 177*

1. During Thanksgiving break, I have to drive to Denver, which is 600 miles away. [nonessential] 2. OK [nonessential] 3. One of these actors is Sonny Landham, who was unsuccessful in becoming the governor of Kentucky. [nonessential] 4. OK [essential] 5. OK [nonessential]

Editing Practice 1, *page 178*

I recently purchased a green-cheeked conure, which is a type of small parrot. It is an intelligent bird/ that is becoming increasingly popular as an exotic pet. *Pyrrhura molinae*, which is the bird's scientific name, is mostly green. The green-cheeked conure obtains its name from the bright green feathers on its cheeks. It is a very playful and active bird. My father, who generally dislikes all birds, even likes my bird, which I named Pepper because she likes to eat raw peppers. Most of the time, Pepper eats a blend of colored pellets that I buy at the pet store. Like many conures, Pepper is capable of mimicking speech but is not a great talker. She mainly whistles and makes a variety of odd noises/ that often wake me early in the morning.

Editing Practice 2, *page 178*

I am rooming with Harold Lee, who is very practical. We couldn't afford to spend much for Christmas gifts this year, so we decided to can some vegetables. First, we made a relish/ that was primarily composed of tomatoes, onions, and cabbage. The tomatoes, which we bought at the local market, had to be completely green. The jars had to be carefully sterilized, and the directions confused us. Luckily, we received advice from my mom, whom I called in a panic. Once we understood the process better, we went on to asparagus, which . . .

LESSON 18: Commas with Appositives

Diagnostic Exercise, *page 182*

Every summer I visit my Aunt Carol, a vigorous woman of sixty-five. Aunt Carol lives in a small town in Minnesota, a state in the northern part of the American Midwest. Even though I love her, we argue about one thing, coffee. Like many midwesterners, she drinks coffee all day, and her coffee is very weak. The problem is that I am from Seattle, the home of Starbucks. Starbucks, one of the fastest growing companies in the United States, has made espresso into a lifestyle choice. My favorite drink, a double mocha, has the caffeine equivalent of a dozen cups of Aunt Carol's coffee. The first time I made coffee at her house, she had a fit. She not only threw out all the coffee I made but also made me wash the pot. From then on, she made the coffee, the kind you can see through.

Sentence Practice 1, *page 186*

1. Ian Fleming, the creator of 007, named James Bond after the author of a book about birds. 2. Ian Fleming also wrote *Chitty Chitty Bang Bang*, a children's book. 3. Tim's mother, a registered nurse, thinks I have a virus. 4. Richard, a guy in my geology class, fell asleep during the lecture. 5. Spanish Fort, a town in south Alabama, was the site of one of the last battles of the Civil War.

Sentence Practice 2, *page 186*

1. Eleven of the twelve astronauts who walked on the moon were in the Boy Scouts, an organization that began in 1910. [specific; nonessential] 2. I rarely see my neighbor, a woman who works the night shift at the hospital. [specific; nonessential] 3. Cuba, a country that struggled for years to produce sufficient electricity, has lifted most of its bans on air conditioners, toasters, and other household appliances. [specific; nonessential] 4. My psychology professor, a noted scholar, suggested I participate in a study she is conducting. [specific; nonessential] 5. Although he was never seriously considered, Adolf Hitler was nominated in 1939 for the Nobel Peace Prize, a prestigious international award. [specific; nonessential]

Editing Practice 1, *page 187*

World War II, one of the best-known wars of all time, was followed a few years later by a conflict that still is not well understood. The Korean War, a conflict between the United Nations and North Korea, was never officially a war. Harry Truman, the U.S. president at the time of the conflict, never . . .

This war caused many problems for the United States, possibly because its status and purpose were not clear. General Douglas MacArthur, the commander of the UN forces, was removed from office for insubordination to President Truman, the commander in chief. After the landings at Inchon, a major turning point, the North Koreans . . .

LESSON 19: Unnecessary Commas

Diagnostic Exercise, *page 191*

Tens of millions of people around the globe,/ contributed to the outcome of World War II. Sacrifice, determination, mistakes, and luck,/ were combined with,/ brains, courage, leadership, and material resources to bring about the Allied victory. Undoubtedly, one indispensable factor was the alliance among the major powers, particularly,/ the United States, Great Britain, and the Soviet Union. Fighting alone, none of the Allies could have prevailed against Germany. But,/ working together enabled . . .

Sentence Practice 1, *page 195*

1. Remember to bring,/ a pen, paper, and your grammar book. 2. Thomas Jefferson is credited with several inventions, such as,/ a revolving bookstand and the first swivel chair. 3. And,/ he sat in a swivel chair while drafting the Declaration of Independence, according to some sources. 4. Each week, Candice paid a tutor to help her pass sociology, but,/

nothing helped. 5. My biology teacher, Ms. Anderson, required a great deal of homework this week, beginning with/ reading three chapters and completing several exercises.

Sentence Practice 2, *page 196*

1. OK 2. But/ there is a comma in this sentence that should be deleted, [OK] unless you intentionally want the sentence to be incorrect. 3. When a city's name is followed by the country's name, [OK] place a comma before and/ after the country. 4. Florence, [OK] Italy, [OK] was the first European city to pave virtually all its streets. 5. For many people, [OK] commas can be a confusing form of punctuation, [OK] along with/ semicolons, [OK] colons, [OK] and quotation marks.

Editing Practice 1, *page 197*

A major development in the evolution of film/ was the arrival of nickelodeons. This was a type of movie theater whose name is a combination of/ the admission price and the Greek word for *theater*. According to media historian Douglas Gomery, these small and uncomfortable makeshift theaters were often converted storefronts redecorated to mimic vaudeville theaters. Usually, a piano player added live music, and/ sometimes theater operators used sound effects to simulate gunshots or loud crashes. Because they showed silent films that usually transcended language barriers, nickelodeons flourished during the great European immigration to America at the turn of the twentieth century. These theaters filled a need for many newly arrived people who faced challenges such as/ struggling to learn English and seeking an inexpensive escape from the hard life of the city. These nickelodeons, which were often managed by immigrants, required a minimal investment: just a secondhand projector and a large white sheet. The craze reached its greatest popularity in 1910. But/ entrepreneurs soon began to seek more affluent spectators, attracting them with/ larger facilities and more lavish buildings.

UNIT SIX

LESSON 20: Apostrophes in Contractions

Diagnostic Exercise, *page 204*

1. On the television show *Seinfeld*, Kramer's first name **wasn't** used often. 2. I **didn't** realize until recently that his first name is *Cosmo*. 3. **It's** too late to eat supper, but let's have a snack. 4. In the original books featuring Tarzan, his pet chimp isn't named *Cheetah*; rather, **its** name is *Nkima*. 5. If **you're** going sightseeing, remember to bring your camera.

Sentence Practice 1, *page 206*

1. My roommate **will not** be awake for at least another hour. [**won't**] 2. **It is** supposed to rain today, but I'm not sure that will happen. [**It's**] 3. The killer whale **is not** a whale; it's actually the largest member of the dolphin family. [**isn't**] 4. A rhinoceros has three toes on each foot, yet you **cannot** see them because they're each encased in a hoof. [**can't**] 5. The British Empire isn't what it once was; the tiny Pitcairn Islands are the last of **its** Pacific territories.

Sentence Practice 2, *page 207*

1. OK. 2. Platinum **was not** highly valued at one time, so Russia used this rare metal in the early 1800s to make coins. [**wasn't**] 3. The town of Hibbling, Minnesota, was entirely relocated because companies **could not** otherwise mine the iron ore underneath it. [**couldn't**] 4. OK 5. OK

Editing Practice 1, *page 207*

Rice might seem to be a common (and perhaps dull) subject to Americans. However, **it's** such an important part of life in other parts of the world that rice has an honored place in many cultures. **You've** probably long known about the tradition of throwing rice at newlyweds when **they're** leaving a church. But you probably did not know that in India rice is traditionally the first food a bride offers her husband. In Indonesia, tradition has it that a woman **can't** be considered for marriage until she can skillfully prepare rice.

Rice **isn't** associated with just marriage. Even the word itself is special. **I've** been to one region in China where the word for rice is also the word for food. In Japan, the word for cooked rice is also the word for meal. **It's** also common . . .

LESSON 21: Apostrophes Showing Possession

Diagnostic Exercise, *page 211*

Paul Ortega has been one of my **family's** best friends over the years. Although he was born in Mexico, he speaks English like a native because his **father's** employer relocated his family to Arizona when Paul was six. In a few years, **Paul's** English was as good as **anyone's**. Nearly every summer, however, Paul and his sisters went back to Mexico City, where they stayed at a **relative's** house. As a result, he is completely at home in either **country's** culture. He and my father have been business partners for many years. The **company's** success . . .

Sentence Practice 1, *page 215*

1. My **husband's** watch is broken. 2. John **Lennon's** middle name was Winston. 3. A **starfish's** eyes are located at the tip of each arm. 4. I need help with **tomorrow's** homework. 5. The student council agreed that the **school's** name should be changed.

Sentence Practice 2, *page 216*

1. The **guppy's** name comes from the name of the man who discovered this species. 2. The **saxophone's** inventor was named Adolphe Sax. 3. Hold the acid at **arm's** length. 4. **Russell's** girlfriend is throwing him a birthday party this Friday. 5. My composition **teacher's** pet peeve is the misuse of apostrophes.

Editing Practice 1, *page 217*

You have probably never heard Alfred **Wegener's** name. Wegener was born in Berlin in 1880. He got a PhD in astronomy, but his **life's** work was the new field of meteorology (the study of weather). As a young man, he became interested in ballooning and, for a time, held the **world's** record for altitude. As a balloonist he was well aware of the fact the **wind's** direction and speed on the **earth's** surface did not correspond at all with the **wind's** movement high above the surface. He was the first person to exploit the **balloon's** ability to carry weather instruments high into the atmosphere and to track wind movement at various altitudes. He was one of a group of early researchers who studied a remarkable current of air that circulated around the North Pole. The researchers had discovered what we now call the jet stream. In 1930, he and a colleague disappeared on an expedition to Greenland. His and his **colleague's** frozen bodies were found a year later.

LESSON 22: Unnecessary Apostrophes

Diagnostic Exercise, *page 219*

Some old **friends** of mine stopped by my apartment for coffee. My roommate's coffeepot was broken, so I made them some instant coffee. I'm not good at making coffee, but everybody had two **cups** apiece. The coffee was pretty old, yet nobody seemed to care. We talked about our **schedules** . . .

Sentence Practice 1, *page 222*

1. I have three **essays** to complete this month. 2. Maria's [**OK**] best friend went on a cruise last summer. [possession] 3. All four **radios** in my apartment need batteries. 4. My parents went to college back in the **1980s**. 5. One of the two Joe **Smiths** in this class is an old friend of mine.

Sentence Practice 2, *page 223*

1. You have several **classes** with me this semester. 2. I need to burn two **CDs** on your computer. 3. When someone's **[OK]** cell phone went off in class, my English teacher became upset. [possession] 4. We aren't **[OK]** ready to leave. [contraction] 5. Did you see all the **cameras** in the hallway?

Editing Practice 1, *page 224*

The word *parasite* comes from a Greek word meaning a flunky who does no honest work but depends entirely on **handouts** from wealthy and powerful patrons. In biology, the term was adopted to describe a huge variety of **creatures** that steal their nourishment from hosts, often causing their hosts' death. The behavior of **parasites** strikes all of us as profoundly vicious and ugly. One of the best fictional **depictions** of parasites is in the 1979 science fiction movie *Alien*. In that movie, the crew of a spaceship investigates a clutch of **eggs** left on an otherwise lifeless planet. As one of the crew examines an egg, a crablike thing bursts out of the shell and wraps a tail around the crewman's neck. By the next day, the crablike thing has disappeared and the crewman seems normal. Later, the crewman clutches his stomach in terrible pain, and a little knobby-headed alien pierces through his skin and leaps out. The alien has laid an egg in the crewman's abdomen; the egg has hatched and has been devouring his intestines. This horrible scenario is in fact based on the real behavior of parasitic **wasps** that lay their **eggs** in living caterpillars. As the **eggs** mature, they devour the internal organs of the caterpillar, sparing only the **organs** necessary . . .

UNIT SEVEN

LESSON 23: Quotation Marks with Other Punctuation

Diagnostic Exercise, *page 232*

1. She described this song as a "dark bluesy gospel disco tune**.**" 2. Are you still writing a paper about Langston Hughes's poem "I, Too, Sing America"**?** 3. OK 4. The sign read, "Keep Out**,**" but I asked myself, "Who would mind if I went in**?**" 5. OK

Sentence Practice 1, *page 234*

1. Gage asked, "When can we eat**?**" 2. OK 3. OK 4. OK 5. Charlene responded, "Why are you following me**?**"

Sentence Practice 2, *page 235*

1. Did she say, "The store opens at noon"**?** 2. OK 3. OK 4. The angry customer screamed, "Don't walk away from me**!**" 5. OK

Editing Practice 1, *page 236*

My girlfriend sleepily asked, "Why are you calling me so late?" It was 2:00 A.M., and I apparently had awakened her.

"Sorry," I muttered, realizing the time. "I've been studying all night and needed a break**.**" This apparently wasn't the right answer.

She yelled, "I was sound asleep!" After another moment, she added, "Do you think I stayed up just in case you needed to call someone**?**"

"Well, I guess this is a bad time to call," I meekly suggested. "I'll let you go back to sleep**.**" She hung up . . .

LESSON 24: Semicolons

Diagnostic Exercise, *page 238*

1. Natural selection resulted in humans having excellent mechanisms to defend against weight loss**;** but poor mechanisms for preventing obesity. 2. As a person's weight increases,

so do the chances of him or her developing several major health problems: diabetes, heart disease, stroke, and even some types of cancer. 3. OK. 4. In the United States, obesity is overtaking smoking as the major cause of death, a trend that is unlikely to change soon. 5. OK

Sentence Practice 1, *page 241*

1. Next week, we will have a major test, one that will be difficult. 2. OK 3. OK 4. Allyson and I went to the same high school, Pine Tree High School. 5. Ken brought several items: napkins, glasses, and forks.

Sentence Practice 2, *page 242*

1. Her truck failed to start because the battery was dead. 2. I read an article about Ralph Bunche, the first African American to win the Nobel Peace Prize. 3. Annie ordered a parfait, a dessert made of ice cream, fruit, and syrup. 4. OK 5. I need to go to the store, which is only about one mile away.

Editing Practice 1, *page 243*

Langston Hughes is one of the best-known African American poets, his fame having begun in 1915, when he was thirteen. At that time, he was elected poet of his graduating class, an unusual selection not merely because he was one of only two African American students in his class but because he had never written any poems. Hughes explained that nobody else in the class had written any poetry either. His classmates elected him, however, because . . .

Even though such reasoning had an element of stereotyping, Hughes was inspired/ and wrote a graduation poem that the teachers and students enthusiastically received. He went on to publish many types of writing: poems, . . .

Editing Practice 2, *page 244*

Something needs to change at my apartment/ because I cannot cope with the mess any longer. Six months ago, it seemed like living with two high school friends would be great; we liked hanging around each other and shared the same interests. What I did not fully understand was that they were (and are) slobs. One likes cooking, which I think is a great hobby. It's not so great, however, when he doesn't clean up the mess that he makes. My other roommate leaves clothes all over the house, even in our one bathroom. One time, I counted what seemed like half of his entire wardrobe on the bathroom floor: four pairs of jeans, three pairs of dress pants, ten T-shirts, and five dress shirts . . .

LESSON 25: Colons

Diagnostic Exercise, *page 247*

1. OK 2. Please remember to pack toiletry essentials such as/ toothpaste, a toothbrush, deodorant, and shampoo. 3. You can probably guess that some of the most common surnames in the United States are/ Smith, Johnson, Williams, Jones, and Brown. 4. OK 5. Nicole suggested that you immediately contact several people, such as/ Maria, Paul, Denise, and Stephanie.

Sentence Practice 1, *page 249*

1. Use the proper form to order ordinary supplies such as/ pens, paper, and paperclips. 2. My friend Kamilah has lived in several countries, including/ Mexico, Brazil, and Ireland. 3. OK 4. OK 5. In the fall, I am enrolling in/ Biology 101, History 101, English 102, and Math 220.

Sentence Practice 2, *page 250*

1. Some famous people had dyslexia, such as/ Leonardo da Vinci, Winston Churchill, Albert Einstein, and George Patton. 2. OK 3. OK 4. Many languages have contributed

to English, especially/ French, Latin, and German. 5. New words in English arise from many sources, including/ gang culture, popular music, and the computer industry.

Editing Practice 1, *page 251*

My college sponsors various trips for students, including/ rafting, skiing, and hiking trips. This fall, I am going on one of the hiking trips. There is a fee involved, but it is still an affordable trip. I have to supply my own/ water container, snacks, and backpack. However, the school provides several things: water, lunch, first-aid kits, and even insect repellent. Some items I definitely plan to leave at home are/ my cell phone, my MP3 player, and my credit cards.

I wanted a few of my friends to come, such as/ my roommate, his brother, and two guys who work with me at the grocery store. They declined. I myself love to go on long walks. Last year, I hiked in several places: northern Alabama, southern Kentucky, and along the coastline in Georgia. Sure, hiking can be a little tedious at times, and you have to be fit to walk several hours a day. However, the rewards include/ getting away from the noise of the city . . .

LESSON 26: Capitalization

Diagnostic Exercise, *page 255*

The name ***Tecumseh*** translates as "Shooting Star." This is a fitting name for the **Shawnee** leader who reached great fame among Indians during Thomas Jefferson's **presidency**. From Canada to Georgia and **west** to the Mississippi, Tecumseh was considered a charismatic **chief**. He was a gifted and natural **commander**, . . .

Sentence Practice 1, *page 259*

1. My father has a job teaching **biology** in eastern Delaware. 2. OK 3. OK 4. Students write in almost every class at this **university,** even **physical education** courses. 5. Tenskwatawa was a **Native American** leader who encouraged his people to give up alcohol along with **European** clothing and tools.

Sentence Practice 2, *page 260*

1. In the 1860s, Montana's present **capital,** Helena, was named Last Chance Gulch. 2. OK 3. Did you say that **Aunt** Iva is arriving today? 4. The **Rhone River** and the **Rhine River** both rise out of the Alps of Switzerland. 5. My **grandmother** believes she can meet with the pope during our visit to Rome.

Editing Practice 1, *page 261*

Last fall we stayed in **New Orleans** for a week. We flew from **Newark** in **New Jersey.** Our trip got off to a bad start because our flight was delayed for two hours because of thunderstorms over the **Appalachians.** We stayed in the **French Quarter,** the oldest part of town. It and the lovely old **Garden District** were not damaged by **Katrina,** the terrible hurricane that did so much damage to the entire **Gulf Coast** . . .

Terrible as it was, we need to bear in mind how much worse the loss of life could have been if not for very accurate forecasting from the **National Hurricane Center** and the **National Weather Service.** For example, compare **Katrina** with the similar hurricane that struck **Galveston** in 1900. That storm killed eight thousand people because there was no ability at the time to monitor off-shore weather. The storm came on shore without any warning at all, killing nearly everyone living along that part of **Texas** where the storm hit.

UNIT EIGHT

LESSON 27: Parallelism

Some answers in this lesson will vary. Sample answers are shown.

Diagnostic Exercise, *page 268*

We all go to college for different reasons: to get an education, meet new people, and **gain** the skills for a job. The best programs are ones that reach several of these goals at the same time. I like to take courses that interest me and **build** skills that will lead to a job. For example, it is great to read about something in a class and then **apply** it in a practical situation. That is why I am doing an internship program. I have the opportunity to get credits, develop professional skills, and **make** important . . .

Sentence Practice 1, *page 271*

1. My boss said that I need to work faster, work harder, and **stop** taking long breaks. 2. A new federal program gives me the chance to take several classes this summer and **get** my degree within two years. 3. Dr. Sanchez helped me to write more clearly, **avoid** grammatical errors, and turn in my papers on time. 4. A common approach to writing a lab report is **to begin** with the materials needed and end with a summary of the findings. 5. My chemistry teacher said that we also need to state the purpose of the experiment, **explain** the procedures, and explain the shortcomings of the experiment.

Sentence Practice 2, *page 271*

1. OK 2. I have to put the cat out, water the plants, and ~~to~~ leave a house key with a friend. 3. This semester, I started working at home in the mornings and **doing** my schoolwork later in the afternoons. 4. I do not want you to lose the directions and **become** lost. 5. OK

Editing Practice 1, *page 273*

My boyfriend, Matt, loves talking on his cell phone and **playing** video games. In fact, he seems to do little else. He spends hours doing both at the same time. I talk on my cell and play video games sometimes, but I also like meeting people face to face, going out with friends, and **having** a little variation in what I do. Just last weekend, I had an opportunity to participate in a blood drive and **go** to a baseball game. During that entire time, Matt managed to run up two hundred minutes on his cell phone and to complete Half-Life 2 for the tenth time. This weekend, I plan to watch a movie with our friends, go for a long walk around the park, and **work** in my garden . . .

LESSON 28: Passive Voice

Diagnostic Exercise, *page 276*

Matt's apartment manager called him, wanting to know why he played his music so loudly. **The phone call surprised Matt;** he didn't think his music was loud. He apologized, but he said his radio was playing at only a fourth of its potential volume. Apparently, **this response satisfied the manager. She told Matt** that . . .

Sentence Practice 1, *page 278*

1. I used this computer. 2. Jim prepared supper. 3. In Japan, cities provide names only for major streets. 4. Until 2008, France prohibited the sale of the energy drink Red Bull. 5. France's government bans television advertisements for wine.

Sentence Practice 2, *page 278*

1. The college president announced the tuition increase. 2. On Tuesday, a massive fire destroyed a dormitory. 3. The recession has affected everyone. 4. In 1993, President Clinton invited the rapper LL Cool J to perform at the presidential inaugural gala. 5. In a 1940 edition of *Look* magazine, future president Gerald Ford modeled winter sportswear.

Editing Practice 1, *page 279*

More and more students have chosen urban campuses in the past few years. At my school, like many others, parking and transportation have become big issues for many students. **The school encourages riding the bus,** but that is not practical for everybody. **Riders can use only** a few bus routes. In addition, **nearly everybody takes evening classes.** Bad as the buses are during the day, at night, they are impossible. **The night buses only cover one route.** And that route has only one bus every hour. **If you missed the last bus,** you would . . .

Editing Practice 2, *page 280*

    The student council has proposed a new plan. Their idea is that **the school could charter several buses.** These buses would shuttle between the campus and the central bus station downtown. **Passengers can access nearly all the bus routes** from the central station. I think **a lot of students would support this idea. The council is putting forward this plan. The council is forming a committee** to see how many students would be interested in this plan. **If we can persuade a reasonable number of students** to sign . . .

LESSON 29: Dangling Modifiers

Diagnostic Exercise, *page 283*

    Studying for hours, **I felt my eyes grow tired.** I walked to the snack bar for a cup of coffee. **When I arrived,** the place was closed. **After I decided** against walking a mile to another place, the thought crossed my mind that maybe I should quit for a while and get some sleep. I returned to my room and tried to decide what to do. Torn between the need to sleep and the need to study, **I heard the alarm clock go off and realized it** was time for class. After struggling to stay awake in class, **I decided** to get . . .

Sentence Practice 1, *page 286*

1. **Because I was well prepared,** passing the test was easy for me. 2. While **I was** sleeping on the couch, my back began to hurt. 3. Since **Jeff arrived** at this school, **his** study habits have changed dramatically. 4. Hurrying to answer the phone, **she hit her knee on** the table. 5. OK

Sentence Practice 2, *page 287*

1. OK 2. While **I was** reading a book on a Kindle, the battery went dead. 3. OK 4. After **I eat** a huge lunch, a little rest is the only thing I want. 5. Realizing we were late, **we knew** our only choice was to take a taxi.

Editing Practice 1, *page 288*

    Last summer I flew from Seattle to New York. Not having flown for a while, **I had an eye-opening experience.** On the positive side, it really is much easier than it used to be to compare rates and schedules. **After I spent** a few minutes (well, quite a few minutes actually) on the computer, the best choice was obvious. That's it for the good news. Everything else was downhill from there. Knowing that I needed to get to the airport in plenty of time, **I knew I had to** get there an hour and a half before departure time. Even then, I very nearly missed my flight. What I hadn't bargained on was how much longer it would take to get through security. Taking off my coat, jacket, and shoes and unpacking my laptop were awkward enough. The real problem was trying to get my shoes back on while juggling all my clothes and my computer. **While I balanced** on one foot and then the other, . . .

    The flight itself was uneventful, though not very pleasant. **Because I was** in the middle seat, it seemed like the flight lasted forever. One thing that had changed since the last time I had flown was the lack of leg room. Even **though I am** of only average height, my legs did not fit into the space. I thought that was pretty bad; then the person in front of me reclined his seat to the maximum. The top of his seat was about 12 inches from my face. I quickly discovered that I could not read. Holding my book so close to my face, **I could not get my eyes to** focus on the page. . . .

UNIT NINE

OVERVIEW: Articles with Geographic Proper Names, *page 293*

No articles for specific mountains or small bodies of water; use *the* **with** the names of mountain ranges and large bodies of water (such as oceans and seas).

LESSON 30: Incorrect Plurals and Indefinite Articles with Noncount Nouns

Diagnostic Exercise, *page 297*

The **modernization** of agriculture has meant a huge increase in just a few crops—**wheat** and **rice** for a̶ human consumption, **corn** for a̶n̶ animal consumption, and **cotton** for industrial **production**. This specialization in a few crops is called a̶ *monoculture.* A̶ Monoculture has some disadvantages: It reduces a̶ biodiversity and requires huge amounts of **energy** and fertilizer.

Sentence Practice 1, *page 299*

1. There is never enough **time** to get my **work** done! 2. It is amazing how much **effort** goes into routine **maintenance**. 3. I have never seen **weather** like this. 4. I am sure they did it for our **benefit**. 5. The **smoke** from the fires was really bothering my **vision**.

Sentence Practice 2, *page 299*

1. The children could hardly stand the **excitement** of going to Disneyland. 2. The company is trying to stockpile basic commodities such as **coal** and **timber**. 3. Most nonprofit organizations are dedicated to the **betterment** of all **humankind**. 4. In many states, grocery stores can sell **beer** and **wine** but not hard **liquor**. 5. We really appreciated his **advice** and **guidance**.

Editing Practice 1, *page 301*

There is almost nothing more important to **people** than meals and **eating**. Every culture has elaborate rituals connected with **food**. After all, we are all interested in the **nature** of the food we eat. Every culture has its own ideas about what a̶ good nutrition is. For example, in some parts of Asia, food is divided into two groups—"cooling" and "warming." In Japan, for example, eels are eaten during warm **weather** because eels are believed to help cool the **blood**.

LESSON 31: Using *A/An, Some,* and *The*

Diagnostic Exercise, *page 304*

Doctors have long known that we need to have iron in our diets. Recently, however, **a** new study has revealed that we may be getting too much iron. The human body keeps all **the** iron it digests. **The** only way we lose stored iron in **the** body is through bleeding. John Murray, **a** researcher at the University of Minnesota, discovered that people who live on **a** very low iron diet may have **a** greatly reduced risk of **a** heart attack. Another study found that diets high in meat have **a** strong correlation with a high risk of heart disease. Apparently, when people have **a** high level of iron, **[the]*** excess iron . . . (*raises error count to 10)

Sentence Practice 1, *page 307*

1. Uniqueness Tip; Uniqueness Tip 2. Normal-Expectations Tip (we expect questions to have answers) 3. Defined-by-Modifiers Tip; Normal-Expectations Tip (exams go with lessons) 4. Uniqueness Tip; Uniqueness Tip 5. Defined-by-Modifiers Tip

Sentence Practice 2, *page 308*

1. Defined-by-Modifiers Tip 2. Normal-Expectations Tip 3. Defined-by-Modifiers Tip or Uniqueness Tip 4. Uniqueness Tip 5. Defined-by-Modifiers Tip

Editing Practice 1, *page 309*

Like many young people just out of school, I recently moved into **an** apartment. I was on my own for the first time. I rented **an** unfurnished apartment because it was a lot cheaper than getting one already furnished. As is normally the case in the United States, **the** apartment came already furnished with **a** stove and refrigerator. (This is not the case in Europe. **Some** friends of mine rented **an** apartment in Rome for **a** semester abroad program. **An** unfurnished apartment there did not even have **a** sink, let alone any kitchen appliances.) I decided that **the** kitchen had to be my highest priority. I bought **a** set of dishes and **some** pots and pans at **a** big chain store. My parents gave me **an** old set of kitchen utensils. I went to Goodwill and got **a** really cheap kitchen table . . .

LESSON 32: Making Generalizations without Articles

Diagnostic Exercise, *page 311*

~~The~~ **Scientists** have long known that ~~the~~ honeybees are somehow able to tell ~~some~~ other bees where to look for ~~some~~ food. In the 1940s, Karl von Frisch of the University of Munich discovered that the type of ~~the~~ dance that ~~the~~ bees make when they return to their beehive is significant. It seems that ~~the~~ honeybees . . .

Sentence Practice 1, *page 314*

1. (1) Adverb-of-Frequency Tip, (2) Present Tense Tip, (3) No-Modifiers Tip (for both *twins* and *families*) 2. (1) Adverb-of-Frequency Tip, (2) Present Tense Tip, (3) No-Modifiers Tip (for both *filling stations* and *automotive repairs*) 3. (2) Present Tense Tip, (3) No-Modifiers Tip 4. (2) Present Tense Tip. (3) No-Modifiers Tip (for *generators*), (4) *Most* Tip (for *people*) 5. (2) Present Tense Tip, (3) No-Modifiers Tip (for both *bees* and *agriculture*)

Sentence Practice 2, *page 314*

1. Most countries tax ~~the~~ cigarettes and ~~the~~ alcohol heavily. 2. His company represents ~~the~~ authors, ~~the~~ playwrights, and ~~the~~ other creative artists. 3. ~~The~~ Disease, ~~the~~ poverty, and ~~the~~ malnutrition are closely linked. 4. ~~The~~ Prices of ~~the~~ glass, ~~the~~ steel, and ~~the~~ cement have actually dropped because of the decline in ~~the~~ construction. 5. Due to ~~the~~ global warming, ~~the~~ winters may actually get much colder in some places.

Editing Practice 1, *page 316*

Deborah Tannen has written extensively about the different conversational styles of ~~the~~ men and women. Males and females use ~~the~~ casual language in quite different ways, especially when ~~the~~ men are talking to men and ~~the~~ women are talking to women. When ~~the~~ groups of men are in a conversation, each speaker tries to control the topic. The most important tool in gaining and keeping ~~the~~ control is ~~the~~ humor. The humor is usually directed at others in the group, often in the form of ~~the~~ teasing. However, the teasing cannot go too far; it cannot be seen as actually insulting. Being able to be teased without getting angry and then responding in kind is a valued skill. ~~The~~ **Verbal** competition among groups of young men is a near cultural universal.

UNIT TEN

LESSON 33: The Progressive Tenses

Diagnostic Exercise, *page 325*

Every weekday morning at 6 A.M., my alarm **goes** off. By 6:15, the breakfast dishes are on the table, and the coffee **is brewing.** I always **get** the children up next. It is very hard for them to get going. On Mondays, they **resemble** bears coming out of hibernation.

While they **are taking** their showers with their eyes still closed, I get everyone's clothes ready. Since the youngest child still **needs** a lot of help getting dressed, I usually **spend** some extra time with her talking about the day's events. By 7 A.M., we all **are sitting** at the table for breakfast. The children **love** pancakes and waffles, but there just isn't time to make them except on weekends. Breakfast goes by quickly, unless somebody **spills** the milk or juice. I **wish** we had more time in the morning, but every morning I am **amazed** when I **look** back and **realize** that . . .

Sentence Practice 1, *page 328*

1. The offer ~~is including~~ **includes** free installation and service for the first year. 2. No one ~~was noticing~~ **noticed** how poorly they were maintaining their records. 3. I ~~am hating~~ **hate** it when people ~~are disagreeing~~ **disagree** about such trivial matters. 4. We ~~are needing~~ **need** more help while we are hosting the conference. 5. It ~~isn't seeming~~ **doesn't seem** to be getting any better.

Sentence Practice 2, *page 329*

1. She is running some errands right now, but she will ~~be calling~~ **call** you back as soon as she ~~is getting~~ **gets** home. (*is calling* is marginally ungrammatical) 2. She certainly **resembles** her mother. 3. I ~~am promising~~ **promise** that I will ~~be considering~~ **consider** it seriously. (*am promising* is marginally ungrammatical) 4. He ~~is belonging~~ **belongs** to all the civic organizations in town. 5. I ~~am hating~~ **hate** that our school ~~is having~~ **has** such a restrictive policy on using computers.

Editing Practice 1, *page 330*

I **think** that I would go crazy if I tried to write the way my husband does. I **spend** just as much time on my papers as he does, but I **write** in a completely different way. I **spend** much of my time thinking through what I am going to say before I ever put a word down on paper. When I **feel** that I really know what I want to say, I sit down and write a complete draft. Then I make an outline for what I have written. Often this outline **shows** me where I need to go back and expand an idea or rearrange something. But, on the whole, I **do not need** to make a lot of changes. My husband **thinks** that . . .

LESSON 34: Two-Word Verbs

Diagnostic Exercise, *page 334*

It used to be that making a plane reservation was a simple matter. You found a travel agency and **called it up.** Since the agency didn't work for any airlines, it looked for the best fare and **found it out.** There was no direct cost to you since the airlines paid the commission; they **built it in** to the price of your ticket. After the airlines were deregulated, however, this system began to fall apart. Faced with much greater competition, airlines identified commission costs as an unnecessary expense, and they **cut them down** by reducing the commission they paid agencies. Some airlines, like Southwest, even **cut them out** entirely. As a result, most travel agencies stopped selling tickets for those airlines. If you want to know about their fares, you must deal with each of the airlines separately. The catch, of course, is that if you call one of them, its representative can talk only about its fares, and you have no way to **check it out** to see if you have the best bargain.

Sentence Practice 1, *page 337*

1. You must be careful to guard **against it**. 2. The policeman straightened **them out** when they crossed the street while the light was green. 3. OK 4. You need to hurry **them up** because it is getting dark. 5. OK

Sentence Practice 2, *page 338*

1. I will **fill you in** on what happened during the meeting. 2. The milk had expired, so I **threw it away**. 3. John finished his algebra homework and asked his tutor to **check it**

over. 4. When Jodie heard the joke, it **cracked her up**. 5. The analyst's associates were helpful. They **backed him up**.

Editing Practice 1, *page 339*

I have two papers due this week, but I can't just **dash them off** like some people (my wife, for example) can. I really have to take my time and **plan them out**. I need to get a bunch of ideas together and then **write them down**. Then, I have to **work them up** into some kind of logical order. Sometimes, when I am trying to work out the relationship of a number of half-formed ideas, I find it helps to **copy them out** onto 3″ × 5″ cards. Then I can **sort them out** in a number of different ways until I get a clear picture of what I am trying to say. Then I put my key ideas into a few short sentences so that I can **sum them up** simply and clearly. If I can't summarize my ideas for myself, I certainly can't **get them across** . . .

LESSON 35: Information Questions

Diagnostic Exercise, *page 342*

ANNA: When **does your flight leave?**
MARIA: At 6:15. Why **are you** so worried? We're not going to be late, are we?
ANNA: I don't think so, but how long **does** it **take** to get to the airport?
MARIA: It depends on the traffic. If the roads are crowded, it will take an hour.
ANNA: How soon **will you** be ready to leave?
MARIA: Don't get upset. I'm nearly done packing now. Have you seen my alarm clock?
ANNA: I don't know where it is. When **did** you **use** it last?
MARIA: For my interview, two days ago. Here it is in the dresser drawer.
ANNA: Where **did I leave** the car keys?
MARIA: Come on! Now you're the one who is going to make us late. Why **didn't we** get started sooner?

Sentence Practice 1, *page 345*

1. How soon **will** <u>dinner</u> be ready? 2. OK 3. Why **won't** <u>your company</u> open a branch in Hong Kong? 4. How long **have** <u>your parents</u> been living in California? 5. When **will** <u>the people you work with</u> know about your new job?

Sentence Practice 2, *page 345*

1. Where **did** you hide all the Christmas presents? 2. What **are** they laughing at? 3. How much **do** you think I should pay for it? 4. How far **can** we drive before we need to get gas? 5. How long **should** we wait for them?

Editing Practice 1, *page 346*

ANNA: What **will** you do when you get back home?
MARIA: The usual things. Why **do** you want to know?
ANNA: No reason. I'm just asking.
MARIA: I think that I will spend most of my time catching up on my writing assignments.
ANNA: What **do** you have to work on?
MARIA: I have to write a paper for my linguistics class.
ANNA: What **is** it about?
MARIA: How children acquire language.
ANNA: Who **are** you going to see?
MARIA: Nobody. Why **do** you keep asking?
ANNA: I called home last night.
MARIA: Oh, who **did** you **talk** to?
ANNA: I talked to Aunt Josie. Guess what she said?
MARIA: I don't know. Anyway, why **should** I . . .

LESSON 36: Word Order in Noun Clauses

Diagnostic Exercise, *page 350*

Many non-Americans ask why the American court system **is** so cumbersome. To understand that, you need to know something about where ~~did~~ it **came** from and how ~~did~~ it **evolved**. Until the Revolutionary War, the American legal system was exactly what the British legal system **was**. Despite the many advantages of the British legal system, colonial Americans felt that the British had used the powers of the government to override the rights of individual citizens. This deep distrust of the ability of the government to use its power fairly explains why the American system **is** so heavily weighted in favor of the defendant. Often court cases in the United States are fought on the ground of what admissible government evidence **is**.

Sentence Practice 1, *page 353*

1. You can get **what you will need** for school there. (**Question**) 2. What **they decide** to do is entirely their own business. (**Question**) 3. OK 4. How often **they were** right proved what **they were** doing was on the right track. (**Question, Question**) 5. What **most people have learned** only reflects what **they have** been taught. (**Question, Question**)

Sentence Practice 2, *page 353*

1. What **they were** offering attracted a lot of customers. 2. What **happened** illustrated how easily **anybody can** make a mistake. 3. You should never ignore how much **something will** cost in the long run. 4. I have no idea where **they went**. 5. We are meeting to discuss what **we should** do about the problem.

Editing Practice 1, *page 354*

One of the many big changes in how we **can** teach writing has been to look at writing as a topic in its own right. For more than a decade now, there has been substantial research on how ~~do~~ students learn to write and what the difference **is** between the way good and poor writers go about the process of writing. Perhaps the most helpful finding is that good writers go through a definite two-step process. What ~~do~~ they write first is an exploration of the topic. Often it starts as a crude draft that wouldn't make much sense to anybody but the writer. But apparently it is how we **are** able to think through what ~~do~~ we want to say. It is really important to get to the point where the writer **can** boil down the key ideas in a few sentences. This first step in the cycle results in a draft that has all the key ideas worked out. The second step in the cycle is a semifinal draft that is very sensitive to how the paper **will** make sense to the audience. Here is where an outline **is** critical . . .

UNIT ELEVEN

LESSON 37: Using Direct Quotations and Paraphrases

Some answers in this lesson will vary. Sample answers are shown.

Diagnostic Exercise, *page 362*

1. One book suggests that New England of the 1600s was in large part governed "by Puritans for Puritanism" (Roark et al. 83). 2. OK 3. OK 4. These historians also write**,** ~~that~~ "The colonists transformed this arrangement for running a joint-stock company into a structure for governing the colony" (Roark et al. 83). 5. OK

Sentence Practice 1, *page 367*

Responses will vary.
1. In a letter written in 1801, Beethoven stated, "I want to seize fate by the throat." In a letter written in 1801, Beethoven indicated that he wanted to take control of fate.

2. Chief Joseph said, "From where the sun now stands, I will fight no more forever." Chief Joseph said that he would not fight any longer.
3. In a review of a book, Ambrose Bierce wrote, "The covers of this book are too far apart." In a review of a book, Ambrose Bierce suggested that the book was too long.
4. Mary Wollstonecraft Shelley wrote in her 1818 novel, "I beheld the wretch—the miserable monster whom I had created." Mary Wollstonecraft Shelley wrote in her 1818 novel *Frankenstein* that the creator looked at the awful thing he created.
5. As John Wayne once suggested to actors, "Talk low, talk slow, and don't say too much." John Wayne once suggested that actors should use few words and say them slowly in a deep voice.

Sentence Practice 2, *page 368*

Responses will vary.

1. Before shooting President Reagan, John Hinckley wrote to an actress, "The reason I'm going ahead with this attempt now is because I just cannot wait any longer to impress you." Before shooting President Reagan, John Hinckley's letter to an actress indicated that he wanted to impress her.
2. Cher once said, "The trouble with some women is they get all excited about nothing, and then they marry him." Cher once indicated that too many women marry boring men who are not worth getting excited about.
3. Former slave Booker T. Washington once wrote, "My life had its beginning in the midst of the most miserable, desolate, and discouraging surroundings." Former slave Booker T. Washington once said that his early life was in a horrible and discouraging environment.
4. Actress Mae West said in one movie, "When I'm good, I'm very good, but when I'm bad, I'm better." Actress Mae West said in one movie that she was at her best when she was bad.
5. Franklin Roosevelt said, "I see one-third of a nation ill-housed, ill-clad, ill-nourished." Franklin Roosevelt said that the country had inadequate clothing, food, and shelter.

Editing Practice 1, *page 369*

My mother told me **that she** believed every marriage was a compromise. For example, my brother Pete has had a lot of trouble quitting smoking. He likes to quote Mark Twain, who said, **"Quitting** smoking is easy. I've done it dozens of times." After my brother got married, his wife told him **that he could not keep smoking inside the house**. She wants him to quit, but she knows how hard it will be for him to do it. She told me that **her** uncle, who had been a heavy smoker, had died from lung **disease**. Naturally, she is very concerned about Pete. Last night, Pete told **us, "I** am going to try nicotine patches**."** We all hope that they will work.

LESSON 38: Citing Sources Correctly

Diagnostic Exercise, *page 373*

1. "But in the sixth century, a new technology emerged that added a new dimension to warfare" (**Volti 257**).
   Volti, Rudi. *Society and Technological Change.* **6th ed. New York: Worth,** 2010. Print.
2. OK
3. The scholar S. A. Nigosian explains, "As a young man Muhammad joined the merchant caravans, and at the age of twenty-five he entered the service of a wealthy widow, **Khadijah"** (415).
   Nigosian, S. A. *World Religions: A Historical Approach.* 4th ed. Boston: Bedford/St. Martin's, 2008. Print.
4. OK
   Nigosian, S. A. *World Religions: A Historical Approach.* 4th ed. Boston: Bedford/St. Martin's, 2008. Print.
5. OK

[Nigosian, S. A. *World Religions: A Historical Approach*. 4th ed. Boston: Bedford/St. Martin's, 2008. Print.]

Sentence Practice 1, *page 378*

1. ... (Roark et al. 283).
   Roark, James L., et al. *The American Promise: A Compact History*. Boston: Bedford/St. Martin's, 2008. Print.
2. ... (Huxley 87).
   Huxley, Aldous. *Brave New World*. New York: Perennial, 1998. Print.
3. ... (Campbell, Martin, and Fabos 189).
   Campbell, Richard, Christopher R. Martin, and Bettina Fabos. *Media and Culture: An Introduction to Mass Communication*. Boston: Bedford/St. Martin's, 2011. Print.
4. ... (McCarthy 287).
   McCarthy, Cormac. *The Road*. New York: Vintage, 2006. Print.
5. ... (McCrone 236).
   McCrone, John. *The Ape That Spoke: Language and the Evolution of the Human Mind*. New York: William Morrow, 1991. Print.

Sentence Practice 2, *page 380*

1. ... (Grunwald 37).
   Grunwald, Michael. "Fire Away." *Time* 24 Jan. 2011: 37–39. Print.
2. ... (Tucker 74).
   Tucker, Abigail. "Invisible Glory." *Smithsonian* Feb. 2011: 74–79. Print.
3. ... (Dobbs 28).
   Dobbs, Michael. "The End Was Near." *Military History* Nov. 2010: 26–33. Print.
4. ... (Manes 154).
   Manes, Stephen. "Where's Wireless Data for the Rest of Us?" *PC World* June 2006: 154. Print.
5. ... (Gibbs 76).
   Gibbs, Nancy. "Sacred Spaces." *Time* 30 Aug. 2010: 76. Print.

Editing Practice 1, *page 381*

Brood, Bob. *What We Really Value: Beyond Rubrics in Teaching and Assessing Writing*. Logan, Utah: Utah State UP, 2003. Print.

Butler, Paul. *Style in Rhetoric and Composition: A Critical Sourcebook*. Boston: Bedford/St. Martin's, 2010. Print.

Haussamen, **Brock**. *Grammar Alive: A Guide for Teachers*. Urbana: NCTE, **2003. Print**.
OK

Shaugnessy, Mina P. *Errors and Expectations: A Guide for the Teacher of Basic Writing*. New **York:** Oxford UP, 1977. Print.

Sheridan, Daniel. *Teaching Secondary English: Readings and Applications*. 2nd ed. **Mahwah: Lawrence Erlbaum, 2001.** Print.

Editing Practice 2, *page 382*
OK

Cubie, Doreen. "Welcoming Travelers and Wildlife." *National Wildlife* Feb./March 2011: **16–19**. Print.

OK

Walsh, Bryan. "Going Green." *Time* **19 July** 2010: 45. Print.

Weintraub, Ariene. "Break that Hovering Habit Early." *U.S. News and World Report* Sept. 2010: 42–43. Print.

Index

If English is not your first language, you may find the ESL index helpful. (The ESL index follows this main index.)

ESL Index

If English is not your first language, you may have noticed the icon (⊕ ESL) as you flipped through this book for the first time. This index offers an alphabetical listing of topics that may be especially challenging for non-native speakers of English.

Correction Symbols

Many instructors use correction symbols to point out grammar, usage, and writing problems. This chart lists common symbols and directs you to the help that you need to revise and edit your writing. The numbers below refer you to specific lessons in this book.

art	article	30, 31, 32
cap	capitalization	26
coord	coordination	13
cs	comma splice (run-on)	2
dm	dangling modifier	29
frag	sentence fragment	1
fs	fused sentence (run-on)	2
no ˅	unnecessary apostrophe	22
no ˄,	unnecessary comma	19
pass	passive voice	28
plan	further planning needed	40
pron agr	pronoun agreement	8
pron case	pronoun case	10, 11
pron ref	pronoun reference	9
revise	further revision needed	42
run-on	run-on	2
sexist pron	sexist pronoun	12
shift	verb tense shift	6
sp	spelling	Appendix E
s-v agr	subject-verb agreement	3, 4, 5
trans	transition	14, 42
ts	topic sentence/thesis statement	40, 41
usage	wrong word	Appendix D
vf	verb form	34
vt	verb tense	6, 7, 33
˄,	comma	13, 14, 15, 16, 17, 18
//	faulty parallelism	27
:	colon	25
;	semicolon	24
˅,	apostrophe	20, 21
" "	quotation marks	23
¶	new paragraph	40, 41
˄	insert	
— or ℘	delete	
⊃⊂	close up space	
∿	reverse words or letters	